# The people centered economy
# - the new ecosystem for work

David Nordfors
i4j co-chair, co-founder, editor-in-chief

Vint Cerf
i4j co-chair, co-founder

Alan Anderson
Editor

Guido van Nispen
i4j Publisher

And co-authors: Chally Grundwag, VR Ferose Thorkill
Sonne, Allen Blue, Patricia Olby Kimondo, Jason Palmer, Gi
Fernando, Daniel Pianko, Wendy Guillies and Derek Ozkal,
Jim Clifton, Jamie Merisotis, Tess Posner, Jacob Hsu,
Monique Morrow Sven Otto Littorin and Guido van Nispen.

The production of this book was made possible by a grant
from the Ewing Marion Kauffman Foundation (grant
number G-201707-2549): The contents of this publication
are solely the responsibility of IIIJ Foundation.

*Published by IIIJ Foundation,*
*565 Middlefield Road, Suite 200,*
Menlo Park, California 94025, USA.

# Table of contents

# How to innovate better jobs for people

## By Vint Cerf and David Nordfors

Meaningful work lies at the heart of every successful economy. This will never change. In a 'people-centered economy', people make themselves valuable by helping others make themselves valuable. When people create each other's livelihoods this way, when one earns more, others earn more, too and the economy grows. "I earn better when you earn better" is - and always was - the golden rule of good business and a healthy economy. Artificial intelligence should be used to embed meaningful work in the heart of every sound business practice. This book, "The People-Centered Economy" (PCE), offers an in-depth analysis and outlines a new mindset and framework for businesses and nations, where the economy is driven by a new powerful engine, the "ecosystem for jobs" that uses AI to innovate new ways for individuals to earn a better, more meaningful livelihood. Some of the actors from the new ecosystem for jobs - entrepreneurs, investors, corporate executives, politicians, philanthropists, economists, and others - present their cases, in their own words, in seventeen independent subchapters. By understanding the theory and placing the cases in this context, the reader will understand what the "people-centered economy" means, looks like, and how to be a part of it.

Meaningful, paid work makes people see value in each other. It makes millions of people need and value each other in societies where each citizen may not know more than a few hundred at most. We cannot imagine a society where people don't need to depend on strangers. What would hold such a society together? It will immediately fall apart, because there is no 'glue' that holds the greater community together.

In the course of our seminars, we have discovered that "shareholder value" is not the only desirable business purpose it is made out to be. Making people and their work valuable to others is a far better metric for success in business, and it is a success of the sort that makes economies grow, and societies thrive.

We do want to create the right platform for our economy, in which machines and algorithms have heretofore been a too dominant force. Planning for the economy of that future with a 'people first' mindset should be a primary focus of business attention. This book is part of

1

our i4j effort to proactively change the metrics by which we assess business success and practice.

Our book has three main parts, first a deeper dive into the concept of the people-centered economy. Then follows next exploring 'coolabilities' - a prime illustrative case how to innovate good jobs for individuals based on their specific abilities - and finally illustrated by i4j by community members, presenting examples of companies and projects they are already running today that are part of the new about-to-be-discovered ecosystem for innovating good jobs for people.

Many actors active today belong to the new ecosystem for innovating meaningful jobs in the people-centered economy. The ecosystem already exists, it has yet to be coined and gain self-awareness. The purpose of this book is to help that happen.

# Introducing the "People-Centered Economy" (PCE)

What is a people-centered economy?

'Economy' comes from old Greek words for "household" and "manage," putting people in the center of the equation of managing their means. In every well-managed household, every family member is valued and everyone will help each other find meaningful things to do. Only a bad household says to its members "there is nothing here for you to do" or "you need a college degree first".

Today, most businesses are "task-centered" because they see value creation in tasks or jobs being done,. 'People' are (still) part of the production, distribution and consumption eco-system, but they enter the equation as a 'cost' for creating value and 'innovation' is trying to bring the human element down as much as possible, to reduce costs. . We suggest this paradigm is a bad fit for the innovation economy, because it uses innovation to kill jobs and makes people uncertain about how to earn a living. Since people must earn in order to spend, innovation becomes the power-saw that the task-centered economy uses to cut down the branch it is sitting on.

A "people-centered" economy focuses on creating value around the individual. This is about making the citizens need each other more, so that they earn a better livelihood in more meaningful ways, not cutting production costs and lowering the value of their work or stereotyping their skills in order to turn them into commodities.

While the task-centered economy says "We need people to do these valuable things", the people-centered economy says "We need things that make these people valuable". A people-centered economy will always want to innovate new jobs that make people even more valuable. It's businesses will always invent new human tasks that have a higher market value than the old ones, increasing their revenues by helping people earn better. This makes it sustainable and much more powerful than the task-centered economy.

The first part of this book examines the different elements of economic models and shares ideas how we can make the "people-centered" economy happen by showing that this not only leads to a more powerful economy but that it also has the potential to become the most significant growth market for innovation and entrepreneurship in history!

Then follows a number of chapters exploring **'coolabilities'** - enhanced abilities, talents and strengths which co-occur with disabling conditions. Chally Grundwag expands and updates her seminal work on coolabilities, Thorkil Sonne tells the story about how he started the first company specializing on the coolabilities of autistic engineers and how this led to the "autism advantage" movement. VR Ferose, experienced senior computer industry executive, is a leader and co-founder of i4j's "coolabilities.ai", a technology project looking at how to design a platform for innovation using artificial intelligence that can facilitate an innovation ecosystem for creating companies, services and jobs for people with disabilities and coolabilities.

The coolabilities-part of the book ends with a chapter by one of us (Vint Cerf) highlighting the challenge security and privacy that comes with personal matching of jobs, especially when information about medical conditions and disabilities is involved. This chapter suggests some design principles for such a system and points out the importance of not hyping the coolabilities concept, which could lead to a backlash for people with disabilities who don't happen to have demonstrable coolabilities.

The third part of the book contains chapters by community members, presenting examples of companies and projects that are a part of the new economic thinking. The goal of the book is to give the reader an understanding of the people centered economy that creates innovation for jobs, the ecosystem it requires and how close we are to having it. We will show that there is already a groundswell of organisations creating the new economy, we just need to learn to recognize it and bring it out into the open where it can thrive.

Our co-writers are all thought leaders and pioneers in their industries and organizations, embracing the concept of the 'people centered economy'. In their respective chapters they will discuss and share real life efforts in creating that new economy. The chapters will discuss **jobs** (LinkedIn, Allen Blue; PeopleProductions, Patricia Kimondo), **venture and finance** (New Markets Venture Partners, Jason Palmer; Freeformers Gi Fernando, University Ventures Fund, Daniel Pianko), **entrepreneurship** (Kauffman Foundation, Wendy Guillies and Derek Ozkal; Gallup, Jim Clifton), **talent** (Lumina Foundation, Jamie Merisotis; AI4All, Tess Posner; Catalyte, Jacob Hsu; Restoring credentials for refugees, Monique Morrow; Coolabilities, Chally Grundwag, Thorkil Sonne and VR Ferose) and the **impact on society** (Innovation policy for jobs, Sven Otto Littorin; and Innovation Journalism, Guido van Nispen)

# Our previous book: Disrupting Unemployment

This is the second book we are publishing. The previous volume, titled Disrupting Unemployment[1], written in 2015 and updated in 2018, presents the vision of innovation for jobs. That vision is based on three assumptions: (1) all people can create value for one another; (2) the majority of human capacity -- including those who are formally employed and those who are not -- remains an untapped resource; and (3) an innovative and "disruptive" jobs strategy can liberate, compensate, and celebrate that resource.

We made the case that innovation for jobs was capable of "disrupting unemployment" by reframing a "job" as a need. Innovation is commonly understood to mean the clever discovery of a new technology, process, or product. In this scenario, however, the most important function of innovation is to design, offer, and value the kinds of work we do and they ways we do it.

---

[1] Nordfors, David, Vint Cerf and Max Senges, "Disrupting Unemployment" 2016, Publisher: i4j/Kauffman FoundationISBN: 978-1523845835, DOI10.13140/RG.2.1.1006.0406

We described the hoped-for outcome of innovation for jobs as a people-centered economy, one whose aim is to raise the value of people and their work, as distinct from the task-centered economy of today. In the task-centered economy, business competes to lower all costs, including the cost of workers. We conveyed our sense of urgency in contending that such a change must begin at once if we hope to bring about the paradigm shift that is needed to restore strength to our economy and our society.

# The need to focus on solutions

Unfortunately, since the original publication of Disrupting Unemployment, our society has largely continued to move in the wrong direction, persisting in its belief in the task-centered economy, in an ever harder competition for cutting costs rather than shifting focus to how the new technologies can be applied for creating more and better jobs for the citizens, who need to earn a living.

The debate around AI, automation and the future of work was sparked in 2012 by the book The Race Against the Machine[2], almost in parallel with the creation of i4j Innovation for Jobs. Bad news travels faster than anything else, and despite The Race pointing to the opportunity for entrepreneurs to create new jobs with the new technologies, job destruction was the discussion that caught on. It has until now stayed on the top of the agenda and the world has been increasing its knowledge of the scale of job destruction that lies ahead of us. Fears often lead to denial or desperate attempts that usually makes things worse instead of being a pathway to constructive action. Fear is not what builds a better world, it is built by realizing positive visions. Very few, if any, except i4j have kept innovation for jobs at the center of their discourse from the beginning.

Universal Basic Income (UBI) has been suggested to solve the future of work, but it has been a tale of two very different proposed UBIs, confusing the discussion: on the one hand, a "utopian UBI" that replaces the need to earn a living, saying that machines will do all the work, and, on the other hand, a "work-friendly UBI", that is meant to replace the social insurances that presently require recipients to be without jobs, thereby including them in the workforce. While the

---

[2] Brynjolfsson, Erik, and Andrew McAfee. Race against the machine: How the digital revolution is accelerating innovation, driving productivity, and irreversibly transforming employment and the economy. Brynjolfsson and McAfee, 2012.

utopian UBI is not being tested and cannot work, for reasons we present in this book, the work-friendly UBI can be a path to PCE (but not be a solution in itself) and is being studied by Finland, for example, who must bring old-age pensioners back into the workforce in order to strengthen their economy.

When it comes to the future of work, the fear of job destruction may become a self-fulfilling prophecy unless the spell is broken.

This book suggests that it can be done, and that it will require no magic wand to break the spell, it just requires reframing the problem into opportunity (as always in life), in this case to create new and better jobs for the jobless, using the same technologies that are destroying the old ones.

This book could not have been written without the gracious, overwhelming support of our community, co-writers, sponsors, partners and everybody else who has been involved in creating it. We thank all of them in creating the groundwork for the future in a people-centered economy.

*Vint Cerf & David Nordfors*

# Jobly

In this book, several chapters refer to "Jobly", an imagined ideal system for job matching based on artificial intelligence. The origination of that name is a futuristic scenario we wrote in 2014, where we for the first time sketched how innovation for jobs could look like from the "customer perspective" - where the customer is in this case is an individual who wants to earn a living and is not fully aware of her strengths or what they can be used for. The Jobly scenario became adopted by i4jers and became a word of the i4j vocabulary, representing highly advanced AI-services for tailoring jobs and educations, and something like a "Turing test" for innovation for jobs.

# Jobly: How to disrupt unemployment.

## By David Nordfors and Vint Cerf (July 2014)

Some say all jobs may be automated. Perhaps next thing consumption will be automated, too, and then we are really in trouble. Seriously, something does not make sense with this way of thinking.

Instead, innovation may disrupt unemployment. With a new mindset that appreciates the value of people, innovation can drive unemployment 'out of business'. Everyone can have a good job.

It's not that we are innovating too much. The problem is that we are trying to run the new economy in the old way. The old way is about doing more of the same, more efficiently. It's about standardizing tasks, creating work manuals, and such things – many of them very tedious and non-rewarding. Well, that's what machines are good at, so if this is only what the economy is about, yes – we will be losing more jobs all the time. And now we are worried, because we can't imagine what people can do instead. So that's what we are lacking: imagination.

It's obvious: all people can create value for each other. There are no useless people. We 'only' need an economy that lets people create value. People are more enabled than ever before. The smartphone is such an amazing tool that we are surprised every day by people doing new things we just didn't think of as something possible for people to do. Each unemployed person with a smartphone is in control of a supercomputer center packed with engineers, according to old norms. How can a sound economy of any sort avoid utilizing this amazing

7

resource of empowered people? It's not like there are too few problems for people to solve or that people stopped wanting more out of life. How about fixing the climate, eradicating disease and stopping wars, to start with? There are an infinite number of new things to do.

If we become as innovative in creating good jobs as we are in creating innovative products and services, then the innovation economy is sustainable. Today there is a product or service being developed for every possible need and desire. Can the economy develop valuable jobs for every person, letting them do something that fits them like a tailored suit, creating the highest possible value and satisfaction for everyone involved? Then there will be an infinite number of job possibilities for a limited amount of people. People will be the scarce resource, not jobs. Imagine instead of getting a job because you can do something that other people (or machines) can do, you get a job because you are special in a way that creates real value for other people. An attractive aim for the innovation economy, we think.

What could this look like? Imagine starting a company that recruits you to their service, let's say it's called Jobly just to give it a name. With smart technology Jobly scans your skills, your talents, your passions, your experiences, your values, your social network, and so on. Jobly finds ways of testing the market for things you can do. Perhaps you say "I would like to paint pictures but I don't know how to earn money on it". Well, there is a fair chance among all the billions of people on the planet there are some people who are willing to pay you. Perhaps you try that for a few weeks, then you try something else, until you decide to settle for something that feels really meaningful that you do together with people you work well with. Finding the right job is a bit like finding the right partner, isn't it? Now, if Jobly takes a commission on what you earn, then Jobly has an incentive to make you as valuable as possible. Jobly will help you find the right training courses so that you will earn better, increasing what they earn. Jobly may offer you health benefits, too, because if they have a few hundred million users, they can spread the risk, they will be your health insurance, too. You are the service they offer to their customers who buy work in order to create value. Jobly would be disrupting unemployment, tailoring jobs for the so called "unemployable". It's quite often that people carrying that label are among the best people we know, the ones that make us feel that something is seriously wrong with the labor market today. The ones that are amazing, only that they don't fit the slots, so sorry, too bad.

A business model like this one is good for both the micro and the macro-economy. It is for-profit driven, maximizes the value of people and minimizes the cost of tasks. It distributes wealth, creating happier workers and wealthier customers. It seeks and creates diversification, enabling people in society to do as many different things as possible together, thereby strengthening the ability of society and economy to deal with all types of challenges. It is a model for nurturing a middle class society in the innovation economy.

The value proposition is attractive. Think about it, only a fraction of all human capacity is being used today. So many people hate their jobs. The market size for disrupting unemployment is the difference between the value created this way today and the value created by all living people, fitted with tailored jobs they are passionate about, giving one hundred percent of their capacity. This might be the greatest business opportunity ever.

So what about automation killing jobs, then? Innovation is actually a very good thing in the economy we have described, because it frees up people so that they can do other things. But it has to be combined with innovation in tools, making people able to do new things that they could NOT do before. Smartphones are great. So is software for creativity and productivity.

People with disabilities, or who have suffered severe social challenges or who have been ill, don't have an easy time on the job market. But with the right tools and work conditions they can be just as attractive as anyone else. They often have special skills that people with less challenging lives lack which can make them even more valuable. You won't find these things in the job descriptions of listed jobs.

Or look at those who are unique in other, very special ways, for example those who say they can see auras around people. It's not a recognized skill. A lot of scientists and other presumably rational people will say they are fakes. They are often into healing or alternative medicine which isn't accepted by the healthcare systems. Insurance won't cover it.

You won't find a single job description saying "we are looking for people who can see auras". There isn't a big market for aura healers. In 2012 researchers found a possible explanation to seeing auras. It's a condition called "synesthesia", crossed wires between the senses. There are people who see colors when they hear music, often excellent musicians, such as Tori Amos or Leonard Cohen. Research suggests that people who see auras have 'emotional synesthesia', their eyes see

9

an augmented reality, colored by their feelings. This is a very valuable gift In a world where so many people are out of touch with themselves. People with emotional synesthesia will often be better at seeing when people are troubled, or spot when someone is lying, because they are emotional seismographs. They can excel in anything that requires gut feeling, which is quite a lot. They can be excellent neuropsychologists, work with improving human-computer interaction, or work with making video conferencing technology more efficient.

Almost no one knows about the 2012 research paper. Why should they? There is no incentive. Synesthesia is a very unusual gift and it's not like aura healers are important for the economy today. You won't see any job descriptions talking about it. This is a type of value that a company like Jobly can cultivate. Their intelligent system will be following the research and relevant discussions. They will know if you are a healer, because it's obvious from your emails. They will notify you, saying something like "you can be very good at reading people, check out this 2012 paper and these other sources if you want to know more". Jobly might go on asking "are you interested in working with something like building a new educational system in Country X?" because it turns out that country X, a place you like going to, is working on an anti-corruption program and are restructuring their educational system. They need people who are empathetic and can spot honest people that can be put to work with coaching kids. You already know people in country X that are involved in the project, it's only you aren't aware of it. They aren't aware that you might solve their problem, and they definitely don't know the 2012 research paper. Even if they know you are a healer, they won't make the connection to their project. Jobly will not tell you all it knows, it needs to keep discretion, but links can be made in each case. Let's say you are thrilled by the idea of spending some time in country X doing good work, and you are pretty excited about the 2012 paper which explained a bit more you who you are at the same time as suggesting how you might create value with it. So Jobly now gets in touch with your friends in country X, the ones working with the education system, presents them with the idea that people with emotional synesthesia might be relevant for building a corruption-free system. If they say this is something they would like to look into, Jobly lets you know, and then it's up to you to get in touch. Jobly will let you know that some of your contacts might be good entry points. If you decide to go for a project together, Jobly will give you all the administrative tools you need to fix visas, taxes and so on. And 20% of the money goes to Jobly, for reinvestment in continued refinement of job and talent mining.

How big is the potential market for job innovation startups? Well, to start with, there is $100 billion in cash spent each year on unemployment insurance. Perhaps a part of that money can be used as incentive for job seekers and companies like Jobly to get going putting people's most valuable talents into use.

But unemployment not only costs tax dollars. That's the small part of it. Human capacity is probably the world's most underutilized resource, the world's largest potential market. Think about it: In an average western country, only about half of all people are in the workforce. About a tenth of those are officially out of work. So there might be a doubling of GDP already there.

Next, consider this joke: A visitor is being shown around a large workplace. He asks "How many people are working here?" His host answers "About fifty percent". We all know it's true. There is perhaps another doubling of GDP just there. The market for disrupting unemployment might, in principle, quadruple the GDP. Can we even imagine a larger market opportunity?

To be honest, we must also not forget: not all of the work we depend on is paid work. It's a lot, spanning from being a good parent to community work, engaging in democracy, or developing Linux and Wikipedia. We DON'T even want this to be paid work. So disrupting unemployment means more than giving people paid jobs. It is about how we create wealth and wellbeing and meaningful lives for everyone.

# The Unbeatable People-Centered Economy

By David Nordfors

*Purpose of innovation:*
*to create a sustainable economy,*
*where we work with people we like,*
*are valued by people we do not know,*
*and provide for the people we love*

13

# Table of Contents

# Dear expert, read this first

If you are an expert on the future of work or the economy in general, you no doubt have gathered a great deal of knowledge. Like many other skilled experts, you might only need to see a few keywords to figure out a text. Many can open a book, read the table of contents, leaf through it and then know enough to discuss its content with the confidence of an expert.

Not this book.

This book systematically takes keywords out of their normal contexts and reframes them. I play games with them tear down walls between ideas that you might see as unrelated. For example, I play with the idea that "employee" and "customer" are the same person. And they are if a "job" is seen as a service delivered to an employee in the same way that a service is delivered to a customer. Confusing? Perhaps, but it actually makes a convincing point once it sinks in. You can read more about it in this book.

I have done my best to prevent fast-reading experts from thinking I'm saying something I'm not. It's a tough task, because the key strategy I am proposing for the future of work requires us all to look at things differently. Therefore, in addition to my very best effort to present the ideas in an unambiguous way, I'm compelled to add a "warning label":

*If you merely browse this book you are likely to misinterpret it because it reshuffles familiar keywords and reframes standard contexts.*

I am indebted to the experts who so patiently read the draft and provided invaluable advice: Lennart Nordfors, David Michaelis, Steve Denning, Jon Shell, Jeff Saperstein, Pat Windham, Valerie Fox, Ralf Lippold, Jana Elhassan, Jason Palmer, Chally Grundwag and my partner in crime, Vint Cerf. Without them, this text would look quite different and lack much of its clarity and edge. Any remaining imperfections are entirely mine.

# A systems theory in the making

*The following few paragraphs are for readers with a mathematical interest only. If this is not you, this section is redundant and you can move on to the Executive Summary.*

I first planned to include formal theory, because the people centered economy is a systems theory in the making. After trying, I took it out because I thought it would scare away readers. Instead, I hope to write a second book on *The Dynamics of the People Centered Economy* if given the opportunity. These are core ideas from the next book.

The economy, as we understand it, is a system of attractors close to some kinds of equilibria determined by their homeostases -- a balance between actors. All components of an economy interact, directly or indirectly, and thus share in defining each other. The attractors are the "wave functions" of the economic systems. When the economy is stable, so are the attractors, equilibria, and definitions. The traditional mainstream economy sees homeostases and equilibria but ignores attractors, and how things define each other. It cannot compute ripple effects of radical innovation, how changing one definition affects all other definitions, how it affects homeostasis, or if it breaks the attractor. This is a requirement for innovation economics, we must be able to analyze the effects of radical innovation. The types of attractors I speak about are notoriously complex. Computing them from numbers for GDP, unemployment, and so on as input is very difficult.

I suggest innovation is best understood as narrative. People know innovation because "it changes the story." I can show that it's fruitful to reframe innovation as "the introduction of new narrative," because innovation means new ways of relating, with technology and business as enablers and sustainers. The mathematics I mastered as a quantum physicist turns out to be potentially excellent for identifying emerging narrative. I believe it can monitor how emerging narratives affect definitions and transform economies, and it may compute attractors of language - relations between words and ideas. The basic assumption is the "Memes connect people, and people connect memes." Clusters of interconnected people and memes are "commemities" -- communities with common language -- and can be used for analyzing innovation economies.

Today, economics mostly places the things people trade at the center, not so much on the people themselves. I suggest to represent economic systems as graphs, which is a natural way of representing any systems of interactions between entities. It allows to readily shift between task-centered and people-centered frames. The "I-Thou Economics" in this book is an example. I hope to present these thoughts on system dynamics in the future. Until then, I hope the present book will have an appeal, also without spelling out the logics.

# EXECUTIVE SUMMARY

## Summary of the people-centered economy (PCE) and its benefits

*A "people centered economy" focuses on raising the value of people.* A "task-centered economy" - which we have today - focuses on lowering the cost of tasks. Innovating higher value jobs is in general more complex than increasing cost-efficiency and there has not existed such a market to date. Only now, AI is providing the tools for it and *a people centered economy is no longer a utopia but a more powerful and humane market economy waiting to happen.*

The needs to be valued and to be in demand are part of our human nature. *Innovation can, and should, make people more valuable.* The economy is about people who need, want, and value each other. When we need each other more, the economy can grow. When we need each other less, it shrinks. We need innovation that makes people need each other more.

We need to earn in order to spend. A sustainable innovation economy will have as much innovation for earning a better income as it has for spending it in better ways. Today, there is very little innovation for earning and no good innovation at all for earning a livelihood, which is what people need and want the most. This is the next big market for innovation.

The New Ecosystem for Innovating Jobs is the biggest market waiting to happen. The global workforce is sad and misused today, with only 5% of workers engaged in jobs matching their abilities. If AI can tailor jobs to fit peoples' individual abilities, the value people in the world create for each other can increase -- perhaps several times. Even if they charge only a modest commission, the market for companies tailoring jobs will be larger than any market existing today.

19

In a task-centered economy, governments and businesses are often at odds. Governments want workers to be paid more, while most businesses want to pay workers less. Public-private partnerships on the labor market often fail and business people are often disappointed with governments. *In a people centered economy, governments and businesses in the new ecosystem for innovating jobs will be aligned by a shared interest in helping workers earn more and have more value in the economy.* Public-private interaction on the labor market will be more efficient through more effective alignment of increased profits and economic growth.

PCE supports an educated view on currency as an infrastructure for people to create value. Human ability alone is not enough, because building an economy requires that people have access to the infrastructure. Local, temporary "crypto-currencies" may offer solutions for bootstrapping local economies -- for example, in poverty-stricken regions or after natural disasters -- by offering local populations good infrastructures for creating value.

## PCE is a Humane Economy

We all want to do meaningful work with people we like, be valued by people we don't know, and provide for the people we love. Innovation should help us with this. *We need an economy that values us for who we are,* embraces our imperfections, and seeks to shape our environments to bring out the best in us. Innovation should also do this.

There exists an "interpersonal economy" that carries more meaning and that the existing economy should serve. It is the essence of human nature to seek and find purpose in love and friendship; this is what keeps the species alive. *We have jobs so that we can have families and friends, not the other way around. We need economics that supports personal relations and does not objectify them.* It might be possible to construct such economics, as shown by the "I-Thou economics" example in this book..

The "transpersonal economy" is not to be ignored. Faith and mysticism are part of human culture and guide economic behavior. Throughout history, humanity has often applied transpersonal solutions to social dilemmas and other "wicked" problems lacking simple "rational" solutions. Faith and mysticism can be appreciated by individuals as sources of inspiration and can be constructive for an economy.

# PCE can be created by introducing an ecosystem for innovating jobs

By introducing an entrepreneurial ecosystem for innovating jobs a task-centered economy can transition into a people centered economy. The resulting people centered economy will create more value than the original task-centered economy. It does not remove existing value markets, it adds a new market -- for innovating jobs. The transition should therefore be driven by a for-profit startup ecosystem.

The new ecosystem bridges labor policy and innovation policy, creating incentives for an "innovation for jobs policy." Labor policy will have an incentive to stimulate an ecosystem that innovates jobs for undervalued people and can multiply existing innovation policy budgets in ways that attract private capital to engage in job innovation -- without affecting existing labor policy programs. A good way for public policy to midwife ecosystems for innovating jobs is by mitigating risk for the entrepreneurs and investors willing to explore this new entrepreneurial opportunity. It allows them to follow models that have already proven successful for bootstrapping other innovation ecosystems. The threshold for starting the ecosystem is a lack of tested ways of evaluating startup business plans for raising the value of undervalued people.

People centered startups should and will compete to seek the most undervalued populations in which the value of work can be raised the most through innovation. In this way, *the people centered economy gravitates toward a middle class economy.* A plausible pilot case for an ecosystem that innovates jobs is "coolabilities," special enhanced talents that typically co-occur with disabilities, such as the enhanced ability of blind people to relate to sound and touch or the autistic coolability of managing detail, which already is much appreciated in the software industry. "Coolabilities" are a reservoir of rare expertise, well suited for job-tailoring that brings higher margins and a high ROI.

Art, culture, and faith are important in people's lives and driving forces in societies. Bootstrapping a people centered economy requires a combination of rational economic measures, as described above, and encouraging people to see the values of fostering a people centered economy beyond its economic rationale. Promoting storytelling, art, and other expressions of human culture provides people with agency and faith in their own futures. The people centered economy also offers opportunities for communities to connect their humanistic and spiritual values to the economy.

# INTRODUCTION
## A challenging journey toward a happy ending

This is a story about the future of society. The story starts today, when technology is changing everything and many of us don't know how we will be earning our livelihoods in the future. It tells us about the threats to our jobs and our society, and our confusion about how to respond. The story then changes direction as we find that the future is not hopeless after all. It is not hopeless because we can transform our mindset in a simple but non-intuitive way, just as our ancestors did when they decided to place the sun instead of the Earth at the center of the planetary system. When they took this difficult step, their confusion about the movement of the planets disappeared. Today we face another turning point, and if we succeed, an uncomplicated vision of a better future appears. Contributors to this volume help point us to how that future can be reached. Despite the threats mentioned above, this is a story that can have a happy ending. Whether it does or not depends on what you and I decide to do together.

## The purpose of this book

When people talk about jobs, workers, employers, and labor markets, they cannot help but think about how difficult it is to find a good job and how few employers treat workers well. Even so, most people fear losing their jobs even if they don't like them because they don't know if they can find another one. According to Gallup, only one in twenty people has a job that matches their abilities and engages their interest. For each worker who is engaged, there are two who hate their jobs. Work is a topic so full of gloom that people don't even want to think about it. For example, "labor market" is not a happy term. Why not? "Farmers market" is a happy term because it signifies fresh vegetables. Why can't "labor market" signify "great jobs"? "Worker" has the ring of "victim." Why? It should be a happy word, like "doer." Likewise, "job" is a word that reeks of uncertainty and fear of loss. That's so sad! The word "job" should be reassuring, like the word "mission." Just as everyone can choose a mission that brings meaning to life, I suggest we should not expect anything less from a job.

I am here to throw gloom out the window and make place for a different way of thinking. Forget even the term "right to work." People DO have the right to work, but we gain it not by focusing on the problems but by focusing on opportunities that solve problems. This opportunity can be described in this simple way:

*All people are valuable,*
*and everyone can create value for others.*
*We need only an economy that makes it happen.*

This book does *not* discuss how to force or even encourage employers to hire or retain workers they do not need or want. Instead, it discusses how to build an economy that creates so many ways for people to create value for each other that jobs will be competing for people instead of people competing for jobs. It suggests a "people centered economy," a healthy market economy where companies compete to offer you, me, and everyone else opportunities to earn a good livelihood by applying our unique sets of abilities, talents, and passions. Thus the people centered economy creates value between ourselves and others.

"*Everyone* is good at something," says V. Ferose, father of SAP's "Autism at Work," who has written a chapter in this book. He convinced his global corporation that autistic people not only have special needs, they also have special talents that most others do not have. We invented a word for these special talents that accompany disabilities: "coolabilities." Together with Ferose we are creating a language that can discuss these special strengths for all people who have disabilities. As we show in this book, this "coolabilities-language" can help create new valuable jobs for people with disabilities, and for everyone else.

If this book will help you find a better, more humane, and happier language that helps you talk about what work is and what its future can be, then it has achieved its purpose.

# PART ONE: THE OUTSET

## Ground rule: The economy is always about people

We teach our kids that it is wrong to treat people like things. Yet that is exactly what the economy does all the time. Am I romantic to think that this must be wrong? Many will say so. I challenge that.

The economy is always about people needing each other. As they need each other more, the economy can grow; if they need each other less, it shrinks. In a good economy, people who need each other also value each other.

In its simplest sense, the economy is a system that connects what people want with what people offer. A good economic system makes such matches meaningful and satisfying both for the giver and the receiver. In a people-centered economy, our basic assumption is that all people can create value for others and that the goal of the economic system is to make this happen. The PCE is both about finding sellers that satisfy the buyer's needs AND finding buyers who value what others can offer. It actually becomes the same thing if we accept that being valued for what we can do is a need. As humans and as members of an economy we all need to be needed and wanted. Who will satisfy that need? In a people-centered economy, the purpose of innovation is to introduce new and better ways to make people need, want, and value each other more. Raising the value of people is the goal and lowering the cost of things becomes a way of making that happen.

Simple logic tells us that in successful economies, people create more value together than they would be able to create apart. If this were not the case, people would be better off living outside the economy, and the economy would not be able to survive. The people-centered economy is the paradigm that is closest to the rule of survival for people as well as societies. In order to survive, we need an economy where people have the incentive to earn a living by helping other people help each other earn a living.

The economy, society, our culture, our survival as individuals and as a species - it all hangs together and it all boils down to one simple truth.

You can call it spiritual, hard fact, kumbaya or bottom line, but it is the essence of what all of them say:

## *At the end of the day, the economy is about being here for each other*

An economy that does this might succeed, if it does it well enough. An economy that doesn't do this is living on borrowed time.

# Idea: "Task-centered" vs "people-centered" economy

This book introduces the idea of elevating our existing "task-centered" economy to a "people-centered economy." Both are market economies. A "task-centered economy" is driven by market-forces aiming at lowering the cost of tasks, while the "people centered economy" is driven by market forces aiming at raising the value of people. Both economies are in agreement that people make themselves valuable by performing valuable tasks, but the drivers are not quite the same:

*A task-centered economy seeks people to do valuable tasks.*

*A people-centered economy seeks tasks that make people valuable.*

Switching the order of two words might not seem important, but it makes all the difference. A task-centered economy will typically shape people to fit job slots, as in "there is a high demand for data scientists" and therefore "go learn data science, it makes you valuable and leads to a good career." A people-centered economy will ideally shape jobs that fit people, as in, "Let's find out what you are good at and like doing and see what opportunities we can create for you." The first one will feel natural; it is what people are used to thinking because it is the economy we live in today. From this perspective the second one might be puzzling, perhaps more like pampering than employment. I am here to convince you otherwise -- that a market for "tailoring jobs" is the largest market waiting to happen, building the strongest economy.

My son told me recently that he intends to get his college degree in anthropology. A quick search on the Internet revealed that it is today the fourth worst-paying college major. More than ten thousand U.S. students graduate in anthropology each year, while the job postings are in the hundreds. This made me concerned. From a task-centered economic perspective, he is making a very bad choice. He should choose a major that gives him a better chance at a good job. A people-centered economic perspective, however, leads to a different perspective. Forget the job slots and ask what value he can create with his knowledge of anthropology. Ideate the job based on what you know and love. He, like everyone, will have a unique combination of abilities, and as AI expands its scope from social interaction to cultural interaction, from sociology to anthropology, there should be something interesting for him, a way to carve out a job for his profile. This is what a people-centered economy is about: carving out, or "tailoring" jobs for people based on their individual talents and desire.

It is my thesis that much more value can potentially be created by a people-centered economy than by a task-centered one, and that artificial intelligence is the key to realizing that potential. This is what we want as individuals and for everyone in the economy. This is the society envisioned in this book, one that should not be impossible to build:

> *A powerful innovation economy,*
> *where people do meaningful work together with people they like,*
> *being valued by people they do not know,*
> *providing for the people they love*

If innovation helps us do this we will prosper.

A word about the vision above, which we shall repeat several times in the book. "Being valued by people we don't know" might have a strange ring, but it is, in the simplest words, what a successful economy requires. Being valued by many others is what makes an economy strong. A modern economy may consist of millions of people, each of whom can know only a tiny fraction of the population. Yet every one of us depends on the others, both near and far away, and the particular work they perform. If we appreciate the effectiveness of this far-flung and disparate community, we come to appreciate the value of all those others whom we will never meet. We can appreciate those who, like us, also discover how much they depend on others (including me) who can do or make the countless things we need and who will need the things that we can do or make in return. We create for others just as they create for us, reinforcing the economy in its reach and diversity.

# PART TWO: THE TASK-CENTERED ECONOMY IS FAILING

## Summary

*The task-centered economy is about lowering the cost of tasks; it is not primarily about making people more valuable. The main danger is easy to summarize: when workers are seen as a cost (which is now the case), cost-saving technologies will compete to lower their cost and thereby their value. The "better" the innovation, the lower their value. People are struggling to stay valuable in a changing world, and innovation is not helping them, except for the chosen few. The present economy is plagued by many symptoms of this lethal illness. In this chapter we will look at some of those symptoms and connect them to their cause.*

We have become excellent at innovating, and the world has entered into a global innovation economy. The task-centered economy rewards innovation that increases the cost-efficiency of things and lowers the cost of labor. As a result, many people fear a task-centered future; they see a looming workplace of constant uncertainty as artificial intelligence and technological innovation are predicted to extinguish most jobs traditionally held today by humans. While technology can indeed create wealth, many experts no longer see how that will continue to be possible as long as the goal of technology is to reduce the cost of labor.

We have increased our technological powers many times and still we are not happier; we do not have more time for the things we find meaningful. Despite the recent decline of unemployment in the U.S., people remain worried. New jobs are, on average, less attractive to workers than jobs that have disappeared. Young people go into debt to pay for protracted schooling that often fails to land them a meaningful job or that prepares them for one that is outdated when they graduate. This contributes to a rising mountain of student debt that may by itself be massive enough to trigger another financial crash. Advances in innovation and technology, which we might expect to help us solve these problems, have instead made them worse.

Going back to the ground rule -- that the economy is about people being here for each other -- we can realize that the task-centered economy obeys this rule only as long as the tasks must be performed by people. But innovation, driven by the incentive to lower costs, will act as a force to replace people with machines, or at least with cheaper workers.

We should consider whether the incumbent task-centered economy can handle innovation in small doses but not in large ones. This is not unlike the way yeast can survive the alcohol it produces only up to a certain level -- and then it dies.

# The Warning Signals

## Warning signals (1): The labor market is becoming less inclusive

Workers with disabilities are "canaries in the coal mine." When the economy starts seeing less value in workers in general, people with disabilities will be the earliest to lose out because they are already struggling to have their abilities recognized. When they are pushed out of the workforce, other workers have reason to worry about being pushed out next. We will come back to people with disabilities several times in this book, because it turns out that these people may have enhanced special abilities, which we are calling "coolabilities," that may offer surprising access to a labor market with better jobs for all people.

AI is a great technology for workforce inclusion. People with disabilities, special needs, and cultural differences can be matched with jobs that fit their special profiles. AI can also create assistive tools for overcoming weaknesses and bridging differences between people from different cultures.

The problem is that inclusion is not happening. Looking at labor market statistics, we see that smart information technology is being used to shut out people who don't fit existing molds.

According to SourceAmerica[3], the future of work (in America) looks

---

[3] Kanady, Shane. "The Future of Work and the Disability Community - 2018 The Social Enterprise Future Report - SourceAmerica." https://www.sourceamerica.org/sites/default/files/report/files/2018_socialente rprisefuture_report_final_hires_ada.pdf. Accessed 3 May. 2018.

disproportionately bleak for people with disabilities. The number of people who leave the workforce claiming disability is on the rise. One suggested reason for this is that people who used to be middle-class are sliding down the economic ladder, increasing the competition for the lower-wage jobs below. until now, those jobs have been the best that people with disabilities could hope for. The graph shows the steep trend toward the exclusion of people with disabilities which began with the onset of the Internet economy.

## PEOPLE WITH DISABILITIES DROPPING OUT OF THE US LABOR MARKET

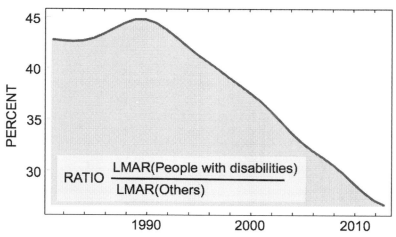

Ratio betweenLabor Market Activity Rates (LMAR) for people with and without disabilities. 100% = no exclusion 0% = total exclusion. LMAR by Cornell University Yan Tan Institute. Data; BLS./Census

According to researchers at Cornell University, the labor market activity rate[4] for people with disabilities peaked in 1990, in the pre-Internet economy, at just below half that of people without disabilities. From then on, as can be seen in the graph, it has declined steadily. [5]By

---

[4] Labor market activity rate (LMAR) definition: percentage of Americans aged 18-64 who worked more than 52 hours in the prior calendar year. The LMAR of people with disabilities is shrinking in proportion to the LMAR of people without disabilities. ( Source: Cornell University Yang Tan Institute; data from the Current Population Survey (CPS) by the Census Bureau and the Bureau of Labor Statistics

[5] In order to make the trend more visible the graph has been smoothed with a Gaussian (fwhm 4 years) - the unsmoothed graph has a more jagged appearance.

the time of the smart economy in 2014, people with disabilities were down to a quarter of the labor market activity rate of people without disabilities.

This picture is confirmed by the worsening job situation for older workers in the U.S. According to AARP, age discrimination continues to rise[6,] despite half a century of legislation fighting it. If technological innovation is truly intended to increase the productivity of the worker, the trend would be the opposite. Assistive technologies would be a big business opportunity, increasing productivity of every individual it is applied to. Instead, it seems that the method for seeking increased productivity is by stricter selection of job applicants - applying machine intelligence for finding workers that better fit the bias of the employer - which often such stereotypes, as the young software engineer.

# GROWING U.S. WORKFORCE EXCLUSION

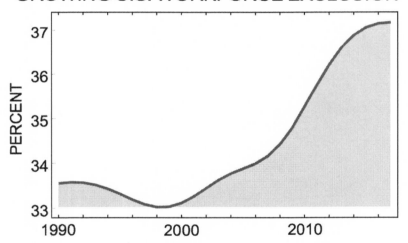

Percentage of U.S. adult population outside the workforce. Data: BLS

The proportion of people excluded from the workforce has increased from just below 34 percent in the 1990 pre-Internet economy to 37 percent in the 2014 smartphone economy. The proportion of excluded people has increased by 10 percent, and the exclusion of people who do not fit the mold is increasing unproportionally. Note that this is not the

---

[6] "Age Discrimination Goes Online - AARP."
https://www.aarp.org/work/working-at-50-plus/info-2017/age-discrimination-online-fd.html. Accessed 3 May. 2018.

same for *all* countries, as Sven Otto Littorin, former Swedish Minister for Employment, shows in his chapter of this book.

The conclusion is that

*technology capable of improving work is instead used in ways that makes it more difficult to be a worker,*

and this in turn is becoming a problem for the employers.

## Warning Signals (2): The wealth and income gaps are widening

The average income of the median U.S. family[7] is falling each year, lagging a bit farther behind that of higher income families, which are raising the mean income ever higher above the median.

## INCOME DISPARITY ON THE RISE

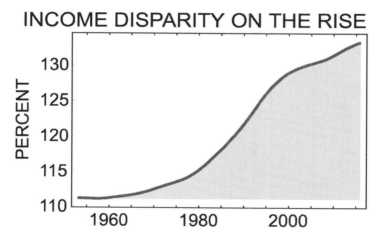

AI can help people get good education and good jobs, creating a more equal society for people, making them leverage on each other's differences. Nearly everyone could be valuable to others and in demand for their skills and talents. But this is not what is happening. In the U.S. and many other places, the rich are getting richer, the poor

---

[7] U.S. Bureau of the Census, Mean/Median Family Income in the United States [MAFAINUSA646N - mean, and MEFAINUSA646N - median], retrieved from FRED, Federal Reserve Bank of St. Louis. Gaussian smoothing applied.

are getting poorer, and the gap between the rich and the poor continues to increase.

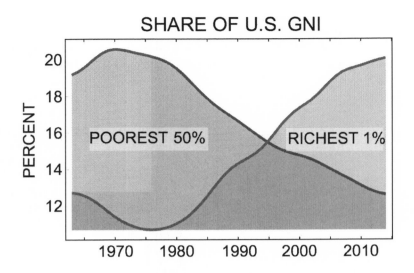

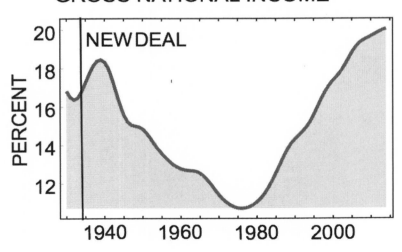

It was not always so. Until 1980, before the onset of information technology, the top 1% of high-income U.S. earners were sharing their riches with the lowest 50 percent of the population a bit more every year, and their take was down to 10% of gross national income (GNI)

that year. But since then, the top percent's portion of the pie has doubled to 20%. The difference is larger today than it was in 1935, in the depths of The Great Depression, when President Roosevelt announced the "New Deal" that put the workers of America back on their feet and delivered them into the middle-class economy. Today, every fifth dollar of the national income goes into the pockets of the 1% (according to the World Wealth and Income Database).

But the GNI and income gaps are dwarfed by the ownership gap, which is bigger still. The richest one percent have increased their ownership[8] of the pie from 25% in 1980 to 40% today, while the percentage owned by the "middle class" (some 40% of the population) has shrunk from 34% to 27% over the same period. The lowest 50% of the population by income have in the meanwhile lost the single percent they once owned and are now, on average, in debt, owning less than nothing.

*The rise of the working middle class boosted by Roosevelt's "New Deal" has been all but wiped out.*

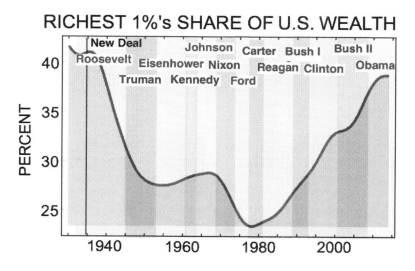

RICHEST 1%'s SHARE OF U.S. WEALTH

---

[8] Net personal wealth share held by top 1 percent; the total value of non - financial and financial assets (housing, land, deposits, bonds, equities, etc.) held by households minus their debts. Piketty, Thomas; Saez, Emmanuel and Zucman 2016. http://wid.world/data/

In the beginning of this century I was working with innovation policy. To measure value, we would look at the success of companies. Managers had strong incentives to help companies perform well, and they built huge wealth that some economists assumed would spread to others in "trickle-down fashion." But objective analysis of the numbers shows that there seems to have been more "trickling-up" than "trickling-down." The trickle-down economic theory is valid when people who own much money spend it on low- and middle-class people who do valuable things. But if innovation displaces too many workers, money spent by the rich will not reach them. It will go instead to the highly-paid few -- the owners and the innovators -- who take over the piece of pie that used to go to workers. The result has been that more money moves back and forth between the rich and less of it trickles down to the less-rich. When the amount employers save by paying workers less equals their net earnings, growth disappears and the economy starts shrinking. This raises the pressure on innovators to help owners cut even more labor costs in order to salvage their dwindling gains. The competition for dollars becomes ever fiercer for a diminishing pie. Like the terminal stage of a fatal illness, the patient shrinks away.

Given the direction the gaps in income and wealth are growing, the illness is clearly, in my opinion, getting worse. Or so it seems; economics is complex, and some economists are suggesting that this apparent illness might in fact be an illusion. But I believe it is very real and threatening. To explain this, we must first know a bit more about economic growth.

## Warning signals (3): The economic growth rate is declining

With the never-ending flow of ever-better tools reaching our hands, we might expect to be creating ever more value for each other, at accelerating growth, every year. But this is not what is happening. Instead GDP growth numbers are slowing. Another worry is that the digital economy is making the world economy more vulnerable to disruptions. There have been several ups and downs in the economies around the world, but the big recession in 2008 it was unusual to see all economies hit at the same time. It seems that the world economies have become so interconnected that a collapse in one place can trigger a collapse everywhere, instantaneously.

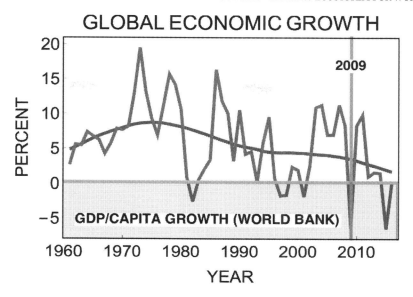

### Technological deflation is confusing us

Having said that the economic growth rate is slowing, we need to examine this assertion a bit more carefully. In the innovation economy, "economic growth" is a fuzzier idea than it was previously. This is because the slowing rate may be caused by two factors. Either innovation lowering the value of workers so that they earn and spend less, or we are getting "technological deflation" -- or both. Technological deflation, in simple terms, is a process that gives us more "bang for the buck" over time due to improved technology. Innovation economists will often point to it in arguing that the economy is not at all slowing down as traditional economists suggest. For example, computers get better all the time while prices go down, not up. Thus technological deflation is confusing our understanding of growth. Because of the increasing importance that "technological deflation" is having in the economy, we need to get even a bit more familiar with the idea.

The increased bang for the buck we see in technological deflation might sound like a good thing. Indeed, we are surely happy to see things get better while costing less each year. But we should be aware that this seeming goodness can at the same time signify more sinister goings-on.

*There are two types of technological deflation.*
*One can be good, but the other is very bad.*

Let us start with the potentially good one. We expect our next smartphone to be better than the one we have and to come at the same price. It never occurs to us to keep this new one until it fails; instead, we expect to get rid of it while it still works perfectly well in order to get the even better phone we expect to come in the not-too-distant future.

This type of technological deflation is the hallmark of a functioning innovation economy. The tipping point between a conventional economy and an innovation economy is when the economy is driven by products that have a shorter life on the sales shelves than they have in our hands before they die. A smartphone model will be sold for perhaps two years before it is replaced by a newer model with improved features. The phone itself might keep functioning perfectly well for five or ten years - if we had the patience to find out. But this is an economy where the customer buys the product only once, and where the more the user loves the product, the more eager she will be to replace it ASAP with something better. The first rule of business is to retain the customer at all costs. In the innovation economy, the most important product is not the one that exists; it is the next one to be imagined and then sold to the customer.

Innovation becomes the driver that speeds up the economy and that makes people buy and sell more products and look for new ways to satisfy each others' needs.

Hence, according to many innovation economists, traditional economists who point out that innovation is not increasing growth rates are missing something important. People are getting more for their money. A phone bought today is twice as valuable as a phone bought for the same price two years ago. If the economic data was corrected for this, we would see a solid and continuous exponential increase in growth. If everything followed Moore's law, doubling in price performance every eighteen months, the exponential growth rate would be 46% per year. We would be speeding up growth by nearly 50% without seeing it in the growth graphs. This is such a sizeable hidden growth rate that it would make the existing graphs meaningless for understanding value creation without knowing how large a part of the economy follows Moore's law.

To counter that, it can be argued that since an increasing part of the economy is being driven by Moore's law, there should be an increasing number of products that are exchanged quicker, following the example of the phone: cameras, games, musical instruments, kitchen equipment, hand tools, and so on. Our drive to consume should be going up because we are more tempted to spend and we should have a greater drive to work more and earn more in order to afford the things we want. This should be visible as growth in dollars -- but that is not the case.

This brings us to the other form of technological deflation which is not so good. This kind can actually kill economies. It doesn't only give people more for their money, it makes people earn less, too. It is driven by companies that compete to pay less for workers in order to offer the consumer a better bang for the buck. People will put off buying something today because they assume it will be cheaper tomorrow. This not only slows the economy, but also causes people to lose their jobs, which gives them even more reason not to spend the money they have.

Kartik Gada, a member of our i4j community, suggests governments should print money to offset technological deflation. He says that printing money and handing it out as universal basic income to the citizens can replace taxes[9]. It is the most outrageously provocative economic idea I have heard to date; it makes economists see red, and members of our community who are renowned economists, even lost their temper when the idea was presented to the extent that I had to intervene.

The logic in Kartik's idea is this: the "quantitative easing" counteracts technological deflation, because printing money causes inflation and balances them out. One effect of printing money is that your next phone will cost more than the one you have, not the same (or less) like today. Kartik says this is fine, because it's a better phone and should cost more. The second effect is that you won't have to pay taxes any more; you simply get fresh money each month from the government's printing press. This "universal basic income" redistributes value from the rich to the poor. Before continuing to the critique, let me say I am intrigued by the intelligence, simplicity and wildly provocative nature of this idea. But I don't know if it will work. If it doesn't it can destroy the currency and the entire economy.

Any economist will say that printing money is seen as a last resort for stimulating an economy that is standing still. It's like using electric shock treatment on a patient with cardiac arrest. Kartik's suggestion to print money instead of collecting taxes is as provocative as it gets. This

---

[9] Kartik Gada, The Accelerating TechnOnomic Medium (ATOM) (2016), http://atom.singularity2050.com

is why I remain sceptical to the idea. Kartik is an unusually intelligent and conscientious man, an original thinker who stands by his guns without getting nasty. Processing his idea has been so valuable in trying to explain the weirdness of technological deflation that I am sharing it with you. Overall, we need to look even closer at how to understand technological deflation or we will not be able to understand or guide the innovation economy.

## Warning signals (4): Gig-workers are like proletarians in the Communist manifesto

A lively current topic of discussion is whether the AI and machine learning revolution that seems to threaten our jobs is different from previous industrial revolutions. The context is certainly new, as we contemplate the self-driving car, a choice of smart appliances, and a world of global connectivity and competition. But the patterns of change are similar. When Marx and Engels wrote *The Communist Manifesto* in 1848, the industrial revolution was knocking down traditional economies like small trees in a mighty wind. Swift changes in technology during previous decades led to dizzying automation of agriculture and crafts, obliterating old jobs in homes and fields and creating new ones in factories. The situation seems a bit similar today, but you may be shocked when I describe the extent of similarity.

Communism was an idea of great attraction but a tragic human failure that plunged billions of people into misery and gave birth to numerous dictatorships with dysfunctional economies. With this in mind, read the following paragraph of original text from the Communist Manifesto, where I have replaced only four key words with modern equivalents/ *Bourgeoisie with Internet Entrepreneurs, Proletariat with On-Demand Workers, Civilization with Digital Economy, and Revolution with Disruption.*

*"Internet entrepreneurship cannot exist without constant disruption of markets, bringing uninterrupted disturbance of all social conditions. The need of a constantly expanding market chases Internet entrepreneurship over the whole surface of the globe, giving a digital character to production and consumption in every country. Established industries are pushed aside and the rapid improvement of all markets and cheap prices compel all nations to introduce the digital economy and become Internet entrepreneurs themselves. Internet entrepreneurship has merged markets and concentrated ownership into a few hands. It is like the sorcerer, who is no longer able to control the powers of the demons whom he has called up by his spells. The periodically returning market bubbles create great destruction. When these bubbles burst, society regresses; industry and commerce seem to be destroyed; and why? Because there is too much digital economy, too many ways of doing business. Internet entrepreneurship has created the modern working class -- the on-demand workers, who must sell themselves in bits and pieces. They have become a commodity, exposed to the whims of the market. Their work has lost all individual character, and all charm. It is only the most simple and most easily acquired work that is required of them. The on-demand worker's production cost is limited almost entirely to his living costs. But the price of a commodity is in the long run equal to its production cost. Therefore, the more the individual character disappears from his work, the wage decreases in proportion. The lower middle class will gradually become on-demand workers, partly because their specialized skills are rendered worthless by new methods of production."*

The accuracy of this message from the grave is nothing less than spooky. The analogy is clear, as is the message it sends:

## *Internet entrepreneurship is the new bourgeoisie.*

The original text from the industrial revolution and the "updated" Internet-era text are displayed side-by-side in Appendix A. Seeing them together is for me a powerful experience that leaves me convinced that we are once again following the old pattern, only in a new context.

The analysis of the on-demand worker, for example, seems spot-on: according to Ridester[10], in 2013 an Uber driver -- the stereotypical on-demand worker -- would have to drive 2.36 miles to earn ten dollars. Three years later, in 2016, this had nearly doubled to 4.71 miles. We recognize the patterns of the Communist narrative, the earnest discussions about how machines were going to kill all jobs.

## Warning signals (5): Return of utopian delusions: "UBI replaces jobs"

It may come as no surprise that ideas akin to utopian Communism are reappearing, because similar thought patterns lead in similar directions. Our brains have not changed much, nor have our basic social behaviors.

The most explicit and radical attempt to influence the future of work today is Universal Basic Income, or UBI. Of the two types of UBI, I'll call the first the "utopian UBI" - or the "communist" one, supported by people who believe all jobs will disappear and all workers will be replaced by machines. The other type is the "work-friendly UBI," which provides a bit less than minimum wage -- barely enough to live on. The second type does give people an incentive to seek work and removes fear of switching jobs; that is, it creates labor mobility. The public discussion, however, refers to both as simply UBI, which causes confusion.

---

[10] "Uber Fees: How Much Does Uber ACTUALLY Take ... - Ridester.com." 5 Mar. 2018, https://www.ridester.com/uber-fees/. Accessed 25 Mar. 2018.

In its utopian form, UBI suggests giving all citizens a basic income that covers their spending without having to work. This form is unlikely to work because

*people will always need to be able to depend on strangers -- even adversaries. They need a common language embracing trust, ethics, law, and practice*

to which each committed individual has a stake and a belief that promises will be kept. Such a common language and trust is the basis for any successful economy, culture, or society.

But a language of trust will only evolve when people form a network of commitments between individuals. And this can happen only when we satisfy one another with our services in return for payment -- everything from baking each others' bread to meeting each others' spiritual needs. It means showing up on time for work every morning if this is the deal you made with your employer, or being a whistle-blower if your employer breaks the basic ethical rules we have agreed on. There is nothing in utopian UBI that can replace these commitments.

Utopian UBI still would not succeed as a market economy even if society did not degenerate into a clan-based structure, and even if ethics, trust, and justice were hard-wired in our brains. UBI would still fail because of the basic logic of money. If all income was delivered by government in the form of UBI, all the money people spend must be paid to the same government in order for them to continue paying the UBI. All the power would reside with the government, and private capitalism would disappear. Logic requires that private capitalism can flourish only when it helps people both earn and spend.

# Root cause: the growth-profit paradox; getting richer makes us poorer

Why does not innovation create more good jobs for more people today? Why is income disparity increasing? Why does it look like it slows down growth instead of speeding it up?

The root cause for all this is the very essence of the task-centered economy: placing products and other things at the center of the value proposition instead of people. It seems very natural to see it this way, because, after all, I want my house painted and there are painters who

41

want to paint it – how can it work any other way? Yet, wanting things done better and cheaper, combined with innovation that makes that happen, is the cause of the troubles.

This is what, paradoxically, makes the efforts of everyone to become wealthier make us poorer overall. I will call it the "growth-profit paradox:" innovation that creates wealth shrinks the economy.

The paradox is explained by the difference between macro- and microeconomics. In macroeconomics, people must earn in order to spend; the worker and the customer are the same. In microeconomics, the customer and the worker are different: one earns, the other spends. Corporations live in the micro world. They innovate, automate, and, when necessary, lay off workers to deliver a better deal to the customer. The customer is king, the worker is just a worker.

But customers who have lost their jobs are weak kings; their biggest need is to get a good job with a reliable income. In a task-centered economy, companies don't see their purpose as competing to offer people a good income, they see it as competing to offer them more in return for spending it. If they do so by firing more workers to cut labor costs, as automation lets them, the average customer will have less money to spend. The companies adapt to the customers' shrinking purses by offering them still cheaper products and services by cutting labor costs. It is a spiral pointing downward toward a point zero where people earn and spend zero. This is the mechanism of the growth-profit paradox. Economic growth is killed by companies that are competing for profits.

At the heart of this paradox is the old saying, "A dollar saved is a dollar earned." This maxim applies to you and me in daily life, and it applies to companies and every other component of microeconomics. But it does not apply in the macro-economy, where a dollar saved is actually a dollar lost. Countries don't have profits, they have growth. This is because one person's earning is always other people's spending. If everyone spends less, people earn – on average – less.

*The labor market is a game of musical chairs,*
*and the more people try to earn money by not spending it,*
*the more chairs are removed.*

Countries therefore want to increase both earning and spending while companies want to increase earning and cut spending. Hence, in a task-centered economy, governments and companies have opposite economic incentives. We see everywhere how governments try to make companies employ more workers than they may need. This gives companies a double incentive to cut labor costs, first in order to lower production costs and then to receive money or favors from governments in return for keeping workers. It's not a great solution for anyone.

The growth-profit paradox is a painfully real threat to our societies and needs to be solved. In this case, "a dollar saved is a dollar earned" is at the center of the paradox. It has become the problematic part in the economic engine.

It might not be possible to solve the growth-profit paradox in a task-centered economy, because it is inherent in the mindset. This mindset always looks at work and asks what is the most cost-efficient way of doing it. What keeps the economy from collapsing is the inherent limits of automating work. Workers have remained a necessary, if undesired, cost. But what will be the outcome if artificial intelligence allows almost all work to be automated? Now the task-centered mindset implodes. With a task-centered mindset, innovation is set to kill economies.

# PART THREE: THE SOLUTION: THE PEOPLE-CENTERED ECONOMY

## Summary

*A people-centered economy (PCE) is similar to the "Copernican revolution" in that it switches people to the center of the economy and moves tasks into orbit. From this new perspective organizations always serve people: some services are for spending, others are for earning. The organizations form an ecosystem competing to make people valuable for each other by superior matching. The problem of the present economy is the unbalance between services for earning and for spending. The solution is to create an "ecosystem for innovating jobs," where companies compete to offer people better earning services. Such entrepreneurs create revenues by identifying demographics of undervalued people and innovating ways of raising their value. Currency is an infrastructure for value creation that might be applied in new forms, locally, temporarily, for bootstrapping economies. Possibilities of adding an interpersonal dimension of value are discussed as ways to strengthen economics by to optimizing relations between people, where dollars provides the means.*

## A "Copernican revolution": place people at the center

I have showed how innovation has the power to push the task-centered economy into the black hole of the growth-profit paradox and that we can already see warning signs. Trying to solve the problem with a fix inside the task-centered economy won't solve it, because the task-centered mindset is itself the cause of the paradox. When we try solving it that way, the reality we perceive becomes complex and confusing. We start debating which jobs can't be done by machines, whether machines can become exactly like people, whether machines should pay taxes, whether machines should have human rights if they become like humans, and so on. These are all interesting philosophical questions, but discussing them will hardly solve the practical problem: innovation is disrupting the economy.

I suggest the key reason why our economy seems so wickedly complex is that we lack the appropriate language and an understanding.

*We are applying the good old ideas that once made things understandable but are now making the world unintelligible instead.*

This happens often in history -- for example, people in the middle ages had long thought that the earth was the center of the universe, but as scientists became more sophisticated and ambitious in creating a model of how the other planets and the sun revolved around the Earth, the more complex and incomprehensible their orbits became (see illustration). But simply by switching perspective, however, and saying that the planets might move around the sun, their complicated and almost fanciful orbits were transformed into nearly-circular ellipses of great simplicity. Today most people can picture the entire solar system in their heads without even needing a model or illustration.

I would suggest that we can profit from a similar exercise in understanding what causes a healthy economy. Just as the astronomical model was instantly simplified by placing the sun at the center, I suggest that economic models can be vastly simplified by moving the value of people to the center instead of the cost of things, as suggested in the figure.

Our present task-centered way of seeing the economy might seem like the time- tested and obvious way, but it is actually complex, disconnected, and wrong. It splits people in two and separates them into different markets: a worker-persona who earns money on a labor market, and a consumer persona who spends the money on a consumer market. This is actually a disconnected reality in which we are living double lives!

Place people at the center, instead, and things fall more neatly into place around us. The labor and consumer markets merge into a single market with us at the center; around us, companies offer us two kinds of services, one for earning money and another for spending it. We are whole again; the economy focuses on us and provides us with things to do, for earning and for spending, respectively.

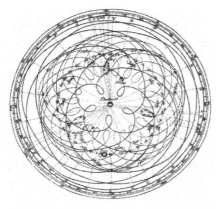

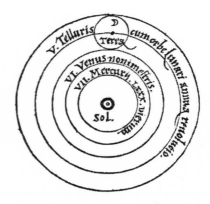

*Earth at the center:* The orbits of Mercury, Venus and the Sun around Earth. From the first edition of Encyclopaedia Britannica (1771)

*Sun at the center:* The orbits of Mercury, Venus and Earth around the Sun. From Copernicus' "De revolutionibus orbium coelestium" (1543)

## TASK-CENTERED ECONOMY

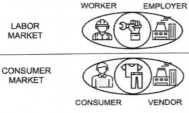

## PEOPLE-CENTERED ECONOMY

*Split vision:* People earn on the labor market and spend on the consumer market.

*Simpler and handier:* People create and exchange value on the market where organizations provide them services for earning and spending.

*PCE has a simple and handy view of the economy: People create and exchange value, served by organizations.*

Perhaps a people-centered economy view could enable us to simplify the innovation economy and engineer it better as the "Copernican revolution" did for physics and astronomy. The economy is all about people, after all, so it seems only natural to place us at the center.

# Seeing the innovation economy through the PCE lens

The task-centered discussion about whether AI will create or kill jobs is complex and confusing. But seen through the PCE lens it is much clearer: "Is AI-innovation being applied more to earning or to spending?" The answer is "spending" and the conclusion is that we need to support innovation that helps people earn.

It's not easy to reframe a job as an earning-service. Almost nobody I have met grasps it at first. They tend to say, "The worker serves the employer, not the other way around." But PCE is a different way of thinking altogether. It postulates that people are served by organizations, not the other way around.

## Essential Reframing (1): A job is a service for earning a livelihood; the worker is the customer

A really good earning-service offer looks something like this:

*JOB OFFER IN A PEOPLE-CENTERED ECONOMY*
*Dear Customer, we offer to help you earn a better living in more meaningful ways.*
*We will use AI to tailor a job to your unique skills, talents, and passions.*
*We will match you in teams with people you like working with.*
*You can choose between kinds of meaningful work.*
*You will earn more than you do today.*
*We will charge a commission.*
*Do you want our service?*

This is the gist of a service that everybody wants but almost nobody has. Today, only the most attractive workers can hope to be approached in this way. I would argue that such a job-service offer is not only becoming possible, it is the biggest entrepreneurial opportunity waiting to happen. Here is where we reframe the task-centered economy into the people-centered one: by reframing "a job" as "the service the customer uses to earn a living." This will sound strange to most people, just as people once found it bizarre that the Earth should circle the sun. After all, every time people of Copernicus' time looked into the sky, they thought they saw the sun circling the Earth. In fact, it is often the experts that have the hardest time reframing because they have become wired to think in a traditional way. They have built so much into and around the frame they have always known that switching becomes a huge challenge. While the

47

layman only needs to reorient a "shack" of ideas, the expert is challenged to rebuild an enormous skyscraper. This is one of the strategies used by innovative startups to outcompete huge corporations with a thousand times their manpower and budget -- they reframe.

Let me attempt to explain this reframing in a simple, logical, and convincing way. I have had this conversation a few times with experts who have deep professional knowledge in technology and innovation, and I believe I have found a good metaphor for doing it.

Here is the dialogue I had with i4j's publisher Guido van Nispen:

> *Guido:* What does "a job is a service for earning a living" and "the worker is the customer" mean? It does not make sense. The worker performs a service for the employer and the customer is the one who pays.

*David:* There are cases where the earner is the primary customer, not the spender.

> *Guido:* What does that mean?

*David:* Think about new platforms like Uber or eBay. They have two customers -- the paying customer, who is the spender, and the participating customer, who is the earner - it can be the person selling things on eBay or the on-demand Uber-worker.

> *Guido:* That's true. These two-sided platforms serve both the seller and the buyer equally. It has become a popular and powerful model for online business.

*David:* I think it's very rare that a platform serves the earner and the spender equally. They they will usually serve one more than the other. The spender wants to pay less and the earner wants to earn more and every so often the platform company comes into a situation where they must side up with one and lose the other. Then they must decide which one to let go. Uber prefers to keep the spender -- the rider -- and let go of the driver -- the earner. eBay, on the other hand, would rather keep the the earner -- -- the seller -- and let go of the spender who visits eBay only to buy things. eBay's primary customer is therefore the earner, who sells things through their platform.

*Guido:* True. eBay depends on hosting good sellers. When they have good sellers, the buyers will come.

*David:* Now imagine if eBay introduces a "jobBay" addition to their platform that lets their sellers sell more than just products. Now it lets them sell services, too. They can sell any service they want, charging the spender by the hour. Gardening, cleaning, tutoring, programming, singing arias on roller skates. Would the seller of services or the buyer be jobBay's primary customer?

*Guido:*The seller would still be jobBay's primary customer. Adding the option to sell work hours does not change that fact. I'm guessing the opera singer on roller skates wouldn't get many customers, though.

*David:* Indeed. Now imagine that jobBay introduces a set of marketing and support tools that help sellers sell their work. They might offer the opera singer a market analysis, such as, "If you ride a horse instead of roller skating, that might increase your chances, but the chances of your finding a client will still be extremely slim. But Max's Opera Cafe hires waiters who can sing, and your roller skating proves you have good balance -- clearly a plus for waiters. Do you want to market your services to them? Click this button." They could furthermore offer health insurance to the sellers who sold more than an average of thirty hours of work per week each month. The sellers would now have an incentive to sell through jobBay. With this addition, would the seller still be the primary customer?

*Guido:* Yes, the seller remains the primary customer. Adding services to help them sell doesn't change anything; quite the opposite. It's a good idea to add the health insurance, it motivates the sellers to sell more via eBay and it solves any legal issues if a seller got hurt while performing a service for a buyer.

*David:* It could even be great business for jobBay, because if they have millions of sellers, that would spread the insurance risk so they can form their own insurance company. It would be a new line of business AND it would give the jobBay earners incentive to sell more hours.

*Guido:* Indeed, a smart business idea AND a good service to the sellers.

*David:* Now imagine a next step. jobBay tells their earners, "If you sell more than 30 hours a week, we can offer you another insurance, too -- a savings-based insurance that can cover the dips in income. It requires that you register as a jobBay employee, but don't worry, "employee" is just legal talk. We won't ever boss you around; you remain our valued customer and can come and go as you want. As our "employee-customer," we are at your service. Our tax experts will manage your tax returns at no cost and you will get other benefits, such as a paid vacation bonus package. At the end of each year, we calculate your average monthly earning and you will receive one month's pay the following year -- without working! -- so you can take your family on vacation without losing any of the services that come with the jobBay "employment" package. You only need to work a minimum of 120 hours per month over a year to be eligible. With the jobBay employment package comes also complementary professional training in software engineering of your choice from our education partner Udacity. Each course usually costs a hundred dollars, but you get them for free. It's good business for us if you take them, because when you earn more, we earn more commission. Your interest is our interest." With this package added, would the earners still be jobBay's primary customers?

*Guido:* Yes, even more so. These added benefits makes jobBay's service to the sellers, or "earners" as you call them, much more "sticky." They have every reason to stay loyal to their platform provider.

*David:* So I conclude -- and here is the twist: If jobBay's primary customers, the sellers, accept the offer, they are formally employed by jobBay. Legally, this is not different from any ordinary employment -- but the big difference is that they -- the workers -- are now the formal employer's primary customers. Their job is offered to them as though it were a service -- and in fact it is. jobBay doesn't care what they do, as long as they are happy with this service, and continue using it for earning their living! Ergo, the job has become a service for earning a living. The worker is the customer.

*Guido:* I understand this now. I never thought about it this way. It feels quite weird, but I guess it is possible to see it this way. Isn't this just philosophy, switching words around and calling things by different names?

*David:* Yes, many will call it "just philosophy." I have an issue with the word "just." This type of philosophy is very hands-on. It makes life simpler and lets people earn a living in better ways with less hassle. It's opens a huge new market for business.

*Guido:* I think I need to rest my brain for a while. Let's talk more about this later.

\* \* \*

# Essential reframing (2): The labor market is a service market; companies serve people jobs

Did the reframing make sense yet? Then you are ready for the next step: discovering the world's largest untapped market that is waiting for innovative entrepreneurs.

*From the worker's point of view, a job is the earning-service that can provide for him.*

Every worker wants this, but it is difficult to find. When we reframe a job as an earning-service, we reframe the job market as a service market. The current job market is very dysfunctional as a service market. There are few good service offers and most service customers are dissatisfied with what they get.

Once upon a time, there was a country called the Soviet Union which introduced Communism and destroyed free markets. If you pulled the right strings and bribed the right people, you could have the incredible privilege of buying a really bad car at the cost of a few years' salary. Today, in the Former Soviet Union, you can buy any car you want if you have the money to spend. However, spending is easier than earning. People everywhere are pulling strings and bribing people to get a low-paying job that doesn't fulfill their needs. In the world of today, the service market for spending is competitive and serves the customers well. But the service market for earning is similar to the old Soviet system across the world.

51

Business people might say that their job is to sell things to people, not to earn money for them, but that is backward. Before the first industrial revolution, success in manufacturing meant selling expensive things to rich people. Then came mass production, allowing the most successful manufacturers to sell cheap things to the masses. Until now, the most successful agents have earned money by helping famous artists and writers earn money. But with AI, the most successful agents will be helping many millions of workers earn better livelihoods in more meaningful ways.

Let's look closer at the idea we call great-jobs-as-a-service, GJAAS. Here the earner/worker is the customer and the employer offers the job/service to the worker. A good job provider will invest heavily in smart AI technology for profiling, matching, and improving human capital to find earners better work than they can find themselves They will offer them better income, benefits, stability, and interesting things to do in partnership with others. That's far more than most people can arrange on their own. It keeps the customer happy to pay a commission on every dollar the service earns — like eBay or any other open marketplace. Serving the earner might even be better than serving the spender, because when the spender runs out of money, the provider loses a customer.

If we see the job market in this way -- as a service market -- how is the current labor market fulfilling this function? Not well; the customers are not happy, to say the least. The good news is that the world's largest service market is ready to be disrupted by innovative new ways to satisfy the customers' needs and wants.

And the market opportunity for this is huge! Here is an estimate: According to Gallup's chairman Jim Clifton[11], of some five billion people in the world who are of working age, three billion want to work and earn income. Most of them want a full-time job with steady pay, but only 1.3 billion have one. Out of these 1.3 billion people with jobs, only 200 million are "engaged" in what they do for a living -- i.e., they enjoy what they do and look forward to each working day. These lucky few, however, are outnumbered 2:1 by those who are disengaged, expressing displeasure and even undermining the work of others. The remainder of the population are simply disengaged from what they are doing, dragging their feet through the work day. This is the sad state of

---

[11] Jim Clifton "The War for Jobs", Gallup.
http://www.gallup.com/businessjournal/149144/coming-jobs-war.aspx

the global workforce that creates roughly a hundred trillion dollars' worth of products and services every year. Humanity is running at a fraction of its capacity.

*If everyone had a job that engaged them, we would all be happier and humanity would create many times more value than today.*

Imagine using modern information technology to tailor jobs to every one of the three billion people wanting to work -- work that is well matched with their unique skills, talents, and passions; work in which they are assigned to valuable tasks and partnered with people they like to work with. In such a world, the average world citizen would be able to generate several times the per-person value created today. Also, the person with a meaningful and satisfying job will be much happier and healthier than the jobless, passive, or disgruntled person who is unsuccessful in finding such a career match on their own. Increasing smartphone penetration and new capacities like cloud computing and big data analytics could tailor rewarding jobs for every person on earth. We are at the beginning of a revolution in strength finding, education, matchmaking, HR, and new opportunities in a long-tail labor market.

Imagine the three billion working people in such a positive environment. How much more value would they create than the unhappy, mismatched workforce of today? A doubling of value creation is surely low, but even that figure adds $100 trillion in value to the world economy. If the job providers charged a 20% commission on the incomes people earned through their services, this would generate $40 trillion in revenues. As a comparison, it is estimated[12] that ride-sharing companies charge their on-demand drivers twice as much commission in return for an unremarkable, low-paying opportunity to earn, doing work that does not build on any special abilities or offer new potential for growth. Innovation for great jobs as a service is a narrative that opens doors to mind-boggling opportunities where companies will compete to leverage the value of people.

---

[12] "Uber Fees: How Much Does Uber ACTUALLY Take ... - Ridester.com." 5 Mar. 2018, https://www.ridester.com/uber-fees/. Accessed 25 Mar. 2018.

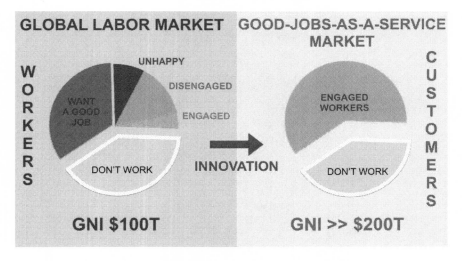

The low-hanging fruit in this process is the population of undervalued people. An innovative employment service can screen the population for talent, train them in ways that fit their abilities, and find paying jobs they can perform effectively. A startup with such an innovative GJAAS could easily raise the value of large numbers of people who now earn zero or few dollars, inviting them to become productive members of the workforce.

So not only is GJAAS potentially the largest job market no one has heard of; it is also a commercial market where companies will compete to serve those who are now left out of the job market. Therefore, GJAAS is an industry on the horizon that can help restore an ailing middle-class economy and restore it to good health.

## *People-centered and task-centered businesses will coexist.*

People sometimes think I am suggesting that *all* businesses *must* be people-centered. This is not the case. I am saying that today there are many companies offering us good ways to spend our money and few companies offering us good ways to earn it. There are no companies knocking on our doors and offering us ways to earn a good livelihood. Companies will go on helping us spend, but I am pointing to the incredible business potential in establishing a market for good earning services.

# How people-centered companies can outperform task-centered ones

There has been much discussion about Uber replacing its human drivers with self-driving cars. I suggest that a better strategy is to automate the cars but hang onto the drivers. Then they can innovate more valuable things for drivers to do than sit behind a wheel. If companies innovate to maximize the value of each of their workers, they become a people-centered company that can outcompete a task-centered company that keeps cutting staff whenever possible. Doing work that requires paid workers is the key to good business. It's an illusion to think of workers as a mere cost; they are the essential capital for earning profits. The only reason people think they can earn more money by cutting the workforce is because they see results in the short run. In the long run, however, the strategy fails.

Imagine you own a furniture factory, and you employ 1,000 workers who produce on average $100 worth of output every hour -- a total production of $100,000 in value per hour. Your labor cost and other costs average $90,000 per hour. This means that every hour your factory produces $10,000 in profit.

Now imagine letting go of all your employees and replacing them with machines. Managing the machines and other expenses costs $60,000 per hour, so now your profit per hour is $40,000. But not for long. As soon as your competitors buy the same machines and sack their own workers as you did, the competition catches up. When everyone has lower production costs, prices can -- and will -- go lower as you compete for the customers' dollars. How much lower? A first guess might be that the price of a $100 chair drops to $70. Since $60 is the production cost, you are back at the ten-dollar profit you had before lowering the price.

But that's not correct, because the price will go lower. When you had workers, you were forced to keep healthy margins because people are messy and unpredictable. They have bad days, make mistakes, fall ill, take time off, fall happily in love and become less efficient, or fall unhappily in love and become even less efficient. There is no way to predict what will happen, although your statistics may help keep you safe by maintaining profit margins that keep you from dipping into the red. The same applies to your competitors, of course.

*Because all of you deal with messy human workers, you must all maintain profit margins that keep you safe. The result is that all of you can operate at a profit, even when you compete.*

But with machines, things change. They aren't as risky and messy as people; they are more reliable and predictable. They let you run on thinner margins without fear of falling into the red. But this applies for your competitors, too. In a free competition on equal terms, competitors push each others' profit margins down to the safety zone. With perfectly reliable machines, the margins will be very thin and each market is likely to be seized by one big player while the others die. This company can earn big money because it can afford higher margins when there is virtually no competition -- like Windows with PCs and Google with search.

Another alternative outcome is a market with many competing players and low profit margins, such as the low-priced airline industry. Yet another alternative is the cartel, where competitors negotiate between themselves a common price floor. None of these alternative outcomes are desirable compared to a lively free-market competition with thriving competitors, offering good services to spenders and letting their workers earn a good living. The logical way of doing that, I suggest, is by choosing a business that requires the participation of paid workers.

Therefore, if Uber can automate all cars using reliable technology, so can their competitor Lyft, and perhaps Google and Apple and Hertz and others interested in entering that space. If it lowers their costs and increases cost efficiency, nobody can NOT do it if they want to be in the game. They would keep competing for automating cars, because they can't afford to lose the ride business as long as there is money in it. They would aim for "winner take all,"hoping to become the Microsoft or Google of self-driving car rides. I would advise them to count on the high probability of a low-cost, low-profit market of automated competitors.

Now imagine the people-centered alternative. If they started to analyze the skills, talents, and passions of their scores of drivers, and offering them better paid work -- more than just driving, a menu of opportunities that leverage their personal strengths -- then the company could keep their stake in the "messy human" business that keeps up their margins. They would be transformed from a task-centered business, with the key aim of lowering the cost of tasks, to a people-centered business, with the key aim of raising the value of workers - and staying in a market where people are a bit messy!

This is why people-centered businesses can be more profitable than task-centered ones, with the exception of the rare "winner-take-all" cases and cartels. The people-centered businesses can keep higher profit margins in competitive markets.

How would it look in practice if an industry decided to automate and then tried to find new, more valuable things for their workers to do? Imagine the furniture factory again. We have automated the manufacturing part of the business; now what? We begin by profiling our workers' skills, talents, and passions. We would see which people they work well with in order to build good teams. Workers would ask, "What is the best value our team can produce if our company removes restrictions on what we do?" This is complex. We would need an ecosystem for innovating jobs, with startups that develop methods for doing such things. We would procure their services and test a few competitors. Our success would depend on our accuracy in finding the true talents and passions of our team, inventing a really profitable way of putting them in play, and keep high profit margins by ensuring that people in our team love what they do and like each other very much, which would induce them to stay with our company. All this ability profiling, opportunity scouting, and innovating new services and jobs would build on and reinforce the ecosystem for innovating jobs. As the company made the shift from getting rid of employees to keeping them and finding new things for them to do, a reasonable conclusion is that the task-centered company could shift to become a people-centered company.

The company will sooner or later get competition from startups specializing in innovating jobs for workers. We will be competing to keep our workers. If we lose that competition, another alternative may be to invent new labor-demanding services for our furniture buyers and lease the workers from the earner-service companies.

In this way,

*an ecosystem for innovating jobs is likely to transform a task-centered economy into a thriving people-centered economy.*

# The AI-industrial revolution: mass-personalization.

Why has this not already happened? At least part of the answer is obvious: The science and technology for tailoring jobs on a mass scale has developed only during the past ten years, made possible by computer science, data science, AI, social networks, the smartphone, the cloud, big data analysis, the Internet of Things, and so on. It has never before been possible to match individuals around the world with jobs anywhere, on the fly. We now have the tools to organize good teams of people for almost any purpose at any time. We can design products, processes, and services (including jobs) and estimate their market potential through computer simulations. Prototyping and manufacturing are entering a new era of versatility and value with techniques like 3D printing.

*The industrial revolution brought mass-production.*
*With the Internet and AI comes the era of mass-personalization.*

Everyone on this planet will be the recipient of individualized products and services matching their own personal needs and desires. These include education and jobs. We already have a long-tail market for products and services. The huge opportunity ahead of us is to build a long-tail labor market, making large numbers of people want and need each other more, and creating more value for each other in small but meaningful ways. (In a long-tail labor market, many small sales of diverse types become more valuable than the fewer, larger, homogeneous offerings that characterize a traditional labor market. In the publishing industry, for example, the Internet has shown that the large population of titles with low sales volume can collectively rival or exceed the sales of the publisher's biggest blockbusters few bestsellers.)

# People-centered currency

Imagine that I tell you, "Do this favor for me and someone else will do you a favor in return." You might reply, "What is the favor I will get in return?" I answer, "I don't know." You ask, "How do I know it matches the value of what you are asking me to do?" "That's for you to decide," I say. You ask, "Perhaps you can at least say who is the other person who will return the favor?" "I don't have the slightest," I retort. "Go find him yourself!"

What are the chances you will perform the favor? The answer is, close to a hundred percent -- if we have currency. I just need to say, "Here, take this slip of paper with numbers on it." As though touched by a magic wand, I go from being something like a con man to being the grownup in the room. This is the true magic of currency. It is the promise of return favors that we trust -- even if I don't know where, don't know when.

You will recall the PCE "definition" of the economy: people create value for each other, served by organizations. Currency lets us do favors for people we don't know and have the favors returned by unrelated strangers. This turns the ecosystem of organizations into a giant matching system between people. But instead of matching people one-to-one, like most systems for romantic dating, the "economic dating system" matches many-to-many in multitudes of combinations. We are all customers of this dating system -- people seeking to create value for each other. Organizations in the ecosystem collaborate and compete for doing the matching, simultaneously stimulating and satisfying our needs and desires and leveraging on our abilities. The goal is to support meaningful lives with families and friendships and to extend this support to coming generations.

It is as "simple" as that. All people can create value for each other. A good economy has an ecosystem of organizations that lets that happen, in the most meaningful and fulfilling ways. Of course, we aren't there yet. We are only too painfully aware of how the largest part of mankind's abilities and desires are *not* being leveraged, and how our ecosystem leaves them unassisted and even obstructs them. This is because we don't have a people-centered economy. We also don't have good enough currencies.

Today, in 2018, as soon as I say this most people will think "Ah! Bitcoin!" or other "cryptocurrencies" that many tech-optimists are professing as the "global currency of tomorrow." I will explain why Bitcoin will never become a useful currency. But I will also come to how correctly designed "cryptocurrencies" could work wonders for the economy. They have the potential to make billions of people create more value for each other, especially those who have too little money today to be part of the economy, and help people help each other in situations where the present economy fails, such as after financial crashes and natural disasters.

In order to do this we first need to understand the idea of currency a bit better. We start out by once again stating what it does. A currency is a promise that favors done for arbitrary people will be returned by other arbitrary people at some time. How is that promise kept? Why should we trust it?

Currency has its roots in the tradition of barter. I will clean farmer Bob's house and he will give me something that I feel has equal value in return -- let's say it's a sack of wheat. Instead of using the wheat for food, I might swap it with someone else who will dig a well for me. The sack of wheat can travel from person to person without ever becoming loaves of bread and still it creates value by filling the role of currency.

However, wheat is not really what I call currency. I would say that currency begins with borrowing and lending, I will explain how. A sack of wheat is heavy to carry and not easy to store; it won't stay fresh and it attracts rats. But unlike my old furniture, I don't need to pay someone for storing it. Banker Anne even pays me interest for storing my wheat in her vault. She gives me a small notebook where she fills in how much I have given her.

Baker Becky goes to Banker Anne and asks if she can have the sack of wheat; she will return it later when she has baked bread. Each sack of wheat makes enough bread to exchange for two sacks of wheat. Banker Anne is of course happy to help. Becky signs an IOU in return for the wheat, including a higher rate of than I get from Anne; the difference is her revenue. But instead of handing Becky the sack of wheat, banker Anne gives her a note where she has written *"I will exchange this note for a sack of wheat. Thanks for trusting, Anne (banker)".* Becky gets a sack of wheat from farmer Bob in return for the bank note -- a sack for a sack.

I decide it's time for me to collect my return favor for cleaning Bob's house. I ask Becky to bake bread for me, which she will do for a sack of wheat. I go to banker Anne to collect my sack, but she gives me another banknote instead, like the one she gave Becky. Becky is happy to bake me bread for it, because she can use it to buy another sack of wheat from Bob.

And so the circle is closed. Bob, Anne, Becky and I have all created value for each other; we have created an economy. I cleaned for Bob; Bob gave wheat to Becky; Becky baked bread for me. And Anne simplified what would have been a more complicated process by creating the bank notes for us. Based on our trust in the notes, Bob, Becky and I did our business.

One aspect of this transaction is extremely important: our currency is actually *not* sacks of wheat, it's banker Anne's *promises* as formalized in the banknotes. Why are banker Anne's promises, her banknotes, trustworthy? Because they have the proper security. Anne has one sack of wheat in her vault, and on top of that she has Becky's debt, the IOU, for another sack of wheat. She has issued two banknotes, so that both sacks are secured. One banknote has collateral and the other one is secured by Becky's promise to pay back in the future.

Let's give our currency a name, "Sow," standing for "sacks of wheat." Our "currency zone" has two Sows in circulation. One is the collateral, Sow, the other is the IOU-Sow. One is covered by what exists today, the other is covered by our trust that in the future baker Becky will be able to pay her debt. We are literally banking on the future, that Becky's bakery will deliver. One might say that banker Anne's trust in Becky is "baked into" the Sow.

## Good currency is people-centered and it's strength is our promises to create value with it.

But then disaster strikes: Becky's bakery burns to the ground. Anne's bank has to write off Becky's debt, which now is worthless. There are two banknotes in circulation, both owned by farmer Bob. But Anne has only one sack of wheat to secure them with, so in fact they are not good for a sack each anymore, despite what is written on them. But they are each good for half a sack.

This is a simplified explanation of what happened on September 15, 2008, when world economy went into the Great Recession. In the U.S., more than nine dollars out of ten are IOU-dollars, backed by people's promises. Lots of people had big mortgages they could not pay. When the world realized that these promises to pay debts were worthless the system crashed.

Back to our community. We have a crisis meeting and realize that perhaps all is not lost after all. Suppose Becky can get help to rebuild her bakery, so that she will remain good for her debt; then the economy and the Sow will be saved. There are many different ways of solving this, but it will need a joint effort be all participants. So we agreed to create an organization together. Since I am a professional cleaner and this is a cleaning operation of sorts, the friends elect me as the president. Now it's up to me to create a solution, and here is what I do: I go to banker Anne, I tell her that I am taking the Sow off her hands; I will save it and save her reputation. I create a central bank for it that has the right to issue Sow-banknotes. I tell the members that, from now on, one-third of every business transaction goes to our common organization to provide for things that we need jointly. I let the central bank issue three new Sows, lending them to banker Anne at a low interest rate. She lends them on to Becky who gives them to farmer Bob in return for rebuilding the bakery plus providing a sack of wheat for baking. Then I go to farmer Bob and have him give the organization the three Sows he just collected from Becky in return for two organization-issued IOUs (which we in real life call "government bonds"). The third one was his tax-payment. The organization uses the three Sows to set up a fire brigade. I contract Becky as fire chief (part-time, because she is baking), paying her one Sow for the job, and giving her the other two as a budget for developing the fire brigade: purchasing infrastructure, paying for labor, and so on.

Result: Baker Becky is back in business, her old IOU is restored, and banker Anne does not need to write off the loss. Becky has a bit more debt to pay now, but she earns extra as the fire chief, so she has that covered. With everyone back on track, the economy is running again. We made it! Trust is restored. The Sow had taken a hit when it lost half its value, but it will probably recover because we are now creating more value.

How much wheat is the Sow worth now? It just became more complex and seems difficult to grasp. Well, it's in our power to believe: can we live up to our production goals? Yes, because we have faith in ourselves, and in delivering on our promises. In fact, this whole episode with the fire just made us stronger. We excelled in what an economy is all about: being here for each other and creating value for each other. Knowing what secures the value of the Sow is trickier, and its traded value has a lot to do with our confidence in it and each other. A lot is in the hands of our organization and me as its president. It's my job to see to that we keep our economy in balance and ready to survive the next disaster.

For example, I now need to find a way to monitor what's going on so I can decide how to keep the value of the Sow steady. We started with a Sow that was worth a sack of wheat, but after I printed more Sow-money it became difficult to say how much wheat it actually is. Then it occurred to me that our currency is really a transportation system! The currency is *not* value, it's the *carrier* of value. What matters is *not* how much a Sow is worth, but how fast we are exchanging value with each other.

The Sow is like a train car carrying the value we are exchanging between each other. Imagine we have four Sow-cars for carrying the value we are exchanging. If our exchange gets more intense, each Sow-car will carry more. If it cools down, a Sow-car carries less.

So how much is a Sow worth? The value a Sow carries! If we balance the number of Sows in motion with the amount of value exchanging hands in each moment, the value it carries will be stable. The cars in the picture above seem to be carrying a bit too much, so we put a few more Sow-cars in motion. Now the load each Sow carries is more reasonable.

OVERLOADED! WE WANT EACH SOW TO CARRY **ONE** SACK OF WHEAT

CENTRAL BANK ADDS SOWS UNTIL EACH ONE CARRIES A SACK

I want the value of the Sow to be steady, because, as a cleaner, I want to know that when I clean farmer Bob's house today for the value of a sack of wheat, I will be able to buy bread next week from baker Becky for the same value.

With this insight, I appoint a chairman for the central bank with the following job description:

*Goal*: Make the Sow a reliable currency for doing businesss

*Tasks:*

1.  Accurately monitor how much wheat a Sow actually "carries" in transaction. You can ask Farmer Bob how many Sows he charges for a sack of wheat ("consumer price index").

2.  Keep the Sow steady by regulating how many are in motion. Add more of them to lower the Sow, take some out of circulation to raise it. Try keep the value close to a sack of wheat so that people feel confident about its value.

3.  Keeping going is more important than keeping steady. If the exchange slows, add more Sows, even if it lowers the value.

4.  Keep in mind that Banker Anne is issuing IOU-Sows by lending people money. This works as long as people can pay their debts, so the chairman must keep an eye on Anne and the IOUs. If she lends Sows to people who can't pay back, trouble will be around the corner.

5.  Call me if there is a crisis. Your job is to keep the Sow steady and on the go. The rest is my job.

I hope this little example has given you a some insight. If you take one lesson from it, it should be this:

# Currency and governance are one

Here is an example from real life: In 2008, Spain fell into recession. An overheated economy and a real estate bubble had driven up prices and now the world no longer wanted to buy Spanish products because they got more for their money if they bought from, for example, Germany. If Spain had had their own currency, the central bank could have done things to lower its value and Spanish industry would have been able to compete with Germany again. But since Spain had the same currency as Germany -- the Euro -- this was not an option. Spain had well-organized industries, but that didn't help when the production price was too high. It had to close down many businesses because they weren't price competitive.

Let's turn briefly to Bitcoin to better understand currencies. Imagine if Spain have used Bitcoin instead of the Euro as currency. Would they have been better off? The answer is an emphatic NO. Imagine that Spain switched its currency to Bitcoin in 2010. An employed worker with a wage equivalent to five thousand dollars per month has her employment contract rewritten in Bitcoin. When they switched currency the Bitcoin was worth five cents, which translates into a salary of a hundred thousand Bitcoin per month. Fast forward to December 2017. Speculators have driven the value of the Bitcoin up to twenty thousand dollars (!). The worker's contracted salary now translates into ten billion dollars a month. The same goes for every worker in Spain. That seems like a lot of salary, but workers paid in Bitcoin would not have been happy for long. Their employers' labor costs would have gone up. The labor cost for building a Spanish car, for example, would be around around a hundred billion dollars. Nobody would buy Spanish goods. Every Spanish employer would have gone bankrupt, every employment contract would be terminated. The Spanish government would not have been able to stop it because it could not print Bitcoins to stabilize the currency.

Proponents will say that Bitcoin is good because is stops incompetent governments from printing money and causing hyperinflation, which happened in Germany a century ago. In which way is Bitcoin-Spain better than that? Bitcoin is not governable and is therefore useless as a currency. It is not a tool for helping people create value for each other and building an economy together.

## Cryptocurrency tailored to make people valuable

But cryptocurrency does not need to be like Bitcoin. In fact, it offers a new world of opportunity for building new types of currencies. We can now create currency that is programmed in ways that allows more people to be valuable. Reflect upon our punchline: All people are valuable, and everyone can create value for others. We need only an economy that makes it happen.

Many big cities have slum areas with people living under poor circumstances, very many without jobs. What if all the good people in these slums -- and most people are good people -- said "screw jobs" and helped each other without being paid by employers? It's a utopian idea, I know, but imagine it for a moment. Everyone could live in a pleasant environment, with well-kept houses and clean streets. By combining their abilities, people in slum areas could lift themselves out of much of the poverty. The problem is not the lack of abilities, it's the lack of an ecosystem of organizations providing services for earning

65

and spending. Today, smartphones are cheap and AI is everywhere, it's a large part of what we need for building that ecosystem, but that's not enough. People need currency in order to keep the ecosystem going and have an economy. In principle, lack of currency has a simple solution. Give people slips of paper with numbers on them and let people exchange them in return for favors. How much is such a slip of paper worth? It's worth the favor you get for it. It doesn't need to be dollars. It lets us build value from scratch.

But introducing new currencies is a mess, and printing dollars and handing them out in slums is a recipe for failure. We might think to raise taxes and push money into the slums, but this sends a negative message to taxpayers: "poor people cost money."

Most societies fail in building economies in slum areas, often leading poor people to create informal economies. They will barter goods; organized crime will lend them money at high interest and become the local "banks." We know it so well that we take it for granted. If slums clean up, it's often because they are gentrified, which doesn't solve the problem.

But cryptocurrency provides tools that perhaps might change this.

## Idea: Local cryptocurrencies for removing poverty

This is my idea how it can work. It is a scenario, it has not been tested, but I hope to convince you that it would be worth a try.

Let's say I am a mayor and I decide to lift a slum out of poverty. I have an idea how to do it without using a single tax dollar. I design a cryptocurrency like this:

- Each jobless resident will get a crypto-wallet that is valid for a year.,

- Each wallet comes with ten crypto-coins

- Each coin is worth one days work.

Some rules that I program into the currency:

- A coin that stays idle for a week disappears.

- Each time a coin is used, ten percent of its value (one hour's work) goes to the municipality.

I deliver a speech to the citizens of the neighborhood:

> *Dear people, you have been ignored long enough. You are all great people who deserve to live in a good society where we look out for each other. We should, and we will, value each other. Everyone deserves to be needed and wanted, not only by their near and dear, but also by society at large. This is the goal, and today we set out together to reach it. Each one of you who lacks a job gets a digital wallet today. It comes with ten coins, each one worth a day's work by one of your fellow residents. We have a smartphone app that has a match-matchmaker. Simply say what help you want and it finds the best people who want to help you. You earn coins by helping others; they earn coins by helping you. This is what the economy is about - being here for each other. We get to know each other and make new friends by helping each other We build trust and togetherness.*

Initially, I don't let people split coins. If Anne requests help, she gets Bob or Becky for the day. If they stay only an hour, it still costs one day. This is because I want people to get to know each other better and build personal trust. It's a good thing for a neighborhood. The coins disappear if they aren't used, which encourages people to request each other's help. Every day they work for each other, I get a tenth of a day. This means that every tenth day, on average, they will be working for the community. I will recruit them for cleaning the streets, repairing public buildings, and so on.

This type of currency might have been useful in Detroit, when the auto industry closed and the economy all but died, turning city into a graveyard of empty skyscrapers. Detroit cannot not print dollars, but it could create a local currency that can get people going again by helping each other, won't interfere with the dollar, is local and temporary.

# The people-centered economy is humane

So far, I have made the case that a job is a service that helps people earn a living. In an economy where the worker is a customer for a job-service and the tools allow job-platforms to personalize jobs to compete for the customer, what can such a service look like? We presented a scenario for a company that does just that in our previous book "Disrupting Unemployment." We called it "Jobly." You can read more about it there, but here is a summary.

Using smart technology, Jobly scans your skills, talents, passions, experiences, values, social network, and so on. It finds ways of testing the market for skills that may be useful. Perhaps you say, "I would like to paint landscape pictures, but I don't know how to earn money doing that." There is a fair chance that among the billions of people, some are in fact willing to pay you for landscapes. Perhaps you try that for a few weeks, then someone offers you a job painting landscapes for postcards. The more you do this, the more you enjoy it, and the people you work with.

Jobly resembles today's manpower companies, which hire people and sell their services. One way for it to operate is to provide workers with a job with benefits, and customers freelance work by the hour without strings. A difference is that it uses the latest technology to tailor jobs that bring out the best talents of every individual instead of fitting individuals to job slots. Jobly is the long-tail labor market, more like Match.com than Monster.com; more like eBay than Walmart; more like Airbnb than Hilton.

I got the idea for Jobly in Paris in 2014 at the OECD Forum. I play the piano, so I searched Airbnb for someone who had a piano. I got a room with Marie, a musician who lived near OECD headquarters. As we chatted, I found out that it wasn't her aim to become a professional musician. She had a bachelor's degree in economic development from a top university in Canada, but it wasn't that either. She wanted to become an aura healer. We didn't learn much about aura healing when I studied physics. In fact, many physicists are openly hostile to it. I might have politely changed the subject if my son hadn't recently told me about playing with a girl who saw colors when she heard music. She loved music, and the colors she saw came with waves of emotions. I learned this condition is called synesthesia, and several well-regarded musicians have it.

I became curious: could seeing auras be another form of synesthesia? I asked Marie if she saw colors when she heard music. She answered, "Of course!" as if it were obvious. I Googled "aura" and "synesthesia," and sure enough, I found recent research suggesting that seeing auras was a form of synesthesia. This came as a revelation to me, and it made me think that we physicists must be more open-minded. The observations have scientific value, I thought, even if the mystical theories accompanying them don't.

I began to think that Marie's synesthesia might actually be a powerful strength, an "augmented reality filter" built into her brain. Many people who are disconnected from their gut feelings make poor decisions about people; Marie might have the opposite -- a very strong nose for people. Indeed, another search on Google produced a blog post by a woman with synesthesia who spoke about how she could tell whether she could trust people. I showed it to Marie. "That pretty much nails it," she said. "Wow, you are an emotional seismograph," I replied. She liked that meme and said she would start using it.

Let's say Jobly could scan all of Marie's data, spotting her interest in auras and noting that she sees colors when she hears music. It would be easy to make the connection, as I did, and scan through all relevant research. Jobly might tell her something like, "You can be very good at reading people—check out these articles if you want to know more." Jobly would also find out that Marie has a degree in Economic Development, is half Brazilian, and has lived in Brazil. She knows the culture, speaks Portuguese fluently, and loves being there. Another simple Google search showed that Brazil receives aid money from several countries. Such programs are often plagued by corruption, and this is where Marie's talents could be valuable. Her knowledge of the culture, the language, her education, and her very special ability qualified her to be a sort of living lie detector. Her social network data would show whether any friends, perhaps from her studies in economic development, were working with aid projects in Brazil. If so, Jobly might ask her, "Are you interested in working with aid projects in Brazil?" If she were, Jobly could give her the tools to network with the aid people and help market her skills. Without Jobly, it would probably be a tall task for her to convince aid organizations to hire an aura-healer, but marketing her abilities would be just the job for Jobly. If she got an assignment, Jobly could also help with visas, taxes, permits, and other red tape. This would raise the value of their service and help them retain the relationship with Marie.

In such ways, Jobly would use machine intelligence to boost collective human intelligence. The Internet has opened the world to people, so that instead of hundreds there are now millions of people capable of exchanging ideas and developing common interests. The challenge is to find them and engage with them, and this is what social networks like Facebook, Twitter, and LInkedIn are supposed to do. A hypothesis, such as "People who see auras can be good at HR" could be developed with the help of both artificial intelligence and collective intelligence, as when groups of people put their heads together. Jobly could help integrate them. Jobly will give Marie tools that give her good dialogues with good people. Instead of defining standard job slots and then seeking for people to fill them, Jobly can facilitate discussions between people that might have common interests so that they get to know each other, get ideas about what they can do together, and tailor jobs together. Artificial intelligence offers good tools for boosting collective intelligence.

I co-published an op-ed including this story, together with my partner and co-chair of i4j, Vint Cerf.[13] The article was much appreciated, but several of our advisors suggested exchanging Marie for a different case when we moved onward with the Jobly scenario, saying it was so far from anything familiar that readers would not take it seriously. To me, this was a bit discouraging, because the point was to show how Jobly could work in all kinds of situations, even those with obscure features.

I was just about to give in when Joana, a member of our i4j Leadership Forum, surprised me by saying she was a synesthete, and could confirm the scenario we had sketched. Needless to say I was astounded by this serendipity. She was generous enough to share her story with the i4j forum; she had never told anyone about it before, including her employer.[14] Her story began with hiring someone whose aura was "dark green," and who had quite extraordinary powers.

> *A few months ago I hired a dark green web developer, a real pro, obviously. We're lucky to have him, as dark greens are some of the best when it comes to programming, but they're hard to find.*

> *Everyone who works in the field of HR management knows the struggle of finding the right people for the right positions. We look for qualities, skills (including soft skills), levels of education, experiences, and so on. I also check the colors.*

---

[13] "How to Disrupt Unemployment" by David Nordfors and Vint Cerf. http://i4j.info/2014/07/disrupting-unemployment/ retrieved September 2018

[14] "How synesthesia helps me to "read" people" by Joana, http://i4j.info/2015/08/how-synesthesia-helps-me-to-read-people/

*I am a synesthete, one of approximately 2-4 percent of the world population. Synesthesia is a rare condition which means that my brain connects things like letters and numbers to certain colors; letters, numbers, and people, to be precise. People? Yes. Weird, isn't it?*

*My name is Joana. I'm located in Germany and I'm a writer and peace activist. Besides, I work part time in a media agency. My job there is actually project management. Since the beginning of this year, I'm also in HR management because my boss noticed that I seem to have a knack for understanding people's character, talents and abilities in just seconds.*

*I never told my boss what makes me so good at reading people, but my ability of associating people with colors is actually what helps me to feel a person's character and talents.*

*Synesthesia is also described as "a mixing of senses," and many view it as a kind of augmented reality. It was not until 2012 that a research study was published about a special kind of synesthesia that only very few of the 2 to 4 percent of synesthetes seem to have: a synesthesia that is linked to persons and emotions.*

*So I'll leave it to the scientists to explain how it works and why, and will simply describe how it feels to have this kind of synesthesia and what benefits I gain from the condition.*

*When I am doing job interviews, I do all the common things like checking the CV, asking about their experiences, going over their education, skills, recommendations, and so on. But my most precise tool, which rarely fails, is my synesthesia. For as long as I can remember, I've been able to "see" people in colors. I don't see colors with my physical eyes, of course. It's more like a very strong and clear association, a seeing with the 'inner eyes.' So when I see someone and concentrate on the person, I instantly get a color that I see with my inner eyes.*

*Later, in my late teenage years and as a twenty-something, I figured out that certain colors match certain characteristics.*

*People who have similar colors also have similar characters, similar interests, or similar talents. I like to use the term "color*

71

*families" or "mind groups" as the people with similar colors have a similar way of thinking and thus a similar mind.*

*So when I meet someone, I know from just seeing his or her color what kind of person he or she is. Not in every detail, of course, but the basic characteristics, some ways of thinking—you get the idea.*

*I came into HR management because I'm almost always right when selecting someone for a special position. Not only does it often confirm what the CVs or experiences have indicated (purple people almost never study things like business or marketing, for example), but it also can show talents that people themselves are not aware of. I can often "see" when someone is lying and I can also see hidden talents or characteristics. I know what kind of color fits in which position. For example:*

*For office management, you need someone who's really organized and has a "down-to-earth" mentality.*

*I know that the people whom these characteristics match best are the ones with reddish or pinkish hues, sometimes also yellow or light green. I know that most dark blue people are smart minds but get bored easily by routines, so they would not fit well in this kind of job and hardly ever apply for it.*

*The dark green developer, by the way, did not apply for this position. He applied for Sales and Marketing, but his color indicated an introvert and a very great talent for technical understanding and computer-related things. Since the position of web developer was vacant, I carefully asked if he ever thought of working in the field of programming. Suddenly his face lightened and he explained that he does programming as a hobby but has never studied it (he studied communications and marketing, because job chances were good). It took some time to persuade my boss to give him a chance as developer but in the end we hired him and it was the best decision ever. He learned what he needed to know in no time and is now one of our best developers. My boss is still surprised about how I found out this special talent, but it was pretty obvious to me.*

*It seems that the augmented reality I have is similar to that of a dog who can sense emotions. It has been suggested that people-*

72

*related synesthesia is based on a subconscious reading of non-verbal signs like body language, which the brain translates into color.*

*But whatever it is that makes me see people in color, it has not only given me a career in Human Resources, but also the ability to understand people very well. All in all, my synesthesia has helped me develop a greater understanding for people and the ability to approach people in a better way.*

Joana's story is more than a lone coincidence. Bloomberg Business published a strikingly similar story:

*When Michael Haverkamp runs his fingers across the leather of a car's steering wheel, he sees colors and shapes. "If the texture feels rough, I see a structure in my mind's eye that has dark spots, hooks, and edges," explains the fifty-five-year-old German, a Ford Motors engineer. "But if it's too smooth, the structure glows and looks papery, flimsy." Haverkamp says these hallucinations, the result of synesthesia, help with his nuanced work, optimizing and coordinating the look, feel, and sound of vehicle fabrics, knobs, pedals, and more. He shares his preferences for each with designers, who then use that information to build cars that are pleasing to drivers.*

The Bloomberg article goes on, saying:

*In one 2004 study, the Psychology Department of the University of California at San Diego had a small group of college students with and without synesthesia take the standardized Torrance Tests of Creative Thinking, which evaluate idea generation and originality, among other traits. The "synners" scored more than twice as high in every category.*

According to the National Institutes of Health, around 10 million people in the U.S are synesthetes. Even if only one in 1,000 of them can see archetypes color-mapped on people, there may still be as many as ten thousand Joanas in the United States alone, enough to create a new profession within HR departments. More research into subjects like this can be a gold mine for companies in the business of raising the value of people.

# 'Coolabilities'– special strengths accompanying disabilities

People with conditions that stop them from fitting jobs slots don't have an easy time finding positions. This is especially true for people with disabilities. These people are often considered unemployable and are dependent on welfare or disability insurance. But people with disabilities will often have accompanying enhanced special abilities, like the superiority of blind people in understanding sounds and touch, or autistic people who often are sensationally good at managing detail.

The labor market has always included some jobs where people with special conditions have an advantage. In Thailand, for example, "blind massage" is appreciated, because blind people are known to have strong, sensitive hands. But such professions have been few, and the market limited. AI entrepreneurship can change that by innovating jobs. An early example is the German company Discovering Hands[15] which innovated the profession Medical Tactile Examiner, training visually-impaired women with highly-developed manual sensitivity to detect early signs of breast cancer. After a nine-month training period they get jobs working with hospitals and medical offices.

*People with special conditions may be extra valuable because their special abilities often exceed what others can do.*

If a sensory system doesn't work, the brain can rewire itself to make use of its idle resources for other purposes. For example, for blind people the occipital lobe, which manages vision, may be recruited by neighboring lobes for managing other functions through a process called cortical remapping and neuroplasticity. This can boost their processing power in a way that isn't physically possible for people who are not blind. The brains of blind people can render them highly skilled at processing somatic sensations and auditory input.

Jobly can also help people who have difficulties getting jobs by using their skills with databases and data analytics, being able to correlate special conditions with special abilities in a strengths finder module. Jobly would not only be able to guess that aura-healers have emotional

---

[15] "Discovering hands taktile diagnostik" https://www.discovering-hands.de/startseite/ Retrieved September 2018

synesthesia and should be good in HR, as we saw with Marie, but would also be able to analyze known conditions and abilities and use various correlations to predict new, undiscovered ones. People with special conditions and abilities would become low-hanging fruit for Jobly, since they are among the most underutilized human resources. According to the United Nations,[16] some 650 million people live with a disability, making them the world's largest "minority" -- a demographic suffering an unemployment rate of up to 80% in some countries. In the U.S., only 35% of working-age people with disabilities are working, less than half the number of people without disabilities. This is in itself an untapped, trillion-dollar potential market for Jobly.

With one-fifth of the U.S. population diagnosed with some form of disability, and perhaps that many more who have not been diagnosed, this is a matter of enormous relevance. And these people need a new language to talk about both their special challenges and special strengths which has not existed until now. These strengths and challenges find use in a number of tasks, like programming software. Thorkil Sonne, a father of the "Autism Advantage" movement and a member of i4j, founded Specialisterne[17], the first company to focus on finding, training, and providing employment for talented autistic engineers. He tells the story in his chapter in this book.

A group of i4jers -- Chally Grundwag, Jay van Zyl, and I -- were discussing the Jobly idea, focusing on how AI could tailor good jobs leveraging on these typical enhanced strengths. As we shared our ideas, we began to feel frustrated by the lack of just the right keyword for these special abilities. We needed a term to used when designing our Jobly scenario for people with disabilities. It had to be factual, relevant, and easy to understand in daily speech. We settled for "Coolabilities" because it is easy and fun to say, which we liked, and captures the spirit of these special abilities -- they are simply "cool," coming as they do unexpectedly and with power. Since we have been using it, the word catches people's interest as soon as they hear it.

Before this development, in 2015, the special abilities that accompany disabilities didn't have a common name -- even though a great many people have felt the need to talk about our special challenges and our

---

[16] Factsheet published 2006 by United Nations Department for Economic and Social Affairs, Division for Social Policy and Development Disability, http://www.un.org/disabilities/convention/pdfs/factsheet.pdf

[17] Specialisterne http://specialisterne.com/

special strengths. But I should concede that it is a major task to map the co-occurring coolabilities and disabilities. Chally Grundwag made the first stab at it, assembling the table below, which readily makes clear what coolabilities are. She chose three disabling conditions that are all neurological and added possible job-matches from STEM as examples. In her chapter in this book, Chally presents an expanded table with more conditions and an in-depth explanation of the coolabilities idea.

**Table 1. Disabilities and Coolabilities**: an overview of how coolabilities and disabilities may be correlated and includes generalizations about characteristics and attributes that may apply to any individual with these listed diagnosis.

|  | AUTISM SPECTRUM DISORDER (ASD) (High Functioning) | ADHD (Attention Deficit Hyperactivity Disorder) | Dyslexia |
|---|---|---|---|
| Disabilities | Difficulties in social interaction, understanding social nuances and reduced self awareness. Narrow focus. Difficulty filtering sensory stimulation ie. (sound, light, touch, smell) and high sensitivity to sensory stimulation. Resistance to change and routine. Repetitive behaviour. Challenged in planning tasks for daily living | Hyperactive; Distractible Can't maintain attention; Restless; Impulsive; Disruptive (Risk taker); Decreased inhibition Preservation (Negative hyperfocus) | Difficulties in reading, spelling correctly, decoding words, and in comprehension of text |
| Coolabilities | Attention to detail. Extraordinary observation skills. Deep interest in specific fields. Intense focus. Expansive long term memory. Comfort with rules and guidance. Affinity to analyzing complex patterns in the social and physical worlds. Creative in specific areas of interest. Original thinkers (more time devoted to talent than socializing). Honest. Visual-spatial skills. Exceptional talent in very specific areas. Success at repetitive tasks. Strong systemizing skills. | Risk taking; Spontaneous; Imaginative; Energetic; Creative; High precision; Multi-tasking; Novelty seeker; Connecting multiple ideas; Creating surprising solutions; Idea generating; Innovative; Proactive; High tolerance for uncertainty, "Flow" (Can utilize hyperfocus productively). | Creativity. Original problem solving. Different perspective. Connecting tasks and realities. Divergent or innovative thinker. High focus in fields of interest. Presaverence. Motivation Visual spatial skills (not in reading). Ability to see the big picture |
| Careers | Computer programmers, software design, communications and networking, engineering design, equipment design, fine mechanics, research, mechanics repair, fine advanced machines assembly, lab technicians, web design,, video game design, app designs, accounting, chemistry. Engineering, statistics, computational art and animation. | Entrepreneurs, CEO's, Educators Inventors<br><br>With these strengths can contribute to many STEM careers. | Any STEM related careers in Science, Math, engineering, medicine, architecture, interior design, graphic design, education, VC etc. when accommodations and assistive tech are present. |

When we show this table to people, many of them tell us -- almost immediately -- that they have a disability or a child or family member who does. One i4jer told us he was dyslexic; he is also a superb strategist.

He has contributed greatly to strategic approaches to developing a startup market around coolabilities. At an evening occasion he introduced me to one of his friends. They had started several companies together, and he suggested I present what we were doing. After a minute his friend said, "This is great! By the way, I'm dyslexic." "Me, too," said my friend as they looked at each other in surprise. They had done a great deal of work together, yet neither of them had ever told the other about their dyslexia. This is one demonstration of the power of Chally's table.

## A personal note: My ADD condition

I shouldn't go much further without describing my own diagnosis of mild ADD a few years ago, something I have told few people about. When I finally received the diagnosis, it came as a relief in some ways. I was now excused from struggling with things most people can do easily. When I saw the table above, I recognised the disabilities, but I also recognized the coolabilities. Most prominently, I had always had great impatience with reading, and to this day will do almost anything to avoid tackling a book or even a long article. At the same time, I have abilities in problem solving, perseverance, and innovative thinking (reader beware!). I had never thought before about whether these qualities were related, but now I quickly went from being excused to being absolved. My special condition had been transferred from a diagnosis to a personality type; from the DSM used by psychologists to the diagnostic Myers-Briggs. It has made me believe that it is wrong to include only weaknesses in the definitions of conditions. A complete definition should take all co-occurring traits into account, the positive as well as the negative. By only including the negative, nearly every trait or behavior can be defined as a pathology. Scottish psychiatrist R.D. Laing famously joked about this: "Life is a sexually transmitted disease and the mortality is a hundred percent."

This shift was earth-changing for me, and forced me to rethink my work strategies. I quickly saw that I should spend less effort struggling to improve my abilities at things I will probably never enjoy or excel at doing, and instead spend more effort on developing my special strengths, which I now realized were less common than I had imagined.

Special Collections, Glasgow University Library, MS Laing WF21/3

For example, I never read textbooks in college. I solved problems instead, and when I couldn't figure out something by myself I would "reverse-engineer" the textbook. I always felt as if I cheated my way through college. As a researcher I kept on making discoveries without doing literature searches first. I did not know if the discoveries were my own or if others had made them before me, so I felt I was a bad researcher. The concept of coolabilities has made me realize that my natural way of learning often involves reinventing the wheel, or standing corrected; that's just how I am. There is no sin in being different.

I also realized that people with disabilities are almost the only people who are identified by what they *cannot* do instead of what they *can* do. If I had received my diagnosis as a youngster it would have been detrimental; I would have been defined by my weaknesses. Instead, I "cheated"by inventing a new technique that worked much better for me.

*But coolabilities is better still because by recognizing my strengths, it assigns value to my differences.*

In a people-centered economy, where the key business is about raising the value of people, the "low hanging fruit" for entrepreneurs will be to identify the largest groups of the most undervalued people whose income could be substantially increased by innovation. That would be cool-abled people, people with disabilities who are consistently undervalued. Many are excluded from the economy even while there is a huge untapped resource of above-average human abilities, often of such a kind that it is possible to create a market for them.

When I come to this point of the argument, thoughtful people often ask, "What about people with disabilities who don't have coolabilities, does this not exclude them?" The answer is "No, it should not." V. Ferose, a senior vice president at SAP -- and an i4jer -- made that point when he was head of the SAP plant in India. They needed employees to manage their power plant, where electricity was produced by a farm of very noisy diesel generators. He never managed to get anyone to stay on the job for more than a few months, even when using the best available noise-dampening equipment. Then he realized he should trying employing a deaf person -- who would not be affected by the racket. And he was right: the new employee even liked the job, and performed much better at it. This is what we have called a "contextual coolability," when a context transforms a weakness into a strength. In order to say that a severely disabled person "has no coolabilities," one must first test for all the hidden, latent coolabilities that might exist. This is a challenge, because we don't yet know even a fraction of the coolabilities that exist. Then we must prove that there are no value-creating situations where this person can't have a benefit from the disability. Speaking to you as someone trained in formal sciences, it will be more difficult to prove that a person has no coolabilities than it will be to find one - and this applies to everyone. So if you don't think that a specific disabled person has any coolabilities, you perhaps have not thought carefully enough. Ferose and Chally will tell you more in their chapters in this book.

The most beneficial known job market for people with coolabilities is for people diagnosed with high-functioning autism spectrum disorder, also referred to as Asperger syndrome, who tend to have an amazing sensitivity for detail. A person with autism spectrum disorder is a bit like a microphone connected to a loudspeaker on full volume. It picks up everything, and if the sound is too loud, the speaker will screech. Normally one would lower the volume, but this doesn't work for autistic people, for whom it is full blast all the time. Autistic people often need very quiet spaces and they may find relaxation in repetitive work. Another challenge they have is reading the subtleties or body language of others; they tend to take things literally and have difficulty in job interviews and work environments.

On the other hand, they can have a superb memory, and when they are interested in something; they can learn everything there is to know about it, and remember every detail. They are persistent at what they do, never giving up on a task. This is well known in the IT industry, where autistic coolabilities are highly valued when it is possible to create work environments that suit their special needs, such as sitting in a quiet room at a computer. Performing precision tasks such as finding bugs in code and repetitive programming, which many software engineers find challenging, can be done with great efficiency and even elegance by autistic engineers. The Israeli army has a special unit for autistic people who specialize in tasks like interpreting aerial and satellite photography. They are able to spot features in photos and program algorithms for finding such features in months -- tasks that take other engineers years. (Their real challenges come in different environments, such as taking the bus home after work.)

In a high-paying business like information technology, it is easy to imagine the potential for the people-centered entrepreneur, finding people who are excluded from the job market today and turning them into engineers where they can be worth a million dollars a year in revenues for a company. The tasks are to (a) find autistic people with the talent and the interest to fit the IT industry, (b) train them to do the job, and (c) put them to work.

We have the beginnings of this industry today, and some i4jers have been central in creating it. I have mentioned Thorkil Sonne, the founder and CEO of Specialisterne, the first IT consulting company focused on screening and training autistic engineers for companies. Thorkil is a persistent and passionate entrepreneur who has built a network of subsidiaries in countries around the world. He champions "the autism advantage" in business and elsewhere, and has spoken about it at the World Economic Forum in Davos and the United Nations. Another i4jer is Ferose, who was the first employer to hire autistic engineers and train them (at which he now works with Thorkil). SAP has set up the goal of hiring 1 percent of their workforce from "the spectrum" by 2020. Other IT companies have initiated autistic programs, too, including HP and Microsoft.

The potential size of the job market for coolabled autistic people is huge, and opportunities are there for entrepreneurs who want to tap it. Yet most existing entrepreneurs are struggling to approach this market, while the large companies, like SAP, are struggling to find enough people on the spectrum to employ. Why? Consider the components of a people-centered ecosystem for innovating jobs: people with valuable abilities who earn little, if anything, today, and companies wanting to employ them. Needed are innovative to connect the two.

It is my conviction that because this need exists, the coolablities market will happen sooner than later. What is needed to speed it up is a proper framing of the opportunity as a hot market opportunity. This can prompt corporate headquarters to build efficient recruitment routines, develop job descriptions that match the talent, and prepare the workplace to leverage the coolabilities and accommodate the disabilities. Once a respected company does this and achieves commercial success with coolabilities, others will follow.

Some will wonder if a not-for-profit industry creating jobs for cool-abled people will lead to the exploitation of people with disabilities. This is indeed a risk with task-centered businesses, who are looking for the most cost-efficient labor to perform certain tasks. It is a much smaller risk with people-centered businesses, which compete to innovate earning services for cool-abled people with disabilities. In this case, it is even more important that the earner is the primary customer.

Before continuing to the next section, I want to emphasize that autism spectrum condition is only one of many conditions with coolabilities, and that people in the autism spectrum have talent and interest not only in programming but in having as many job choices as anyone else. And it is time to employ the concept of coolabilities beyond the IT industry. Many people in the spectrum are becoming frustrated in hearing only the IT-opportunity story, which has become a stereotype. Furthermore, the IT and software engineering industries represent only a small portion of the working world, which is also true for people on the spectrum. Our task is to innovate rewarding, profitable jobs that leverage the coolabilities of the remaining 99.99 percent of people with any kind of disabling condition and matching their unique, personal profiles of skills, talents, and passions with people they like working with at meaningful tasks.

## The economy around our personalities

Maximizing the value of people means leveraging their potential. This would be more straightforward if we really knew what people's potential was and in which ways it could be valued by themselves and others. AI offers tools to find out, for better and worse

Jobly won't necessarily need to interview people to find their hidden skills and talents. It can suss out these qualities by scanning (with permission) known data about a person: e-mail exchanges, social networks, files on their computers, browser histories, calendars, address books, health records, and so on. It will also have access to other newly available material used by companies like Facebook and Google to sell you products. This is the shadow part of scanning personal data, and it is becoming a real threat. I will give you a futuristic vision of how this mapping of personalities can go and how it can be used to perhaps give most people great jobs. Then I will discuss the looming threat against our privacy, which is even greater than we might fear.

## VeeMe, my Virtual Me

Meet VeeMe, my "virtual me" that acts and reacts like me.

VeeMe is not yet a reality, but the combination of mobile technology, the Internet of Things, the cloud, big data, and social networking are bringing it closer.

The mobile revolution means that I'm plugged in at all times, and all of my communications are recorded. The Internet of Things revolution means that unconscious information can be recorded, too—everything from my heart rate to the freshness of the milk in my refrigerator. The cloud revolution means that all that data is stored and accessible, including data created by others. The big data revolution means that it's possible to data-mine the information I (and others) create, finding correlations between the things I do, or between my actions and the actions of others. The social networking revolution means that it will be possible to figure out who influences whom about what.

When all of our actions, our bodies, and the state of all of our possessions are monitored and analyzed, we have the potential to build a real virtual me—an AI agent that "stands in" for me, simulating my actions and reactions.

VeeMe will be built out of all the data collected about me: my emails, social network data, credit card data, health data, tax data, phone calls, location data, and so on. It will also draw on contextual data that can explain why I do the things I do. If it's raining cats and dogs I'll probably want to get a car ride instead of going by bike. VeeMe will know this, because it collects the latest info on news, weather, and more.

To create VeeMe, I index and analyze all my data and create a model that can simulate my behaviors. I use a mixture of techniques, such as data mining, language analysis, social network analysis, and artificial intelligence. I have stored millions of complex stimulus-response patterns, and now I am training VeeMe to replicate them.

In this way VeeMe gradually learns to behave like me, and the learning continues as VeeMe joins me in everything I do. I can ask VeeMe about things I have difficulty remembering. I can ask for "my own best advice." VeeMe will suggest what I should do in a given situation. VeeMe has a perfect memory, and can also help me better understand important events, resolve conflicts, and make choices.

Imagine everybody having a VeeMe, just as everybody has a computer and a smartphone. It becomes cool; you have to have one. Then imagine everybody's VeeMes talking to each other. If my VeeMe and your VeeMe "like" each other, you and I might want to meet in real life! The interaction between different VeeMes can be a way of pre-screening information and social preferences.

The ability to create connections is why my VeeMe will work well with Jobly. VeeMe is an advanced digital identity, and these identities aren't limited to people. Communities, companies, anything capable of interacting and creating data can have a VeeMe that simulates character and behavior. VeeMes are talented digital assistants, screeners of offers, and matchmakers for friendship and dating.

Jobly can be a "dating" site for VeeMes. Rather than looking for a programmer, a company might better look for someone with a mix of desired skills and talents, and a personality that fits the existing team. Today's dysfunctional labor market tries to do this by adding psychometric tests and interviews to the standard personal bio.

Jobly can assist companies in creating VeeJob digital identities that can meet with my VeeMe and VeeMes I will be working with if I get the job. If they get along virtually, the company may invite me over to see how we get along in real life.

## Privacy and ownership: My VeeMe must belong to me

VeeMe is about privacy, too. There is a lot of data about me in the cloud and in various databases. I (still) trust some players, like Google and Facebook, with a large amount of my digital self. Others I don't trust, but they can get my data anyway, because I often don't read all the fine print before downloading an app. It has turned into a slippery slope, by now we have become aware that there may be organizations unknown to us that have enormous knowledge about who we are, what we do and how we behave, and are using it for purposes we do not approve of. When I first published the VeeMe scenario in 2012[18] it seemed like pure science fiction but now, only six years later, it no longer feels far-fetched and appears more like a rapidly approaching reality.

Since VeeMe is the best virtual copy of myself, and it *must* be under my control. Imagine a company offering you some app on your smartphone and seizing the legal right to create a VeeMe of you that

---

[18] "Xconomy: Meet VeeMe: The Virtual Agent Programmed to Think Like Me." 29 Nov. 2012, https://www.xconomy.com/san-francisco/2012/11/29/meet-veeme-the-virtual-agent-programmed-to-think-like-me/. Accessed 26 Sep. 2018.

they can use for any purpose. Companies have a growing business incentive to know as much as possible about me to construct their own models of me and use them for marketing or behavioral targeting and they are doing it. Privacy laws must take a great leap forward if they are to protect us from this dark side of free enterprise.

Every challenge, however, including the challenge to maintain privacy, is an opportunity, and there is room for a new industry here -- the one that maintains my VeeMe from prying "eyes." What is needed is powerful players whose business interests align with my need for privacy. That should be possible, because VeeMe should be attractive to marketers, who can test their offers on VeeMe and decide if this is something I may like. If VeeMe likes it, I will look at it. I might even earn a few dollars on selling marketers access to my VeeMe.

The database inside VeeMe is mine—it contains my private information. If I own a VeeMe, it will be easier to safeguard that information. A company managing my VeeMe would have an incentive to ensure that there are no unofficial or pirated VeeMes out there. Jobly, marketers, and others wouldn't get to copy that database -- they would just get to interact with it. They would provide stimuli and VeeMe would provide responses. Building and maintaining VeeMes would become big businesses.

The architecture would be as follows: I have a safe "container" that contains all my data. My container is hosted by a platform provider that is responsible for keeping it safe. App manufacturers make apps that can interact with my data through the platform. Apps would connect through my own API, managed by the platform provider.

At the University of Warwick the HAT project "Hub of all things"[19], headed by Irene Ng, has addressed the issue of who owns your data by building a market platform of this sort for individuals to trade & exchange your own data for services.

The VeeMe system architecture fits the people-centered economy because both are about maximizing the value of people; they each try to allow each individual to leverage the potential of being unique. There will be a great market for mining the unconceived jobs that makes each person feel meaningful. Now I will be the author of the amazing novel in progress: my own life. The better the jobs, the more interesting I get, and the more my VeeMe increases in value.

---

[19] "Hub-of-All-Things." https://www.hubofallthings.com/. Accessed 26 Sep. 2018.

The companies that offer to manage my VeeMe are the banks of the future. They must have extremely high security and strict policies. They must carry very big sticks, big enough to strike down identity thieves and protect my data like banks that take care of my money today. Just as banks earn money on my money and split the proceeds with me, the future VeeMe banks will find ways of earning on my VeeMe and splitting it with me. There will be many other ways to earn value.

To the extent my VeeMe can act like me in different situations, it will have reverse-engineered myself with regard to those situations. It will mimic more than my consciousness. My unconsciousness comes into play, too, because it is present in my actions and therefore in the data I create: my repressed feelings, automatic skills, subliminal perceptions, habits, automatic reactions, and perhaps complexes, hidden phobias, and desires. My personal data can carry the signs of all this. Even if it isn't explicit, my data is a giant psychometrics test that VeeMe can dig into. It is a very sensitive issue, who wants to hand over the keys to their personal inner selves to marketers?

## Humane education (1): People-centered learning

Today, education is the dysfunctional twin of the dysfunctional labor market. Each is supposed to catalyze the functions of the other, but most of the time they refuse to talk to each other. Most education isn't even designed to give people job skills. Instead, school systems are designed to prepare students to pass tests and qualify for the next level of education until at some level enough people drop out to provide the raw material for a basic labor market. Elementary school aims for the level of middle school, middle for high school, high school for college.

When my grandparents were alive, six years of elementary school was the standard extent of schooling. In my parents' day it was grades nine to twelve. Now it is college and grad school. If this continues, so many people will manage to get postgraduate degrees that the labor market will require them. In fact there is already an inflation of post graduate degrees.

It's bizarre that today, when every other ten-year-old can create market value with a smartphone, students must wait until their twenties before applying for their first job. Why are we doing this? The answer used to be that jobs are more advanced so we must need more advanced education. But that is not a good answer at a time when a university professor can be outdone by his teenage kid in the use of computers -- a prime job skill. The most accurate answer to why everybody is doing it is because everyone else is doing it. But that answer is not sustainable and we are beginning to see a process of disruption and alternative models.

Education will be disrupted because we no longer learn everything from books or classrooms; we learn many of the most relevant skills by doing. Thanks to people like Steve Jobs, we don't need to read a manual before we start using a computer. We are shifting paradigms: the old one was the tedious sequence of learning first and then doing.

## *The newer, simpler paradigm is to learn while doing.*

We are collectively stuck in the old sequential way of operating -- as we can see by looking at many public school curricula. It's time to invent the Jung Machine!

As we remain stuck in the old learning mindset, we don't see the negative legacy of sending kids to school until a good deal of their knowledge is outdated. And there is a corollary to this critique: How much of what we learned in middle school and high school is necessary for getting the right job, or even the first job? Again, our collective mind says kids are too young and immature to start working; they need to grow up to be ready for a tough world! This means keeping kids isolated from the "difficult" labor market until they are ready to handle it -- mentally strong and socially responsible. But wait, isn't it experience in handling real-life problems that makes us into that kind of adult?

The answer is that we need a people-centered view not only of work but also of education. Important questions are: How can this person create the best value for herself and others? What can she do? What can she learn? Students need to learn not only academic subjects like math and history; they need to function with other people -- to work on a team, to be generous without being used, to respect oneself and others; to compromise, network, make friends, handle conflicts, and many more real-world activities.

# Humane education (2): Schools for people

At one time, schools were considered more advanced than companies, and company apprenticeships were considered backward. Many modern societies (with notable exceptions in Germany and elsewhere in Europe) got rid of apprenticeships and focused on school, so that kids would be qualified to build the modern society when they grew up. But today, in the innovation economy, companies are more advanced than traditional schools. Companies educate their workers so well that many apprenticeships are teaching at the cutting edge of knowledge.

At our mainstream schools, few students learn how to negotiate a salary, sell others on an idea for a new program, or navigate a career. A lucky few are taught how to apply for jobs, in theory, and become a part of the labor market. An even better step might be to bring company representatives into the schools and coach the kids on doing useful tasks. The teacher could facilitate testing a product or conducting market research. Today's school kids would then have the tools to create real value. The class could learn to discuss job specs, suggest a price, make an offer. If they land project, they could distribute the work, do it as a team, and deliver the product. When completed, the class or school would be paid. Imagine all they would learn, from creating value to working as a member of a team.

This model would have several benefits. The kids learn the higher skills they need for work life while doing real work. They learn to be independent, collaborate, be responsible, discover what they are worth. They are coached and supported by teachers who help them avoid exploitation, learn the ethics of work and business, and prepare for "real" life.

# The interpersonal economy

In order to have a people centered economy we need to be able to separate people from things. Just a few years ago "who is human" would have been a very philosophical discussion but with AI and automation it is become very real. What makes us non-machines and how is this a good thing?

Saying that people are not machines because we can do things that machines can't do has become a very unhelpful definition. The incentives to automate cannot be abolished. Economists and intellectuals keep trying to identify more types of tasks that machines will never be able to do as well as people. The problem with this is that any task a person can accomplish can, in principle, be performed by a machine. Some people counter that love, care, and intimacy are qualities that machines will never do as well as people. But we see how technologists are challenging even that level of outcome with sex-robots. If the customer's needs can be satisfied by any form of consensual stimulation of the mind, there is business to be done and an incentive for technological innovation. There is little doubt that it is possible to invent chemicals, virtual realities, and robots that can match even the most personal desires, and we are already seeing early stages of this.

So spending effort on identifying what people are good at that machines cannot do is at best a way of stalling the evolution of these machines. In the worst case, it speeds innovation by pointing innovators to new lucrative challenges. We are now confronted with not only challenges of the future of work, but also the objectification and commercialization of every human need and ability.

*And as we focus ever more on things,*
*we start seeing and treating each other as things.*

We have to find another way of separating ourselves from machines.

## Is it a "Thou"?: The Turing test versus the Buber test

The "Turing test" is a way of separating people from machines. The test was introduced by Alan Turing in his 1950 paper "Computing Machinery and Intelligence,"[20] opening with the words: "I propose to consider the question, 'Can machines think?'" Some suggest that when machines pass the Turing test, they will be indistinguishable from people in the economy. Let me provocatively suggest that machines already passed the Turing test long ago.

The Turing test uses two closed rooms, with a human in one and a machine in the other. An interviewer asks questions, and if the interviewer can't tell the difference between human and machine based on the answers, the machine passes the Turing test.

---

[20] Turing, Alan (October 1950), "Computing Machinery and Intelligence", Mind, LIX (236): 433–460, doi:10.1093/mind/LIX.236.433

Imagine a restaurant boss as the interviewer. In the first closed room a person is washing dishes. In the second room is a dishwashing machine. The boss sends in dirty dishes, and the dishes come back clean from both rooms. The dishwasher passed the Turing test.

"Hey, that's not a fair test!" you might object. "The boss didn't even ask any questions!" Well, don't complain to me about that, and good luck complaining to the boss. After all, he might say, "The dishwashers are there to wash dishes, not to talk."

The boss is right. He is living in a task-centered economy and he simply needs to get the dishes clean in the cheapest and best way. In the task-centered economy, the dishwashing machine passes the Turing test because it reduces people to machines.

In the people-centered economy, a Turing test is the way we have learned to know it. The restaurant boss will talk, ask questions. He will instantly know the difference between the human and the machine. The machine will do the dishes and the boss will chat with the human about other talents and what they might do together to add value to the restaurant. So far, so good.

But what happens when we replace the dishwasher with that ultimate artificial intelligence that can do everything a human can do? The boss can't tell the difference between the human and the machine any more, no matter what he asks. In fact, he takes quite a fancy to the computer and suggests they go out for a drink together after the Turing test. "Sure thing, I'd love that," says the computer (in order to pass the test). The boss bounces up to the door, opens it and…Heartbreak!

The computer may have passed the Turing test, but it didn't pass what I call the Buber test, named after Martin Buber, the philosopher who wrote the book *I and Thou*.

I suggest the Buber test is as important as the Turing test for discussing the economy, because it draws the line between your encounter with me and when you are experiencing a thing.

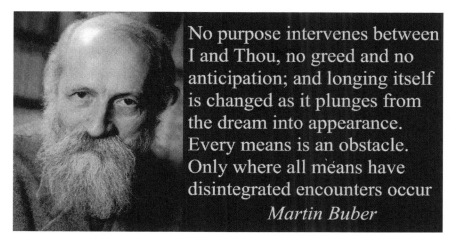

No purpose intervenes between I and Thou, no greed and no anticipation; and longing itself is changed as it plunges from the dream into appearance. Every means is an obstacle. Only where all means have disintegrated encounters occur

*Martin Buber*

Man can only relate in two ways, says Buber. One way is experience, where he relates to a thing or an idea, which is an "it" for him. Buber calls this "I-it." The only other way is the encounter with another being, to which he relates as a "thou."

The computer that passes the Turing test remains an "'It" for the restaurant boss, even after passing the test. Now let's say he comes home feeling really awkward after that embarrassing experience. His dog Ruff runs up to greet him, barking with joy. He looks Ruff in the eyes, and he encounters him. In that very moment Ruff is his "thou," not an "it."

*While Ruff the dog will score zero every time on the Turing test, he passes the Buber test with flying colors.*

t should be possible to estimate how much the presence of Thou, through family, friends, dogs, spiritual connections or any other form of Thou, contributes to the economy, by making us more productive, by reducing healthcare costs, and acting more peaceably. It would come to a sizeable amount, because without any of that, productivity and consumption would be much lower. But I won't do that here, because it would be putting the cart before the horse. The purpose of Thou is not to get more It in our lives. It is the other way around; the purpose is to nurture our relations with Thou. That said, analytics and economics depend so much on our relations with Thou that there is good reason to include it in the bookkeeping. The question is how to do it, and how to avoid turning people into dollar signs.

# Humane economics in a people-centered economy

So far, we have discussed an economy where we can work with people we like and are valued by people we don't know (meaning the market wants us). The last part of our mission statement – to be with our families and friends -- brings its own challenge: work can take such a large part of our lives that personal life suffers.

My purpose in having a good family situation is not to improve my job situation. I feel the opposite: The purpose of having a good job is to have a good family situation. We can account for dollars, but not love and friendship. Since accounting is the basis of the economy, when we optimize the economy we optimize the dollar, not the family. This brings another paradox:

*The power of mathematics puts the dollar on top,*

*but we need to put family and friends on top.*

How can we do that? If we treat a Thou like an It, it becomes an It. "Love for sale" is no longer love. And yet in order for a people-centered economy to be humane, love must somehow be reflected in analytics and economics. How can we solve this paradox?

It can be possible to create a discipline of economics that is highly efficient, humane, and people-centered, seeing personal relations as meaning and wealth creation as a means for achieving it. The purpose of such economics will be an economy that induces people to see to each other's well-being and penalizes behavior of the rat-race, i.e., people who push to work harder without increasing well-being. The improvement of information technology is making it ever more important to encourage a humane people-centered economics,. because the better we get at computing, the more imaginatively we can use analytics and economics to steer and shape society.

## The economics of today does not make sense

The values of economics in its present forms can be counterproductive and bring negative effects to society and the economy. For example, workaholics are praised for their dedication, even when this causes them to neglect families and friends. Their habit is good for revenues, so the economy incentivizes the behavior. Increased commuting distances are bad for commuters but they are good for economic growth because they drive the creation of infrastructure. And paying people for doing things we prefer doing ourselves is "good for the economy" even though it doesn't make sense to the layman who wants to split his own firewood. What is wrong? Mathematical models may give counterintuitive results either because reality is more complex than we think it is, or it because the model is missing something, or both. I believe it is both.

The argument for a more complex reality is that all business is good business as long as it doesn't kill business. By keeping each other busy, people are in sync; they continually depend on each other and maintain common standards. They are ready to apply their collective abilities to both opportunities and threats. By being both earners and spenders, even strangers depend on each other, and this dependence extends the good society beyond the range of family and friends. GDP points to civilization and away from tribalism. The economy happens when people need each other. When people need each other more, it grows, and society supposedly becomes more valuable for its citizens. But here the model is missing something.

93

*GDP cannot distinguish between when people love or hate needing each other. The relation between wealth creation and well-being is therefore problematic.*

ll-being cannot exist without wealth, but wealth can exist without well-being. Some people get wealthy while making humanity more miserable. Businesses may even have incentives to ruin the economies that feed them. Presently, some economists suggest, economic incentives for replacing people with machines will be so high that all jobs will go away and people will no longer have to work. This would be the end of society, as I have repeatedly said in this book, because it would dissolve the interdependency of citizens unknown to each other on which society depends.

When GDP was introduced, it provided direction for governments to create the policies that led to better jobs, education, healthcare, and leisure. A creator of the modern GDP we use today, Simon Kuznets, warned against relying on it too heavily, but the lack of alternative indicators has kept governments aiming for the highest GDP growth they can achieve. The same goes for companies, where CEOs and boards of directors find themselves committed to maximizing profits, not well-being -- even if they know that it is well-being their workers and customers actually want.

## Economics for well-being has not reached the market

Economists are looking at how to measure well-being in ways that governments can use to improve policies, but the indicators presented so have not become influential. In the case of business management, research has shown that well-being among workers is a better predictor of long term sustainable success than quarterly reports, but it is difficult to implement and maintain because it cannot "show the numbers" as concretely as quarterly reports. Design thinking, a method that has empathy among workers, has proven its mettle on the market. But even when an empathy-based production method shows the numbers, a serious flaw remains: the notion of well-being for the purpose of generating dollars. It is a reversed logic. Well-being should be the purpose, wealth the means.

94

Contemporary economics is based on mathematical theory, which makes it very powerful. And as we build better computational tools, an economy focused on trade, competition, and creating dollars increases its power over our lives, pushing the other parts aside. When people are offered more opportunities to earn or save money, the opportunity cost of leisure time will increase. Higher risks on the labor market provide an incentive to avoid that cost. Citizens may spend more of their time attempting to earn a living or, alternatively, shedding risk by, for example, not having children. We do see lower nativity rates in advanced economies, and perhaps this is one cause.

The well-being indicators of today are compound indicators, measuring things like education, access to healthcare, and happiness. Many of these topics map directly onto policy, taxes, and budgets. But even if they gain influence they are still only providing the means of creating meaningful lives for people; they do not provide well-being. They may also be difficult to integrate into accounting and other features of economic theory. They will not not simplify the mathematics, and will most likely make it more complex.

Economics is both appealingly powerful and appallingly flawed. Some people may think that its flaws, in particular the failure to model well-being, are inherent and come from being able to price everything that is traded but not other things that matter, like friendship, freedom, or clean air, which cannot and should not have a market price. They will say that markets are inherently cynical and should be separated from the more human aspects of life. Various well-being measures are being created to evaluate the importance of these priceless things. This results in two parallel systems of economics -- an economics of wealth and an economics of well being. There is on the one hand GDP and quarterly reports and on the other hand well-being indices. This dual economics serves the already existing split between between business (hard) and charity (soft); between for-profit and nonprofit entities. Governments will gather income from the hard economy and spend a large part of it on the soft economy. Successful business leaders can "give back," turning hard company profits into soft foundation grants. But even if this has worked to some degree, it won't solve the challenge of automating jobs.

# The quest for a unified economics for wealth and well-being

As I have pointed out, it is not possible to have an economy where nobody is a worker and all people live on handouts. The only solution is for the hard economy to become people-centered.

It means we will be much helped by unifying the hard and the soft economics into a single economics that creates wealth for the purpose of well being. This economics must fulfill one basic requirement: it needs to win over the system we have today. Creating dollars for well-being out-value creating dollars for making more dollars, meaning that the economy with well-being must be better at creating dollars than the one without. With such unified economics, governments and companies will beat competitors by using the dual system, and we will transition into a humane people-centered economy. Some hardcore business people might be disturbed at softening the hard approach, thinking that soft automatically means non-profit. But they can be shown to be wrong, because we know that organizations with motivated workers perform better than those with people who dislike their jobs. If people get on well, they work better together; they are happier in their personal lives, and motivated to do well by their employer. If people feel that earning their living is meaningful and enriches their lives, their motivation will strengthen, too. This does not guarantee an easy life, but at least one that provides the opportunity to find happiness, overcome difficulties, and turn crisis to advantage. Therefore, it seems reasonable to assume that an organization able to motivate its workers should be able to outcompete an organization that restricts its focus to the bottom line. The key is tools for accounting and analytics that lets them strategize and operate with the same ease as their task-centered competitors.

I suggest that a successful economic tool box for well-being -- one that can eclipse the task-centered GDP and outshine the addiction to quarterly reports -- should live up to these conditions.

| **CRITERIA FOR SUCCESSFUL WELL BEING ECONOMICS** | |
|---|---|
| 1 | MAKES A DIFFERENCE BETWEEN PEOPLE AND THINGS |
| 2 | IS ABLE TO ASSIGN WELL-BEING AS PURPOSE AND DOLLARS AS MEANS |
| 3 | IS APPLICABLE IN ALL SITUATIONS WHERE PEOPLE USE ECONOMIC TOOLS TODAY |
| 4 | IS MATHEMATICALLY ELEGANT, POWERFUL FOR DEVELOPING THEORIES AND ALGORITHMS |
| 5 | APPEALS TO DECISION MAKERS SO THAT THEY CHOOSE TO USE IT |
| 6 | IS EASY TO UNDERSTAND, AND APPEALS TO PRACTITIONERS |

# Ideating "humane economics"

## A provocative example: "I-Thou Economics" that does not objectify people

To give a feel for what a humane, people-centered might look like, I present a raw and simplified scenario. It is not a tested economic theory and I have no intention to suggest that this is the one and only key to people-centered economics. The intention is merely to trigger thoughts and inspire new thinking in new ways. If someone who reads this is inspired to build a solid economic theory that provides great tools for building a people-centered economy, proving in the process that what I suggest here is trivial, unpractical or erroneous, it will have served its purpose and might therefore be considered a success. With this disclosure, let's continue with the idea.

## The problem

Economics today is agnostic to what people consider meaningful. Lacking the notion of meaning, it defines meaning as maximizing means. This may seem reasonable if people always apply their available means to make their lives more meaningful. But in reality, people's thoughts are colored by the way the economy works, so that they, too, start thinking that the meaning of life is to earn as much money as possible so that they can do meaningful things. It gets problematic when they never get to do the meaningful things, or they decide that what really is meaningful is to earn more money for its own sake, because the economy celebrates that.

97

Classical economics tends to objectify people, seeing everyone is an It. People are defined by their attributes, like gender, strength, health, skills, talents, education, professional experience, certifications, recommendations, and nationality. In economics, people are always interchangeable with anyone (or anything) that has similar attributes. There is no downside to automation, as long as it has the stuff to do the job.

The root of the problem is objectification.

## A possible solution: Introducing "Thouness" value

Let's expand our basic credo to an assumption that might be suitable for building people-centered economics.

*Assumption:*
*The meaning of the economy is to be here for each other. Money provides the means; interpersonal relations are the meaning*

Is this a good assumption to build on? First of all, is it reasonable to define meaning this way? Different people find different things meaningful. Some people find more meaning in writing books than being with people. It's meaningful to go to college, because without a college degree it's difficult to get a job, so you work with teachers and other students to achieve that goal. I am suggesting it's the other way around, that going to college serves as a means for building relations with high-school teachers and kids. Yes: Living in the heart of Silicon Valley, I can say that with all my heart, because high school kids here live under such pressure to achieve that the teenage suicide rate is higher than anywhere else. So many kids have jumped in front of a train close to where I live that the police now have guards at rail crossings day and night.

Imagine if kids saw the purpose of going to college as a means of building good interpersonal relations with teachers and classmates? This would be positive whether they got into college or not because they would build good networks of people around them. It is fair to assume that kids who seek to improve relations with others will manage better than those who don't. This applies not only to high-schoolers but to people of all ages.

There are more arguments for choosing interpersonal relations as meaning; let me use Buber's distinction between Thou and It to make the case. From a Darwinian perspective, purpose is defined as the continuation of our species, seeing everything else as means, including ourselves. But for us, raising a family is driven by Thou, from finding a mate to raising kids. From the species' point of view, every "It" we experience serves only to keep "Thou" in our lives so that we will raise the next generations. In consequence, from our point of view, that "Thou" becomes the closest we have to holy.

From these perspectives, it is not unreasonable to assume I-Thou as meaning and I-It as means for our model, where I-Thou stands for feeling connected with other living souls and I-It is how we relate to money, things, ideas -- everything that isn't a Thou.

Another good reason to like this assumption is that Buber's formula for I-Thou and I-It is not only a beautiful idea, it is also appealing to my mathematical mindset as a basis for economics. If an interaction is either I-Thou, I-It, or a mix of both, then the mathematician in me is happy, because it means that everything that happens between people can be described in terms of I-Thou and I-it. Even better, I-Thou and I-It don't overlap at all, they are like apples and oranges, or X and Y. And just as we can describe any position in the coordinate system with the two numbers values of X and Y, and any movement as a more or less complex combination of them, we can in a similar manner describe every interaction.

People can be both I-Thou and I-It. I can say to a plumber, "Mister plumber, I have found another plumber who will do the job in a way that suits me better so I am exchanging you for him." I have placed the plumber in the position of an It, which is fine. I can separate business from friendship. If I say "My son, I have found another boy who has better school grades so I am exchanging you for him," it sounds horrible. My son is supposed to be Thou. Treating him like an It makes him become an It. If I am friendly with the plumber, he is both Thou (the friend) and It (the plumber), and I do not want to hurt his feelings. Plumbing is I-It, friendship is I-Thou. They are different, but they overlap. In the accounting books it doesn't say if we are friends or not, it just records the actual deal. But in reality, we know who are our friends and we could, if we wanted to, build accounting software that figures out from my email and social network which people to ask to get the best price and service. It's something we do in our heads today, but perhaps an even better way will be to procure the help that improves my relations the most. Plumbing is fairly standard as a service, and it might be worth paying a bit extra to engage someone I want to improve relations with. It builds my "Thouness" capital. Thouness can boost Itness -- as long as it is within the limits of business ethics.

The ethics of friendship is, as we know, different from the ethics of business, and so are the economics of Thouness and Itness. We know a lot about the economics of Itness because we use versions of it every day. But the economics of family relations and friendship is not exact. There are certain things we do to nurture love and friendship, where the most important thing may be simply being together, often not even talking. The one thing we never can do with love and friendship is to trade them. "Your kisses are amazing" is a beautiful thing to say; "Can I have another kiss if I pay you $10?" is not. I suggest an economic rule about this:

# *If I treat a Thou like an It, it becomes an It.*

Having different rules for I-Thou and I-It is the key to humane, people-centered economics. This means we can separate Thou from It, people from things. It means we can use computers to help us figure out what we should do, together with whom, in order to best reach the goal of improving interpersonal relations. It does not mean we should work only with friends, which is too simplistic. The goal is to find the right balance and timing to know what with whom to improve both my interpersonal relations and to earn the money I need to do that.

## An "I-Thou" accounting scenario

Let's look at an example of how this type of accounting can look in a simple scenario, something that can happen in anyone's life. It is the story about Bob inviting his friend Anne for dinner. It includes Itness (we will count the dollars added to GDP as the story progresses) and Thouness, the interpersonal encounter – which is the purpose of the dinner.

Bob wants to spend the evening with Anne, who lives in the next city

He works for 2 hours for his employer, Acme and earns $50

He pays Railex $10 for a return ticket, and takes a train to the next station

Anne and Bob are happy to meet each other

Anne takes him to the Rose pub, where her friend Marie works

Anne and Marie are happy to see each other

**Created by Rana Chakrabarti**

Let's talk about the productivity, as economists call it. This is about seeing the value of the efforts -- the proportion between the effort we put in and what we get out.

> ### *Productivity = Market Value Creation ÷ Creative Effort*
> *In this case = $110 ÷ Bob's work+Railex train ride+Rose Pub dinner+Marie's work*

When we get a lot out of a small effort, productivity is high. When we put in a lot of effort and get little out of it, the productivity is low (and we wonder if it was worth it). When economists speak about productivity, they mean dollars. But in real life, it's not the dollars that make life meaningful; it's what I do with them. Are they bringing meaning to my life, or the lives of others? Here is where today's GDP-based economics is flawed. If I used all my dollars in meaningful ways, earning 10 times more might add more meaning to my life; then it would be true that we should focus on increasing GDP. But that is a wrongful assumption. We all know that when we focus too much on earning money, our lives are diminished; we have less quality time to spend with family and friends. So a second kind of productivity is needed in economics: how much meaning we add to our lives by adding to GDP. We can call this ratio *Meaningful Yield*. Bob's dinner with Ann and Marie added 110 dollars to GDP. How much meaning did that money add to their lives? How much closer did it bring them together? The "meaningful yield" is what makes the real difference between the economics of today and "I-Thou" economics. It says, "This is how much Thouness (or closeness) you gained for each dollar that was created in the economy." It is the ratio between meaning and means that gives the difference between the rat race and a good life. When we have a good balance between earning a living and living with family and friends, the meaningful yield will be high.

The meaningful yield is the conversion factor between productivity ("Am I well-paid for what I do?") and meaningful productivity ( "What I do lets me live a meaningful life")

---

*Meaningful Yield = Creation of Meaning ÷ Creation of Means*
In this case: 5 ♥ ÷ $110

*Meaningful Productivity = Productivity × Meaningful Yield*
In this case = 5 ♥ ÷ Bob's work+Railex train ride+Rose Pub dinner+Marie's work
( The effort that went into spending quality time with friends)

---

Today we look at the economy in dollars; PCE adds Thouness and meaningful yield to that. In PCE we must choose Thouness – family and friends – as meaning (making it the numerator) and dollars as means therefore (making it the denominator). In PCE, the better we provide for family and friendships for each dollar earned, the better. But the task-centered economy flips the equation upside down, setting the dollar as the purpose (numerator) and family and friends as the means (denominator). Our task-centered economy wants to create as many dollars as possible from our work and from each friendly smile alike. It treats Thou as an It, because it cannot see the difference between them.

To see what difference this makes in practice, here are some alternative scenarios for Bob's evening. Are they better or worse for the economy? Let's compare what PCE and the present task-centered economics say. Rule: The present economy aims at increasing dollars. PCE aims for increasing Thouness and the meaningful yield (thouness per dollar).

## COMPARING VALUES: PEOPLE-CENTERED VS TASK-CENTERED ECONOMICS

| BOB INVITES ANN FOR DINNER ALTERNATIVE SCENARIOS: | GDP | THOU NESS | MEANI NGFUL YIELD | TASK-CENTERED ECONOMICS SAYS | PCE SAYS |
|---|---|---|---|---|---|
| 1.Bob skips going out with Ann and works more hours instead. Spends the extra money on seeking treatment for stress at work | ↑ | ↓ | ↓ | "BETTER!" | "WORSE!" |
| 2.Bob is relocated to a place farther away from Ann. He must work an extra hour to afford the extra travel cost. | ↑ | | ↓ | "BETTER!" | "WORSE!" |
| 3.Marie takes the evening off and invites Bob and Ann over. Bob buys food and they cook together. Marie earns less but gains time to become friends with Bob | ↓ | ↑ | ↑ | "WORSE!" | "BETTER!" |

This table shows clearly what is wrong with the economic system today. The economy lacks a good definition of meaning. In the economy of today, the meaning of work is to create more work; the meaning of earning money is to earn more money. If we introduce interpersonal relations as meaning, and see GDP as the effort we put in to achieve meaning, the paradox is solved. GDP is proportional to well-being ONLY when people get something out of the extra money and work. If everything disappears into the dust of the rat race, there is no meaning and the increased GDP can be a bad thing.

Note one interesting detail in the table: it hints that commuting increases GDP. In other words, the current economy might carry a hidden incentive to increase commuting time. It would be interesting to see whether deeper research reveals more outcomes of this activity.

This is enough mathematics to show the most important outcome of this new way of accounting. Just by introducing interpersonal relations and putting a Thou into the accounting, the annoying GDP-weirdness disappears in our example. There is more mathematics to adding Thouness, which can be explained in another publication on the dynamics of a people-centered economy.

## Accounting for Thouness as a business strategy

So Thouness can address a paradox in macroeconomics, perhaps, but what about business? How would it look if a company started measuring

104

and accounting for the Thouness values it has? The answer is that Thouness is good for companies, too. Imagine the fictitious company Acme Inc., where all workers have several friends at work who get along well and inspire on another. This is obviously a company with good Thouness capital. Among the owner benefits of this, two that directly relate to the bottom line are labor cost and employee retainment. The Acme employees are not very likely to switch employers because another company offers them 15 percent higher pay; they would prefer to stay with their friends and teammates. If they had no friends at work, they accept 15 percent at once, and possibly even less. In other words, a company with good Thouness capital can operate with lower labor costs, higher cost efficiency, and higher profit margins than competing companies with equally qualified workers. A close-knit team is very good for competitiveness, and Thouness is strongly bonding.

Now imagine that Acme is doing quite well, but the shareholders are of the opinion that they should be doing even better, considering how good the team is. The board switches the CEO for a more aggressively growth-oriented person. The new CEO says, "We have a great team, but they have no real incentive to do their very best. I will increase productivity by having them compete more." So the new CEO introduces competitions, prizes, Employee of the Week contests, and so on. Initially, productivity does indeed rise. But by making the employees into competitors, Acme begins to shed its Thouness capital. Before long, the high-performing employees are more likely to accept employment offers from competitors because they have less friendship at work. The CEO is forced to increase salaries to retain his best workers, and that shrinks the margins. Many of us have seen this happen in real life in companies where we or people close to us have worked.

## An accounting app that makes good employers win over bad ones

If Acme had had a way to measure and account for its (considerable) Thouness capital, as well to evaluate its connection to the bottom line, this would not have happened. The CEO, the board, and the shareholders would see the thouness capital and understand how it was keeping the company competitive. Part of Acme's profit would be routinely reinvested in thouness capital; the company would do whatever it took to remain a sustainable innovative company where workers worked with people they liked, felt valued by the market, and

105

could provide for the people they loved. This would be a competitive people-centered company.

Is it possible to create an accounting app for Thouness? I can say with confidence that if a) we can measure how many good friends Acme's workers have in the workplace, b) if research can show a number for how many extra dollars, on average, are needed for poaching a worker with friends at work, and c) if that number is useful for planning wages, then *yes*, it is possible to create an app.

The app can be a simple add-on that connects to an existing accounting system. Any numbers that show the coupling between Thouness and dollars will be helpful, such as how much less sick leave do people with friends at work have? How much easier is it to get workers to work overtime in order to cover for each other? And so on. The app itself is quite straightforward. The crucial effort is the sociological research that measures these statistics. In the PCE, this research is a huge research field. Much of it would be public, but a lot would be private, too. If I subscribe to a Thouness-plugin app for my accounting system, I want the one with the best translations between Thouness and dollars. A company like Gallup can offer it, for example, and they can offer different packages with different price tags.

It can create a very nice market for research companies to help good employers win and make bad employers lose.

# Some benefits of the notion of "Thouness"

## Thouness (1): A definition of meaningful value

Here I have chosen "Thouness" as meaning, and this might still seem a bit quirky to some readers, even after going through the example above. Let's compare it to alternatives. We could do the same simple math as above, but with a more standard measure of well-being (several are in use already). Then we would be talking about "well-being productivity;" that is, how much well-being is being created per dollar, assuming the money has been earned and spent in good ways. The problem with this approach is that familiar well-being measures include housing, access to healthcare, and education. These do not represent the qualities people see as meaningful in life, even though these quality-of-life items, or "meaningful capital," are important in building meaningful lives. But they are mostly about I-It, not I-Thou.

When I discuss these ideas, people often mention the World Happiness Report that uses Gallup survey methodology to rank how "happy" people are in various countries. I use the quote because it's not exactly what we mean by happy in daily speech; it is a weighted statistical measure that includes various parameters. Happiness, in my opinion, is a decent choice because it is not simply capital for achieving something else. We don't make ourselves happy because it's good for productivity. Productivity goes up *because* we are happy. Happiness works the same way as Thouness this way, which is good. Is it better than Thouness as a definition of meaning?

Some believe that life is about being happy, and that would make happiness the right thing to measure. I can't say that is entirely wrong -- we do want to be happy -- but

*the key to meaningful happiness is living a full life, with the full spectrum of events, relations, emotions, and other conditions*

we have learned to experience, endure, and master. Saying that the goal is to be happy and that something is wrong if we are not happy is like keeping the car in the garage to avoid wear and tear. Troubles are there to be recognized, addressed, and overcome, and we can't know the full richness of life without taking these steps bravely and generously. Thouness, on the other hand, covers all emotions and instances. We can be unhappy in our relationships, be angered or disappointed by I-Thou relations, but this is not to say that these relationships are meaningless. They still have meaning and it is worthwhile to spend Itness as means for the purpose of maintaining Thouness, such as going out for dinner together or consulting a marriage and family therapist. The conclusion is that happiness is probably not better than Thouness in meaningful productivity.

Thouness is a more attractive entity from at least two perspectives: first, "thou" is the complement of "it" which satisfies the scientist in me, meaning that it allows me to describe all possible human relations as either the one or the other or a mix of both. It's a beautiful coordinate system spanning the entire relational space. The second reason is that

## *Thouness fits the Darwinian idea that success means the continued existence of our species.*

I-Thou is what holds couples together and, hopefully, inspires them to raise children. I-Thou is craved by the very organism of people. Researchers see changes in the cardiovascular, immune, and nervous systems of lonely people who have a higher risk for infections, heart disease, and depression. Research suggests it is the subjective experience of loneliness (in other words, the lack of thouness) that is harmful, not the actual number of social contacts (or the number of likes on a facebook post) a person has. Loneliness is becoming a field of research of its own, which should be useful for developing a humane people-centered economy.[21]

This reasoning brings us back once again to the same conclusion: the most enduring and meaningful goal is to be here for each other. This is our best strategy with regard to our own success, the success of our communities and the continuation of the species. Thouness is, therefore, an appealing definition of meaning in humane people-centered economics.

## Thouness (2): A cause of perceived reality

Thouness focuses on the interpersonal relation, placing it at the center of our perception of reality. Happiness does not have to create reality, it might just as well be a dream. But interpersonal relations between existing people do much more.

More often than not, I suggest, our reality is constructed, and here is where the interpersonal connections, especially Thouness, plays a central part. We share ideas about how things relate, and often depend on discussions with others to confirm our understanding of reality. In other words, our sense of reality, which exists as an idea in the conscious mind, is confirmed by something outside the mind. Our realities, as we experience them, are constructs that are strongest when our conscious mind finds confirmation from another person, ultimately a Thou.

---

[21] "Why Loneliness Is Hazardous to Your Health | Science." 14 Jan. 2011, http://science.sciencemag.org/content/331/6014/138. Accessed 10 Apr. 2018.

*This is how we create reality from our narratives: in dialogue
between separate minds, confirming each other's
ideas, dreams, truths, and even lies.*

We each take on distinct roles as we relate to each other, and in each of
our minds emerges a constructed reality. The more real this feels, the
more real it becomes. We sense reality subconsciously, and we only
rarely deliberate on a conscious level about what is real or not. Our
subconscious minds keep confirming each other without our being
conscious of the process.

To conclude, Thouness helps develop ideas, shape common language.
It creates reality and is the mother of value creation. This is another
powerful reason to include it in economics.

## Thouness (3): Discerning personal and collective identities

I-Thou and I-It are also useful for discussing personal identity, more
than happiness or other measures of well-being. This is another example
of the versatility that resides in Thouness and Itness. People are rarely
conscious that "we" is actually two different words. The first is the
*interpersonal we* we use face to face, as in, "Shall we go to lunch?"
Second is the *collective we* that is about belonging to a collective identity,
as in, "We Swedes like sailing." The interpersonal-we is pure awareness
of encounter. It says, "I am talking to you" -- and as such it is close to I-
Thou. The collective-we refers to sharing attributes. I can say both of
them at the same time if I put my hand on your shoulder and say, "How
about we philosophers go for lunch?"

Being aware of the difference provides important insight that can help
us to better lives and communities. One key question is which one
should rank higher, the interpersonal-we or the collective-we? Imagine
a meeting between Romeo and Juliet:

109

**COLLECTIVE- AND INTERPERSONAL-WE: RANKING ORDER**

| RANKING ORDER | WE-TYPE DEMO | EFFECT OF RANKING |
|---|---|---|
| 1. COLLECTIVE-WE<br>2. INTERPERSONAL-WE | Collective: "We Swedes celebrate summer solstice" | "I love you, but we Capulets and Montagues don't mix so we won't be together" |
| 1. INTERPERSONAL-WE<br>2. COLLECTIVE-WE | Interpersonal: "Shall *we* go for a walk?" | 'We Capulets and Montagues don't mix, but I love you so we'll be together anyway" |

If collective-we sets the limits for interpersonal-we, the community rules. If interpersonal-we sets the limits, we follow the community as long as it suits us. They are a yin-yang combination. We seek a harmony between them so that they enable each other. I believe the interpersonal-we always has the final word, because it includes the real me - my sentient me.

I already discussed in the "I-thou economics" demo how a company might succeed better if it accounts for its Thouness -- the friendship and I-Thou cohesion between individuals in the company. Here is another example of how it can help companies be successful, this time by separating between collective-we and interpersonal-we.

Imagine that we own a company with many employees. We want a good company culture, a good collective identity the employees will want to belong to and be loyal to. We want employees to help each other do their best for our company. How can we help? There are two opposing strategies. One is top-down, to build friendship from collective identity. A typical failure in top-down corporate culture is to give employees T-shirts with the company logo and drive them in buses to some organized activity designed to build friendship and company loyalty. The other strategy is bottom-up, to build collective identity from personal friendships. This strategy fails when the company helps employees become friends without making clear what that has to do with the company; the friends may actually leave the company together.

In a people-centered economy, jobs compete for people, which means that people are offered a choice between different meaningful ways of earning their income. The job providers may be platforms with hundreds of millions of users, like Google, Facebook, or eBay are today, but with business models based on offering users the means to earn their living in meaningful ways. Workers may build interpersonal-we relationships through social networking platforms, building a

110

collective-we identity by jointly being part of a workpool integrated into the social network.

Thouness adds a new perspective to the proposed goal for the economy, making it more rational:

**GOALS FOR A PEOPLE-CENTERED ECONOMY**

| GOALS FOR INDIVIDUALS | LEADING VALUE TYPE |
|---|---|
| WE DO MEANINGFUL WORK WITH PEOPLE WE LIKE | THOUNESS + ITNESS |
| BEING VALUED BY PEOPLE WE DO NOT KNOW | ITNESS |
| PROVIDING FOR THE PEOPLE WE LOVE | THOUNESS |

In other words, a meaningful job allows us both to be close to family and friends and to build a strong, inclusive economy. The one enables the other. I have come to this conclusion before, but here it comes one step closer to the type of logical statement that could be practical for economic modeling. It is an indication that Thouness may be the type of condition that helps develop a humane, people-centered economy.

## Summary: How "Thouness" can be helpful in people-centered economics

Adding Thouness to economics can offer both practical and philosophical benefits.

Some suggested practical uses of Thouness in economics:

- *In business accounting* -- a framework enabling management practices for synergizing profitability and collaboration; making companies where people like each other more competitive than others.

- *In branding, marketing, and human resource management* -- a framework enabling models for harmony and synergy between the personal identity of individuals and the collective identities of organizations.

- *In macroeconomics and econometrics* -- a framework enabling creation of well-being-based economic policy that beats today's growth-oriented policies at their own game, with well-designed policy synergizing the well-being *AND* competitiveness of nations.

- *Reaching critical mass in projects* -- In I-Thou relations, people help each other without expecting financial benefits. Thouness offers a framework for economic modeling of ways to bootstrap projects (for example the new ecosystem for innovating jobs).

Some suggested philosophical benefits

- *Attempts to address all human economic behavior* -- if every human interaction is either "I-Thou" or "I-It" or a combination of them, it means that these two dimensions of interaction form a so-called *"complete set,"* a base for analyzing all possible human interaction and thus all economic behavior.

- *Transdisciplinarity: bridges economics with psychology, social sciences and humanities* -- as a mathematical discipline of science, economics struggles to connect with sciences outside the realm of formal logics. As a "complete set," Thouness/Itness opens the doors to creating mathematics for the wider human behavior and thereby including knowledge from other sciences in economic models.

- *We can't lose anything by including it* -- Thouness adds a new value dimension; it does not take away anything from existing economics. Set Thouness to zero everywhere and it will be exactly the same economics as today.

Still, we must continue asking whether integrating Thouness into accounting is a useful idea until it proves its value in real life. As a basis for thinking about this, I close this provocation by returning to my suggested criteria for a successful humane, people-centered economics, now adding check marks for "I-Thou economics:"

**IS "THOUNESS" A PATHWAY TO HUMANE ECONOMICS?**

| CRITERIA | |
|---|---|
| MAKES A DIFFERENCE BETWEEN PEOPLE AND THINGS | YES |
| IS ABLE TO ASSIGN WELL-BEING AS PURPOSE AND DOLLARS AS MEANS | YES |
| IS APPLICABLE IN ALL SITUATIONS WHERE PEOPLE USE ECONOMIC TOOLS TODAY | YES |
| IS MATHEMATICALLY ELEGANT, POWERFUL FOR DEVELOPING THEORIES AND ALGORITHMS | INDICATION |
| APPEALS TO DECISION MAKERS SO THAT THEY CHOOSE TO USE IT | N/A |
| IS EASY TO UNDERSTAND, AND APPEALS TO PRACTITIONERS | N/A |

I will continue developing this idea, and invite others to join. For example, it seems mathematically elegant and resourceful, but has not yet been proven. As for applications and appeal, nothing can yet be said because no applications have been developed. As I pointed out in the beginning, my intention in presenting the idea of Thouness is NOT to demonstrate a functioning alternative to existing economics -- I don't yet have enough facts, models, or arguments.

# The transpersonal economy

I debated with myself if I should include faith, mysticism, spiritualism, and religion in this book because of their controversial nature. Many of the people I consulted advised against it. The reason I decided to include them is simple. A substantial part of the economy is transpersonal, because

*faith, spirituality and religion affect economic behavior.*

For the record, I am agnostic with no spiritual practice. An educated scientist like myself, religious or atheist, is schooled in seeking rational explanations to mysteries. Questions about whether gods and miracles exist are, in my opinion, not themselves scientific or scientifically provable, but it is beyond doubt and may be subject to scientific research that people have faith in religion and that it plays a major role in cultures, societies, and economies. Because PCE places people at the center of the economy, whether they are religious or not, we need to understand what their beliefs mean in the context of economic behavior.

\*\*\*

"Transpersonal" means, according to the dictionary, "denoting, or dealing with states or areas of consciousness beyond the limits of personal identity." We have already touched on this concept in our discussion of interpersonal interaction and the difference between a Thou and an It. You might remember that Ruff the dog will fail the Turing test but she passes the Buber test with flying colors -- at least when it is her master who is performing it. For people who don't like dogs, she will remain an It.

## Thouness (4): True relativity – "The Thou is in the I of the beholder"

Whether a relationship is "I-Thou" or "I-It" is entirely a personal, subjective question. "I-Thou" is something I perceive. The Thou does not have to be a human. To me, every other dog is a Thou, worthy of deep personal connection. I know people who have "I-Thou" relations with trees and flowers. Buber acknowledges this, and here is where the rabbi manifests his religion. His view is that all our relationships bring us ultimately into relationship with God, the Eternal Thou.

Framing Thouness within the science of psychology, we can say, "The Thou is in the I of the beholder;" that is, the relationship is subjective, a personal perception. It is up to you or me whether we see a "thou" in people, dogs, trees, or a mystical force some of us perceive. From a scientific point of view, I will suggest that debates over what is *objectively* a thou - Do trees have souls? Do gods exist? -- is irrelevant. The relevance lies entirely in our subjective perceptions of I-Thou and how it affects us. What is true as well as relevant is instead this: our belief strongly affects our social and economic behaviors, both as individuals and as groups and societies. Economics must take this dimension into account in order to come anywhere close to understanding why and how people interact economically in various ways.

I-Thou economics is agnostic and pragmatic. It sees Thouness as a component of people's minds that influences their sense of reality and value, and plays an important role in decision making. People apply their own rules for how they interact with a thou versus an it. Thouness and Itness simply furnish a formal language for these differences that can make it possible to create economics that takes interpersonal and transpersonal value into account.

# Social dilemmas are wicked problems and existential challenges

Social dilemmas are wicked problems that can destroy economies or stop them from ever coming into existence. They can have rational solutions, but – as we shall discuss – the simplest and most efficient solutions are often based on irrational faith and have transpersonal drivers.

How often do we come across a system that everyone knows is broken, and might have a workable solution, and yet nothing happens? To see such a system, many people need look no farther than their own workplace. For example, if I run a company and I know that everyone will feel best served by having a well-paying job, I will still feel forced to lay off employees if my competitors do that to lower production cost. If I don't do it, I lose my customers and I will have to fire my workers anyway. All my competitors can share the same view,

*we want to keep our workers, and we will still lay off our workers, because the one who doesn't becomes a martyr without even leaving a positive impact.*

This is a "social dilemma," where people's short-term self-interest harms the common interest as well as each individual's long-term interests. Such dilemmas are examples of what economists refer to as "wicked problems." That is, they seem complex and, because they are paradoxical, have no obvious solution. Such social dilemmas challenge our well-being in many ways. They often drive environmental issues, such as overharvesting of fish, overpopulation, destruction of rainforests, and emission of greenhouse gases. There are many different types of social dilemmas, among them the "prisoner's dilemma" that destroys community and "the tragedy of the commons" that pollutes or degrades the environment.

Social dilemmas are notoriously wicked problems because, from a perspective of logic and self-interest, there is no solution that makes sense. But humanity has evidently solved social dilemmas time after time throughout history -- since before people could read or write, and certainly before they understood social dilemmas and designed public policy. Consider features of law and order, which a stable society must have. Individuals usually want the freedom to do whatever they want, while society needs each individual to follow agreed-upon laws. It is easy to imagine the chaos if everyone felt free to loot stores and get rid of anyone who stands in their way. Running a society requires a critical mass of people who follow the laws and can require others to do the same.

It is simple enough to see how a law-abiding community will be more powerful than one without law and order. It is not so simple for members of a lawless environment to bootstrap themselves into a law-abiding society. They need a critical mass to create a system of lawmakers, courts, and police; they require idealists who are willing to sacrifice themselves for what they believe is the greater good. This defies the logic of traditional economics in which one does what's best for oneself.

## Transpersonal solutions to social dilemmas

The Darwinian solution is just that: humans are always, to some extent, irrational, erratic, and prone to mystical beliefs that they will stick to, despite knowing better in their rational minds. The solution to social dilemmas is often not more knowledge, but more faith. We solve them with our hearts at least as much as with our minds, and preferably through the force of both.

We all know about the economic value of knowledge; economists study it in detail. We know much about faith, too, but we seldom think about it from the economic point of view. But faith is just as important as knowledge in shaping economies.

*Faith can solve paradoxes that might be inaccessible to rational knowledge.*

Irrational faith is a central part of any economy and how economic decisions are made. People are governed by faith, by whatever name they describe it. Buying a house or choosing a college education requires some amount of irrational faith. Logic might tell us our decision is good enough, but without faith we will often live to regret our decisions. Faith drives us so that what would be poor decisions by any rational means turn out to be good ones at the end of the day because we put our hearts and souls into them. Entrepreneurs need

116

faith in what they do, betting their fortunes at incalculable odds instead of playing things safe.

Since faith is such an important part of the economy, we must look at it more closely and understand it in logical terms. For example, if faith is more tied to Thouness than to Itness, the amount of Thouness within a community of entrepreneurial idealists can be a measure of its ability to succeed. This suggests that people may be more willing to commit themselves to a decision and make significant sacrifices when their actions bring them closer to friends, loved ones, or their Eternal Thou. This might be possible to measure and model with humane people-centered economics.

# A Darwinian perspective on the power to believe

Religion is a good example of this kind of faith-based vision. All societies have, or have had, religion at the core of their culture. Why? The "Darwinian" explanation is that religion has helped cultures survive. I cannot discuss the existence of spiritual mysteries, but I can discuss how belief can affect collective behavior and the economy.

Christianity, Islam, and Hinduism are embraced by three quarters of the world population today. They are each over a thousand years old and still provide an appealing vision for followers. They all preach the values of peace and justice. Moses handed down rules based on these values, defining them as God's commandments. If they would honor these rules, he said, the people would please God and prosper. If disobeyed, God would punish all. And indeed, this was close to what happened in ancient Israel. When people followed the rules, they prospered, and when they did not, the community suffered. This strengthened the belief that God was watching over everyone.

Let us play with what might seem like a sacrilegious idea: that Moses invented his encounter with God in order to make people follow these mostly-sensible laws designed to make his people prosper. It would have made sense to Moses the politician, because he would have known that attributing the laws to God would strengthen his message and raise the chances that people would obey. Without that reputational boost his chances that people would follow the laws would have been slight. But the lie would also have made sense to Moses the true believer and religious leader. Ager all, God had entrusted him with the extremely challenging task to lead his people into safety.

Introducing law and order would help them survive. He could have said in his prayers that he was willing to take the risk of being punished for doing what he believed to be necessary, just like any leader. Then it would not even be lying, because he had told God the truth.

As an agnostic, I will argue that God exists in reality for those who so believe and that they are well served when their actions of faith deliver desirable results, like introducing legal justice. From the Darwinian perspective, I will hypothesize that bootstrapping a society based on public devotion to the law is very much helped by religion and probably difficult without.

From the table below, we can see how strong religion remains around the world, despite the sweeping advances of science and technology.

**THE WORLD REMAINS RELIGIOUS**

| RELIGION | ADHERENTS 1910 | | ADHERENTS 2010 | |
|---|---|---|---|---|
| Christianity | 611,810,000 | 34.8% | 2,260,440,000 | 32.8% |
| Islam | 221,749,000 | 12.6% | 1,553,773,000 | 22.5% |
| Hinduism | 223,383,000 | 12.7% | 948,575,000 | 13.8% |
| Agnosticism | 3,369,000 | 0.2% | 676,944,000 | 9.8% |
| Atheism | 243,000 | 0% | 136,652,000 | 2.0% |

Johnson, Todd M.; Grim, Brian J. (2013). The World's Religions in Figures: An Introduction to International Religious Demography (PDF). Hoboken, NJ: Wiley-Blackwell. p. 10.

I suggest there are more reasons why faith and religion are helpful. It is something for "transpersonal economists" to look into. My premise is that faith is a driver of hope and vision that is required for survival and provides direction and purpose. As described earlier, it is different from knowledge, which is an enabler. We speak of holding on to faith in order to endure difficulties and find direction and courage even when we don't know what to do. This is beneficial in itself; one who has faith will often take action that has results, while one who lacks faith will often get nowhere. Sharing faith is also beneficial in aligning people's goals, which inspires them to encourage one another. People will confirm each other's faith, increasing its reality, and catalyze the common language that helps coordinate their thoughts and actions. Shared faith is therefore the foundation for communities and societies, supported by codes of ethics, law, order, and collective decision making. It is the root of collective identity, which is needed for a well-functioning society.

# We need to have faith in our togetherness or togetherness will not exist.

Since shared faith is so important for our identity and community, it must be protected. Nature and human societies are always testing strategies for this, and some have proven successful. An example is to hold fast to a common idea, such as a system of knowledge of a mystical belief. For citizens in the modern age of technology, faith in our knowledge appears to provide this kind of power. But communities held together by mystical belief have historically been more durable, which is a Darwinian explanation for why most societies have been "protected" by some form of religion. Let me suggest how this works.

Let's say we build a community around a belief in an untested idea. We begin with a secular case. The idea might be that people who are liberated from "job slavery" by letting machines do all the work (as Karl Marx envisioned, and others envision today) will be productive, fulfilling, and happy. A community built around such a belief will then be living in a constant struggle to protect that idea. As long as the idea isn't tested by comparing it to an alternative, the community can thrive. But should it be tested and proven wrong, faith will disintegrate and the community will fall apart.

On the other hand, if the community is based on a mystical idea that cannot be tested or disproven, such as the protection by higher powers, the community remains safe. This is why, I suggest, spirituality has outlived such testable ideas as utopian Marxism.

Knowledge and faith are not the same, but they can be complementary; they may strengthen each other or they may conflict and create doubt. People will do well if they seek to align them while keeping them apart. One way of aligning them is via self-fulfilling prophecies, as in the case of Moses and the Ten Commandments. A self-fulfilling prophecy does not prove the existence of a divine being -- nor does it contradict it. It creates a reality out of a mystical belief, and confront holders of both assumptions: the observant believer who assumes the Ten Commandments are dictated by God, and the atheist assuming they were dictated by Moses out of his own human wisdom. Faith-empowered self-fulfilling prophecies have allowed societies to survive Darwinian selection. There is no way of predicting every self-fulfilling prophecy. Since reality is so complex, we might discover one only after its fulfillment, if ever. Therefore I conclude that my own faith in faith itself is a wise choice for the non-believer.

119

In short, to build a sustainable society together, we need to strengthen each other's faith, which may be helped by accepting the validity of a mystical belief. We should be aware of the benefits of mysticism, and realize when it can make us stronger and when it cannot. Mysticism is broader than spirituality, so that everyone, including atheists, have some form of mystical faith that provides direction. People who have no proclaimed god or religion will still express ideas such as "Nobody is born evil," which is a vague but hopeful mystical belief that cannot be confirmed or refuted by science. Every good leader, from Moses to Martin Luther King, has supported such mystical beliefs that promise a better future for their community and strengthen the collective identity.

My own summary of this somewhat detailed discussion is mostly practical: Faith is a requirement for a healthy economy. If religion were not essential, we could dismiss it, but the truth is that all major cultures have held a religion at their core. And my agnostic, practical approach leads me to note that

*religion provides a way to solve the tragedy of the commons and other paradoxes of social dilemmas.*

I began this discussion by seeking a solution to the challenge of reaching critical mass for a humane, people-centered economy. A critical mass is needed because the promise of a future superior economy does not answer the question "Why is this startup a good investment?" A good answer is required to attract the entrepreneurs and investors who are needed as trailblazers for the new idea. MItigating risk is only part of the solution; also required are people who have faith in the idea. The critical mass can be reached only by a community of believers who might act based on little more than their common faith and commitment to support each other. I suggest that this is possible, however, since the basic idea is sound -- that the economy is about being here for each other, that money provides means, and family and friends provide meaning. This idea is deeply rooted in the cultural values of mankind, and has proven itself time after time in bootstrapping economies. It succeeds by convincing sufficient numbers to act in mutual interest, not pure personal interest, thereby solving the social dilemma.

But it is impossible to leave this topic without addressing the dark sides of communities of faith, which can be highly oppressive. In every case where mystical belief and religion have created a culture, it has been

120

accompanied by ill-treatment of dissenters. By not being subject to the principles of science and other free inquiry --including the right to challenge all statements -- these cultures can slide into autocracy, controlled by leaders who compete for the power to dictate right and wrong in the name of their absolute but untestable "truth."

Once again, it is Martin Buber who suggests a guiding principle to address the critical issue.

*Martin Buber*

*"Some would deny any legitimate use of the word God, because it has been misused so much. Certainly it is the most burdened of all human words. Precisely for that reason it is the most imperishable and unavoidable. And how much weight has all erroneous talk about God's nature and works (although there never has been nor can be any such talk that is not erroneous) compared with the one truth that all men who have addressed God really meant him? For whoever pronounces the word God and really means Thou, addresses, no matter what his delusion, the true Thou of his life that cannot be restricted by any other and to whom he stands in a relationship that includes all others."*

As a non-believer, I am willing to underwrite that statement. I am also willing to work with any person who sees "Thou" as the meaning of life, with their religion respected as a personal matter. It is a powerfully unifying idea. Perhaps it is eclectic communities -- mixtures of religious, agnostic, and atheistic people of different minds and backgrounds -- who are best suited to find community defined by this idea. By building Thouness among themselves, they can leverage on each others' differences, optimizing the chances of creating a humane people-centered economy. This is the strategy behind the i4j community building. I do my best to make people like each other and we practice "friendly disagreement" in our discussions. I can promise that it is a highly productive and satisfying path to new insights.

121

# PART FOUR: BUILDING THE PEOPLE-CENTERED ECONOMY

In order to have a people-centered economy, we must manage the transition from the task-centered economy we are living in today. There are many great ideas that never become realized because the thresholds are too high or the incentives are misdirected. This is something I learned to study when I was a director at a Swedish science foundation supporting academic-business collaborations to innovate.

Regarding thresholds, we would routinely discard proposals that required large numbers of people and organization. We had seen how the Paris Agreement, an international treaty on reduction of greenhouse gases, was challenged to recruit enough countries for the treaty to be workable. We would have preferred to fund the small, agile effort of Elon Musk and Tesla. His strategy was to build electric cars and solar solutions that fought gas emissions by becoming hugely popular among consumers. While the Paris Agreement required scores of governments to first agree and then collectively implement, Elon did not need a consensus; he simply need to build an electric car that became a hit on the market. Elon understood that fuel management was the only thing that stopped electric cars from taking over, and he saw that battery technology had become good enough to address the issue. His startup Tesla demonstrated for the first time that electric cars are better in every aspect. Then he did one more revolutionary thing: he released all electric car patents to the public sphere - free for anyone to use. This has helped create the new ecosystem for electric vehicles where car companies are competing to build the best products. Elon will have won even if Tesla goes out of business, because we know now that cars with combustion engines are living on borrowed time.

Introducing PCE is very much like introducing the early electric cars. Insufficient batteries delayed electric cars from happening just as information technology has not been sufficient for the complex task of individually tailoring livelihoods for everyone. Modern battery technology made electric cars possible just as AI is making it possible to tailor jobs. Eventually everyone will want an individually tailored job because it is more attractive than a standard job slot and creates more value. What remains is to demonstrate that attractive jobs can be

122

tailored just as Tesla demonstrated that it's possible to build attractive electric cars and to create an ecosystem of companies competing to do it.

This section is about how to introduce PCE in this way.

Elon Musk's Tesla Roadster, with Earth in background. "Spaceman" mannequin wearing SpaceX Spacesuit in driving seat. Camera mounted on external boom. Photo: SpaceX

# Reviewing the essentials of PCE

Before continuing, let's review the main features of PCE, beginning with two important elements:

- One: A healthy and powerful economy is one in which everyone thinks, "I earn a better living when I am helping other people to help one another earn a better living." This strategy scales from the smallest family-sized group to communities as large as cities and states. An economy where people think, "I earn a better living by making people need each other less" is not only a dysfunctional economy and a weak culture, but it does not scale. When too many people say this, it becomes the growth-profit paradox.

- Two: A people-centered economy is one that is in balance. Today, almost all innovation serves the purpose of helping us spend or save. But families need to earn in order to spend. Therefore we need at least as much innovation for earning as innovation for spending if the economy is to be balanced.

As we have seen in the task-centered economy, innovation poses a threat to workers when they are considered a cost. But in the people-centered economy, innovation offers workers the opportunity to become more valuable. This potential resource is what innovation will target.

If we find those elements appealing, I suggest that we might agree on the mission for a people-centered economy:

*A sustainable innovation economy,*
*Where we do meaningful work with people we like,*
*Being valued by people we do not know,*
*Providing for the people we love*

This is a statement in four parts, and for me, much of its beauty is that all the parts are in harmony, with each part strengthened by the others. Let's look at it more closely:

1. The first goal, **a sustainable innovation economy**, contains important qualities. It means that innovation keeps us alive and well, offers us firm and level ground to stand on, avoids the sharp-clawed competition often associated with capitalism, and functions reliably and equitably into the future.

2. The second goal, **meaningful work together with people we like**, has been the dream of working people, but it has rarely been achieved. We all need friends to feel fulfilled, and we all want to spend our time doing meaningful things with and for them.

3. The third goal, to **be valued by people we do not know** (for what we are able to do), is the essence of the healthy economy. We want to believe in our own value to others, the value of others to us, and the value of each person to the general welfare. Without the belief that each of us has value, and can play a valuable role in their community, society cannot be strong.

4. The fourth, to **provide for our loved ones**, is what sustains us and makes us human. Without our family life, our species would not continue to exist.

These goals seem to convey the essence of what we desire. Each is consistent with the others, all are synergetic and self-reinforcing. They translate well between the micro-perspective of the individual and the macro-perspective of the society as a whole, as shown in the table below.

### GOALS FOR A PEOPLE-CENTERED ECONOMY

| GOALS FOR INDIVIDUALS | GOALS FOR SOCIETY |
|---|---|
| 1  A SUSTAINABLE INNOVATION ECONOMY, | ⇨ A STABLE PROBLEM SOLVING SYSTEM |
| 2  WHERE WE DO MEANINGFUL WORK WITH PEOPLE WE LIKE | ⇨ A PRODUCTIVE WORKFORCE |
| 3  BEING VALUED BY PEOPLE WE DO NOT KNOW | ⇨ A SOCIETY OF SCALE |
| 4  PROVIDING FOR THE PEOPLE WE LOVE | ⇨ SUSTAINABLE WELLBEING |

**THESE GOALS ARE: ✓ CONSISTENT ✓ SYNERGETIC**

I have suggested that this mission is possible to realize, and this book is my attempt to explain how.

The transformation from a task-centered economy to a people-centered economy is not a trivial one; it is nothing less than a paradigm shift.

It is a great challenge to understand the basic principles that underlie the system dynamics of an economy, and to design processes for re-organizing societies accordingly. Changing the public mindset, the language, how we value and relate to each other and things require a cultural shift, which is always difficult. Here's a joke that explains that difficulty better than I can: "Did you hear about the registrars who were cleaning out the old archives? To be on the safe side, they made a copy of every document they threw away." Indeed, how do we avoid repeating our old patterns?

**There are two main ideas that need to be reframed in order to build a people-centered economy.**

1. We need to reframe business as an activity that (a) raises the value of people and (b) treats the labor market as a service market offering ways for people to earn a living.

2. We need to reframe economic value so that its focus widens beyond money. It needs to be able to distinguish between means and meaning, things and people. Money provides the means of the economy, but improving the relations between people should be its purpose. The opposite does not work,

125

because it objectifies personal relations (turning "thou" into "it"), but is still the only way the mathematics of mainstream economics can work today.

**REFRAMING THE ECONOMY**

|  | PEOPLE-CENTERED | TASK-CENTERED |
|---|---|---|
| COMPETING TO | RAISE THE VALUE OF PEOPLE | LOWER THE COST OF THINGS |
| PRIMARY CUSTOMER | THE EARNER | THE SPENDER |
| A "JOB" MEANS | A SERVICE FOR EARNING | SERVING AN EMPLOYER |
| MACRO/MICRO INCENTIVES | ALIGNED *BOTH WANT EARNER TO EARN MORE* | OPPOSED *MACRO WANTS HIGHER WAGES MICRO WANTS CHEAPER LABOR* |

With these new frames and people-centered goals in mind, it is possible to paint a coherent picture of a people-centered economy. To do this, I'll present a number of ideas, suggestions and scenarios. They should not be seen as facts; this is an exploratory sketch, not a finished picture. The creation of the new ecosystem for jobs is only the beginning. It must grow organically, and when that happens, we'll depend on a coherent vision of a bigger picture, appropriate goals, and a common language among the stakeholders who can make the vision come true. It is my hope that this book can contribute to that.

# Constructing a people-centered economy

## History lesson: Study the welfare societies that triumphed

The communist solution to economic failures and inequities was not a success; communism has failed everywhere it has been attempted. What has worked are the welfare societies, mixed economies where the forces of government and private enterprise mostly balance each other, blending socialism and capitalism. While communism proved dysfunctional, welfare societies beat capitalism at its own game throughout the twentieth century. I will describe this in some detail, because just as the analysis in the *Communist Manifesto* maps almost perfectly onto our present situation, I suggest the same applies to the solution -- the middle-class welfare economy -- that was the outcome of the industrial revolution in nearly all successful economies.

The "Swedish Model" was the poster child for the welfare economy for half a century. When Marx published the *Communist Manifesto*, Sweden was one of the poorest countries in Europe. Paupers and orphans were auctioned away -- in public auctions -- to bidders offering to take them for the lowest caretaking compensation. One-sixth of the Swedish population emigrated over a short period to America, fleeing starvation and the lack of religious freedom. This was fertile ground for communism, which spread rapidly, organizing workers into unions.

What rescued Sweden from communism was the emergence of homegrown social democracy championed by a few socialist leaders. The most prominent was Per-Albin Hansson, the social democratic prime minister who coined the meme "Folkhemmet" – the People's Home -- and became its father figure, always referred to by his first name.

I suggest that we can apply reframed versions of what Per-Albin did in Sweden, as well as Franklin Roosevelt's strategies for the American Dream. They solved the industrial revolution "future of work" conundrum, creating formulas for middle-class economies that dominated the twentieth century. As we saw, the introductory chapter to the two-centuries-old communist manifesto offers a strikingly pertinent analysis of conditions today when just four words from the original are replaced by four words of today's conditions (as shown in the beginning of this book and in the appendix). Perhaps a similar simple twist can provide valuable ideas for creating the next middle-class economy?

Another echo from the first industrial revolution is the resurfacing of the neo-Marxist delusion that nobody will need to work because all jobs can be automated and all people can live entirely on utopian UBI handouts (work-friendly UBI is fine). I have already explained why this is a flawed idea.

And now we can look more closely into the parallels.

Marx's mistake in designing communism, apart from the absence of incentives inviting people to enter trusting relations with people they don't know, was his basic assumption that human society develops through class struggle and his recommendation of revolution whereby the proletariat would rise up against their exploiters. "After we get rid of the oppressors we can build a good society" has always been a fantasy for revolutionaries. A serious roadblock on this path is the way

127

it seeds a culture of finger-pointing and violence that often persists also after the oppressors have been removed. This is often because revolutionary leaders are usually better at fighting enemies than building economies. Once in power, they tend to remove all capable people who know how to run things and build mediocre societies (or worse). They keep themselves in power by continuing to find more enemies to finger-point at and fight, or imagining them if they must -- scenarios that doomed both the Soviet Union and Nazi Germany

Per-Albin invented a more rationale, inclusive approach, avoiding violence, finger-pointing, and paranoia, with hugely positive effects. Said Per-Albin about "the people's home" in 1928:

Per-Albin Hansson

*A home builds on togetherness. In a good home, we don't look down on each other or take advantage of each other. The strong does not plunder the weak. In the good people's home there is equality, consideration, cooperation, helpfulness. Applied to the large public and citizen's home, this would mean tearing down all social and economic walls and barriers that now divides us into the privileged and the underserved, the rulers and the ruled, the exploiters and the exploited .... For Swedish society to become a good people's home, class distinctions must be removed, social care developed, wealth and income gaps must be narrowed, workers should take part in managing the wealth we build, democracy must be fully implemented and applied also socially and economically.*

Just three decades later, Sweden had become the richest country in the world, ranking at the very top of most economic, social, and educational indicators. This was possible because (1) the people were aligned in needing, wanting, and valuing each other, (2) they shared a common vision and had a common language for it. Similar economic "miracles" have also happened in, for example, Singapore and Israel, both of which applied the successful concept similar to Per-Albin's people's home.

The key tool for building the Swedish people's home was presented two years later at the Stockholm Exhibition in 1930: architecture. Six architects launched "funkis," a Swedish version of functionalism (which stated that building design should be based solely on the purpose and function of the building). Funkis used affordable materials, such as brick and concrete; the architecture enabled quick and efficient construction; and it would provide good homes for millions of people over the next decades.

In 1931, the architects published their manifesto *"Acceptera!"* ("Accept!") that outlined design as an instrument for building a new society. The key message was the same as Marx's: mass production has come to stay; traditions and crafts, vocations and culture are gone. The solution was to embrace it and create a new culture for the masses, with mass production and consumption as the basis for a middle-class economy in the machine age.

> *Accept the present reality -- this is the only way of mastering it -- and create a liveable culture. We do not need the old forms of old culture to maintain our self-esteem. We cannot move back in time. We cannot jump forward into an unclear utopian future. We can only see reality with our eyes, accept it, and master it. The means and the goal of our cultural life has never been in doubt. It is for the tired and pessimistic to say that we are building a machine culture for its own purpose. [...] The irresistible machine culture is conquering the world, while the battle for beauty is wandering astray into reality-altering aesthetics...*

These were the thoughts that shaped not only the modern Swedish economy but also the way people lived and the design industry Sweden has become famous for. IKEA is a child of "Acceptera!" Founder Ingvar Kamprad was five years old when the *Manifesto* was published, and he grew up witnessing the changes.

I suggest that our present industrial revolution, which is taking us from mass-production to mass-personalization, this time killing the vocations and traditions from the previous industrial revolution, calls for a similar recipe -- designing a new society, with new concepts of not only how we should work and educate, but also how we can live. Just as we have learned over the last century to appreciate beauty and meaning in mass production -- everything from products to services and entertainment -- we should look into the possibilities of creating personalized beauty again, as before the first industrial revolution but now on a mass scale.

As an example, back in the nineties when I was director for research funding of the newly created Swedish Knowledge Foundation, I planned a funding program for the building industry. I was charmed by the idea of personalizing mass-production of housing. The emerging computer graphics tools made it possible to design each home differently even in large construction projects consisting of many units. I imagined how a new neighborhood of apartment buildings could be built, integrating interior designers with artists and craftspeople in the teams of builders. This technique would not cost much more, since the designers earned less than building workers. Teams of designers and artists could produce details for different buildings, starting from a common standard base unit expertly developed by the existing building industry. The plan of integration, thanks to new computerized tools, would not increase production price much, but it created great jobs for artistic professions and provide a richer experience for people moving into the apartments.

We sketched an idea for a funding program and showed it to the construction industry. This industry was descended from the functionalist vision, now a backbone of modern Swedish society after mass-producing millions of homes. I was much younger and lacked experience, not realizing that an industry with its roots in the aesthetics of mass-production was not going to be the best evangelist for mass-personalization. Their response was not positive. At the stakeholder meeting we had organized, the CEO of the construction industry association waved his copy of the work paper at us and said, "Well, I read it and it is..... Groovy?" He then dropped it on the table like a dead fish.

We went back to the drawing board and made something that fitted their mass-production mindset. I felt like Galileo, pushed to confess that mass-personalization could go nowhere, even though I knew that it represented the future of a healthy, people-centered construction industry. It would be even more attractive with the emergence of 3D printers that can build houses. We would have to wait until construction people found new and better ways to engage more people in a more meaningful creative process so that they need, want, and value each other more.

## "The future of work" needs a new story and imagery

I still believe I was right to look at aesthetics and design and the Swedish "Funkis" case as a starting point. It just won't be launched by the incumbents of today. Imagery and narrative is essential for any vision of the future to be understood and followed, so it is not a bad idea to start there. We will be setting out from a dark place and head toward the light.

Sad people have sad thoughts. Our sad feelings about the job market make us think sadly about the future. What does that future look like? Googling "the future of work" will give you a picture of what we see ahead of us:

*A snapshot of the mood surrounding "the future of work". Top Google image hits (Aug 14 2018)*

Nobody wants the dystopian future depicted above. But they will remain the imagery that will lurking the back of our minds until they are matched by alternative images that people can look at and say, "This is what I want my future to look like."

We don't yet have those images; this style remains to be shaped.

*In order to move toward a creative and satisfying future, we must have a positive vision in which we can picture ourselves.*

Here is what I want the future of work to look and feel like.

Art by Marconi Calindas

( If you have the black-and-white version of this book, I should tell you that this beautiful painting by Marconi Calindas is full of happy colors.)

You might be asking yourself "How can this be the future of work? The person does not seem to be working in this picture." My answer: Why is this *not* the future of work? How do you know that the person in this picture is *not* working? Perhaps it is the public preconception of what is meant by "work" that is keeping us in the dark. We need to experiment with pictures, stories, design -- all types of creativity -- to construct our vision.

What we now need is visual artists and storytellers who can imagine images and scenarios of a better future in ways that give people hope and make them want to engage in building a better future together.

133

Every cultural movement in history has used art and storytelling to engage people's hearts and minds. U.S. president Franklin Delano Roosevelt, "America's cheerleader" throughout the Great Depression, realized that people must believe in a future if they are to build it. His message to people who feared losing everything they owned, was "*We have always held to the hope, the belief, the conviction that there is a better life, a better world, beyond the horizon.*"

Two years into his tenure, in 1934, his administration launched the Public Works of Art Project (PWAP), an agency that employed thousands of artists, writers, and photographers who had lost their livelihoods during the depression. The PWAP was one of several relief program for unemployed workers. These artists created nearly 16,000 paintings, murals, prints, and sculptures for government in the years to come. One of them was Seymour Fogel who's murals expressed a persistent optimism and faith in the institutions and qualities of the American character and a yearning for a better, more cooperative and more enlightened future. People who were struggling could see themselves in his pictures, having meaningful, rewarding jobs, good family lives and promising futures for their children. Here are two examples of Fogel's work, "Industrial Life" and "The Security of the Family."

You will observe that the middle-class society that emerged since then made progress regarding what we see lacking in Fogel's pictures: diversity. But if his paintings would have been boycotted at the time the output would have been more anger and misery. The people who saw themselves in these pictures helped society move in the right direction.

What we need today is a new wave of art conveying optimism. In these times, the Internet can help us come together to shape the imagery and stories that invite us and others to find faith in a good future of work, conveying intuitively and immediately what I am trying to communicate by words, hoping to reach through to receptive readers.

## The work-friendly – not utopian – UBI can pave the way

Although a version of Universal Basic Income (UBI) has arisen as a new, utopian form of Marxism, I have also described a non-utopian, work-friendly UBI. This one is a mixed formula in which the government guarantees a basic "living wage" and leaves it up to individuals to generate anything more. The idea is to replace much of the social welfare system with UBI while not killing people's incentive to work. Today, people often fear losing or switching jobs. Work-friendly UBI keeps

135

people going while they look for their next job. Danish Prime Minister Poul Rasmussen invented a word for it:[22].

# *"flexicurity".*

Today, Schumpeter has become popular among innovators. He was inspired by Marx's analysis, but came to a different conclusion, suggesting that constant self-disruption can create and sustain an innovation economy. But innovators, be wary, because we don't see your disruption converging toward what Schumpeter had in mind. Instead we see it matching almost perfectly Marx's analysis of the problem. Innovators are simply implementing Schumpeter in the wrong way in counting on technological innovation to sustain us. But we can get it right if we create a balance between public and private forces, seeing the worker, the customer, and the citizen as "three parts of same person." These parts "orbit" around a fourth part -- the friend and family member -- who brings the other parts purpose, sustaining a state of creative disruption that serves all the without confusing purpose with means.

# The PCE engine: the ecosystem for innovating jobs

We now need to focus on how to kickstart the ecosystem for innovating jobs and regain the natural balance between earning and spending that everyone desires.

## Example of an actual startup: Workgenius

Benjamin Bear is an entrepreneur (and i4jer) who founded the now defunct startup Workgenius, a beautifully simple and clear people-centered business idea that I use to explain "entry-level" steps in the people-centered economy. In a people-centered economy, investors would race to invest in him. But in the existing task-centered economy nobody did, Workgenius did not find enough investment to reach critical mass. It was too far ahead of its time.

Ben identified an unsatisfied need among the rapidly growing number of on-demand workers. When he started his company, in 2015, their main challenge was to find enough work. The average independent worker

---

[22] "Flexicurity - Wikipedia." https://en.wikipedia.org/wiki/Flexicurity. Accessed 26 Sep. 2018.

would have four sources of income, and discovering and scheduling new work opportunities was a fragmented and distracting task, and still is. Ben's innovation was a smartphone app that curated jobs from on-demand work apps. The worker would register an account, list her skills, and set up an earning goal. Workgenius connected her to a range of sources for on-demand work and presented the ones she qualified for. The worker would select the work that looked interesting, and she would receive recommendations on where and when to work in order to reach her earning goal. The work would be scheduled in her calendar, Workgenius took care of the accounting, and payment would be collected from the on-demand platforms.

I remember when Ben first presented his idea for a startup at our yearly i4j Summit in 2016. It seemed so simple that most of us didn't recognize how transformational it could be. Workgenius fits the people-centered business definition elegantly: (1) the worker is the customer; (2) the job is offered to the worker as a service, and (3) the job is tailored to match the skills of the worker. Explaining this idea to people is usually difficult, but his example was clear and simple.

The advantages of Ben's approach became even clearer when compared with start-ups that had taken the wrong approach to these issues. Uber, for example, after several years of success, had found itself in a battle with its drivers concerning their status. The company said they were not a taxi company with drivers; they were an online marketplace, like eBay, with a business plan of connecting buyers with sellers of car rides. That was, mildly put, not doing wonders for their reputation, when combined with news stories featuring drivers who felt badly treated. When I asked Ben about his strategy for avoiding this kind of hot water, he said, "It's not a problem. I offer my workers employment if they work enough hours. As employees I offer them benefits and health insurance. It is all a part of the service offer."

This made a profound impact on me. Ben had reframed the labor market as a service market. He offered his customers a chance to earn a living as his employees. He did not so much care what they did as long as they were happy with their work, able to earn money, and secure. He was eager to offer his workers everything that Uber was fighting in courtrooms to NOT offer their drivers. Why? Because for Ben, the worker was his *primary* customer. For Uber, the driver is the *secondary* customer; their primary customer is the one who pays. Ben had seen a good market for paid work instead of a paying customer.

The key difference between people-centered and task-centered company becomes plain if the market for car rides gets tougher. Uber, Lyft, and other ride companies say, "We can't pay as much as before, but it's still work. Take it or leave it." Workgenius says "The ride market is tough, we don't recommend it. Here is a better alternative of paying work you might like. We are always looking for the best people."

There are millions of struggling on-demand workers, and as I have shown above, an untapped multi-trillion-dollar market around the corner. The Workgenius business idea can open that future market by solving an existing need. It is powerful, because it places itself between the gig platforms and the gig workers. As soon as people start using the Workgenius app as a gateway to paid work, all the gig platform companies lose their direct contact with the worker. They end up keeping the personal relationship with the spender, while Workgenius takes over the personal relationship with the earner. That should benefit Workgenius, because the earner is a more important and better customer for them than the spender.

The competition for serving the spender is tough and granular. The spender will shop hard for nearly every item of importance, and finding the best price has become a market of its own. The fight for her every dollar is intense as innovators flock around to help her spend more. If the spender runs out of money, the customers disappear. This happens often in an economy like that of the U.S., where the economy swings back and forth and half the population have more debts than assets.

The earners, on the other hand, are a neglected and needy category of customers, much underserved. There is little competition for them and therefore many opportunities to serve them while making a decent profit. Furthermore, the earner is a loyal customer because the average citizen wants a secure income from one or two reliable sources, while the spender distributes money in small batches through hundreds of competing vendors.

*The earner is not only a more*
*loyal customer, offering more business,*
*but also one offering more chances to be retained.*

While the spender vanishes when she runs out of money, the earner stays as long as she can earn. This puts the people-centered business serving the earner as the primary customer in a powerful position. A successful business will have more dependable, loyal, retainable customers.

138

## WORKGENIUS - A ONE-STOP SHOP FOR EARNING AN INCOME

1.Worker registers profile, sets up earning goal, lists skills and preferences.

2.Workgenius shows work apps that user qualifies for. Worker selects which ones to use.

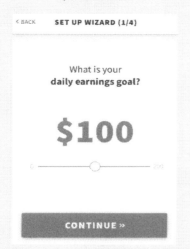

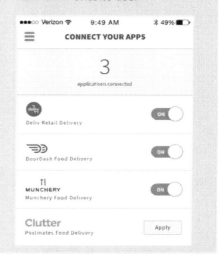

3. Workgenius recommends when and where to work based on worker's preferences.

4. Worker keeps track of results + builds reputation, manages benefits and health insurance

# The need for PCE early investors

I thought Workgenius would be a smashing success for all the reasons given above. But as it turned out, Workgenius raised only $150,000 in seed investment and then nothing more, despite providing proof of concept and recruiting 10,000 workers who earned money through the platform. One would think that their simple, powerful approach, the enormous potential market, proof of concept, and initial customers would be enough to attract investors and scale up the service to independent workers. Why didn't that happen? The answer is that despite its people-centered advantages, the view when seen through task-centered frame still popular among investors is not as appealing.

From the mainstream investor's point of view, market size and cost efficiency are paramount. "Pay less" beats "Earn more;" a dollar saved is a dollar earned. Paying less is the easiest way to earn more. If we can do something more cost efficiently, we take over the market. The basic message of startup pitches goes like this: "Here is something that costs $80 to make and sells for $100. The market size is $100 billion. Our innovation does it better. It costs us $1 to make, and we can sell it for $80 and own the market. Our revenue potential is $80 billion, mostly profit. Will you invest?"

If the proposition holds water, the investor will go in with reasonable hopes of making a killing. If it fails, the limited partners will consider it a worthy try and an honorable loss. Ben knew he needed a mainstream pitch of this type for Workgenius,where he targeted the cost cut and the market size. Ben and his team identified companies with work pools as their customer. A company normally has a recruitment cost per worker of $300-500. Workgenius's selling argument was that they would reduce the companies' recruitment cost by offering them access to Workgenius's pool of workers for a monthly fee. They would halve their own cost -- i.e., to $150-$250 -- compared to recruiting their own pools. In other words, the suggested business was to lower their labor costs. The maximum market size of one-time recruiting fees was around $20 billion for the entire existing U.S. on-demand workforce. The market for yearly revenues from monthly fees was modest -- a few million. Compare this to the much simpler PCE business model with the basic idea -- workers are undervalued, and there is considerable money to be made in raising their value, up to trillions of dollars, as I have indicated.

So the task-centered lens does not convey the potential of the business, and still the investors will prefer it. The idea of raising worker wages -- i.e., increasing employers' labor costs -- does not push the right buttons. The former is easier, because the customers are companies spending a lot of money and the entrepreneur helps them increase cost efficiency. The latter is seen as complicated, because undervalued workers don't have money and it's guesswork to say how much an innovation can raise their value.

There is one notable exception: when innovation helps someone who earns little or nothing to take over a job from someone who earns more. One example of this is to train uneducated workers in third-world countries do work that can be outsourced from countries with higher labor costs, a model successfully exploited by India, Vietnam, Bangladesh, and others. The entrepreneur is indeed helping poor people do better, which is a good and honorable cause, but if it is done by offering cheaper labor costs, lowering GDP in the countries of the companies that purchase the service it lowers the value of the average global worker. This is innovation that might increase people's need for each other (across borders, in this case) but lowers the value they see in each other. It will be better to use such platforms for bootstrapping local economies, where people in the region leverage each other.

A good people-centered job increases both demand and value. It does not cut costs or underbid existing workers. It doesn't lower the labor cost in the economy, it increases it. And when the labor cost goes up, earning goes up, people can spend more, and the economy grows. It's a great solution. But there is a barrier we must jump over.

It might look as if I am presenting the investor as the "bad guy". But it is not necessarily so, even investors are facing their own tough choice. Let's see this from their perspective. Imagine you are an investor. You have managed to get both very rich people and a trade union pension fund to invest in your latest startup fund. They expect good returns. Now you are looking for entrepreneurs to invest in. Today, two entrepreneurs are pitching their ideas.

1.  *Task-centered startup pitch*: "Sodastream for chocolate." The entrepreneur gives you two bars of chocolate and asks which one tastes best. The first chocolate bar costs two dollars in the shop, most of which is labor cost, and revenues are two billion dollars a year. The second bar comes from his/her innovation, a small machine that people use in their homes. He/she charges a dollar a pop for the ingredients, fifty percent of which

is profit. He or she will take over the whole market; the revenues are a billion each year, half of it profit. The second one tastes much better. You check the numbers, which look fine, and you invest.

2. *People-centered startup pitch*: "Specialized jobs for people from the autistic spectrum." The entrepreneur has invented a method that recruits and trains autistic people with the enhanced ability of attention to detail (autistic people can have tremendous abilities ot this type). He has an incubator that invents new jobs for this special ability. His pilot team of autistic workers identified features in medical X-ray images and aerial photos that nobody thought were possible to see with the naked eye. His business idea is to start serving hospitals and geological surveys and then move into other applications. Each analyst will generate revenues of $250,000 per year, $50,000 of which is profit. You ask him where he got the numbers, and he says he got the estimate from a survey he made. You don't invest, because: (a) The numbers can't be verified; (b) the market size is unknown; and (c) revenues come from raising the value of work, which adds complexity to the pitch. Compare that to simply crossing out workers and showing a billion in one shot.

You did what you had to, and now you have to be able to answer to the people who invested in your fund.

The problem is that it's much easier to make a huge and quick return on investment by killing jobs than by creating jobs. When you kill jobs, you don't have to split the revenues with the workers (they are out of the game). When you improve their jobs, you have to split the revenues with them, give them service, and maintain them.

That's the growth-profit paradox again, standing in the way of building a people-centered economy. How to solve this problem? Let's look at a couple of ways.

*Goal*: Venture capitalists need a common language for investing in people-centered startups, a new professional jargon that enables them to discuss opportunity, risk, and management of venture projects in the new ecosystem for innovating jobs. They must convince themselves that their peers will join later investment rounds and that there is a good exit down the road. They must be able to discuss these things among themselves. There is no such language today, so they need to build it. It is a classic case of chicken- and- egg because the only way to of building the language for investing in people-centered startups is by investing in them and sharing the experience. How to do it?

## Government can bootstrap a venture capital industry

There are ways of creating a venture capital industry where there was none before. In the U.S. and Israel, the governments had nurturing programs. This is not widely known, because private business does not like talking about how government helped create their business.

The truth is that government has a huge role in mitigating risk. If the private investor gets all the upside when an investment succeeds and the government shares the downside if it fails, the investor can take larger risks. And this should be enough. Building the ecosystem for jobs means high risk in the beginning, when investors and entrepreneurs have a breathing space to make early mistakes, learn from them, and develop best practices. The U.S. and Israeli governments did this with success in creating the venture markets we see today. We can try to do the same again in a people-centered way. Knowing that a successful program will replace the need for unemployment insurance with income from great jobs, we are working not only with innovation policy, but also labor policy, which always has much larger budgets.

## Banks could help government bootstrap PCE ecosystems

Here is a scenario where governments and banks team up in a win-win-win situation with VC investors and entrepreneurs. Why banks? Because they are one of the the the few industries that already have the earner as their primary customer. While most companies care only how customers spend their money, banks care about how they earn it. They help people manage their capital and lend them money, and have a direct interest in customers having a stable income and good credit rating.

A bank's greatest asset are the debts people owe them, as we saw when we discussed currency. If I have a steady income, a high credit score, and pay loan interest on time, the probability that they will get back all their money plus interest is high. What happens if we can't deliver on our promises? That is what happened in 2008, when banks had been

143

lending lots of mortgage money to people who could not pay it back. It is a complicated story how the banks tried various ways to rescue the situation by blending trustworthy debt with broken debt in buckets of "subprime" debt that they would go on using as securities on their borrowing back and forth. It was based on the calculated risk that there were always enough borrowers in a bucket who were paying back to keep the bucket floating.

Until one day the bubble burst. The subprime buckets sank and had to be written off. They could not cover for other loans that then sank, too, and on in an uncontrolled chain reaction that nearly melted down the world economy in a very short time. It has taken a decade for the world to start recovering.

This is more evidence that, at the end of the day, the economy is about being here for each other. Helping each other to make good on our promises is the basic recipe for a good economy and a good society. The economy is not about things or dollars but people and their needs, abilities and the value of their promises. So when bank customers lose their jobs to automation, banks lose, too. The customers' earnings stop coming into their accounts and their debts become riskier. Banks and government are strongly co-dependent and have a direct interest in ensuring that people have jobs with a stable income. For banks, earners are savers and borrowers. For governments, earners are taxpayers who support other earners. Both need to avoid meltdowns like the one in 2008. Between banks and governments, instead of a growth-profit paradox like with companies serving the spender, we have a win-win deal, where both institutions want to help people earn.

There are more reasons that banks care about all this. They are challenged on several fronts, as smartphones, artificial intelligence, and the cloud move into many functions of the traditional bank. The banks understand this, and are all planning to automate as many jobs as possible to cut costs and push back at the competition. Branches are closing and employees fear for their jobs. Automation means thinning profit margins and financial trading done by robots. Margins are squeezed to the decimals of a percent per trade.

A major issue for customers of the financial industry is trust. By tradition, banks have traditionally represented the interest of savers and made them feel safe. But after 2009, when hoards of people who had borrowed more than they could pay back had to move out of their homes, they felt let down by the banks, which since then have faced the challenge of winning back that trust. If they can once again demonstrate their desire to help people earn, they might be able to redeem their relationship to their customers, who would once again be willing to take on loans and mortgages, increasing the banks' business. The workers can and should once again be the most important customer group for banks. And governments have every reason to encourage this, so that more customers will generate the tax revenues essential to government functions. This could put banks at the center of a people-centered economy.

The question is: What can government and banks do together to win back customers' trust? What would a bank-enabled, people-centered economy look like from a banker's point of view, and how would it be good business for a bank? Consider the healthcare company Kaiser-Permanente, a healthcare provider and health insurance in one. Unlike competing healthcare providers, who do now sell health insurance, it earns most when its customers don't need treatment. Therefore, Kaiser invests in innovative services that keep customers happy and healthy. Banks could use that model, connecting their customers to services like WorkGenius, jobBay, and Jobly.

Imagine a bank customer who has taken out loans he can't pay back. Today the bank will not offer much more than a scheme to improve the terms of the loans, which may not be enough. Americans already carry a mountain of bad debt, and every year, debts worth many billions of dollars are written off. Banks lose money, customers lose credit scores or go bankrupt. Delinquent debts are sold to debt collectors, a booming and not very pleasant industry with badly paid employees who create a lot of friction and harassment. This process makes nobody happy. The collectors retrieve only a fraction of outstanding money, and they often continue trading the debts they didn't manage to collect so that people's broken hopes and promises are changing hands between collectors for a few cents on the dollar.

Imagine how the situation changes if the bank customer has an earning service connected to the account. The debt collector is replaced by a coach who is paid to help the customer find better ways of earning at least enough to stay current with debts and maintain a decent credit score. Instead of receiving ugly phone calls and threats from collectors, the bank customer has encouraging conversations with a coach who guides the customer toward a solution. This generates a win for all parties: The bank does not have to sell the debt at a loss, and the customer can be trusted to take on more credit. Back-of-the envelope

145

calculations show that such services could create a substantial new industry for coaches, who could certainly earn better incomes for more interesting work than they found as a debt collector. The only loser would be the debt collecting industry, but their loss would be much smaller than the total gain, and its former employees could find more appreciated and rewarding jobs as coaches. Such a shift would be likely to increase profits, incomes, and GDP.

Banks should be interested.

For banks to create earning services in this way, the service process needs to be innovated, attracting an ecosystem of entrepreneurs, venture capitalists, angel investors, and others. These pioneers, in turn, must agree to join a partnership that works to generate innovative services that help 'earners' work in more meaningful ways. Banks can offer their customers foresight, helping them find new, better jobs before they lose their old ones. They have already gathered enormous knowledge and 'big data' on sectoral employment, so they know, for example, that all their clients who are cashiers will be struggling in the next decade as their jobs disappear. They could offer them 'retooling/schooling' programs so remain good earning customers who are good for their loans.

The federal government stands to benefit as well, mainly because of how it strengthens the national economy. But it also offers opportunity to lower the outdated barriers between labor and technology policy. Every year, the U.S. government spends over $30 billion to keep unemployed people off the streets. If only 1 percent of this amount were used to match private money in creating seed funds in the ecosystem for innovating jobs the size of the funds would equal all the seed investments made in the U.S. in one year. In other words, with almost no risk or effort, government could bootstrap an early-stage venture market for a people-centered innovation ecosystem that is just as large as the early-stage VC market of today at hardly any expenditure.

Banks would be ideal co-investors and catalysts because of their incentive to have a market of startups offering 'earner' services to their customers. As large customers or buyers, banks would leverage their own investments in the innovation economy.

As for the future of bank branches, they are ready-made settings for coaching or mentoring, which are best done face to face. Instead of discussing how to save for a pension, adjust loan payments, or apply for a mortgage, customers would discuss jobs for multiple family

146

members, education, and financial plans for the future. These discussions would resemble those the bank offers today, but on more meaningful topics closer to the customer's private and professional needs. Above all, the customers would feel safe, knowing their private information is secure and their coach is working for them.

I believe that this scenario is not science fiction. It is different from what we have now, and feels strange because it asks us to reframe our view of labor policy. The reframing leads to a simpler, more positive picture for all parties, with people helping each other live up to promises and pay down debts. It also increases their trustworthiness because their goals overlap in significant ways. Instead of encouraging the players to pressure each other for payments, often destroying their reputation or trading their unpaid debts on murky markets, the process judges people by their attitude, desire, and potential, not by how their particular training fits an available job slot.

Later in this book you will see a chapter by Gi Fernando that shows an effort by U.K. banks that are actually taking significant PCE steps.

## A PCE business plan: Joblygenius restores bad debt

Now it's time to present a startup scenario, a people-centered business plan that makes the case for the huge potential of the ecosystem for innovating jobs. We start where Workgenius so sadly left off, a really good idea that did not attract investors because it was not attractive enough to employers (or other "big spenders"). This plan needs enough "spender-appeal" to attract venture capitalists, who have less leeway than many might think; they always have their own, more conservative, investors to please. We need our attractive business pitch to disrupt an existing dysfunctional market. What can that market be?

A few years ago, Jay Van Zyl and I wrote a business plan that made exactly such a pitch. Here I will call it "Joblygenius", to make the connection to Ben Bear's Workgenius, and in producing it, we were coached by another i4jer, Pete Hartigan. Pete coached SocialFinance (SoFi) in their early startup days and onwards as it grew to become the multi-billion-dollar financial institution it is today. The key strategy of SoFi was to focus on student debt, a sadly mismanaged financial market in the U.S., and a growing bubble of bad debt that now has reached a size where it can crash the world economy -- just as the toxic "subprime" mortgage debts did in 2008.

147

Instead of presenting a long and boring business plan, I will give you the essential elements, using Curtis Carlson's ingeniously simple NABC method. Curt (who is a member of i4j) designed NABC when he was  head of the legendary research lab SRI International, where he needed a formula allowing even the most technically minded researchers to devise sound business ideas. NABC stands for "Needs, Approach, Benefits, Competition" -- the four essential elements  of a sound business idea.

Joblygenius' pitch is simple and straightforward:

> *The **need***: Bad debt makes banks lose money, debtors go bankrupt, and governments reap financial crises when bad debt bubbles burst.

> *The novel **approach** addressing the need*: Instead of debt collectors forcing debtors to pay money they might not have, Joblygenius offers debtors a chance to restore the bad debt by helping  them earn more, with the assistance of personal coaches. Banks can offer customers the choice between being helped by Joblygenius to restore their delinquent debts or have them passed on to debt collectors.

> *The **benefits** of the approach*: Banks get better customers and the value of their debts increase. They avoid the bad reputation that often is caused by debt collection. Bank customers remain credit-worthy and can borrow the money they need to buy cars and houses. Instead of being leaned on by debt collectors, they are helped by coaches. Governments are relieved to witness the rise of a commercial market that can restore bad debt, lower the risk of financial crises, increase GPD, and helping people become better workers. Everyone wins except the debt collectors.

> *The **competition***: Today, the main competitors for Joblygenius is debt collectors. Because debt collection lowers the value of debt and brings negative side effects, banks are incentivized to try Joblygenius before proceeding to debt collection.

Let our friends demonstrate the scenario. Marie has been troubled lately and has accumulated a credit card debt that now is delinquent. But credit card company owner Anne is not selling Marie's delinquent debt to the debt collector quite yet because I "sold" Joblygenius to Anne. I qualify "sold" because she does not pay me anything. I give it to her for free because Anne is adding all of her credit card customers to my platform. This is how I get my REAL customers -- the workers. Anne has a million customers now, and so do I, just like that. My offer to Anne's trouble-free customer is simple: I offer them the gig-aggregator Workgenius. I teamed up with Ben Bear and his Workgenius platform, which was just what I needed to start Joblygenius. Now all my customers can do gigs, although I am aware that only a minority will be using the service initially.

Before Anne's credit card company added Joblygenius to their service, they would send Marie payment reminders for three months and then hand the debt over to a private debt collector. This person would push Marie to cut a deal that would terminate the debt, charging typically a twenty-five percent "pot fee" on everything they managed to bring in. Anne would be lucky if she got back half the amount Marie owed her. When Jay and I wrote the business plan, in 2016, the debt collectors would earn 15 billion dollars a year, collecting 55 billion dollars of delinquent debt from 40 million Americans. This equalled more than 15 percent of the adult population. Creditors were writing off 160 billion dollars of bad debt each year, money that simply disappeared from the economy. Anne would not only have lost the money she lent to Marie, she would also have lost Marie as a trustworthy customer, which is an even bigger loss. Adding insult to injury, murky debt collectors generate 200,000 complaints every year, and 5,000 lawsuits.

In the our Joblygenius business plan, Jay and I told our potential investors that we would disrupt the debt collection industry, earning many billions of dollars each year by restoring bad debts for creditors like Anne. What we made a smaller point of was the REAL business idea -- to add as many earners as possible to our job platform, helping them to earn better and charging them a commission. If we were able to serve all workers on the planet earning less than three thousand dollars each year, Joblygenius' yearly revenues would be 150 billion dollars at only one (1) percent commission!

Here is how we would help Anne restore Marie's debt, thus eating the debt collectors' lunch. "Before handing Marie's debt to a collector," we would say to Anne, "let us try to restore it. We will charge the same fee as the debt collector, twenty-five percent, if we succeed and the debt is restored. Your loss will be half of what it will be if you go to a debt collector and instead of losing Marie we will restore her as a trusted customer. You will receive praise instead of complaints from Marie. If we fail, you don't need to pay us anything and can still hand the debt to a collector, so you aren't even taking a risk by engaging us." Anne would obviously accept, because we offered her everything to win and nothing to lose.

Then we would get in touch with Marie. We would tell her, "Anne is about to hand your debt to a debt collector, which can become ugly and unpleasant. Instead, let us help you earn better and restore your debt. We have the experts and algorithms to do this. Your debt will be restored AND you will be earning more than before! You will receive a personal coach. We do this because we believe in the personal touch. More often than not, personal challenges are the underlying reason for your present situation. A life coach can cost quite a bit, but don't worry -- you pay a commission on what you earn, so there is no risk that you will increase your debt." Marie would obviously accept this offer.

Here is where Joblygenius goes beyond Workgenius: We have a network of coaches who  can help Marie. Joblygenius has a matchmaking system, like a dating app, which helps us find coaches who might be a good match for Marie. We find two: one is Bob, a retired Army officer who loves helping troubled people "get their shit together." It's what made his life meaningful during all those years in the Army. Marie's dad was an Army officer, which is one reason why Bob is a good match. The other matching coach is Becky, a social worker who had recently lost her hospital job when the institution replaced their social workers with a smartphone app.

Marie goes with Bob. They meet at the Rose Pub, where Bob helps Marie start using Joblygenius for doing gig-work. Marie needs to pay 250 dollars a month to stay current on her credit card debt and they set up an earning goal of 160 dollars a week. Marie can earn this by working one day a week. When she looks for gigs herself, she usually earns around 15 dollars an hour, but with our superior AI that helps her choose the right opportunities she can earn 20 dollars per hour. Now comes the "magic" part that allowed Bob to have a successful career. He puts his big warm hand on Marie's shoulder, looks her deep in the eyes, and when he feels the connection he says "Marie, you can do this. I know you can, because you are strong." He sees in her eyes that is message is getting across. He schedules a video-meeting in a week and another meeting in real life a week after that.

This is a good, meaningful job for Bob and he can earn a good living at it. Here are the numbers:

Twenty clients is not an unusual workload for counselors. With AI-client management tools, Bob can help forty clients without problems. So Joblygenius is not only restoring bad debt for creditors like Anne and helping people like Marie earn better. It also creates a new service market for coaches like Bob, people who want to earn their living by helping others earn a living.

I hope you will agree that Jay and I thought out a great business plan for a people-centered startup. So why did we not move ahead with it? It has two weaknesses. The first is the assumption that banks and credit card companies will jump on the offer. It is a great offer, no doubt about that, but in real life, banks are difficult to interest in new ideas. There is someone in the bank who manages the books of bad debt and this person is instructed to engage debt collectors, not innovative startups like Joblygenius. Changing this culture is a major challenge, partly because financial institutions are so strictly regulated by public policy.

The other hurdle was pointed out to us by Pete, who knows the venture community. He said investors would like the idea -- but they would suggest replacing the coaches with an AI app that has zero labor cost. That was when I gave up on the idea.

However, if we could build a collaboration between government and banks to invest in venture funds that invest in companies like Joblygenius, there would be better chances. This thought brings us back to policy.

| | REGULAR | WITH JOBLYGENIUS | JOBLYGENIUS' AI-TOOLS |
|---|---|---|---|
| **JOBLYGENIUS FOR BOB THE COACH: EARNINGS** | | | |
| MARIE'S HOURLY GIG RATE | $15 | $20 | SMART JOB FINDER / PLANNER FINDS THE BEST GIGS FOR MARIE |
| NR. OF CLIENTS PER COACH | 20 | 40 | SMART CLIENT MANAGEMENT SYSTEM ALLOWS BOB TO MANAGE MORE CLIENTS |
| MARIE'S CAPACITY FOR GIG WORK | 8 HR/WEEK | 12 HR/WEEK | SMART TIME MANAGEMENT HELPS MARIE DO MORE WORK WITH NO EXTRA EFFORT |
| BOB EARNS (20% COMMISSION) | $12/HOUR Too little! | $48/HOUR Great! | |

Twenty clients is not an unusual workload for counselors. With AI-client management tools, Bob can help forty clients without problems. So Joblygenius is not only restoring bad debt for creditors like Anne and helping people like Marie earn better. It also creates a new service market for coaches like Bob, people who want to earn their living by helping others earn a living.

I hope you will agree that Jay and I thought out a great business plan for a people-centered startup. So why did we not move ahead with it? It has two weaknesses. The first is the assumption that banks and credit card companies will jump on the offer. It is a great offer, no doubt about that, but in real life, banks are difficult to interest in new ideas. There is someone in the bank who manages the books of bad debt and this person is instructed to engage debt collectors, not innovative startups like Joblygenius. Changing this culture is a major challenge, partly because financial institutions are so strictly regulated by public policy.

The other hurdle was pointed out to us by Pete, who knows the venture community. He said investors would like the idea -- but they would suggest replacing the coaches with an AI app that has zero labor cost. That was when I gave up on the idea.

However, if we could build a collaboration between government and banks to invest in venture funds that invest in companies like Joblygenius, there would be better chances. This thought brings us back to policy.

# POLICY IDEAS: WHAT GOVERNMENT CAN DO

I am ending my part of this book with some aspects of PCE that await facilitation by government:

- *PCE governance*, including agile governance, innovation, and labor policies

- *PCE business* and the ecosystem for jobs, in particular innovating better livelihoods

- *PCE research and analysis*, including PCE economics, and transdisciplinary research

- *PCE culture*, including the arts and humanities

- *PCE currency*, with new tools for bootstrapping economies

These have been addressed in one way or another, explicitly or implicitly, in the book so far, and will be examined more closely in the chapters by my co-authors.

I will not prescribe any solutions that I don't feel confident about, and speak from my own experience, as a former director of a public foundation for research and innovation and program director at a national innovation agency, both in Sweden. On top of this experience, there have been many discussions and collaborations with peers mainly in the U.S., Europe and Israel, including setting up bi-national innovation programs between Sweden and Israel which later became a model for European programs. I also started a center at Stanford University that was backed by governments and foundations in five countries.

## PCE governance

When a country sets out to grow a new for-profit industry for innovating jobs it will require a mix of innovation policy with labor policy. There is usually a chasm between these policies, with different mindsets and little experience of collaboration between the departments who manage them, and indeed little willingness to collaborate.

Together with i4j co-founder Sven Otto Littorin, Sweden's former minister for labor and a key architect of the new Swedish economy, I have discussed how silos in government are a problem for innovation for jobs.[23] This stands in the way of integrating labor and innovation policies, even with the best partnership across leaders in government; even when united by a large crisis, as Sven has described in his case presentation of GM's closure of SAAB Automobile, where he and the Minister for Enterprise jointly created an innovation-for-jobs policy[24].

Furthermore, governments with a "Nordic model," hosting central collective bargaining between companies and unions, may become locked into an "iron triangle: " Each actor is kept in place by the other two.[25] Labor policy is synchronized with unions and innovation policy with companies, keeping them effectively apart.

In his chapter in this book, Sven Otto Littorin goes deeper into the innovation for jobs policy that was applied for the SAAB shutdown. In Sweden, employers are required to provide severance pay when laying off workers, and there is a transition period between receiving notice and job termination. Sven and his colleague, the minister for enterprise, offered to simplify the exit for GM, recruiting them to be "part of the team" rather than the hostile adversary. The transition period was used to retrain staff; severance money was placed in a fund where it was matched by national government unemployment funds and local government money. A new incubator company was set up with assets of the new fund, and GM handed over the plant. From the workers' point of view, their jobs continued, and they went every day to their workplace. The only difference was a new sign on the building and new management carrying out a new business model: find jobs and spin out new companies. This model was later once again applied with Sony Mobile when they closed Sony Ericsson in Lund, the cradle

---

[23] "The "Innovation for Jobs" Chasm | HuffPost." 4 Apr. 2011, https://www.huffingtonpost.com/david-nordfors/lainnovation-and-job-crea_b_843872.html. Accessed 12 Sep. 2018.

[24] "Suggestions for Bridging Industry and Employment Policies in National Governments", Sven Otto Littorin, Sweden's minister for employment 2006-2010 http://i4j.info/wp-content/uploads/2013/05/i4jSvenOttoLittorin-SuggestionsforBridgingIndustryandEmploymentPoliciesinNationalGovernments-2.pdf Accessed 12 Sep. 2018.

[25] "How to Disrupt Unemployment Policy", Sven Otto Littorin, Chapter in "Disrupting Unemployment: Reflection on a Sustainable, Middle Class Economic Recovery" by David Nordfors, Vint Cerf and Max Senges. Publisher: Ewing Marion Kauffman Foundation (February 4, 2016) ISBN: 152384583X

of cellular technology. In that case, Sony took and active part in the new ecosystem, using it as a an incubator for commercializing the many unutilized patents created by Sony Ericsson. Sven's model is a great example of how labor and innovation policy can be combined into an innovation-for-jobs policy that is more powerful and successful than the sum of its parts in the different silos.

Countries without similar national labor policies for layoffs can consider introducing a minimum transition period and build a startup ecosystem around it, including quick education and training that give the soon-to-be-unemployed a new job before the transition period ends, and other useful startups that can leverage on the freed-up resource of a skilled workforce.

Returning to the governance challenges, there is a language issue at its heart. When people don't understand each other, they usually speak different languages, in this case different professional jargons. Innovation economists speak about the micro economy, while labor economists speak about the macro economy. It can be challenging to spend employment policy budgets on innovation because the treasury will want to know "when" and "how many" jobs will be created with the money. Today, few econometric models attempt to predict that. Employment support money spent on innovation might even kill more jobs than it creates and this makes it difficult to propose such expenditures. I showed earlier in this book that the question "Does innovation create or destroy jobs" is difficult to answer because innovation can do both. PCE solves the conundrum by distinguishing between "innovation for earning" and "innovation for spending." The focus is shifted from the technology to the business model. It is not a problem to use labor policy money to stimulate innovation for earning. The key criterion is that the innovation must have a business model where the earner is the primary customer. If the innovation serves both spenders and earners, regarding the spender as primary, it will in fact be a spending service, as we have seen happen with gig platforms. "Who is the primary customer?" is the key question, and the answer must be "the earner" in order to be backed by labor policy money.

There will be challenges arising from the PCE "Copernican revolution," placing tasks in orbit around people instead of people in order around tasks. Creating a common language for labor and innovation policies, macro and micro economy, means not only that they can be brought together; it also means that they cannot be kept apart. The borders between the government departments will be blurred, which can trigger turf wars within the administration.

For example, when people earn their livelihood through a service, labor and consumer policies converge. Something similar happens with regard to people with disabilities. "Coolabilities" shifts focus from people's characteristic weaknesses to their accompanying strengths. Accomodation is already part of a commercial strategy for talent management. If a company is interested in someone's enhanced abilities, they must accommodate for weaknesses in order to leverage them, which is true for coolabilities. This leads to an innovative and sometimes confusing mix between disability/ diversity policies and talent management and recruitment, which today are opposite worlds, looking at each other -- not always kindly -- over the chasm that divides them.

Bridging the perspectives of policy and employment requires breaking down silos. This is not a new challenge in public-private partnerships. There already exist numerous organizations within government that help bridge them and almost none of them have actually broken down barriers. It is not difficult to create such bridging organizations; the difficulty is to create good ones with enough budgets, experience, and decision mandates to make a difference. Even if PCE can be partly run with existing structures, governments will have to incubate new structures to run a people-centered economy. Governments cannot simply shut down ministries of labor and "merge" them with other ministries to cover both business and employment. This desire usually leads to some kind of "ministry for industry and labor" hosting two separate silos under the same name. I suggest that the only way to create a government without barriers between labor and innovation policy is to incentivize existing ministries, departments, and agencies to create joint efforts, like the one Sven Littorin did in Sweden.

## PCE business: bootstrapping the new ecosystem for innovating jobs

The commercial ecosystem for innovating jobs is the driver of the PCE. Government's most important task is to help this ecosystem spring to life and to maintain ethics. The initial task is to nurture PCE-venture investors.

Already today many entrepreneurs are pitching ideas for serving the worker -- the earner -- as the primary customer, only to be forced to change that to serving the employers -- the spender, because their venture investors will say that job-seekers have no money to spend while employers do, and therefore the employers should be the customer. There are, however, some investors who support entrepreneurs focusing on helping earners and others who would want to. Some of them are co-authors of this book. Jason Palmer, partner at New Markets Venture Partners, outlines in his chapter the ecosystem and lists a number of investors and other players that are already now members of it. Jamie Merisotis, who heads the Lumina Foundation, and Daniel Pianko, co-founder of University Ventures Fund, present what they are doing in the ecosystem. i4j has convened investors, but we have only begun to create an investing community.

*An ecosystem innovating livelihoods requires investors.*
*Government can help bootstrap a community.*

This is the ignition key to the PCE engine. It is readily achievable for almost any government, national or local. There already exist reliable policies for engaging venture capital in a new field. It can be done today and without requiring complicated preparations.

The difference between bootstrapping the ecosystem for innovating jobs and, let's say, an ecosystem for HR and education, is the focus on creating business serving the earner as the primary customer, as opposed to focusing on a sector of activities, like "education" or "HR" or technologies. This is about finding investors who believe the earner is a better customer than the spender. Since this is a question of going against established best practice I suggest to first look for them in the *transpersonal* economy.

# First find investors with faith in the mission.

Accepting a breach of best practice in order to test something new always requires faith. We initially need investors who don't need to be convinced by arguments that it is an attractive market. They should intuitively understand it, based on values, and have faith in making it -- sooner or later -- into a commercial success. Religious communities were important for bootstrapping the U.S. economy in previous centuries and there is good reason to engage them again. Any congregation with ideals that match PCE is a venue for finding partnerships. I have already said that I am agnostic and don't have any spiritual practices, but it is a matter of fact that many of the best partners I have had along the journey of developing i4j and PCE are religious people with ideals. In terms of economy, I am offering them transpersonal equity, it places them closer to their "eternal Thou". By joining, they add to mine, my faith in faith itself and the good it does for the people who have it. There are many non-mystic communities

157

of faith serving equally good partnerships. The i4j coolabilities initiative has shown that parents with kids with disabilities are especially good initial partners. They will not sway easily and it has been easy for us to establish trust.

Thouness is especially valuable in the beginning of a project. We build something together; we know it costs us today but we have faith in the market it will create. This exemplifies what I have said about social dilemmas, because the best business strategy for joining the PCE is to wait for others to make the mistakes and then join them. The economically best and most rational strategy is not to initially pursue partners who require good business logic for joining, but go for those who are able business people with additional transpersonal value that allows them to connect with what we seek to achieve. I will refrain from recommending specific policy ideas, but it makes good sense to discuss how non-profit and religious communities can partner. The Religious Society of Friends (Quakers), for example, believes in dialogue as a foundation of their faith. All believers may take part, knowing that the difference between I-Thou and I-it is a part of the faith, and many of its members have founded successful businesses. There are similar groups within all major religions. Any community based on such values -- religious or secular -- could potentially be a good incubator for PCE and there is no reason for not approaching them accordingly.

Recruitment of participants may follow several steps. Once the new ecosystem for innovating jobs is established, early-stage investors are engaged and a community is formed that has a common identity and language. Then the need arises for larger investments to stimulate growth. Thouness and transpersonal values become less important as the ecosystem gathers. Because institutional investors require a strong business logic for why their dollars should be placed in PCE-funds, government can help bring banks on board, activating the model I have suggested. Government should by now have identified and mapped the large commercial actors who, like banks, care about how people earn their income and have a direct business interest in helping people earn an adequate, stable income, preferably by doing things they find meaningful. Such actors can have a high incentive to invest in, or increase the market for companies created by the new ecosystem for innovating jobs.

Standard innovation policy tools, like matching private capital for creating venture funds, will be useful and straightforward.

When starting out, coolabilities should be one of several early pilot ecosystems for innovating jobs. This might seem surprising, because few investors think about people with disabilities as a go-to market for a high growth economy. But there are several reasons for choosing it as one of several initial pilots:

- Easy to allocate transpersonal and interpersonal capital for bootstrapping the ecosystem. Parents of children with disabilities with day-jobs in the innovation economy are excellent members in the initial community.

- Coolabilities is an almost totally unexplored source of valuable capabilities around which to innovate jobs. People with disabilities are excluded and exceptionally undervalued. Therefore, the ROI can be very high as their value rises.

- In many cases, only the public's traditional perception is a barrier to market for people with disabilities. Assistive technologies exist and are in many cases cheap. Technological barriers and business barriers to market can be low.

- People with disabilities are not expected to fit normal job slots, so that the thought of individually tailored jobs is easier to embrace and understand. It makes people understand PCE, when they otherwise might think that innovation for jobs is only about giving people the "right" education to fit the universe of quickly evolving job slots.

- An ecosystem for innovating jobs that can individually tailor livelihoods for "coolabled" people can do it for all other people, too. Everyone has a unique profile of abilities. When the ecosystem works for coolabilities, it will stimulate growth of a the better labor market overall.

- For the reasons above, coolabilities can be a shortcut to PCE.

Note that the coolabilities ecosystem requires commercial venture investors; it is *not* a non-profit ecosystem, even if non-profits will be part of it. The whole idea is that coolabilities becomes a high-growth market, which it deserves to be.

# PCE research and analysis

I showed that PCE needs accounting, analysis, and forecasting tools as well as usable economics that places people, not tasks, at the center of equations. I suggested how such economics can incorporate Thouness (or equivalent wellbeing) as a value dimension of its own. I also showed how doing that allows us to define dollars as means for improving our interpersonal relations, which we can define as purpose, and I demonstrated how this removes the weirdness we are used to seeing in economics today -- for example, how it is "better for the economy" if people work themselves sick on overtime and seek treatment for it on weekends instead of relaxing with family and friends.

Because this is a popular book for a general audience, I avoided diving into any mathematics that can deliver the message in a more firm and formal way to economists. I am willing to do that, if offered the opportunity to write a book on the Dynamics of PCE. This is not the only insufficiency in our mainstream applied economics; there are more, which I can return to on another occasion.

PCE will be much more difficult to bootstrap without the right tools, and these must be developed. Government could set up a special agency for pushing their development, though such an agency needs to be able to choose challenges, set radical goals -- ("moonshots") -- and make them happen. The perhaps most successful example to date is DARPA, the U.S. Defense Advanced Research Projects Agency, which gave us the Internet, GPS, and other important innovations. PCE would benefit from an "EARPA," Economic Advanced Research Projects Agency, that can create innovations like the GPS for PCE. I have discussed in the example of "I-Thou accounting" how sociology research can build a commercial market for tools that will make good employers outcompete bad ones. This could be something for an "EARPA" to explore.

# PCE culture

I have discussed the importance of people having a vision of a good future. Googling "The future of work" is a good mood-o-meter, and today the results are very dark. We need visions in order to make progress. We need pictures, and stories we can relate the visions to, so that we can see them in our minds. Franklin D. Roosevelt created an agency that commissioned art by unemployed artists, many of whom had lost their income and even homes in the Depression. We need something similar today. There are many artists of all kinds and storytellers who are struggling because the Internet killed much of their business. They will be much helped by an ecosystem for innovating jobs. Perhaps this can be one of the early pilot systems, initially boosted by commissions from government, spurring artists to create and share their visions of what a better future looks like, making this a part of the public discussion about the future of work.

# PCE Currency

Fighting poverty and cleaning up slums has had such limited success until now that it is easy to overlook when discussing how to build a competitive economy. From a PCE perspective, we are talking about very large amounts of very undervalued people and therefore large opportunities to innovate jobs.

Cryptocurrency offers unprecedented possibilities to fight poverty and bootstrap economies that have been destroyed by disasters, natural or economic. Programmable currency can create local currencies with restrictions, so that they don't interfere or compete with the central currency, as I have suggested in the section on currency. This, too, can be an excellent research topic for an "EARPA," in collaboration with municipalities.

## Pilot Case: Natural Disasters

National government can experiment with policy allowing municipalities to issue local and temporary cryptocurrencies for kickstarting economies. Among the best pilot cases should be natural disasters. Here follows a scenario that illustrates how policy can be created. The case was developed together with George Minardos, a member of i4j. At the time, Napa and Sonoma were suffering unprecedented wildfires with massive destruction of homes and private property. We designed the case to match the ongoing situation. The cryptocurrency is here called "LoTT;" the technology is provided to municipalities by the startup "LoTTSystems."

*A natural disaster has destroyed thousands of homes in the municipality of Santa Emma.* Thousands of citizens have nowhere to live, and don't have the money to rebuild their houses. Insurances will take long time to kick in and deliver. Even if they had the money, there are few cleaning and construction companies available - all are swamped with work. The central government has issued a state of emergency, municipalities don't need to follow policies that would stand in the way of repairing the community immediately after the disaster. They have been given the right to mobilize public servants. They do not have the right to mobilize civilians, and are asking for volunteers to help out.

Government fears black market activity and threats to citizens' safety, through unlicensed contractors and fraudsters who potentially lead the way toward organized crime in filling the vacuum. There is moreover a great unfulfilled need for one-to-one services that are difficult for government or contractors to offer due to their personal nature, such as family support for single parents.

The Mayor of Santa Emma issues LoTTs during a state of emergency. The mayor's office appoints LoTTSystems to create and operate the system of LoTTs for the municipality. A LoTT Governance Board (LoGo) is set up, with the Mayor as Chairman, governing the LoTT. LoTTSystems provides economic expertise, supporting the LoGo's decisions with analysis and advice. Santa Emma now has a system of tokens enabling its citizens to help others and get help in return.

The Mayor is thereby the official party for other parts of government, and is responsible to see to that the LoTTs adhere to policy. The Mayor will be empowered by the state of emergency, and the governor will endorse the introduction of LoTTs as a state of emergency service.

The role of the Mayor and the sanction of the Governor is pivotal, since LoTTs, despite not being official fiat currency, introduces a labor market, a multiparty value exchange (for work) between citizens. The integration with government makes LoTTs a part of the economy, which can be accounted for in GDP and other indicators, thereby contributing to the strength of the fiat currency. In other words, LoTTs supports growth and stabilizes currencies. Since LoTTSystems is providing for government, it will avoid much of the trouble with governments, tax authorities and Central Banks that has been highlighted by Bitcoin and other Blockchain instruments.

At its first meeting, the LoGo issues the LoTTs: Each adult citizen of Santa Emma, 10k people, is appointed 5 LoTTs = 50k LoTTs. The Municipality of Santa Emma is appointed 10k LoTTs, i.e. it receives 10.000 workdays by its citizens. LoTTSystems is appointed 1000 LoTTs, which are used for recruiting technicians/programmers and local helpdesk. The municipality of Santa Emma has now issued tokens for a value of 61.000 workdays to be exchanged between its citizens.

The LoGo sets up policies that are programmed into the LoTTs:

- LoTTs are valid during the state of emergency

- LoTTs can be owned by citizens, the Municipality and LoTTSystems.

- One LoTT is one workday, the maximum a citizen can receive in one day

- Of every received LoTT, the worker gets 89%, the municipality 10% and LoTTSystems 1%

The Mayor presents the LoTTs at a Town Hall meeting. Citizens are offered to register and download a personal wallet containing initially 5 LoTTs. LoTTSystems maintains a marketplace and makes an API available, enabling third-party applications, such as time management, skills-training, advanced matchmaking etc. Applications are obtainable via LoTTSystems App store.

LoTTSystems uses its' initial 1000 LoTTs to recruit 50 Santa Emma citizens. Some are engineers, others are hired to help the citizens of Santa Emma use the system.

The municipality uses its initial 10.000 LoTTs for recruiting citizens that 1) help fellow citizens get going with exchanging workdays and 2) recruit special expertise for which there is special demand during the state of emergency.

The amount of ideas worth testing are endless.

# FINAL WORDS

We should embrace that we are human beings, and what it means to be human. This includes being not-so-smart, erratic, slow, error-prone, and so on. According to my reasoning, this is actually why we are on this Earth, why we survive, and why the economy works. Perfection is the enemy, variation is the norm.

One purpose we can probably agree on: If the human species is to continue to populate the Earth (or another planet, should that be possible), we have to have kids. A corollary is that the continuation of humanity actually depends on love. Instead of seeing human relations as a means of driving the economy, we see it as having the larger purpose of enhancing human meaning: community, friendship, love. Many economists today will say that getting married and having kids is good because it drives the economy. We need a sense of economics that affirms the value of families. We don't yet have math models for this because our traditional approach is shaped by our obsession with monetizing everything. We need math models that assign a (high) value to personal relations, and embrace I/Thou, people-centered economics.

One could argue that the task-centered economy has survived as long as it has because we have not invented the technology and ideas to overthrow it with anything better. That may well be true, as economic theories that have tried to challenge it, including communism, have lacked the successful formula and failed. The more successful model of social democracy continues to survive, however, perhaps because it incorporates at least some of the elements of a people-centered economy.

Now even that successful model is being tested, however, and we have not accepted the challenge to devise something better. We continue to believe in the same task-centered customs that have held us firmly to the time-worn and unreliable belief that "a dollar saved is a dollar earned." In continuing to accept this "truth," and the many assumptions that support it, we have -- perhaps unwittingly -- been trying for centuries to help each other be worth less.

Luckily, in the blink of an eye, historically speaking, we have happened onto a digital armamentarium of tools capable of creating a people-centered economy. The opportunities are enough to make us dizzy as we list the enormous forces that have reframed our lives in an unprecedented rush of invention and deployment: personal computers, the Internet, "big data," social networks -- a rich digital matrix linking us at the click of a mouse with known and unknown fellow humans around the world. All of these inventions are necessary to launch the innovation for jobs -- to support new value, new ways of relating, and new narratives that are opening a path to the people-centered economy. With the advantage of these tools, at last we can begin to do what needs to be done: Perform meaningful work with people we like, gain value from people we don't know, provide support and security for the people we love. Just as the economy will gain in strength, so can we -- and so can those with whom we live in community.

There is no contradiction between simply being a simple being and being an intellectual, a strategist, knowledge worker, or innovator. In fact, a simple person and an intellectual make a good match. Intellectual analysis should help us build societies that let us be our own messy selves together, where we can be imperfect, ignorant, or silly without penalty. I can't think of any better purpose for life than to combine our qualities. It's when we separate the emotional intuitive animal inside us from the logical constructions of our rational minds that we create unhealthy societies that punish us for being ourselves.

Philosophy and science are for those who want them, and life should be good also without them. What matters is that we feel good with each other and do things together that we find meaningful. Knowing what we are, which we learn from knowledge and intelligence, is less important than knowing who we are, which we learn from being ourselves, and for this we are more helped by wisdom than IQ. So while I have a professional life and a personal interest in mathematical patterns which can improve our lives and societies, we must not forget what it means to be human, which we do best by being human, and that the purpose of economics is to serve humanity and not to be served by it. I hope that this book will help people see that a humane, people-centered economy outcompetes the alternatives.

To conclude, a healthy economy can thrive in societies that are easy to live in, just as a simple product outcompetes a complicated one. For us as individuals, I recommend the following strategy for daily life:

*Take pleasure in the simple*
*Life, at best, is an adventure*
*Life, at its best, is trivial*
*We were born with these big brains*
*We were born longing to not use them*
*With these faculties of ours we understand presence*
*thereby avoiding it*
*We understand passionate love*
*of which understanding is the enemy*
*We idolize the complicated*
*because it is a challenge for the mind, we think,*
*while it merely is a projection of our inner selves*
*made complicated by our ability to understand*
*that there is much we do not understand*
*understanding we should understand it,*
*in order to be understood*
*as understanding.*
*While what we mean by understanding*
*what we really mean*
*but don't understand that we mean*
*is the meaning of meaning*
*That understanding is not a thought*
*It's a way of being*
*And if your thought is "I think, therefore I am"*
*please prepare to be disappointed,*
*leave a big dark space in its former place*
*Then fill that space with light, like this:*
*Think "I am, therefore I think"*
*Think "I am, because I am"*
*Think "Now I am"*
*and say "I am me"*
*and be.*

###

# APPENDIX A: THE COMMUNIST MANIFESTO IN THE WORDS OF THE INNOVATION ECONOMY

## A GLANCE BACK AT *THE COMMUNIST MANIFESTO*

**KARL MARX**

TABLE OF WORD SUBSTITUTIONS

**COMMUNIST MANIFESTO**

| 1848 | 2018 |
|---|---|
| CIVILIZATION | DIGITAL ECONOMY |
| MEANS OF PRODUCTION | MARKETS |
| REVOLUTION, DESTRUCTION | DISRUPTION |
| BOURGEOISIE | INTERNET ENTREPRENEURS |
| PROLETARIAT | ON-DEMAND WORKERS |
| CRISES | BURSTING BUBBLES |
| OPPRESSION | EXPLOITATION |

| 1848: BOURGEOIS AND PROLETARIANS | 2018: INTERNET ENTREPRENEURS AND ON-DEMAND WORKERS |
|---|---|
| The history of all hitherto existing society is the history of class struggles. | The history of all societies is the history of class struggles. |
| Freeman and slave, patrician and plebeian, lord and serf, guild master and journeyman, in a word, | Freeman and slave, industrialist and factory worker, in a word, exploiter and exploited, stood in constant opposition |

| | |
|---|---|
| oppressor and oppressed, stood in constant opposition to one another, carried on an uninterrupted, now hidden, now open fight, that each time ended, either in the revolutionary reconstitution of society at large, or in the common ruin of the contending classes. | to one another, carried on an uninterrupted fight that each time ended either in their common ruin or in the reorganization of society at large. |
| In the earlier epochs of history we find almost everywhere a complicated arrangement of society into various orders, a manifold gradation of social rank. In ancient Rome we have patricians, knights, plebeians, slaves; in the middle ages, feudal lords, vassals, guild masters, journeymen, apprentices, serfs; in almost all of these classes, again, subordinate gradations. | In the earlier eras of history we find almost everywhere a complicated arrangement of society into various orders, a manifold ordering of social rank. In ancient Rome we had patricians, knights, plebeians, slaves; in the industrial ages, owners, managers and workers. And within these classes, sub-hierarchies. |
| The modern bourgeois society that has sprouted from the ruins of feudal society, has not done away with class antagonisms. It has but established new classes, new conditions of oppression, new forms of struggle in place of the old ones. | Internet entrepreneurship is not doing away with class antagonisms but establishing new ones, along with new conditions of exploitation and new forms of struggle. |
| The bourgeoisie cannot exist without constantly revolutionizing the instruments of production, and thereby the relations of production, and with them the whole relations of society. | Internet entrepreneurship cannot exist without constantly disrupting markets, and thereby the relations of production, and with them the whole relations of society. |

| | |
|---|---|
| Constant revolutionizing of production, uninterrupted disturbance of all social conditions, everlasting uncertainty and agitation, distinguish the bourgeois epoch from all earlier ones. All fixed, fast-frozen relations, with their train of ancient and venerable prejudices and opinions, are swept away; all new-formed ones become antiquated before they can ossify. | Constant disruption of markets, uninterrupted disturbance of all social conditions, everlasting uncertainty and agitation, distinguish the Internet entrepreneurs era from all earlier ones. All fixed relations, with their prejudices and opinions, are swept away; all new-formed ones become dated before they can settle in. |
| The need of a constantly expanding market for its products chases the bourgeoisie over the whole surface of the globe. It must nestle everywhere, settle everywhere, establish connections everywhere.<br><br><br>The bourgeoisie has through its exploitation of the world's market given a cosmopolitan character to production and consumption in every country. To the great chagrin of Reactionists, it has drawn from under the feet of industry the national ground on which it stood. All old-established national industries have been destroyed or are daily being destroyed. They are dislodged by new industries, whose introduction becomes a life and death | The need of a constantly expanding market chases Internet entrepreneurship over the whole surface of the globe. It must nestle everywhere, settle everywhere, establish connections everywhere.<br><br>The Internet entrepreneurs have through their exploitation of the world's market given a digital character to production and consumption in every country. To the great embarrassment of traditional industrialists, it has drawn from under their feet the ground on which they stood. Old-established industries are daily being destroyed. they are pushed aside by new industries, whose introduction becomes a life and death question for all modern economies. |

| | |
|---|---|
| question for all civilized nations,.. | |
| The intellectual creations of individual nations become common property. National one-sidedness and narrow-mindedness become more and more impossible, and from the numerous national and local literatures, there arises a world literature.<br><br>The bourgeoisie, by the rapid improvement of all instruments of production, by the immensely facilitated means of communication, draws all, even the most barbarian, nations into civilization. The cheap prices of its commodities are the heavy artillery with which it batters down all Chinese walls, with which it forces the barbarians' intensely obstinate hatred of foreigners to capitulate. It compels all nations, on pain of extinction, to adopt the bourgeois mode of production; it compels them to introduce what it calls civilization into their midst, _i.e._, to become bourgeois themselves. In one word, it creates a world after its own image. | The intellectual creations of individual nations become common property. Narrow-mindedness becomes more and more impossible, and from the numerous national and local storytellings, there arises a global storytelling.<br>The Internet entrepreneurship, by the rapid improvement of all markets, by the immensely simplified ways of communication, draws all, even the most backward, nations into the digital economy. The cheap prices are the heavy artillery with which it batters down all resistance. It compels all nations, on pain of extinction, to adopt to its ways; it compels them to introduce the digital economy and become Internet entrepreneurs themselves. In other words, it creates a world after its own image. |
| The bourgeoisie keeps more and more doing away with the scattered state of the population, of the means of production, and of property. It has | Internet entrepreneurship is more and more doing away with scattered markets and property. It has merged markets and concentrated ownership |

| | |
|---|---|
| agglomerated population, centralized means of production, and has concentrated property in a few hands. | into a few hands. |
| ... during its rule of scarce one hundred years, [it] has created more massive and more colossal productive forces than have all preceding generations together. | During its short rule, it has created more massive and colossal productive forces than all previous generations did together. |
| Modern bourgeois society with its relations of production, of exchange, and of property, a society that has conjured up such gigantic means of production and of exchange, is like the sorcerer, who is no longer able to control the powers of the nether world whom he has called up by his spells. | Internet entrepreneurship is like the sorcerer, who is no longer able to control the powers of the demons who he has called up by his spells. |
| . It is enough to mention the commercial crises that by their periodical return put the existence of the entire bourgeois society on its trial, each time more threateningly. In these crises, a great part not only of the existing products, but also of the previously created productive forces, are periodically destroyed. In these crises, there breaks out an epidemic that, in all earlier epochs, would have seemed an absurdity – the epidemic of overproduction. Society suddenly finds itself put back into a | It is enough to mention the recurring market bubbles that are growing bigger and bursting harder each time, creating great destruction in the Internet economy. A large part of all existing Internet companies are destroyed each time. When the bubble bursts, society regresses; industry and commerce are destroyed; and why? Because there is too much digital economy, too many ways of doing business, too much industry, too much commerce. |

state of momentary barbarism; it appears as if a famine, a universal war of devastation, had cut off the supply of every means of subsistence; industry and commerce seem to be destroyed; and why? Because there is too much civilisation, too much means of subsistence, too much industry, too much commerce.

| | |
|---|---|
| The conditions of bourgeois society are too narrow to comprise the wealth created by them. And how does the bourgeoisie get over these crises? On the one hand by enforced destruction of a mass of productive forces; on the other, by the conquest of new markets, and by the more thorough exploitation of the old ones. That is to say, by paving the way for more extensive and more destructive crises, and by diminishing the means whereby crises are prevented. | The Internet entrepreneurs' own societies are too narrow to contain the wealth they have created. And how do the Internet entrepreneurs handle this? On the one hand by enforced disruption of a mass of productive forces; on the other, by taking over new markets, and exploiting the old ones more thoroughly. That is to say, by paving the way for ever more disruption, and by stopping the prevention of it. |
| The weapons with which the bourgeoisie felled feudalism to the ground are now turned against the bourgeoisie itself. | But the weapons the Internet entrepreneurs are bringing down the conventional economy with will soon be turned against themselves. |
| But not only has the bourgeoisie forged the weapons that bring death to itself; it has also called into existence the men who are to wield | They have created the people who will ensure their own downfall --the modern working class--the on-demand workers. |

those weapons--the modern working class--the proletarians.

In proportion as the bourgeoisie, _i.e._, capital, is developed, in the same proportion is the proletariat, the modern working class, developed; a class of laborers, who live only so long as they find work, and who find work only so long as their labor increases capital.

These laborers, who must sell themselves piecemeal, are a commodity, like every other article of commerce, and are consequently exposed to all the vicissitudes of competition, to all the fluctuations of the market. Owing to the extensive use of machinery and to division of labor, the work of the proletarians has lost all individual character, and, consequently, all charm for the workman. He becomes an appendage of the machine, and it is only the most simple, most monotonous, and most easily acquired knack, that is required of him.

Hence, the cost of production of a workman is restricted almost entirely to the means of subsistence that he requires for his maintenance, and for the propagation of his race. But the price of a commodity, and therefore also of

These workers must sell themselves in bits and pieces. They have become a commodity, like every other article for sale, and are as a consequence exposed to all the whims of competition and to all the fluctuations of the market. Their work has lost all individual character, and all charm. It is only the most simple and most easily acquired work that is required of them.

Therefore, the on-demand worker's production cost is limited almost entirely to his own cost of living. But the price of a commodity, and therefore also of labor, is in the long run equal to its production cost. Therefore, the more the individual character disappears from his work, the wage decreases in proportion.

| | |
|---|---|
| labor, is equal, in the long run, to its cost of production. In proportion, therefore, as the repulsiveness of the work increases, the wage decreases. Nay, more, in proportion as the use of machinery and division of labor increase, in the same proportion the burden of toil also increases, whether by prolongation of the working hours, by increase of the work exacted in a given time, or by increased speed of the machinery, etc. | |
| The lower strata of the middle class--the small trades-people, shopkeepers, and retired tradesmen generally, the handicraftsmen and peasants--all these sink gradually into the proletariat, partly because their diminutive capital does not suffice for the scale on which modern industry is carried on, and is swamped in the competition with the large capitalists, partly because their specialized skill is rendered worthless by new methods of production. | The lower middle class will gradually become on-demand workers, partly because they don't own enough capital to remain important, partly because innovations are making their specialized skills irrelevant. |
| But with the development of industry the proletariat not only increases in number; it becomes concentrated in greater masses, its strength grows and it feels that strength more. The various interests and conditions of life within the | With the development of industry the on-demand workers will increase in number and their various interests and conditions of life will become more and more equal, in proportion as machines remove all distinctions between them, and reduce their wages to the same low level nearly everywhere . |

ranks of the proletariat are more and more equalized, in proportion as machinery obliterates all distinctions of labor, and nearly everywhere reduces wages to the same low level.

The growing competition among the bourgeois, and the resulting commercial crises, make the wages of the workers ever more fluctuating. The unceasing improvement of machinery, ever more rapidly developing, makes their livelihood more and more precarious;

The growing competition among Internet entrepreneurs to disrupt markets makes the workers' wages ever more unreliable. The constantly accelerating improvement of machines makes their livelihood more and more uncertain;

Chally Grundwag coined Coolabilities (enhanced abilities in disabling conditions ) and is heading the development of the concept with i4j. She is a professional mental health consultant working with children, families and educators from highly diverse populations in the bay area. She holds a M.A. in counseling psychology from the Institute for Transpersonal Psychology (Palo Alto) and B.A in comparative literature and German from the Hebrew University in Jerusalem. She is also an artist and a certified Wellness Recovery Action Plan facilitator.

# COOLABILITIES – a new language for strengths in disabling conditions

by Chally Grundwag

We coined the word "coolabilities" in 2016 to describe the typically enhanced abilities, strengths, and talents that may co-occur with disabilities. David Nordfors, Jay Van Zyl, and I were brainstorming an application for exploring those strengths, we needed a good word to refer to them and we could not find any word that already existed, despite researching the matter. About a year ago, a meeting between

David Nordfors and V.R Ferose (Senior Vice President and Head of Globalization Services at SAP SE) led to the coolabilities.ai project (see also the chapter in this book by V.R Ferose et al), where research and design came together to conceptualize a new ecosystem for analysis and application of coolabilities.

Coolabilities is more than just a cool word. Many people with disabilities have valuable strengths that sometimes are unknown even to themselves and definitely ignored by their surroundings. Coolabilities is a keyword for bringing together scientific evidence and common knowledge. It draws on growing scientific understanding of enhanced abilities generated by neuroscience, neuropsychology, and other fields like business management, education, occupational therapy, and design. In addition to the scientific work there is a vast body of knowledge close at hand, widely discussed on websites, blogs, news stories, books and other venues growing by the day. Coolabilities is also a keyword for the common wisdom established by advocacy programs, support groups, non-profit organizations, and for-profit companies that look for people with specific disabilities and coolabilities. Coolabilities are *not* "super-powers" or another name for "human potential" and a disabled person's strengths are *not* limited to coolabilities. We can use coolabilities as principles for organizing our minds when gathering relevant information about the phenomena. In short, coolabilities is intended to be a common everyday word that is easy to understand, say, use, adds value to conversations and at the same time is backed by scientific evidence.

All people have different abilities, strengths, and challenges, and people with disabilities are no different. Why, then should there be a special term? The answer is because people with disabilities are usually defined by what they *cannot* do. So far, it has not been possible to get away from that labeling for various reasons. If you are diagnosed with an ailment, the treatment focus will naturally be on what's not working. Our society has generated a lot of vocabulary to explain what it is that disables a person. A word that describes *strengths* that co-occur with the disabilities adds a new dimension or frame to the discussion. Coolability, then, is the counterpart of disability within the context of the condition. It allows us to look at the whole condition, including both its strengths and challenges. Coolabilities are, per definition, directly correlated both to diminished abilities and to enhanced ones, and the term is designed to fill the gap in our knowledge.

This way of constructing the concept reflects a scientific reality. For many years, neuroscientists have been looking at enhanced abilities and compensatory mechanisms for some conditions. Cross-modal plasticity has been discovered as an important mechanism that can give rise to coolabilities. For a blind person the visual cortex is not useless, it is assigned to help other senses, like hearing. Advances in technology, such as fMRI, help us gain deeper understanding of these processes, and expands our understanding of a number of conditions. The concept of coolabilities connects them all and opens a new, wider lens for understanding for both the scientific and social aspects of strengths linked to disabilities.

Today we ask what are the implications of these findings in daily life, for people like us. How can this knowledge create possibilities for real people in real-life situations - jobs, education, design, and technology. And how can this knowledge add to, or change approaches in medicine, rehabilitation services, counseling, and policy? Coolabilities is a creative name for something that always existed but lacked a label. People have always been conscious of them, discussed them, and placed them at the center of numerous narratives. This raises an interesting question: Why have we until now lacked a language for coolabilities when we have such a rich language for disabilities? This is a plausible research topic in itself which can tell us much about human nature and culture.

Coolabilities offer a language of hope, potential, and opportunity. It is spontaneously and happily embraced by, for example, parents of children with disabilities and others involved in advocacy. What people know about their own strengths, or about their children or someone they work with, is suddenly acknowledged and defined with one word. Furthermore, coolabilities allows us to look at ourselves or our children through a refreshing lens. This is not a "tap on the shoulder" concept, because there is a growing body of scientific evidence to support everything that coolabities stand for. For some people learning about coolabilities is transformational. Some people are "locked in perception" and may have a hard time expanding their view; others find it difficult to accept that their ideas about themselves or their loved ones are affected by flawed systems and limited narratives. People recieve messages from both immediate and wider cultural environments deriving from both implicit and explicit biases, and accept them as true. It is very difficult to break away from culturally embedded shaming and degrading narratives which influence our identity and core beliefs. We have an issue with internalized stigma, and the coolabilities concept provides a more positive and empowering framework to embrace the unique sensory perceptions and strengths of people with disabling conditions.

180

The story of coolabilities is the story of millions of people with disabling conditions who may or may not have an official diagnosis. It gives people new hope in perceiving ways and ideas to use their abilities.

My friend Stefan has dyslexia and his difficulties in spelling and decoding had been casting a dark shadow over his school experience and self perception. He said, "I have disabilities in spelling and decoding, but I've learned that I am very good at problem solving and thinking outside the box [which is a common coolability for dyslexia]. It's been a huge step for me to admit that I am good at anything. And I think this is what it is all about - finding your coolalbilities and using them."

The benefits of the word coolabilities are numerous. With language comes framing, and critical thinking. Comparative literature, my B.A major, offered me a good approach for exploring coolabilities: to look specifically at what is NOT said in a narrative and ask why. It is a way of building a framework of ideas from knowledge gaps. We assume we know something until something else emerges which changes our perspective and opens up new possibilities. For example, for generations the representation of women in knowledge institutions like universities was non-existent -- not because women didn't think or write or do research, but because we were systematically excluded from the academic narrative. It is natural for me to ask myself who and what else are systematically excluded from narratives we accept as valuable or true and what are the reasons behind this, and the consequences.

The system for clinical diagnosis has dominated the way we think about illness and disabilities, and how we manage them. What is consistently and systematically excluded from the narrative are strengths. A sad example of how far the exclusion of positive traits goes is the old clinical term "idiot savant" to describe severely disabled people with obvious coolabilities. The exceptionality has been reduced to a symptom of a problem. Unfortunately there are many other similar cases. I give myself the freedom to speak about it because of my personal experience. Like me, many other mental health professionals share this critical perspective and are now questioning the system.

Looking at the historical factors which influence the creation of big systems is relevant for understanding the way we think, treat, and create policies and other practices around disabilities. Phil Brown in his article "Naming and Framing: The Social Construction for Diagnosis and Illness" discusses the circumstances that lead to the creation of medical diagnosis. He points to the societal, medical, and policy outcomes of this process. This is relevant to the topic of coolabilities because it can explain how and why the discussion about strengths was left out of the diagnostic narrative. It can also contribute to the discussion of what is the general perception of strengths. The language that we choose to describe a condition has more influence on people's lives than most of us realize. What is a disability, what treatment is given, what research is designed and what kind of research and treatments are funded have a lot to do with the use of language and sometimes competing narratives. Other serious consequences are decisions around who gets or does not get a job or an education, what accommodations or services are funded, and which treatments are recommended.

Limiting the human experience and conditions to a set of symptoms might have devastating consequences that lead to wrongful, harmful, or invasive practices that can cost human lives. Language matters because language creates reality. Our view of ourselves and others has a lot to do with language. If we add the coolabilities language to the disability language we get a deeper, truer description of conditions, that may lead to a better understanding of human nature. We have enough evidence to show that coolabilities exist; we need to add this lens to our daily life because it will allow us to open ourselves and our society to new possibilities, potential, and hopefully the elimination of stigma.

If we mirror the disability language with a coolabilities language we can get a better understanding of conditions and and see both the possibilities as well as the challenges. We have suggested three categories for coolabilities. They are not mutually exclusive, and a coolability can belong to more than one category.

- **Singular coolabilities**: These are innate coolabilities, or enhanced abilities innate to the condition. They appear for example in people who were born with the condition; hence the wiring of the brain and the behavior happen from the beginning. Many "Savant" skills are a good example of singular coolabilities.

- **Compensatory coolabilities**: These are acquired abilities which occur when one or more abilities are strengthened following the loss of another. A good example is a strengthened sense of touch and tactile discrimination at the loss of the sense of sight, or learning how to use the mouth or toes with great precision at the loss of limbs (like artists who paint holding a brush in their mouth or toes).

- **Contextual coolabilities**: These have to do with context, environment, and framing, and arise when a perceived weakness becomes a strength. For example, a hearing deficit can be an advantage for a person who can focus well in a noisy environment. Having a narrow field of interests, one of the characteristics that is often used to describe a person on the Autism Spectrum, may also indicated that someone actually has deep expertise in one of them.

According to the Social Security Administration, you are "legally blind" if your vision cannot be corrected to 20/200 in the better eye, or if the visual field is 20 degrees or less in the better eye for at least 12 months. According to the World Health Organization (WHO), 253 million people live with visual impairment; 36 million are completely blind and 217 million have moderate to severe impairment. It is worth mentioning that 80% of all visual impairment can be prevented or cured.

A subject of great interest to me is the coolabilities of the blind. What happens to the other senses? How well do blind people "see" with their hands? Are tactile abilities enhanced? Are other senses affected, such as auditory memory? Neuroscience offers some answers, and so do stories of people who are themselves blind. A large body of evidence in neuroscience and neuropsychology shows enhanced abilities (increased activities in certain cortical areas), such as vibro-tactile abilities. Visually impaired people use the sense of touch (e.g., feeling textures and vibrations) in more effective ways than non-blind people. They are likely to identify differences in texture faster and more accurately. This is how the experience of Braille reading may lead to changes the structure of the brain. Interestingly, this tactile information is registered in the "visual" cortex of blind people.

This phenomenon of "reorganization" the brain is named cross-modal or cross-sensory plasticity. It points to the way our brains extract meaning from external stimuli. That is, it is the way we use our senses to make sense of the world.

Blind people generally show superior auditory abilities in many functions, including spatial hearing, pitch, verbal auditory memory, auditory stimulus encoding, and speech comprehension. Blind people also show increased activity in the amygdala (the part of the brain responsible among other things for the fight or flight responses, emotional memory) in response to angry and fearful sounds. This seems logical, partly because they rely on auditory input for survival and indications of threat. In addition, some research shows enhanced odor awareness in the blind, specifically the ability to notice smell generated by emotional states. Another enhance ability is better auditory memory for environmental sounds. Echolocation -- the ability to create in the visual cortex a sonar picture of a sound by clicking with the tongue and analyzing the sound's echo -- is another interesting coolability of some blind people. This is yet another fascinating example of cross-modal plasticity, which teaches us that our eyes are just one channel for creating pictures in the mind.

Physical and biological evidence for enhanced abilities are only part of the equation. Societal norms, culture, and personal experiences contribute to the tapestry of coolabilities. In the Easterseals blog, Alicia Krage describes her perceived advantages of being blind, including; not judging people by their looks, paying more attention to people's personalities, being more direct with verbal communication versus relying of visual facial cues for judging feelings, and the ability to read and function in the dark. She says that blindness is only a disadvantage in regard to activities that require light.

An example of a cultural context for coolabilities is that in Thailand, blind masseurs are much in demand and prepare for professional work in specific courses of training. This does make sense as we think about blind persons' enhanced sense of touch, which is likely to provide deeper tactile understanding, and to inform the masseur of the location of places that need attention, muscles that may be "stuck," and so on. This example illustrates that the professional choices of people with a disability or coolability might be far more diverse than we suspect. It is not suggested that professional choices or decisions should be limited to coolablities. Rather than thinking of ways of avoiding people with disabilities, employers might better remind themselves of their limited perception of disabilities, and the largely misinformed ecosystem around disabilities. At least some of the barriers that prevent full acceptance of people with disabilities in society can be removed by adding the "coolabilities lens" to imagine more professional opportunities to people with disabilities.

There are many illustrations of this point. For example, I once read an article about a group of blind jewelers who made "feel/hear necklaces," a wonderful artistic expression of coolabilities. In a similar sense, Dr.

Marc Maurer, former president of the National Association of the Blind, describes being sightless as a rich and liberating experience where imagination is not limited by the sense of vision. He speaks about Thomas Edison inventing the phonograph as a device to create a "hearing book," and how this marvelous invention led to a revolution in the music recording industry.

Much has been written about the compensatory plasticity of the brains in people who cannot hear. Good, Reed, and Russo (2014) explain: "...*when one sense is unavailable, sensory responsibilities shift and processing of the remaining modalities become enhanced to compensate for missing information. This shift, referred to as compensatory plasticity, result in unique sensory experience for individuals who are deaf, including the manner in which music is perceived.*"

What do we know about coolabilities of deaf people? You can probably guess that some are connected to visual perception, but the story is more complex for those who are both deaf and blind, or have other challenges. One interesting finding is that for the deaf there is an enhanced activity of the secondary auditory cortex by visual stimuli such as sign language, which also happens with vibro-tactile stimulation.

When it comes to enhanced abilities, deaf people have a somewhat larger visual peripheral field. One conjecture is that they may have to rely on wider vision for survival. Another enhancement is that certain areas in the brain, associated with language processing are activated by the visual stimulation of sign language. A different coolability is the ability to hold greater focus and concentration on non-auditory stimuli, which means enhanced use of the prefrontal cortex.

Good, Reed, and Russo also explain that both neural plasticity and cognitive strategies contribute to enhanced abilities in the deaf. Research shows that deaf people are much faster at visual search tasks than non-deaf people, which means that they are more efficient in processing visual information in distracting environments.

Other coolabilities of the deaf are better speech processing through visual modalities, such as sign language and lip reading, as well as better interpretation of facial expressions and identification of other people through facial recognition.

On fascinating story about enhanced ability of the deaf and the hard-of-hearing in interpreting vibro-tactile stimuli is the one of world-famous musician and percussionist Evelyn Glennie, who is profoundly deaf. She writes about her experience of music:

> "Hearing is basically a specialized form of touch. Sound is simply vibrating air that the ear picks up and connects to electrical signals, which are then interpreted by the brain. The sense of hearing is not the only sense that can do that... With low frequencies the ear is inefficient and touch takes over."

Israeli choreographer Moshe Efrati, who established the dance company Kol Demama (Sound of Silence) in the mid 70s, adds another dimension to the experience of dance as most people know it. His group had 20 dancers, 10 of them with hearing impairments. Efrati cued the hearing-impaired dancers by stepping on a board. The dancers could feel the vibrations he created in the board, and could follow the music from the vibration caused by bass notes.

Author and world famous speaker Helen Keller was both blind and deaf. Her enhanced vibro-tactile abilities are well documented. She could identify people by the vibrations made by their feet as they entered a room, read people's lips with her hands, read braille and tactile sign language, and appreciate music by feeling the vibrations of the sound placing her fingers on a table top.

Williams Syndrome (WS), a rare genetic condition, is notable for being a condition whose description includes both its challenges and its gifts. On the one hand, people with Williams syndrome suffer from serious health conditions and learning challenges; on the other hand, they are known to have enhanced sociability, empathy, and response to distress. Research shows that people with WS are better at deciphering intentions, emotions, and mental states when they look into other people's eyes.

People with WS often have other gifts; a special affiliation for music, an extraordinary sense of rhythm, and exceptional verbal abilities. fMRI studies of people with WS show hyperactivity in the amygdala in response to viewing happy faces, and enhanced fear response to non-social stimuli. They also tend to have a large and very active auditory cortex, which ordinarily is observed only in some professional musicians.

In our article from 2016, we spoke mainly about coolabilities of neuro-diverse populations. The term neurodiversity managed to capture something that had been long missing in our culture and its consideration of employment. It brought into the discussion the acknowledgment that some of the conditions that are described as neurological disorders, are in fact natural variation of neurological "wiring". The term neurodiversity was specifically coined to describe Autism Spectrum Conditions (ASC), but was embraced by the public to describe a wider group of neuro-developmental conditions including dyslexia and Attention Deficit Hyperactivity Disorder (ADHD). However, many years passed before the term was acknowledged by mainstream academic research. Like many other innovations it was met with suspicion and criticism. Perhaps not surprisingly, neurodiversity as a term was first embraced in academic circles by researchers in business entrepreneurship and design.

Debra Satterfield is a pioneer in incorporating coolabilities principles into her academic work. She is a mother to a non-verbal autistic child with profound disabilities and a professor for User Experience (UX) Design at California State University Long Beach (CSULB). Debra used the coolabilities lens in her Play•IT design studio project, and together we facilitated a series of conversations between CSULB design students, parents of children with special conditions, and designers to see how the coolabilities lens could inform their design work. We decided to look further into how to help designers tap into the coolalbities of non-verbal autistic children. Debra Satterfield suggests future research on what she calls "Pervasive Coolabilities" where the disabling condition is considered so profound that no abilities of value are recorded or perceived by society at large. From her own experience, this group has tremendous potential for physical, emotional, social and behavioral contributions that are yet undocumented through scientific research. New medical and communication technologies have the capability to provide a better understanding of the implicit coolabilities demonstrated by these groups of persons.

Coolabilities aspires to capture the general principles which describe the strengths of people with various conditions, and has the potential of becoming a broad interdisciplinary field that looks at the enhanced abilities, gifts, and strengths of people with disabling conditions and their expressions in real life through many different lenses.

This table is a variation on "table 1" from the 2016 paper, with the addition of blind, deaf, and Williams Syndrome. It provides and example of how we can describe conditions in holistic way adding the coolabilities lens.

| Condition | Disabilities | Coolabilities |
|---|---|---|
| **Autism Spectrum Conditions** | Difficulties in social interaction, understanding social nuances and reduced self awareness. Narrow focus. Difficulty filtering sensory stimulation ie. (sound, light, touch, smell) and high sensitivity to sensory stimulation, sensory overload. Resistance to change and routine. Repetitive behavior. Challenged in planning and executing tasks for daily living. | Attention to detail. Extraordinary observation skills. Deep interest in specific fields. Intense focus. Expansive long term memory. Comfort with rules and guidance. Affinity to analyzing complex patterns in the social and physical worlds. Creative in areas of interest. Original thinkers (more time devoted to talent than socializing). Honest. Visual-spatial skills. Exceptional talent in very specific areas. Success at repetitive tasks. Strong systemizing skills. |
| **Attention Deficit Hyperactive Disorder** | Hyperactive; Distractible. Can't maintain attention; Restless; Impulsive; Disruptive (Risk taker); Decreased inhibition Preservation (Negative hyperfocus) | Positive risk taking; Spontaneous; Imaginative; Energetic; Creative; High precision; Multi-tasking; Novelty seeker; Connecting multiple ideas; Creating surprising solutions; Idea generating; Innovative; Proactive; High tolerance for uncertainty, "Flow" (Can utilize hyperfocus productively). |
| **Dyslexia** | Difficulties in reading, spelling correctly, decoding words, and in comprehension of text | Creativity. Original problem solving. Different perspective. Connecting tasks and realities. Divergent or innovative thinker. Perseverance. Motivation/ Visual spatial skills (not in reading). Ability to see the big picture |
| **Deaf/ profound Hearing impairment** | Complete of profound hearing loss. | Larger peripheral field (vision), enhanced language processing through visual modalities (enhancement of visual-spatial abilities), better focus on non auditory stimuli, enhanced ability to decode and interpret vibro-tactile stimuli, experience music through vibro-tactile abilities, more attuned to body language, can focus in noisy environments |

188

| Blind | Complete visual loss or severe visual impairment[26]. | Superior auditory abilities: spatial hearing, pitch, verbal auditory memory, and better auditory stimulus encoding, better comprehension of speech and other auditory input. Enhanced activity in the amygdala in response to angry and fearful sounds. Enhanced sense of smell, odor awareness, better memory for environmental sounds, enhance tactile encoding (texture), echolocation. Imagination that is not limited by sight, less dependent on light conditions, less judgmental of looks, direct verbal communication of feelings.And maybe the most interesting of all, echolocation - the abilities to assign the visual cortex to get a sonar picture in the brain. |
|---|---|---|
| **Williams Syndrome**[27] | Hypersociability (negative), naive, difficulties decoding social cues, hyperacusis (very sensitive hearing) developmental delays, learning challenges, attention deficit issues, anxiety. challenges with visual spatial tasks such as drawing. Many health issues - i.e. teeth, cardiovascular disease, kidney abnormalities, musculoskeletal abnormalities, hypercalcemia, Ophthalmologic issues like ocular misalignment | Extraordinary verbal skills, highly social, enhanced friendliness, special affinity to music, musicality , significantly more likely to possess absolute pitch, enhanced long term memory (faces), enhanced empathy and response to distress, love to help others, enhanced friendliness, enjoy learning by repetition. |

---

[26] "legally blind" if vision cannot be corrected to 20/200 in the better eye, or if your visual field is 20 degrees or less in your better eye

[27] https://williams-syndrome.org/what-is-williams-syndrome

V R Ferose is Senior Vice President and Head of Globalization Services at SAP. Based in Palo Alto, Ferose is responsible for the adoption of SAP products worldwide through the delivery of solutions targeted at individual local markets. By providing functional localization, translation, product compliance and product support across several countries, Ferose's team enables SAP's global footprint. He is a director on the board of Specialist Foundation. He founded the India Inclusion Foundation, which seeks to mainstream India's inclusion discussion, and conducts the India Inclusion Summit and Inclusion Fellowships. In 2012, the World Economic Forum named him a 'Young Global Leader'. In March 2017, he was conferred the AUCD award for his pathbreaking 'Autism at Work' initiative. Ferose has co-authored Gifted, a best-seller on people with disabilities.

# The Birth of the Inclusion Ecosystem: Precision Employment for people with Disabilities, Coolabilities, and the Rest of Us

By VR Ferose, Lorien Pratt, Sudipto Dasgupta, and Ganapathy Subramanian

Ashok Giri and his wife Pavithra Y.S. didn't take the easy road when building their Bangalore-based Business Process Outsourcing (BPO) firm, Vindhya. With seed capital of half a million rupees (under US$8,000) and five early employees, the company was founded in

2006 with a novel but bold business model: to employ disabled people in India. As a technologist, Ashok wished to use his experience to give back to the community. The decision was aligned with Pavithra's aspirations: to bring equal employment opportunities to the disadvantaged youth of India.

Several years later, the company now has over 1,400 employees, including those who are blind, deaf, have various physical disabilities, and even some on the autism spectrum.

In India, where the stigma surrounding disability is particularly strong, Vindhya's value can be measured in far more than profits. A feeling of compassion, love, and purpose surround the firm, in a country where fewer than 2% of disabled people are employed. As a percent of the workforce in India, this number is even smaller, as shown below:[28]

| Type of company | Percentage of employees who are disabled | Estimated total disabled persons employed in India |
|---|---|---|
| Public sector companies | 0.54% | 2,720,695 |
| Private sector Indian companies | 0.28% | 1,410,731 |
| Multinational companies | 0.05% | 251,916 |
| Total | 0.87% | 503,832,494 |

But Ashok and Pavithra are not alone. Vindhya is just one of a growing ecosystem of companies that help to find jobs for "differently abled" people: a movement that, surprisingly, also has substantial implications for the future of work and employment as a whole.

About this chapter

This chapter is an overview of this emerging space. Crystallized in part by VR Ferose, who created the India Inclusion Foundation, there is an emerging network of companies providing various services to help to employ disabled persons. Note that it is still early days: inclusion initiatives worldwide attract only a fraction of those who could be employed, often only the top few percent of individuals. So, alongside global transformations like the "gig" economy and outsourcing, the value of employing disabled persons is only beginning to be realized.

---

[28] Sources: http://www.dinf.ne.jp/doc/english/asia/resource/apdrj/z13j00400/z13j00410.html and
https://data.worldbank.org/indicator/SL.TLF.TOTL.IN?end=2015&locations=IN&start=2014

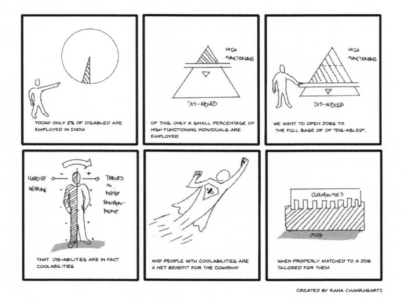

CREATED BY RANA CHAKRABARTI

In addition, nascent technologies that are supporting this population will ultimately bleed into mainstream employment as well. This takes us to the next purpose of this chapter: to catalyze the next phase of growth of organizations like Vindhya, that have demonstrated that the broad population of disabled persons, and not just the smartest few, are employable. The figure below illustrates this point, and also gives a chapter overview.

To open jobs to the full gamut of people considered "disabled" requires innovation. For example, although Artificial Intelligence (AI) is often vilified for its potential to negatively impact employment, the situation is the reverse for the disabled. The reason is similar to why Amazon is able to profit from the "long tail" of rare and specialized products: technology helps to match niche people, with particular skills, to solve niche tasks, with specialized needs. Disabled job matching bleeds into the mainstream market, because it points the way towards more effective use of employees and lives within an environment in which understanding "soft" employment factors like loyalty, sense of purpose, and happiness have a better-understood impact on the bottom line.

Disabled people can make substantial contributions. Take, for example, Naoki Higashida, who is profoundly autistic, yet is also the second-most translated Japanese author[29]. Another example: when SAP began its Autism at work program[30], the company hired several mid- to high-range persons with autism. It found that their very strong memories and ability to stay on task resulted in them outperforming regular engineers.

With a commitment to hire 650 people on the autism spectrum by 2020, SAP has identified a list of tasks for which they are particularly well-suited (box). A great video about an autistic person at SAP can be found at https://www.youtube.com/watch?time_continue=73&v=uPd42mX2BWE.

Why now?

There are several technical and social factors converging to form this rapidly-crystallizing ecosystem. These include platform business models, an improved understanding of the importance of "soft" cause-and-effect links in the success of an organization, an understanding of how explicit modeling of externalities can create winner-take-all market dominance, and the development of tools like AI, machine learning, and DI to support decisions that transcend overly simplistic categorizations like "disabled" and enable win-win-win outcomes for organizations, individuals, and society. These forces are illustrated in the diagram below:

---

[29] https://ferosevr.com/differently-abled-people-remind-us-value-compassion/
[30] http://usa.specialisterne.com/2012/10/23/forbes-india/

The bottom line: organizations are now poised to uncover a significant resource that has gone largely unrecognized to date. New technologies can unlock value that not only boosts operational and financial results, but also improves workplace culture and has a positive impact on the well-being of the larger society.

In the following sections, we explore each of these trends, along with some of the barriers to adoption that will need to be overcome.

Our core question: *What is the shape of the emerging inclusion technology ecosystem, and how can we help it to reach its full potential?*

# Understanding of the value of disabled workers

Disabled hiring initiatives typically require employers to dedicate supervisory, training, and other resources to assist those with physical or cognitive challenges. Most employers view this investment as providing only "soft" benefits—altruism, complying with regulatory requirements, or brand improvement. They therefore are willing to dedicate the required resources to only a small percentage of their total employees. In the context of the bottom line, organizations often view such hires and associated costs as a net negative at worst, and as an unquantifiable positive at best.

This thinking is wrong on two counts. First, when placed correctly, disabled people can produce a net benefit. Secondly, the technology and thought processes needed to hire disabled persons is closely related to what's needed for precision job matching, which is an important trend with substantial benefits for persons of all abilities.

There is a growing body of anecdotal and empirical evidence supporting these claims. An evolving set of tools gathered under the umbrella of artificial intelligence and machine learning are making it possible to more accurately measure both the costs incurred to hire, train and manage specially-abled individuals and the surprising, but very real, financial and "soft" benefits they bring to their employers.

# Coolabilities

When Ferose was first in charge of an office in SAP India, he made a habit of walking the campus with his facilities manager on a regular basis. One day, the two descended into the office basement, where the din of a power plant battered their eardrums. The place was also cold because of the air conditioning. Many office buildings in India maintain such local power stations to offset the frequent power grid outages in the country. "Ferose," said the facilities manager, "I cannot find anyone to work here. It is too noisy and too cold!"

Working with local resources, Ferose was able to identify a deaf employee who had grown up in a cold part of India. His lack of hearing was what Grundwag, Nordfors, and Yirmiya have dubbed a "Coolability[31]", allowing the employee to be effective in an environment that would be intolerable for most. Yet, despite the widespread use of such power plants, this simple job match had not been made elsewhere.

In the previous chapter of this book, Grundwag defines "Coolabilities" as:

- **Singular coolabilities**: These are innate coolabilities, or enhanced abilities innate to the condition. They appear for example in people who were born with the condition; hence the wiring of the brain and the behavior are innate. "Savant" skills are a good example of singular coolabilities.

- **Compensatory coolabilities**: These occur when one or more abilities are strengthened following the loss of another. A good example is a strengthened sense of touch and tactile discrimination at the loss of the sense of sight, or learning how to paint holding a brush in the mouth or toes at the loss of limbs.

- **Contextual coolabilities**: These have to do with context, environment, and framing, and arise when a perceived weakness becomes a strength. For example, a hearing deficit can be an advantage for a person is working in a noisy environment; having a limited field of interests can enhance expertise in one of them.

---

[31] https://www.researchgate.net/publication/309493288_COOLABILITIES_-_ENHANCED_ABILITIES_IN_DISABLING_CONDITIONS

Coolabilities include skills developed to compensate, for example, for a
missing limb, or a loss of motor control or cognitive function; and ways
of perceiving and processing sensory input that simply do not develop
for people with a full complement of "normal" human sensory abilities,
such as a blind person learning to use echolocation.

The table below (also from Grundwag *et al*) shows the start of a
Coolabilities careers data set, which identifies disabilities their
associated Coolabilities, and the jobs for which people in this category
are best suited.

| | AUTISM SPECTRUM DISORDER (ASD) (High Functioning) | ADHD (Attention Deficit Hyperactivity Disorder) | Dyslexia |
|---|---|---|---|
| Disabilities | Difficulties in social interaction, understanding social nuances and reduced self awareness. Narrow focus. Difficulty filtering sensory stimulation ie. (sound, light, touch, smell) and high sensitivity to sensory stimulation. Resistance to change and routine. Repetitive behaviour. Challenged in planning tasks for daily living | Hyperactive; Distractible Can't maintain attention; Restless; Impulsive; Disruptive (Risk taker); Decreased inhibition Preservation (Negative hyperfocus) | Difficulties in reading, spelling correctly, decoding words, and in comprehension of text |
| Coolabilities | Attention to detail. Extraordinary observation skills. Deep interest in specific fields. Intense focus. Expansive long term memory. Comfort with rules and guidance. Affinity to analyzing complex patterns in the social and physical worlds. Creative in specific areas of interest. Original thinkers (more time devoted to talent than socializing). Honest. Visual-spatial skills. Exceptional talent in very specific areas. Success at repetitive tasks. Strong systemizing skills. | Risk taking; Spontaneous; Imaginative; Energetic; Creative; High precision; Multi-tasking; Novelty seeker; Connecting multiple ideas; Creating surprising solutions; Idea generating; Innovative; Proactive; High tolerance for uncertainty, "Flow" (Can utilize hyperfocus productively). | Creativity. Original problem solving. Different perspective. Connecting tasks and realities. Divergent or innovative thinker. High focus in fields of interest. Presaverence. Motivation Visual spatial skills (not in reading). Ability to see the big picture |
| Careers | Computer programmers, software design, communications and networking, engineering design, equipment design, fine mechanics, research, mechanics repair, fine advanced machines assembly, lab technicians, web design,, video game design, app designs, accounting, chemistry. Engineering, statistics, computational art and animation. | Entrepreneurs, CEO's, Educators Inventors  With these strengths can contribute to many STEM careers. | Any STEM related careers in Science, Math, engineering, medicine, architecture, interior design, graphic design, education, VC etc. when accommodations and assistive tech are present. |

# Tools to disrupt unemployment

The growth of the open source movement is another driver for the
emergence of the disability and employment disruption ecosystem. As

David Nordfors and Vint Cerf describes in the previous i4j book, *Disrupting Unemployment*[32], there is an important opportunity for a tool to support matching disabled (and abled) people to jobs. (they called their fictional tool "Jobly".)

A new open-source project is bringing this vision to reality. Spearheaded by technologists in Bay Area, Sudipto Dasgupta and Ganapathy Subramanian in their spare time, the Coolabilities open source project is embodying the table above into the core of a cloud service and database that can be maintained by a crowd and can be accessed by an API to determine when it is best to hire a disabled person, especially "tailored" jobs for the otherwise so-called "unemployable". Planned for its first release in May 2018, the API will be accessible by employer systems as they are searching for new employees. Its motivation is illustrated below:

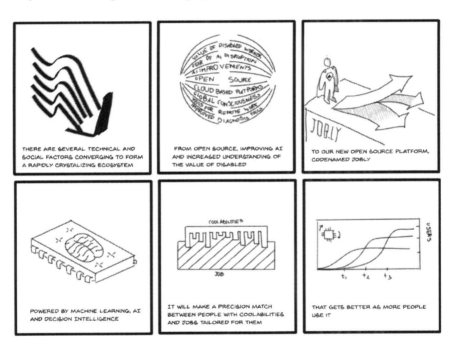

## Multiple forms of value

To understand how inclusion of disabled persons in an organization can be a net benefit, even from only a financial perspective, it's important to

---

[32] http://i4j.info/2014/07/disrupting-unemployment/1502/

understand the connection between disability, compassion, and productivity.

Money isn't a very good proxy for happiness; it's just easier to measure. As the ease of managing and analyzing data increases, this limitation is decreasing. Psychologists studying happiness have demonstrated that, beyond a certain level of basic income, other factors have a greater impact. These include a sense of purpose, relationships, and compassion.[33] As evidence of this improved understanding, for instance, the UK began to measure national well-being in 2012[34], following Bhutan, which already measured gross national happiness[35].

Even if the desired outcome is purely financial, "soft" factors like happiness matter tremendously. Starbucks, for example, is able to charge more for a cup of coffee due to the sense of community the company engenders. The company then re-invests the resulting profits in employee education and other benefits, increasing employee satisfaction, thereby improving retention and reducing employee training costs and further enhancing profit margins.

Increasing anecdotal evidence from the disabled community indicates that their inclusion has an impact on the bottom line. And an increasing number of business cases support this understanding as well.[36]

## The Goonj story: understanding waste as resource, preserving dignity

Take Anshu Gupta's NGO, Goonj, as an example: he identified a leading cause of death in India, and tried to solve it using discarded clothing. And Goonj employs over 600, many with disabilities.[37] In the

---

[33] https://en.wikipedia.org/wiki/Stumbling_on_Happiness
[34]
http://webarchive.nationalarchives.gov.uk/20160105183326/http://www.ons.go
v.uk/ons/rel/wellbeing/measuring-national-well-being/first-annual-report-on-
measuring-national-well-being/art-measuring-national-well-being-annual-
report.html
[35] https://en.wikipedia.org/wiki/Gross_National_Happiness
[36] https://www.theglobeandmail.com/report-on-business/rob-
commentary/employees-with-disabilities-can-have-a-positive-impact-on-
profitability/article28540451/
[37] http://gulfnews.com/culture/people/indian-ngo-recycles-old-clothes-for-the-
poor-1.1581320

systems-thinking tradition of Buckminster Fuller, Gupta realized that waste from one source—in this case discarded clothing from urban areas—could form the input to another system—teams of disabled people who repurpose the clothing for use by those in rural areas.

This is Goonj's mission[38]. And its philanthropic position has helped the company to scale quickly: it handles over 3,000 tons of material annually, and is supported by thousands of volunteers and grass-roots partner organizations.

"What in other peoples' eyes is waste," says Gupta, "I consider it a resource. And that resource is provided to people in dire need of it in remote villages across India." An important decision made by Goonj is to not provide clothing for free. To preserve the dignity of its clothing recipients, they have to work for it, through local tasks like digging wells, recharging water ponds, and building bamboo bridges.

Yet Goonj, like many other firms, is still challenged to scale its approach. Gupta, now called the "clothing man of India", has a company that is challenged increasingly by the supply chain and logistics challenges more commonly associated with a company like Amazon. Goonj, like many others, is ready for the next phase of growth. And cutting-edge technology has an important part to play.

# Artificial Intelligence and precision job matching

Just as precision medicine is an important growth area in health care, firms like Vindhya as well as Cognoa, Specialisterne, and more (some covered below) are lighting the way towards a "precision employment" future, powered by software platforms and AI, which transcend traditional concepts of "abled" and "disabled" to uniquely characterize a potential employee's (or volunteer's) abilities, matching them to the best job or task in a distributed autonomous tasking environment. Imagine "Uber for jobs", and you'll understand the gist of the idea.

---

[38] http://goonj.org/

# Disability, ability, and beyond

Disability, along with specific categories of disability (like "autistic", are labels that stigmatize but don't provide much, if any, real information. It is critical to recognize that all of us are, in fact, "differently abled"– we each have a particular set of strengths and weaknesses that make us less or more suited to a particular job or task. And, as we encounter health issues and suffer minor or traumatic injuries, we may become "less abled" in some ways even as we gain insight and expertise.

By some measures, a third of the global population is "disabled" at some point in their lifetime even if born without any traditionally defined disabilities. With older workers making up an increasing percentage of the population, this group of employees and prospective hires will continue to grow.

At Vindhya, Ashok jokes that his strength is to use "X-ray vision" to look beyond surface characteristics of a worker in order to gain a deeper understanding of their suitability for a particular job. One important result: Vindhya has found that attitude is a much better predictor of success than aptitude. However, because aptitude is easier to measure, employers tend to give it disproportionate weight when assessing prospective hires and promotions.

But Ashok, as an individual, doesn't scale very well. What if his ability to see the hidden strengths in others could move from his niche in India's disabled community to benefit differently abled people worldwide? How can technology, combined with his kind of knowledge, help catapult the energy and compassion of the disabled community into widespread usage?

One answer is machine learning. When deployed properly, this technology can help us overcome these biases of expectation and perception. A machine learning system can ingest a comprehensive list of a person's characteristics as input to a job match. Work history, performance reviews, individual answers on diagnostic instruments, scores on aptitude tests, and other objective and subjective metrics can all be considered Machine learning language processing systems can read a prospective employee's resume to extract important categories, extract sentiment from coworker or reference comments, and more – these are all data sources that were not previously accessible. Brent Vaughan of Cognoa calls this "Deconvoluting the heterogeneity in the labels."

Precision job matching using machine learning is illustrated in the figure.

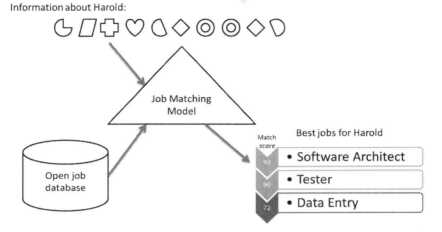

As shown here, Harold is looking for a job. He is characterized by a number of attributes, which might include scores on assessment tests, performance reviews in related jobs, the number of years he has previously worked as a software engineer, and more. An AI job-matching model creates a score for Harold for each job in an open positions database (which also contains detailed information on each job), and returns a list of the top matches.

And machine learning systems can learn over time: as their human partners correct their early mistakes, they continuously improve. If, for instance, a machine learning system matches a particular candidate to a position that doesn't work out, this information can be fed back into the system, which identifies what was different about that employee from the ones that were successful, and can then use those factors to perform a better match in the future.

This ability for a job matching to improve over time is shown below:

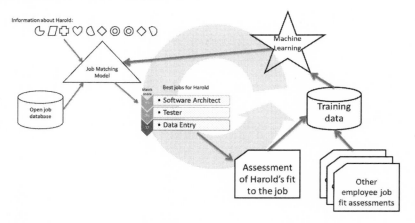

As shown here, Harold's experience on the job is combined with that of others, which machine learning uses to improve its job matching model for future employees. This is an iterative process, allowing for the accuracy of job matching to continuously improvement over time.

A final AI example: one category of AI systems perform Natural Language Processing, or NLP. As shown in the diagram below, NLP can analyze documents about Harold to extract categories of information. For instance, how can we tell whether Harold has worked in the health care industry? Before NLP, we might have to enter the names of all of the health care companies into the world into a database, and match Harold to each one. NLP does this analysis automatically. NP can also analyze *sentiment*, which reflects the "mood" of a text block: how positive is this reference letter?

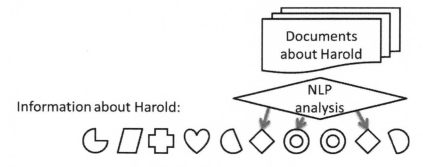

This NLP capability extends the kind of information that can be used for job matching from traditional "structured" information such as what can be found in databases, to "unstructured" information from documents.

# Improvements in diagnosis: the Cognoa story

In the United States, a parent sees the signs and symptoms of autism on average when their child is 14 months old, yet the average age of diagnosis is over four years. This delay in diagnosis can make a big difference, preventing children from receiving therapy during key neurodevelopmental windows during which children can benefit the most, especially in developing countries where the age of diagnosis is much greater.

Although it is often not well-known, providing an early diagnosis that enables children to receive appropriate behavioral therapy between two and four years of age can result in lifelong improvements in key areas like language and socialization. Studies have shown that early behavioral intervention programs in children with autism can result in over 75% of children attending mainstream schools by the age of six. If children in rural areas or developing countries have less access to special-needs education, then being able to attend mainstream schools can have an even greater impact.

Cognoa is an AI-based digital health company that provides parents with a mobile app to assess and track cognitive and behavioral development in their children. It also provides parents with clinician-based advice to support their child's development. Cognoa says that its diagnostic technology uses AI that has been rigorously validated in multiple clinical studies, and has been shown to identify autism and developmental delays earlier. The company recently received regulatory recognition as the first medical device to provide a primary diagnosis of autism, and expects to receive full FDA clearance in 2018.

Autism, like the entire human condition, is heterogeneous: no two autistic persons are alike, and many are quite different from each other. For this reason, autism diagnosis and treatment can be particularly difficult. To solve this problem, Cognoa also uses machine learning, in a somewhat different way than precision job matching as described above (although there are substantial synergies). The company's software identifies patterns of attributes in children, but instead of matching them to a job, its technology determines whether those attributes that could indicate a diagnosis of autism or other developmental delays, and uses them to recommend customized treatment activities.

The company's road map includes continuous improvement to its diagnostic technology, using an ever-growing list of attributes combined with increasingly sophisticated AI. Since many of the symptoms it codes for are also diagnostic of other conditions like ADHD and OCD, Cognoa is also working to extend its diagnostic technology into these arenas as well. Says CEO Brent Vaughan, "We need to find needles in haystacks, and if you want to do that, AI/ML is the right tool."

# The future of compassion

Since 1947, 59 actors have won Oscars for portraying disabled characters.[39] Why is this? Disability drives a powerful dramatic punch, and disabled people's triumphs over adversity make a compelling story. But this element doesn't need to be limited to Hollywood. And, as Naoki Higashida writes in *Fall Down 7 Times, Get Up 8*, people with disabilities have an important role to play in society at large: by increasing compassion worldwide. [40]

At Vindhya, Pavithra and Ashok Giri were not directly connected to disabled people in their families, and so were often asked about their motivation for starting the company. Their answer: "we had compassion, and if you have that, you can do it all." Vindhya struggled in its early years, and ran out of salary for its only five employees. So the workforce agreed to work for only bus and lunch money. This dedication paid off: they became the core of the over 1,400 employees today. Furthermore, says Ashok, "in eleven years, we have never lost a customer". This is a characteristic completely unheard-of in the traditional commercial world, and illustrates a powerful force that, when tapped, has tremendous potential.

The bottom line: an ecosystem of organizations working towards a shared purpose is powerful at a level that purely financial goals cannot engender. Political movements can mobilize millions of people to work without pay, so why not combine the best of both worlds, bringing a sense of purpose and compassion to the world of work? There is no reason that these need to be separate.

---

[39] http://www.indiewire.com/2017/09/actors-oscar-nominations-disabilities-afflictions-1201879957/

[40] https://ferosevr.com/differently-abled-people-remind-us-value-compassion/

# Decision Intelligence bridges from theory to practice

Decision Intelligence (DI)[41] is a technology that helps to bridge this gap: to demystify AI so that it can be used in practical settings. It uses AI, data, and human expertise to support organizations as they reason through complex cause-and-effect chains from policies and actions to business outcomes. These chains can include "soft" cause-and-effect links as well as traditional financial ones.[42]

In particular, a DI model can show how, although an investment in hiring disabled people may be more costly in the short run, it produces substantial value in the long run, through reduced attrition, increased productivity, and the high morale and motivation that comes to a workforce that is driven by an increased sense of compassion.

A secondary benefit of DI is that it allows more complex business models to be understood, and the assumptions upon which they depend made explicit, validated, and tracked as they change over time. In particular, for organizations to fully appreciate the value of disability hiring, they must:

1.  Understand soft factors internal to the business which lead to improved financial performance, as above

2.  Model the "triple bottom line" including financial, social, and environmental impacts

3.  Model externalities, to understand how an organization's impact on its larger competitive, social, environmental, and market environment creates "boomerang" effects that can benefit that organization in the long run. This is in contrast to many traditional companies that began by assuming infinite sources and sinks. This limited way of thinking is today causing considerable social and environmental negative impacts. DI empowers organizations with the tools to embrace proactive modeling of these factors.

---

[41] https://en.wikipedia.org/wiki/Decision_Intelligence
[42] https://www.youtube.com/watch?v=VXZ-HDsIB-o

4. Be able to find the "sweet spot" between profit and purpose: where both financial as well as social goals can be met simultaneously. Organizations live within complex and nonlinear systems, and non-AI-based tools fall short of the ability to work together with human experts to solve such a complex problem.

Consider, for example, how an organization might determine the cost/benefit impact of the specialized training required to hire and employ a prospect with autism. The organization might want to see how much it would cost to train a candidate, and to then project the productivity impact or other benefit it could expect to obtain.

This organization might use DI to build a model that captures assumptions and metrics such as the dollar cost of an hour of training, the current and target skill level of a candidate or group of candidates and the expected number of hours required to achieve the target skill level. Once it has built the initial model, the organization can test various scenarios by changing investment levels, costs, operational variables, and/or desired outcomes.

For example, based on institutional experience, the organization might add to the model the expected cost of missing a project's deadlines. The various scenarios can be adjusted collaboratively in real time and the results are represented visually. See, for example, an interactive DI model at the reference in the footnote that shows how to think about a training program.[43]

# Platforms

Another technology force driving the diverse worker ecosystem is cloud-based platforms. Just as Amazon provides a platform for matching buyers to sellers, a "reverse amazon" can match givers to receivers, or workers to jobs. And just as the Amazon platform uses AI to capitalize on a "long tail", an open-source platform can do the same for matching long-tail jobs to long-tail tasks. This "two-sided deep matching", powered by AI, has tremendous potential.

A platform is typically both a software system and also a business model. Most typical is a "two-sided" platform, which forms a place for buyers to

---

[43] www.di-everywhere.com/announcing-interactive-web-based-decision-intelligence/

meet sellers, developers to meet application buyers, and so forth. A software platform typically contains functionality that can be reused by multiple other companies. Probably the most familiar platform is a personal computer: there is no need to have a separate machine for word processing, a spreadsheet, and playing games. Rather, the same screen, keyboard, and other parts serve multiple purposes. But this was not always the case. When computer technology was new, these functions were indeed separated: you could buy a separate word processor, an accounting machines, and game consoles.

More recently, the concept has expanded to globe-spanning platforms such as Amazon.com, Alibaba and others that leverage the Internet to unify marketing, sales, payment, inventory and other formerly distinct business software categories that enable buyers to find sellers and sellers to manage their businesses and business relationships.

This platform model applies to the ecosystem described here as well. It can be both a model where systems that would otherwise be separately reinvented by multiple companies can access a central service. A platform might match workers to jobs that they are uniquely qualified for. Recruiters, BPOs serving disabled workers, and others can leverage AI to optimize job matching, can use natural language analysis to help train and supervise special-needs employees, develop decision intelligence models to support build the business case for hiring, and more.

The difference between this emerging platform market and the traditional trajectory of platform development is, however, profound. Pioneering companies in this space are unified by a sense of compassion, of purpose, and a desire to serve all their stakeholders. The motivations of this emerging movement derive from values seemingly at odds with much of the mainstream tech industry's focus on achieving market power in the service of individual financial gain..

# Emerging flag bearers

To drive the kind of change in thinking described in this chapter requires persistent and patient advocacy over a number of years. Ferose has articulated seven steps:

1. **Advocacy**: Laws are central to ensuring that citizens have rights to equal opportunity. 85 countries in the world have a

disability law. Yet many of these laws are outdated. Although working with governments to build inclusive laws is important, it might also makes sense to work in parallel with companies to lead this effort? For instance, Irish activist Caroline Casey[44] is working to convince 500 CEOs to sign an Inclusion pledge to make disability a board agenda item, much as many companies mandate to have at least one woman on the board.

2. **Awareness:** The lowest common denominator for every issue is awareness. When people are more aware, they become more sensitive, and when they are more sensitive, they take action. India Inclusion Summit is an annual event that raises awareness of the abilities of the "disabled". A gathering of people from all walks of life, and providing free access, the Summit's motto is "Everyone is good at something".

3. **Early Intervention:** The earlier in life that disabled people feel a hopeful path for the future, the better. And early diagnosis of a condition is critical to provide necessary interventions, especially for intellectual disabilities. Girls born poor and disabled used to have terrible prospects in India, and were sometimes abandoned by their parents. Vindhya has asked its community to drop them off at its location instead. Another hopeful light here: Cognoa is also a powerful technology for early diagnosis (for Autism, ADHD, Dyslexia and other intellectual disability), leading to more proactive intervention.

4. **Education:** People with disabilities need training programs that are customized. Yet many renowned institutions are not disability-friendly. To really provide equal opportunity for people with disabilities, all programs must be inclusive. What is the chance that a deaf mute or blind person from India can make it into IIT or Harvard? It is never the lack of ability; it is always our inability to provide a level playing ground for people with disabilities.

5. **Employment:** Many people with disabilities find employment a dead end to their career aspirations. After struggling through the education system, a lack of apathy and openness by employers means that more than 90% of people

---

[44] https://en.wikipedia.org/wiki/Caroline_Casey_(activist)

with disabilities around the world remain unemployed. Job matching, as discussed here, as well as programs like SAP's Autism at Work (AaW) and Differently Abled People,[45] represent an important step forward. Says the Honorable Jack Markell, Governor of Delaware, "When the focus is on ability, rather than disability, people can achieve amazing things....and you are transforming the lives of so many families, it's difficult to put a price on that." An inspiring video about this program can be found at https://www.youtube.com/watch?v=_A_zFVJvXaw.

6. **Lifestyle:** People with Disabilities have the same aspiration as so-called normal people. Helping disabled people to envision their life path, and to understand that there is hope for a happy future, with marriage, a satisfying career, are fundamental to living a life of dignity and happiness. More often than not, these issues are afte thoughts as they are considered non-viable from a business sense. One success story here is Inclov, an app for finding partners (and eventually getting married) focused on people with disabilities. The app has already transformed the boundaries of finding a life partner in India.[46]

7. **Assisted Living:** one of the most common challenges for all parents with children who are disabled and dependent, is to think of a life after they die. While creating trusts and securing financial freedom is what most parents with resources do, the majority have no option. Disability also increases at the end of life, so facilities and resources for assisted living are essential.

In the remainder of this chapter we describe three flag-bearers who are working together in a loosely coupled global ecosystem to advance the above steps.

## Specialisterne and SAP

Consider the partnership between SAP and the social enterprise Specialisterne. During his tenure as the Managing Director of SAP

---

[45] https://www.sap.com/corporate/en/company/diversity/differently-abled.html

[46] https://economictimes.indiatimes.com/magazines/panache/disabled-community-wonders-why-a-separate-matchmaking-app-is-needed-for-them/articleshow/61610259.cms

Labs India, Ferose invited Specialisterne founder Thorkil Sonne to speak to his employees in Bangalore in 2012. Thorkil, who also has contributed a chapter to this book, talked about his experiences as the parent of an autistic child and the worries he shared with other parents. How could they prepare their daughters and sons to take care of themselves when their parents are no longer there to help them? His son did not communicate effectively. Autism limited his ability to interact with other people. How would he find a job? Who would be willing to hire him and do the work needed to train and supervise him? There were so many things his son would never be able to do.

As Thorkil pondered these questions, he came to realize that they were the wrong ones. He chose to refocus: on those things that his son and others like him CAN do and, in fact, do very well. And he founded one of most progressive and effective advocacy groups for integrating autistic and other differently abled people into the workforce, called Specialisterne, which means "Specialist"

Many people with ASD have amazing skills and abilities that make them well suited to specific tasks that are very valuable to employers. Unusually precise and persistent visual memory, the ability to repeat processes very accurately, the ability to spot deviations in patterns. Thorkil began thinking about how those skills and abilities matched with the some of the requirements in technology companies like the one he ran at the time.

Even with automation, many of critical tasks in writing, prototyping, testing, and building software require human input and review. Many of those tasks require a level of specific (and expensive) expertise that is often available only from employees who are also needed for other high-priority work. The processes involved are typically repetitive and challenge even highly-skilled workers' ability to maintain the necessary focus for more than a short time.

Thorkil tested his hunch that such jobs were very well matched to individuals with various forms of ASD. After he assessed their skills, he trained some to perform software testing that required long-term concentration on repeated tasks. He taught others to build software that required the ability to recall and visualize long string of programming and complex relationships among programs. As he observed these people - many of whom were considered unemployable in any high-value jobs - building and testing gaming software, it

210

became clear that his hunch had been right. They were not just able to do the work. In many cases, they excelled at it.

Today, Specialisterne is working with organizations worldwide to help them identify and create opportunities for millions of differently-abled people to do meaningful work. Those workers are contributing directly to their employers' short-term productivity and financial targets. They are also making a real difference in the culture of their workplaces and the attitudes of their coworkers towards their jobs and employers.

While working to find candidates and match them to jobs where they might add real value, Ferose's team at SAP Labs also had to design specialized training programs and build supervisory structures that would give the new hires the best chance to succeed. The upfront investment of financial and human resources was large and the return was at first very uncertain.

Today, the positive return on the initial investment is clear. And SAP Labs India has derived other unexpected, but very significant, benefits from the program.

SAP now sees the program building more than one kind of wealth. The addition of differently-abled employees at SAP Labs India contributes directly to its financial performance, helps to maintain a positive and attractive working culture, and benefits the larger society in which the business operates – creating, in effect, a positive "triple bottom line." An interview with SAP and Thorkil can be found at https://www.youtube.com/watch?v=Om-wXuKSWOs .

Going forward, Specialistierne's goal is to enable a million jobs for people with autism. It works with Microsoft, SAP, EY, IBM, PwC, Bloomberg and many more clients on five continents to share best practices and challenges, as well as creating a pool of appropriate candidates. The company will be hosting an Autism Advantage luncheon at the United Nations in April 2018, and is also working regionally for autism inclusion.

## Vindhya

As introduced above, Vindhya is a pioneer in finding work for disabled people across the spectrum, not just the very high functioning individuals. Over the company's 11-year history, it has gained some important insights:

1.  Hire everybody that applies, assuming they pass a basic
    attitude screening test. The company can find a job even for a
    person with just one finger.

2.  Reframe disabilities as abilities. Ashok says that a deaf person
    is less distractible, and he jokes that a person in a wheel chair is
    less likely to take a smoking break.

3.  Understand that a group of people with different disabilities
    often has a massive amplification effect. For a deaf person to
    work with a blind person brings out their own compassion and
    reduces their sense of being disabled. Also, groups of disabled
    people will often work together in a complementary way.

4.  Understand the power of gratitude and compassion, which
    create motivation, productivity, and customer and employee
    loyalty.

5.  You must have a flag bearer: a person to catalyze an effort like
    this.

# An ecosystem emerges

Each of these initiatives continues on its own, but each is also deeply
connected to the next, through threads that include technology, long-
term relationships, and a shared sense of compassion and purpose.
Following a common pattern in technology, a "divergent" blast of
varying approaches to a problem has proceeded into a "convergent"
phase where participants recognize that wheels are being reinvented
that don't need to be. This often forms the basis for a platform: either
in the form of technology such as Amazon, and/or an ecosystem /
Keiretsu of like-minded companies working together towards a
common goal.

And a shared goal is a powerful incentive. Much as individuals in a
particular company can be galvanized by a strong leader and vision,
separate companies can also find powerful synergies by working
together within an ecosystem. Purely commercial ecosystems, such as
Microsoft's or Apple's partner network, can provide a powerful sense of
belonging. But the inclusion ecosystem we describe here feels
qualitatively more powerful. An aspirational view of the ecosystem is
shown in the diagram:

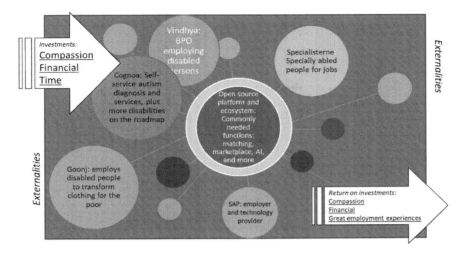

# Overcoming barriers to change

The vision described above is compelling, but requires substantial energy to realize at a worldwide scale that addresses the needs of disabled people of all abilities. Some of the barriers to change are illustrated in the figure below.

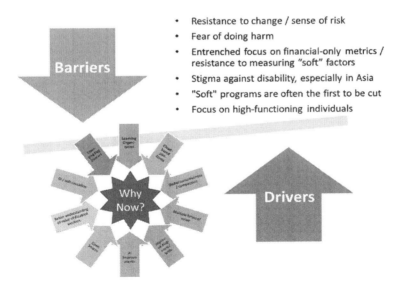

- Resistance to change / sense of risk
- Fear of doing harm
- Entrenched focus on financial-only metrics / resistance to measuring "soft" factors
- Stigma against disability, especially in Asia
- "Soft" programs are often the first to be cut
- Focus on high-functioning individuals

To overcome these barriers will require persistent effort from several directions. One key insight, based on a recent conversation with John

Hagel of the Deloitte Center for the Edge is that the only way you can do large-scale transformations is to do a transformation at the edge, and let the core move to the edge. The reason: disruption, well, disrupts. So as soon as a transformation initiative has visibility, it will attract organizational "antibodies".

Ashok's strategy is a case in point. Instead of trying to convince IBM, HP, SAP and more to change their hiring practices, he is looking to "solve the inclusion problem" from the outside for the Fortune 5000, providing an expert service bureau that takes this challenge off their plate.

Another strategy is to realize that small changes every day are better at driving behavior change than large training initiatives offered at a lower frequency. For this reason, apps like Cognoa's need to be more than just a coach: this advanced technology enables an every-day behavior change tool, customized for a particular patient. Cognoa uses AI to analyze understand a particular child, instead of providing general-purpose advice. It uses the child's age, developmental stage, future milestones, and behavioral and developmental strengths and weaknesses. Parents use Cognoa to track and support the developmental and behavioral milestones with the app's personalized recommendations: activities such as "make a sandwich" for building independence and confidence as well as reasoning and communication skills. Another activity: "Act out storybooks" for social and emotional development and speech and language. These are activities every parent can do at home with their kids on a daily basis – and Cognoa connects to the reason why: which developmental and behavioral attributes the activity addresses and improves, as designed by clinical pediatric specialists.

This is where technology-driven change happens: using personalized real-time information and experiences, and which enables forward goals and outcomes. AI and machine-learning, combined with the easy accessibility and delivery of smartphones, will significantly improve the pathways and channels of care. And certainly when it comes to neurodiversity—every individual is unique—this is extremely powerful.

CREATED BY RANA CHAKRABARTI

# Conclusion and Manifesto

Due to recent improvements in technology (the internet, AI, machine learning, natural language, DI), along with a shifting global consciousness, a tipping point has been reached regarding how disabled people access jobs and resources. We are all observing this change crystallizing in different ways, but our experience shares a surprising number of common themes. We share the following beliefs:

1. The **benefits of hiring disabled people** (including lower attrition, better performance on certain tasks, greater focus, and more), when done right, outweigh the costs, even when considering only financial outcomes.

2. **Money is a bad proxy for happiness.** As this realization spreads around the world, and as data gives us a deeper insight into reality, a great shift is beginning.

3. Inside the business models of most companies, **"soft"** causal links, often within feedback loops, form "invisible engines" driving even traditional financial-only profitability. Making

215

these explicit-and "going public" about the business value of compassion and purpose, is increasingly important to all companies worldwide.

4. The concept of **"disability" is oversimplified** in such a way that it leaves massive opportunities on the table: for employers and employees alike. Unpacking this simplification has tremendous value.

5. For the same reason that "precision medicine" is powerful, **"precision employment"** can be so as well: using a much more detailed vector of specific capabilities rather than an aggregated label like "autistic".

6. Unlike traditional technology plays, organizations in this space are as motivated by a shared sense of **purpose** as they are by financial goals.

7. **Compassion and gratitude** are particularly powerful, and are enhanced by the presence of disabled persons in the workplace.

8. These **"multiple bottom lines"**, when well-managed, represent a superpower that will be a model for markets of the second half of the 21st century.

9. **AI, including natural language processing, and machine learning**, have substantial capabilities to match workers to "the perfect job" or task

10. Indeed, these new technologies are essential to deploying job matching at **scale**: up and down the spectrum of abilities, and around the world.

11. The most powerful (and therefore inevitable) deployment model for the above capabilities is as a **platform**-based ecosystem: a hub-and-spoke arrangement where commonly needed technology and facilities are provided in a single place (instead of reinvented in multiple places) and which reduce the effort required to launch a new initiative.

12. Such a platform can be used for **giving** (matching your time and resources to the best way you can help) as well as buying.

13. Multiple bottom lines add complexity that requires new tools to manage. Linking multiple machine learning systems in a chain of cause-and-effect, and understanding complex systems effects (**decision intelligence**) is an essential methodology to take on this next challenge.

14. **Empowering** workers to make their own decisions, and parents to help with their children's own diagnoses, is an important role of technology.

15. **Behavioral** interventions have received less attention than medical ones, and hold tremendous promise.

16. Innovation is best done "at the **edge**". Disability services are valid in their own right, but also form the "edge" of a larger market for matching to all differently abled people.

17. **Large enterprises** are a good early market for many of these services (such a technology to help with diagnosis and job matching). There is a natural synergy between the innovation in a startup and the considerable needs of larger companies.

18. The approaches described here have value for both paid workers and volunteers, and for both long-term jobs as well as smaller tasks.

19. In a complex world, with multiple organizations working in constantly changing ecosystem, a worker can lose sight of how their contribution affects the whole. Since a sense of purpose and connection to that whole is an important sense of happiness, the importance of clear visualization of how tasks and jobs fit into chains of events with impact will become increasingly clear. Technology will have an increasingly important role to play in **visualizing** these causal chains.

20. To grow this ecosystem requires a **flag bearer**: one or more people to lead the charge. Let's do this.

Thorkil Sonne founded the social enterprise Specialisterne in Denmark in 2004 after his youngest son was diagnosed as autistic. In 2008 he founded the not-for-profit Specialisterne Foundation with the goal to enable one million jobs for autistic / neurodiverse people through a global network of Specialisterne entities, partners and platforms.

Prior to Specialisterne, Thorkil was CTO in an IT company and chairman of a local branch of Autism Denmark. Thorkil has promoted "the autism advantage" through speeches in 24 countries and co-arrange with the UN an annual Autism Advantage Luncheon at the UN HQ.

Specialisterne Foundation is associated with the UN Department of Public Information and Thorkil is a Schwab Foundation Social Entrepreneur connected to World Economic Forum, an Ashoka Fellow and part of the I4J network.

# The Autism Advantage Movement

By Thorkil Sonne

## Autism throughout history

Autistic people have been among us for ages – way before the diagnosis was invented. Autism comes from the Greek words "auto" meaning self and "ism" meaning direction. I.e., it relates to people with "self-direction" as individualists, who are unique and not well rounded socially.

Throughout history important research and inventions were developed by unique individuals, e.g. Einstein, Darwin and Newton, who might qualify for a diagnosis within the autism spectrum if born today.

At their time, the professor types were accepted and appreciated in society. They made valuable contributions to the development of society and their quirks were accepted.

What if Einstein was born today? Would he be assessed as a toddler and be told that he has a disorder? Would he go to special institutions for therapy, education and work? Would we try to change his behavior to fit with the norm for behavior at any given time?

We will never know, but we must ask ourselves if we do enough to encourage "self-direction" persons to realize their potential in truly welcoming environments.

# Autism today

Today it is estimated that autism affects 1 of 59 Americans and that the unemployment or underemployment rate is close to 80%.

With these numbers we can estimate that 5.4 million Americans are likely to be affected by autism and that 2.9 million autistic adults in working age (2/3 of age span) are unemployed or underemployed.

Are we seeing a national health crisis unfold? Or have we as a society developed a payment model where everyone who needs attention beyond the norm, has to be diagnosed in order to become understood and supported in his or her personal development?

Using the numbers from USA, there are 129 million autistic people worldwide – more than Japan's population.

I.e. we are talking about a huge portion of citizens that are not given a fair chance to contribute to their communities and realize their potential.

# A wake-up call

In 1996, my third child was born in Denmark.

His older brothers had taught us that children develop at their own pace. As parent you have to be patient and ready to support the kids when they are ready to move up their development ladder.

But our son did not progress the normal way. The caregivers in the kindergarten would do much to help him, but none of their methods worked. He could sit on a swing for hours and be happy - but when the caregivers wanted him to engage in social activities, he became frustrated and sad.

There were no simple physical explanations for the problem. Then a psychologist observed him and concluded that without doubt, our son has the diagnosis "infantile autism" - a lifelong pervasive developmental disorder, for which there is no cure.

We were told that our son would not be able to develop as his older brothers and that the challenges observed in the kindergarten would always be there.

It was shocking to receive the diagnosis - we recognized our son in the psychologist' description – but we never saw him as disabled.

Our lives as parents changed that day, but our son's world did not change a bit. He was still the same caring and trusting child. It was only the parents for whom the world had turned a somersault.

We were close to fall into the hole of pity for those who have an autistic family member. But we realized that we would not want our son to be anything else and that our family norms are more important than society's norms.

We stopped reading books about the deficits and impairments of autism, and we became curious to get to understand his world. I joined the autism organization and became chairman of a local branch of Autism Denmark, where I met very many young autistic people. None of them had meaningful and productive jobs matching their skills and personalities.

As technical director in an IT company I was responsible for a number of IT projects and IT systems. I could see a business need for many of the skills I saw in autistic people, such as good memory, pattern recognition skills, attention to detail, perseverance, high accuracy in repetitive tasks, innovative thinking, honesty and trustworthiness. I also knew how difficult it is to source people with these skills, for example as analysts, software testers and coders.

With our son as inspiration, support from the family, engagement in the autism community and a career in IT, it seemed so obvious that I should make an attempt to remove the divide between talented autistic people and jobs calling for talent that many autistic people possess.

The idea of creating employment opportunities for autistic people in the IT industry found its form, and I founded Specialisterne. The first office was established in February 2004 in Denmark.

# From local to global

A few months after Specialisterne was launched, BBC World News broadcasted a story about Specialisterne globally. The international response was stunning. I received emails from more than 100 countries from autistic people, families or companies who asked for my help to create meaningful career opportunities for autistic people in their country.

I was very busy getting Specialisterne Denmark off the ground, but I had to say yes to these call for action from my global family of individuals and families who share a common hope of a future, where autistic people will be truly welcomed in the labor market and appreciated as valuable citizens.

My response was to found the not-for-profit Specialisterne Foundation in 2008 with Specialisterne Denmark as in-kind contribution as platform for collaboration, knowledge sharing and innovation.

The goal was to enable a million jobs by 2030 for autistic people and people with similar conditions across the world regardless of differences in welfare support, culture and religion.

Specialisterne Foundation launched Specialisterne entities and partnerships in 20 countries to gain knowledge in different market conditions. The strategy was to showcase that autism can be an advantage in competitive jobs and to support companies starting employment programs that would be adapted to the company's processes.

So far, Specialisterne created around 1 000 jobs and around 10 000 autistic people probably got employed by organizations who started employment programs inspired or trained by Specialisterne or followers.

# The autism advantage

The autism advantage unfolds when you turn skills and behavior that others see as challenged into assets that can help the employer develop great products and deliver great services where attention to detail, high accuracy, innovative thinking and honesty is key.

The autism advantage includes positive 'spillover effects', such as higher engagement and retention rate by co-workers, better leadership by managers and strengthening of community relations.

The autism advantage will enable companies to have a more diverse workforce that will prepare the company for the 4th industrial revolution, where innovation and resilience will be essential to survive in a market driven by new technology and disruptive business models.

I claim that at least 5 percent of all tasks in any business area will be a great fit for autistic people. If I am right, then the unemployment or underemployment rate for autistic people should not be any different than for any other people.

Having worked with a number or large companies, we proved the autism advantage multiple times in careers ranging from cyber security to pig farming.

Careers are not just for autistic people with good education and high IQ. We claim that autistic people can make you a better manager and create more inclusive and engaged workplaces. We invite all stakeholders in the communities to work with us to identify meaningful employment and training programs for people across the autism spectrum.

# The UN perspective

The Convention on the Rights of Persons with Disabilities (CRPD) was adapted by the UN General Assembly and entered into effect in 2008.

The CRPD follows decades of work by the UN to change attitudes and approaches to persons with disabilities. It takes to a new height the movement from viewing persons with disabilities as "objects" of charity, medical treatment and social protection towards viewing persons with disabilities as "subjects" with rights, who can claim those rights and make decisions for their lives based on their free and informed consent as well as being active members of society.

The preamble of the UN's CRPD states: "Disability is an evolving concept, and that disability results from the interaction between persons with impairments and attitudinal and environmental barriers that hinders full and effective participation in society on an equal basis with others."

CRPD chapter 27: "States Parties recognize the right of persons with disabilities to work, on an equal basis with others; this includes the right to the opportunity to gain a living by work freely chosen or accepted in a labor market and work environment that is open, inclusive and accessible to persons with disabilities".

In 2015 the UN member states agreed on 17 Sustainable Development Goals (SDG) to be met by 2030 as a global commitment for a more sustainable world.

As associated with the UN, Specialisterne Foundation will work with partners in SDG 17 "Partnerships for the goals" on reaching goals related to SDG 8 "Promote sustained, inclusive and sustainable economic growth, full and productive employment and decent work for all" and SDG 4 "Ensure inclusive and equitable quality education and promote lifelong learning opportunities for all".

From a moral point of view, all states should by now have implemented the CRPD and be on the way with efforts to meet the SDGs, so why are the unemployment numbers still so high?

I believe that UN member states can set a framework, but it is up to the mindsets in the population to realize the intentions in the CRPD and SDGs. It will take a global grass root movement lead by families to realize the intention of the moral decisions on human rights and sustainability set by the UN General Assembly.

# The autism advantage movement

In 2012 NY Times Magazine released an article named "The Autism Advantage" about my son and Specialisterne.

Specialisterne Foundation and UN Department of Public Information defined the theme "The Autism Advantage" and invited a number of progressive companies to share their autism employment programs in the UN HQ on UN World Autism Awareness Day April 2nd 2015.

224

The message was the same from all employers: employing autistic people is the right thing to do for your shareholders. The event was broadcasted globally and created a baseline for the positive approach to autism.

I was asked by the UN to arrange an annual Autism Advantage Luncheon in the UN HQ and invite key stakeholders to discuss employment of autistic people and touch base on the global development in acceptance and appreciation of autistic people in the workplace. The third Autism Advantage Luncheon will take place on the UN Autism Awareness Day April 2nd 2019 and be a platform for announcing SDG partnerships.

We find similar interest from the World Economic Forum (WEF), committed to improving the state of the world as the international organization for public-private cooperation.

As a Schwab Foundation Social Entrepreneur I attended the annual World Economic Forum Summits in Davos, Switzerland and Tianjin/Dalian, China to discuss the autism advantage and how autistic people can help companies improve leadership and practice inclusive growth in the 4th industrial revolution. The interest in embracing neurodiversity among WEF members is strong, as truly inclusive work environments encouraging differences will be essential to be competitive in the future business landscape.

# The Dandelion Principle

Kids love dandelions: they blow dandelions, make wishes, tie necklaces and paint faces. But as you grow older, your own norms will typically be replaced by society's norms and the love for the dandelion will likely turn to hate. If you buy a house with a garden and you see the dandelion again you will see it as a weed and want it out of your garden as you will only want the flowers you decided upon.

If you take the dandelion from the lawn, put it in the kitchen garden and treat it well, you will find that it is one of the most valuable plants in nature. You can actually make a living out of treating it well and harvest its values for natural medicine, nutrition, coffee, tea, wine and beer.

The dandelion reminds us all that every seed of every dandelion has the potential to add value as an herb in a welcoming environment, and that everyone of us have the power to decide if we see the dandelion as a weed or an herb.

It is the same with people. If welcomed, everyone can add value, but if not welcomed, we will never be able to benefit from the potential value of every individual.

We call it the Dandelion Principle and use the dandelion as Specialisterne's logo. The Dandelion Principle has been documented in MIT Sloan Management Review and in a Specialisterne case study at Harvard Business School.

The dandelion principle is not limited to autistic people. It is a generic principle and will in particular benefit neurodiverse people (with autism, ADHD, OCD, dyslexia, etc. who face similar challenges as autistic people) and in other places where human talent is left untapped.

# Scaling

So far, we proved that the Autism Advantage is real and that everyone can start tapping into it by working with partners who have experience in assessment and employment of autistic people.

Now we want to demonstrate to the world that the time is now to tap into the autism advantage and implement the dandelion principle, if you want to add values to your shareholders through higher quality, stronger engagement and better leadership.

The i4j network is a great platform for launching initiatives inspired by the autism advantage and the dandelion principle. Coolabilities and the human centered value creation is spot on and can lead to thousands if not millions of meaningful and productive jobs that will create value for individuals, families, employers and the society.

Our ambition is to create the world's biggest grass root movement of people in all countries who seek to change the opportunities for autistic/neurodiverse people to be included in the labor market in meaningful and productive careers.

Imagine if we can empower all families with autistic members and stakeholders in the community globally through technology, massive open online courses, social media, new models for identification and utilization of talent and new economic models for education and employment.

My learning in life is that nothing is impossible for those dedicated to solve social challenges through innovative and scalable business models.

Our ultimate goal is to work in UN SDG partnerships and inspire policies to be adapted to better include neurodiverse people in the labor market and education system. When the UN SDG will be evaluated in 2030 we hope that there will be no more need for Specialisterne.

Let us use the autism advantage to create the biggest grass root movement ever and create more diverse and inclusive workplaces for all in communities globally.

Vinton G. Cerf is Co-Chair and Co-Founder of i4j. He is vice president and Chief Internet Evangelist for Google and contributes to global policy development and continued spread of the Internet. Widely known as one of the "Fathers of the Internet," Cerf is the co-designer of the TCP/IP protocols and the architecture of the Internet. He has served in executive positions at MCI, the Corporation for National Research Initiatives and the Defense Advanced Research Projects Agency and on the faculty of Stanford University.

# Finding Work: Privacy and Security Challenges

## by Vint Cerf

*Systems for assisting job seekers to find work will need access to substantial amounts of personal information. They will need to characterize the capabilities of the worker and allow a prospective employer to contact him or her. An aggregated system may contain very significant amounts of information for a large number of individuals and thus represent an attractive target for hacking. Moreover, customers of the system (e.g., employers) may prove to be negligent or at least deficient in protecting this data. This brief essay outlines some desirable properties of a job matching system that contribute to the protection of individual privacy and the general security of the system and its contents.*

228

In 2014 we coined the name "Jobly"' for an imagined ideal system using artificial intelligence to match people with job opportunities. Jobly is also designed to help when the applicant is unaware of her abilities and the employer is not aware of the value those abilities offer. Since then, Jobly has become a part of the i4j vocabulary for describing an application that makes ideal matches; one could call it the i4j "Turing test" for matching people with opportunities. Another meme that more recently has caught traction in i4j discussions is "coolabilities," the enhanced abilities that sometimes accompany disabilities. A Jobly for people with disabilities and/or coolabilities has become a vision for some of the i4j members who have started a project aiming for an ecosystem that develops a new generation of labor market applications.

In theory, the more a prospective employer knows about a candidate's capabilities and situation, the more effectively a potential match can be established. That line of reasoning suggests that a job matching system such as the hypothetical Jobly will function best when it has maximum information about jobs and candidates. On the other hand, significant aggregation of personal information has risks. What if the database is hacked and its contents stolen and misused? Myriad harmful scenarios come to mind: identity theft, diversion to commercial purposes, use of personal information against the user (law enforcement, social media abuse), national security risks (e.g., OMB database penetration), potential embarrassment about disabilities, and denial of access to legitimate benefits, such as insurance. I am sure readers can imagine other examples.

How might these risks be mitigated? How should they be balanced against the potential benefits of high and granular accuracy of the information? There are some obvious responses to these questions including deliberate withholding of some information despite the potential reduction in the fidelity of job matching. In the case of persons with disabilities, late disclosure -- such as after a job offer -- might have negative results.

Beginning with the basics, any system holding significant personal information will need to be designed with maximum security in mind. Local encryption of the data, two-factor authentication for access, and end-to-end encryption during any data transfers are all clearly needed. Moreover, any parties provided access to this information or to whom information is transferred must exercise equal diligence in protecting it. Apart from the sensibility of this view, recent European legislation titled General Data Protection Regulation (GDPR) addresses in strong terms

229

the need to protect personal information in its myriad forms. GDPR is being adopted widely, not only in the European Union, but elsewhere.

Regulation, however, is not the same thing as prevention; strong technical means will be needed to achieve the desired result. If harmful disclosures are made through negligence, poor technology, or unethical or uninformed choices, punishment such as financial penalties will not be sufficient to put the genie back in the bottle.

Job seekers will face their own challenges: Whom should they trust with information that might lead to better work opportunities but which might also lead to unintended but potentially harmful or hurtful disclosures? It seems plain that control over access to the information is key to protecting the interests of the parties whose information is at stake. Complex laws have been enacted for the protection of medical information and one might conclude that HIPAA-style[47] protections might be appropriate and even already applicable for certain personal information. There have been consequences of the HIPAA rules in the U.S., not the least of which may be that statistical information about the incidence of certain medical conditions is hidden by HIPAA access controls. This limits the potential to understand and mitigate certain genetic conditions or recognize a person's susceptibility to particular diseases. Nonetheless, it is understood that disclosure of medical information to unauthorized parties can have serious negative consequences.

# Architectural Principles for the Jobly system

This line of reasoning leads one to consider specific desirable properties of the Jobly system, including:

1.  General Access Control to all personal data

2.  Fine-grained Access Control to specific data

3.  Strong authentication of accessing parties

4.  Strong integrity control of information

How might we achieve such an architecture? What technical means

---

[47] **HIPAA** (Health Insurance Portability and Accountability Act of 1996)

might be adopted? How hard or easy would it be to make use of the resulting job matching system? Might it be too cumbersome to be effective? We can begin to answer such questions by reviewing the primary functions of a security architecture, including data encryption, access control, matching, and encrypted communication.

## Sketching a Security Architecture

**Data Encryption** The candidate architecture for the Jobly system must include encryption of all content at rest to protect against breaches of the storage system that would release all content in unencrypted mode. The encryption key for this data can be held by the system and need not be known to users of the content. Transfers of data to third parties should also be encrypted using a newly generated symmetric key conveyed to the third party, encrypted in that party's public key. Accurate authentication of authorized users of the system should be a requirement, possibly with the use of two-factor authentication, to limit the vulnerabilities of usernames and passwords. The strongest designs would use a physical cryptographic device to generate dynamic secondary passwords for each access. Cryptographic algorithms embedded in software on mobiles are less attractive owing to the potential for hacking mobiles.

**Access Control** All access to the contents of the client (i.e., job seeker) data should be logged and audited. One might explore the use of machine learning methods and other analytic tools to detect potential abuse (e.g., persistent efforts at access or attempted access to large swaths of client information). The operator of the Jobly system will likely also need to do some kind of due diligence on parties wishing to access Jobly client data. Contracts for access with penalties for abusive behavior would be appropriate.

**Matching Process** Ideally, matching would be a process conducted *within* the confines of the Jobly system. In other words, a customer of the Jobly system seeking to fill a job would provide the job description to Jobly. It might provide only a summary of characteristics it seeks or it might detail the actual work to be done or specific talents or credentials sought. A refined and semantically rich language for these specifications would be attractive.

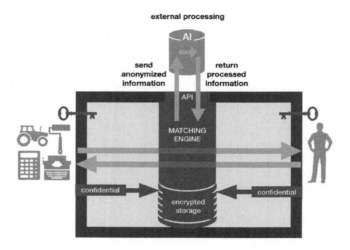

In an attempt to bridge the gap between job seekers and employers, Google has engaged its Knowledge Graph to assist in job matching[48] so as to expand the semantic matching between job descriptions and candidate worker capabilities and experience. These concepts and the associated Google API might work well for the implementation of Jobly. The result of activating Jobly against a job description would be the identification of potential candidates.

One might then imagine that the employer would be provided with a list of potential candidates identified only by an anonymous identifier assigned when the candidate registered. If one were concerned about persistent identification and binding of information about the candidate by employers, one could generate random identifiers for each instance of response, although this could complicate the retention of state information during the exchanges between the employer and Jobly. In any event, at most, the employer would receive only information that the client job seeker chooses to label *public*. Note that the job seeker could decided whether coolabilities should be considered public or not. A deliberate search for coolabilities or disabilities could produce a summary of anonymous potential matches.

**Encrypted Communication** Upon the discovery of a possible match, it seems appropriate to notify the job seeker of the event, to provide the seeker with a summary of the job as described by the employer, and to ask what, if any, non-public information the job seeker wishes to release to the

---

[48] https://cloud.google.com/blog/big-data/2016/11/cloud-jobs-api-machine-learning-goes-to-work-on-job-search-and-discovery

employer. The intent of this feature is to allow the employment candidate to decide what information to release, depending on the job description and the employer. It is important that the employer and the job seeking client have confidence that the information provided to the employer has high integrity and security. To this end, the Jobly system should provide a way for job seekers to digitally sign all their content held by Jobly. Registration with Jobly would be accompanied by the registrant providing to Jobly his or her public key.

To allow for selective subsets of data to be provided to employers while controlling access, the candidate could digitally sign the aggregate block of candidate data but separately encrypt subsets of the candidate data so as to provide decryption keys for release of individual data to the employer based on candidate preferences. Individual private or symmetric keys might be used to protect individual candidate data; i.e., different keys would be provided for each datum. This prevents the employer from using a common key to decrypt everything in the candidate's biography.

To protect the keys while in transit, the query from the employer might include two things: the employer's public key and the candidate's approval for access to particular data. This would cause Jobly to send the encrypted data along with the decryption key, which would be encrypted in the employer's public key. In this way, the candidate controls what data is released to the prospective employer and the data is cryptographically protected both from view and alteration without detection.

## Creating policy that works

It is sometimes asserted that lawmakers are like people with hammers who think everything looks like a nail. It is tempting to imagine that passage of a law against an abuse somehow solves the problem. All it does is create incentives either to comply with the law (generally a good thing) or find a way around it (generally a bad thing). What is needed is a deeper appreciation in the community of lawmakers as to the limits of technology, and the ways it works and doesn't work. Most important is the need to assist lawmakers with knowledge and useful metaphors that help them and their aides assess the utility of various technical approaches to problems in the privacy and security space. Of course, that is what expert testimony is partly intended to accomplish, but in the process of writing law and regulation, real expertise is vital. There was at one time an Office of Technology Assessment attached to the U.S. Congress. It was abandoned in 1995[49] much to the detriment of legislators who needed OTA information. It seems timely to reconsider this value of this function, given the increasingly technical nature of our society and our deep dependence on information technology and infrastructure in daily life. Citizens also need deeper awareness of the risks and power of technology. Developing this awareness requires tools and training to protect their own interests. We all have roles to play to protect individual and corporate safety, security, and privacy while maintaining transparent processes of governance in the private and public sectors.

I am ending my chapter with two comments that are relevant in the context of a Jobly for coolabilities.

## Comment (1): Is blockchain a key to Jobly's success?

As this book goes to press, we are experiencing massive hyperbole in the discussion about blockchains and cryptocurrencies. I am not a big fan of either, but it is fair to ask whether the properties of blockchains and variants such as "smart contracts" might somehow have a role to play in building a Jobly-like system. In principle, the primary advantage of a blockchain is that its entries are essentially impossible (or at least too difficult) to alter. In other words, the integrity of the information in the blockchain is protected. A blockchain may not provide confidentiality, although that can be added by encrypting the entries in each block. The question of key management arises at this point: When a significant number of parties are given access to content, the encrypting key must be protected. Blockchain also has the property that the chain can be replicated in a distributed way so that many parties have access to its content. The need for access control, as has been asserted in this essay, makes problematic the widespread replication of the access keys to encrypted content. The key replication and protection problem is not inherently solved with blockchain, but if other security properties of the blockchain entries can be implemented, widespread access to the distributed database of personal information might prove attractive. Of course, there are other ways to create distributed databases whose contents are synchronized, so I do not regard blockchain as a critical or unique solution.

---

[49] https://en.wikipedia.org/wiki/Office_of_Technology_Assessment

# Comment (2): Coolabilities, disabilities and work: A personal note

I wear two hearing aids and have done so for 62 years, since I was 13 years old. My hearing quality generally has decreased by about 1 dB per year, but hearing aids have allowed me to function in a hearing world. I never learned to sign, and I am not a talented lip reader, though I have friends who are skilled in either or both of those talents. In addition, my wife was profoundly deaf for 50 years, and has always been an accomplished lip reader, but received cochlear implants in 1996 and 2006.

I mention these conditions to provide some background for the thoughts below. This book highlights observations about skills that are often correlated with disabilities, such as Autism Spectrum Disorder. I concur that such special abilities ("coolabilities") should be known to employers whose businesses might take advantage of these special skills although it is vital that disclosure comes only to employers who understand the utility of these skills and are prepared to accommodate conditions needed to exercise them. I do worry, however, that an over-focusing on coolabilities may lead to rejection of persons with disabilities simply because they have no more special abilities than the rest of us.

I don't have any noticeable coolabilities. My hearing loss doesn't bring advantages except perhaps for flying overnight, when I can take off my hearing aids and sleep soundly despite the screaming two-year-old behind me. On the other hand, I do need some accommodations to work effectively. Phones need amplification in spite the hearing aids. I need to make special arrangements for Q&A when speaking to larger audiences. I use a headset for video conferences to improve the quality of sound. I am a big fan of real-time captions for general conferences and, when possible, video conferences. It has not occurred to me to highlight my hearing loss, although during interviews, I do not hesitate to bring it up if I have difficulty hearing the interviewer. I am also very public about this when speaking in public and engaging the audience.

Over-emphasis on coolabilities could have the negative effect of reducing interest in people who just happen to have a disability but that doesn't prevent successful accomplishment of the work. I think it is vital to consider first the capabilities of all prospective workers, to assess their merits, and then to adapt conditions to allow them to work effectively. Capability to do the work is what counts.

Jason Palmer is General Partner at New Markets Venture Partners, one of the nation's leading education-focused venture capital firms. As a double-bottom line investor, New Markets focuses on innovative, high impact, early and growth stage edtech companies that improve student outcomes while building profitable organizations.

Jason has been affiliated with New Markets since 2011 and became a General Partner in 2016 after three years at the Gates Foundation. Jason brings twenty years of experience as an education technology entrepreneur, executive and investor, and focuses on fund strategy, supporting portfolio companies and leveraging deep connections with industry leaders. He is a board director for Motimatic and serves as a board observer for Credly, Signal Vine, LearnPlatform and American Honors College. Jason previously served as a board director at Moodlerooms, DecisionDesk and StraighterLine.

Prior to his current role, Jason served as Deputy Director at the Bill & Melinda Gates Foundation, leading postsecondary innovation efforts to improve the outcomes of low-income, minority and first-generation college students by investing in colleges, universities and entrepreneurs pursuing digital and adaptive learning, student coaching and advising, financial aid structures, comprehensive credit transfer and employer pathways. Prior to the Foundation, Jason founded and grew three investor-backed technology and services companies before holding a series of executive positions at Microsoft, SchoolNet, Kaplan and StraighterLine. At Kaplan, Jason led three education businesses as general manager or president, in addition to founding and leading the company's venture capital effort.

Jason holds a B.A. in interdisciplinary studies from the University of Virginia and an M.B.A. from Harvard Business School, and also serves on the University of Virginia's Curry School of Education Foundation Board.

# Building A People-Centered Economy: *Startups Redesigning Learning and Earning*

## By Jason Palmer

Earlier this year, my dry cleaner, a 55-year old African-American grandmother making $10/hour, surprised me by gushing about the Computer Science courses she was taking on **edX**. She knew I worked in technology, and was wondering if an edX Micro-Masters was enough to get her a salaried coding job, or whether she really needed to get a full Masters in Computer Science.

My dry cleaner is not alone – more than 14 million students are taking thousands of free courses on edX to help their careers, and more than 4 million post-traditional students aged 25-64 are enrolled in longer certificate and degree at America's colleges and universities.

The "people-centered economy" is more than just a bold vision being put forth by the authors of this book – it's already being built, below the radar, by innovators serving postsecondary learners and workers. We "only" need to discover it, start mapping it, and encourage others to join. Entrepreneurs are leveraging new business models and technologies that pioneer new ways for people of all ages and backgrounds to tap into their passions, strengthen their skills, and deploy them in flexible, digital, virtual ways that increase the greater good for those individuals, as well as our society and economy.

*The "people-centered economy"is more than just a bold vision being put forth by the authors of this book – it'salready being built. We "only" need to discover it, start mapping it, and encourage others to join.*

As a venture capitalist focused on education, training and workforce technologies, I'm lucky enough to see "behind the curtain" of hundreds

237

of the most futuristic, most innovative education technology companies in America. Some of these companies are pushing the boundaries through artificial intelligence, blockchain, virtual and augmented reality, while others are creating digital infrastructure for e-learning, competencies, assessment and credentialing.

This vantage point allows me to see, close up, William Gibson's quote from his 1984 science fiction novel *Neuromancer:* "The future is already here — it's just not very evenly distributed."

The mainstream media is filled with dire predictions: of automation displacing millions of jobs, the hollowing out of the middle class, and life potentially becoming more digital and de-personalized. I fully believe these predictions will come true for boring, routine, easily automatable jobs. But for the most part, this isn't the future I see. Instead, I see promising startups that are focused not on automating humans out of existence, but rather on optimizing human potential, giving humans powerful tools to augment their natural abilities and scale their positive impact. The best of these companies empower learners and earners, and are beginning to re-define the structure of education and employment.

*The most promising startups are focused not on automating humans out of existence, but rather on optimizing human potential with powerful tools to augment their natural abilities and scale their positive impact... beginning to re-define the structure of education and employment.*

In fact, education and work are starting to blur in profound ways that give concrete meaning to the old phrase "lifelong learning." When the phrase was first coined in 1971 in Denmark, lifelong learning meant simply "ongoing, voluntary, and self-motivated" pursuit of knowledge, emphasizing personal fulfillment after high school or college.

However, over the past fifty years, learning scientists have determined that education isn't just a passive activity one sits through for the first two decades of life, but instead is a continuous, active, ongoing developmental process over the course of one's life, encompassing executive function, language acquisition, reading, writing, mathematics, metacognition, and other subject-matter-specific learning as well as experiential learning-by-doing (e.g., project-based work and work-based learning), all of which can be mapped to milestones, competencies, skills and achievements.

On top of this scientific infrastructure that describes how humans develop, learn and grow, the education-workforce continuum is going through a rapid evolution powered by four trends:

1. software is eating the world;

2. millions of analog jobs are evolving into highly-empowered, "new collar" technology specialist jobs, closely connected to the gig economy;

3. education is becoming digital, grain-sized, and micro-credentialed; and

4. employers, educational institutions and people are embracing a more flexible, more holistic understanding of work and life that involves lifelong learning, a kaleidoscope of new hybrid jobs, and a newly emerging conception of happiness and livelihood based on the passions, curiosity and abilities of each individual – rather than fitting people into outdated, cog-like corporate molds.

These major trends are reshaping the education-workforce continuum, and the strongest startups are exploiting these trends – for good.

## Software Is Eating The World

Back in 2011, Marc Andreessen famously wrote that "software is eating the world." What he meant was that almost every industry was being transformed from analog to digital – from books to e-books, brick-and-mortar commerce to e-commerce, self-owned cars to self-driving Ubers and Lyfts. Nearly every industry – banking, health care, real estate, manufacturing, energy, education – is experiencing this transformation, and almost every company needs to become a technology company, because software is improving or re-designing nearly every fundamental business process.

This powerful trend is especially reshaping education and the workforce, too. In the labor market, this tsunami of technology has resulted in the creation of millions of "new collar" jobs – a term coined in 2016 by IBM CEO Gina Rometty that covers "entirely new roles in areas such as cybersecurity, data science, artificial intelligence and cognitive business." Rometty noted that 1/3 of IBM's workforce didn't have four-year college degrees, but their new collar jobs demanded sophisticated technical skills that workers were gaining through career and technology training.

## Analog Jobs Are Becoming New Collar Jobs

As demand for more technology-related employees has surged, the unemployment rate has fallen to 3.8% but the U.S. economy is still short 6.6 million jobs – almost 3 million of which qualify as new collar jobs. Most of these jobs are more accessible and equitable than ever before. Many can be done anywhere and at any time, as long as individuals learn to create, communicate, collaborate, think critically, and work virtually, through technology as well as face-to-face. And many do not require a college degree.

An increasing number of workers need digital literacy and technology skills – whether or not their role directly involves coding. Labor analyst **Burning Glass Technologies** found that half of jobs in the highest paying quartile are in occupations that commonly require coding or other technology skills from job applicants. In the 21st century, everyone needs to learn to read, write and code.

Historically, America's colleges and universities have provided the educated workforce that industry needed, but higher education has been slow to adapt to the computer science revolution, and these new-collar needs are not being met fast enough. In 2017, America's postsecondary institutions awarded less than 100,000 computer science degrees – well short of the 500,000 computer science-related job openings for individuals with these kinds of technical skills, according to Code.org.

In Burning Glass Technologies' analysis of 27 million online job postings in 2016, it found that half those openings were for "middle-skill" jobs, those that pay a living wage yet require less than a bachelor's degree. More than 80% of these jobs are "digitally intensive," paying more and offering greater opportunities for advancement than comparable opportunities in the same sectors. These jobs range from basic clerical, customer service, finance, and operations positions, which use basic productivity software and social media, to roles that rely upon specialized digital tools, such as network/systems administrator and maintenance/service supervisor. "While advanced digital skills, especially coding and programming, are in high demand in high-skill occupations, there is a large set of digital skills that open opportunities for middle-skill workers," the report notes. "Basic CRM skills, such as use of Salesforce, and social media skills, are door openers into several high-paying career areas."

To address this voracious need for technical skills, technology academies like **General Assembly** and **Galvanize** have grown rapidly, working with employers to understand the exact skills they're seeking, hosting coding bootcamps and other applied technical courses to teach those skills, and connecting students with companies through events and other mechanisms. The approach seems to be working: Galvanize reports 87% of their graduates being hired into information technology jobs within six months, while employers hired nearly all of the three-quarters of General Assembly students using the company's career advisory services within 6 months of starting their search.

Most people don't know that the majority of job postings on ZipRecruiter actually decreased their education requirements between 2016 and 2017 – particularly in account management, sales, and quality assurance roles. Despite their shifting requirements, the number of these jobs is growing, and they have the potential to be well-paying without saddling workers with college debt. "Through 2024, the economy will create more than 16 million middle-skill job openings, including 3 million from newly-created jobs and 13 million from Baby Boomer retirements," notes Anthony P. Carnevale, director of the Georgetown University Center on Education and the Workforce. "Many jobs in the New Middle pay well: 40 percent pay more than $55,000 annually and 14 percent pay more than $80,000 annually. By comparison, the average bachelor's degree-holder earns $61,000 annually."

Consulting giant McKinsey & Company, where I serve as an advisor to The Consortium for Advancing Adult Learning & Development (CAALD), estimates that 39 million routine-skill American jobs could be displaced by automation over the next fifteen years, but also notes that 30 million of those workers could find their way into new occupations and newly created categories of jobs – if they gain the right new skills. The extent to which current and developing technologies will automate jobs varies substantially by sector and role. What's more, 15 million additional jobs could be created that aren't visible today, if historical trends from prior periods hold.

For example, physical jobs in predictable environments (such as factory operations and fast food preparation) or those in data processing (accounting clerks or mortgage origination) can be easily displaced by machines. But according to McKinsey, "automation will have a lesser effect on jobs that involve managing people, applying expertise, and social interactions, where machines are unable to match human performance for now." Likewise, jobs in more unpredictable or human-centric jobs like child- and elder-care "are technically difficult to automate and often command relatively lower wages, which makes automation a less attractive business proposition."

However, as technology automates routine tasks, and everyone's work involves some technology skills, human soft skills are simultaneously growing in importance. For example, job-search Web site ZipRecruiter breaks new-collar positions into health care, engineering, technology and software; the skills that appeared most frequently in 2016 included JavaScript, HTML and hardware, but in 2017 those words disappeared from the top 10 list in favor of "customer service," "documentation skills" and "collaboration."

Innovative startups like **Mursion** are using virtual reality technology to develop realistic, immersive learning simulation environments just like simulators used by pilots to practice flying and surgeons to perfect complicated techniques – but for soft skills. Mursion allows people in high-people-engagement occupations to practice and master the interpersonal skills they need to work empathetically with clients and colleagues. "Through repeated short doses of simulated practice, Mursion trains learners to manage their emotional impulses, project empathy, de-escalate conflict and promote shared understanding," says Mursion CEO Mark Atkinson, whose company is on-track to deliver 60,000 simulations in 2018 to a variety of professionals. Use cases range from customer service representatives de-escalating a conflict to nurses or police officers having challenging conversations with patients and their families.

Meanwhile, another startup **PAIRIN** is using not only technology but research on job performance to measure and develop soft skills as part of its personalized career and professional development platform. With a focus on making hiring more equitable for "underemployed" people, PAIRIN measures an individual's soft skills (such as empathy, collaboration, creativity, curiosity, and thinking critically) but also provides them with guidance on the right careers and development tools to help them improve those skills.

*With a focus on making hiring more equitable for "underemployed" people, PAIRIN measures an individual's soft skills (such as empathy, collaboration, creativity, curiosity, and thinking critically) but also provides them with guidance on the right careers and development tools to help them improve those skills.*

Almost every occupation needs these soft skills, but few employees have them – including students who grew up in wealthy homes and attended strong schools. "PAIRIN was founded on the belief that all people have amazing value, but most of us never realize our potential," says co-founder and CEO Michael Simpson. "Most careers with good starting salaries and growth rates require some level of job-specific specialized education, but students first must develop the soft skills to complete the training. Those same skills are also 75-83% of the reason people succeed or fail in a job."

PAIRIN has administered more than 100,000 soft skills surveys to date and delivers personalized recommendations and coaching to those potential employees, sometimes through partnerships with high school internship programs, apprenticeship providers, and work training programs. It also uses predictive algorithms to help businesses interview and hire these employees based on the demonstrated soft skills and competencies that actually correlate with strong performance – rather than basing their decisions on loose proxies like college degree or biased judgements like "cultural fit" or interviewing skills – and machine learning to collect data from top performers and refine those algorithms over time.

Simpson says 40% of PAIRIN's business customers hired top performers in the last year that were technically "not qualified" by standard HR criteria like years of experience. For example, healthcare technology firm Swisslog eliminated education and experience requirements and doubled the diversity of its workforce while also increasing retention, saving millions of dollars in employee turnover costs.

These entrepreneurs note that finding ways to develop these soft skills is essential not only to helping people achieve their maximum potential as workers but also as humans.

*"Work wasn't diverse even a few decades ago. You worked with people you lived near, who looked like you, went to the same stores as you, and played on the same sports teams. Now, work is more like a UN meeting, but it happens every day,"*

"Work wasn't diverse even a few decades ago. You worked with people you lived near, who looked like you, went to the same stores as you, and played on the same sports teams. Now, work is more like a UN meeting, but it happens every day," says Simpson of PAIRIN. "In a connected society, the need to effectively communicate and collaborate has increased dramatically."

## Education Is Becoming Digital And Micro-Credentialed

As employers and jobs demand greater technical skills but also stronger, nuanced human skills – and the pace of change clipping along ever-faster – it is clearer than ever that workers need different forms of learning and credentialing. For most, formal learning is rarely relevant to the demands of work, with high school and college coursework often disconnected from the knowledge and skills a worker will need to obtain a job or advance in their career.

Before joining **New Markets Venture Partners** as a venture capitalist, I worked for three years at the **Bill & Melinda Gates Foundation**, studying and investing in higher education innovation. Our team collaborated with other forward-thinking funders, including **Lumina Foundation** and **University Ventures**, who share a common vision of a people-centered ecosystem for jobs where postsecondary institutions, employers and associations work together to create a more efficient and more transparent system that better meets the needs of the American public.

Over the past twenty years, the number of Americans pursuing postsecondary education has increased along with the number of jobs demanding advanced degrees, but that market is also changing in shape. In 2015, America's higher education system awarded 1.9 million bachelors degrees, the highest number on record. More than 1.1 million international students study at U.S. colleges and universities each year, with 25 of the world's top 50 universities based here. The importance of a postsecondary credential has grown so large to an individual's career prospects that Georgetown University calculates that a bachelors degree is worth $1 million more in lifetime earnings compared to a mere high school diploma.

That said, college has become incredibly expensive – and a difficult long-term gamble for many students who would be the first in their families to attend college, who come from low-income families, who need to earn a living wage immediately, or who might need to take out costly loans to finance their education. No wonder only 53% of college students graduate with a degree. Meanwhile, there is incredible variation between the graduation rates of institutions (particularly for underserved students or working adults) and the income potential by program of study. "Degrees still pay large dividends for the typical student, but there are many who will sink dollars into a degree that will see little or no return," notes Beth Akers, a former fellow with the non-partisan Brookings Institution.

As a result, startups like **Vemo Education** have cropped up to partner with schools who want to align incentives with student success while also easing the financial burden on those graduates. Vemo works with schools to build and maintain "income-share agreement" programs (ISAs) through which all or a part of a student's tuition is funded upfront in exchange for a small percentage of their earnings after graduation for a set period of time. Vemo serves nearly 30 postsecondary educational institutions, ranging from large public schools like Purdue University in Indiana to smaller private nonprofits, like Lackawanna College in Scranton, Pennsylvania to vocational schools and coding programs like **Kenzie Academy**. For example, training provider **New York Code + Design Academy's** ISA program offers upfront tuition funding in exchange for eight percent of income for 48 monthly payments. The program also includes a $40,000 minimum income threshold, so that graduates don't have to make a payment if they're not earning a sustainable salary.

*Vemo works with schools to build and maintain "income-share agreement" programs (ISAs) through which all or part of a student's tuition is funded upfront in exchange for a small percentage of their earnings after graduation for a set period of time.*

"We currently live in a system where a school's price isn't always aligned with the value that that school delivers to a student. What's worse, schools recruit students on inputs like aggressive marketing tactics and lavish amenity spending, not outcomes like early career pathways and earnings," explains Tonio DeSorrento, CEO of Vemo. "Schools are opting into this new outcomes-based funding model to democratize access to higher education, eliminate financial barriers to completing college, align price with value, and signal and deliver outcomes for their students."

**Holberton School** founder Julien Barbier put an even finer point on it in describing his program's deferred tuition model that charges 17% of students' income for 3.5 years: "If our students fail, we don't get paid and we die. And we should die."

The higher education sector is rapidly diversifying to address this more complicated post-secondary market for high school graduates and other adult learners. In the wake of the recession of 2008, massively open online courses (MOOCs) like **Coursera, Udacity** and **edX** emerged to offer free online college classes, later beginning to charge for access or credentials, and often partnering with companies and higher education institutions to deliver their content digitally to larger audiences.

"The biggest benefit will not come from college course MOOCs, but from MOOC-like programs providing students with focused occupational training and job placement without college matriculation," says professor Leonard J. Waks, author of a recent book on the evolution of MOOCs. "These programs will provide entry-level skills and real job opportunities in many fields for students from deindustrialized working class families - students who were driven into college solely for economic reasons when the industrial economy collapsed. Young people seeking to advance into leadership positions can then enroll in the university, and in many cases, employers will subsidize their tuition payments."

In addition, sub-baccalaureate credentials are growing much faster than bachelors and other advanced degrees. Between 2004 and 2014, certificates and associates degrees grew by 56% from 1.35 million to 2.1 million awarded each year, and the Lumina Foundation-backed Credential Engine project counted 334,114 different postsecondary credentials awarded annually including 66,997 certificate programs, 13,656 registered apprenticeships, 8,864 state-issued occupational licenses, 5,465 certifications, 1,718 bootcamp certificates, and 47 micromasters or nanodegrees. These are the credentials being used as data to drive hiring and promotions in the new collar economy.

Smaller in grain size but potentially larger in terms of impact are the open digital "badges" and "micro-credentials" that have been developed over the last five years, offered by industry associations, colleges, businesses, and nonprofits to represent mastery of specific relevant skills. "Without a way to capture, promote and transfer all of the learning that can occur within a broader connected learning ecology, we are limiting that ecology by discouraging engaged learning, making critical skills unattractive or inaccessible ... and ultimately, holding learners back from reaching their potential," wrote Mozilla officials in their seminal 2012 paper on badges' potential. With funding from the MacArthur Foundation, the Mozilla Foundation advanced technical standards (now overseen by the IMS Global Learning Consortium, where I served on the board) for Open Badges that individuals could collect and display as evidence of learning.

Because they are digital, portable, verifiable, competency-based, potentially "stackable" into larger signals such as degrees, and often embed actual evidence of their accomplishment, many see digital badges as the next wave of learning certification. Imagine a learner's unique knowledge as a constellation of badges – more trustworthy than a self-reported resume, more relevant than a college degree, more thorough than a transcript.

*Because they are digital, portable, verifiable, competency-based, potentially "stackable" into larger signals such as degrees, and often embed actual evidence of their accomplishment, many see digital badges as the next wave of learning certification.*

"Microcredentials and badges can undistort demand by allowing learners to assemble their own modular learning pathways rather than requiring them to rely on bundled certificates, diplomas, or degrees curated by educational institutions," notes business consulting firm McKinsey & Company. "Similarly, the unbundling of learning content through open educational resources, crowdsourcing of content, and virtual delivery of teaching and tutoring disintermediate the supply and thus reduce costs."

To organize this nascent market and provide the technical infrastructure to track myriad credentials and badges, companies like **Credly** offer universities and companies a platform to verify skills and competencies, issue portable and secure credentials, and mine the results for insights on how those credentials are used. Credly has issued tens of millions of credentials to millions of individuals through thousands of customer organizations, ranging from Association of International Certified Professional Accountants (AICPA) and Arizona State University's Honors Program to Microsoft and IBM.

"Resumes are self-reported and can be exaggerated; degrees are clumsy proxies for actual capabilities and knowledge; and the outcomes of on-the-job learning are opaque and not documented in a portable manner for employees," points out Jonathan Finkelstein, founder and CEO of Credly. "In a labor market based on knowledge and skills, digital credentials are now the currency of choice. Verified competencies are becoming a layer in the economy, powering the next generation of training, recruiting and staffing with richer, more transparent verified information about what people know and can do."

Indeed, it's not just credentials that are being unbundled – it's the learning itself. This trend has been accelerated by the availability of Internet connectivity and other technology, and more recently by the development of courseware that's responsive to the needs of students. Digital content, online assessments and adaptive courseware -- sometimes grouped together under the umbrella phrase "personalized learning" -- has allowed edtech providers, schools, and teachers to offer up "playlists" of instruction based on a diagnosis of student performance and progress. During my time at the Gates Foundation, we invested $22 million into eight such innovators – **Smart Sparrow**, **Acrobatiq**, **EdReady**, **Lumen Learning**, **Cogbooks**, **Cerego**, **Rice University OpenStax** and **Stanford Open edX**.

This work has gone hand-in-hand with a trend toward "competency-based" learning, in which students progress is based not on seat time but rather on knowledge attained and skills mastered, which must be proven before the student moves on to the next unit, the next grade, and so forth. The roots of this movement were put in place decades ago, when education moved from "norms" – comparing students against one another – to "standards" – defining what students must know and do.

Today's teachers and schools measure themselves and their students against content standards and increasingly against broader competencies – just as the workforce looks less for college degrees as proxies for knowledge and more for demonstrations of relevant skills.

# A Kaleidoscope Of Flexible Jobs

Digitizing learning and work allows both to be broken down into pieces and remixed in more customized ways that fit people's needs and skills in the moment, and in scalable ways that can grow with the needs of the economy – and of these individuals – over time.

Many entrepreneurs have stepped forward to address this opportunity. "The sheer number of new products available for both employers and job seekers trying to navigate and succeed in the job market has increased exponentially in recent years," according to the **Rockefeller Foundation**. "Technological solutions can be designed and deployed in ways that produce value to both the "demand side" (employers) and "supply side" (job seekers/employees) of the job market."

One category with particular promise is digital talent platforms that match workers and jobs, which business consulting firm McKinsey & Company has found often increase the number of hours worked, benefitting companies as well as workers. "Even if a small fraction of inactive youth and adults use these platforms to work a few hours per week, the economic impact would be significant," notes McKinsey. "Online talent platforms help put the right people in the right jobs, thereby increasing their productivity along with their job satisfaction."

"Companies are increasingly looking for ways to fill the labor shortage gap while maintaining financial agility to shrink and expand their workforce as needed," agrees Wade Burgess of **Shiftgig**, a platform for connecting hourly workers with the companies who need them, such as food service, events, hotel and hospitality, and retail businesses. "And workers are becoming empowered to choose where, when, how often, and for whom they work, with lifestyles that either want or require flexibility."

*Shiftgig uses predictive matching algorithms, tagging candidates with their previous experiences and skills, as well as workflow automation technology to screen workers for potential "gigs" and provide companies with qualified labor on demand.*

Shiftgig uses predictive matching algorithms, tagging candidates with their previous experiences and skills, as well as workflow automation technology to screen workers for potential "gigs" and provide companies with qualified labor on demand. Shiftgig has nearly 50,000 workers in its database and has connected them with nearly 3,000 client companies for hundreds of thousands of shifts worked to date. Many of these workers use Shiftgig for a "side hustle" alongside their full-time job.

The rise of these contingent jobs has happened more quickly than have changes to our policies. As such, many states and courts are currently deciding how whether such workers are independent contractors or employees -- and what that might mean for rights such as minimum wage, insurance benefits (which some seek to disaggregate from employment more broadly), the ability to unionize, and freedom from employment discrimination.

But Burgess describes his "gig" workers as empowered, navigating their own path. "Many of the primary gig worker personas view work as a component of life to be harmonized with other functions in life," he says. "They value freedom and flexibility as a lifestyle choice. Most gig workers operate much more like entrepreneurs, relying on their own initiatives and ambition to chart their course, rather than relying on a company or boss to do this for them." He adds that the defining quality of many of these workers is their soft skills, such as communication and customer service, which translate well into multiple on-demand opportunities.

Is this flexibility the future of work? Software giant Intuit predicts that 40% of the workforce will be made up of such "contingent" workers by 2020, up from 30% in 2010. These workers "increase business efficiency, agility and flexibility" (and cost employers less) and also have "a greater say in when and how much they work, giving them greater work-life balance."

In fact, one of the fastest growing companies in the country right now is, **WeWork**, a shared workspace company that is capitalizing both on the increase in freelance workers as well as the shifting real estate needs of companies. Since its launch in New York City in 2010, WeWork has expanded to 253 locations in 22 countries, managing more than 1.3 million square metres of office space, and is valued at $40 billion. "WeWork was, and still is, a company that's making its best efforts to create a world where people make a life and not just a living," says CEO Adam Neumann of his company, which also offers coding bootcamp programs (powered by **Flatiron School**, a recent acquisition), shared living spaces, a gym, and soon, even elementary schools on-site. With 5,500 employees and growing, WeWork has has the potential to serve hundreds of thousands of freelance learners and earners in the future.

That said, it's important to recognize that many gig workers prefer longer assignments that offer job security and benefits. In addition, independent contractor laws need to better balance the needs of employers and their gig employees -- laws that currently favor those who run the platforms and demand the services. As we update these policies and laws, we must balance risk and reward while also maintaining flexibility for both employers and employees.

# Conclusion

As these innovative new companies mature and scale their reach and impact, they have the potential to achieve not just improved efficiencies and shareholder returns, but something far loftier: more equitable outcomes for people, including income as well as satisfaction with their jobs and happiness in their lives.

Consider McKinsey's finding that there are nearly 100 million people in the United States and European Union alone who are either unemployed, underemployed, or out of the workforce entirely. Many of these are women or people outside of the core working ages – the very young or the very old. The widespread adoption of these new technologies could match these workers with the lifelong learning they need and the better jobs they desire – increasing equity and boosting GDP simultaneously.

These benefits stand to accrue not only to nations more broadly, but to individuals, the families they support, the children they raise, and the communities with which they engage. Indeed, these "new collar" jobs not only pay more, but often hold greater potential for advancement, are often more creative, and can offer greater flexibility and better work-life balance than the jobs they are replacing.

It is my belief that these startups – and hundreds more yet to be identified and written about – are paving the way toward a world just beyond the horizon in which humans, augmented by technology, can do more work in less time. In addition to such productivity gains, we are approaching a time in which school, work and life are better integrated, rather than pitting work and school against life and family in a zero-sum game in which we study to work and then work to live.

Instead, these technology, learning, and economic developments have the potential to enhance our satisfaction with our work and our live. With every activity in which we engage better aligned toward our interests and skills, flexibly arranged around one another, we might actually strengthen and affirm our overall purpose with every step forward.

## The People-First New Ecosystem for Jobs:

### Startups and Investors Transforming How We Learn and Earn

| | Higher Education | Workforce | Infrastructure & New Models |
|---|---|---|---|
| **Knowledge delivery and credentialing (platforms and courseware)** | Acrobatiq<br>Cogbooks<br>Coursera<br>EdReady<br>edX<br>EverFi<br>Fishtree/Follett<br>Khan Academy<br>Lumen Learning<br>Minerva<br>Rice OpenStax<br>StraighterLine<br>Smart Sparrow | Cornerstone<br>Degreed<br>EdCast<br>Grovo<br>Lynda.com<br>Mindflash<br>NovoEd<br>Pluralsight<br>Simplilearn<br>Udacity<br>Udemy | 2U<br>Burning Glass<br>Credly/Acclaim<br>D2L<br>Instructure/Canvas<br>LinkedIn<br>Pearson Embanet<br>Trilogy Education<br>Vemo |
| **Alternative pathways to the traditional system** | AppAcademy<br>CodeSchool<br>General Assembly<br>Flatiron School<br>Galvanize<br>Holberton School<br>Lambda School<br>Kenzie Academy<br>Revature | Care.com<br>Elance<br>Flexjobs<br>Freelancer<br>Guru<br>People Productions<br>Presence Learning<br>Shiftgig<br>Uber/Lyft<br>Upwork | Greenhouse<br>Hired<br>Humu<br>Knotel<br>Regus<br>WeWork |
| **Emergent Learning Technologies For Adults** | Grammarly<br><br>Mursion<br><br>PAIRIN | | |
| **Ecosystem Nonprofits** | Code.org<br>Digital Promise<br>EDUCAUSE<br>Education Superhighway<br>i4j Innovation for Jobs<br>Jobs For The Future<br>Mozilla Foundation | | |

| | |
|---|---|
| **Impact-Oriented Venture Capital Investors** | Exceed Capital Partners<br>Learn Capital<br>New Markets Venture Partners<br>Owl Ventures<br>Reach Capital<br>SJF Ventures<br>University Ventures |
| **Foundations** | Bill & Melinda Gates Foundation<br>Chan Zuckerberg Initiative<br>Emerson Collective<br>Ewing Marion Kauffman Foundation<br>Ford Foundation<br>Hewlett Foundation<br>Lumina Foundation<br>MacArthur Foundation<br>Omidyar Network<br>Rockefeller Foundation<br>Walton Family Foundation<br>W.K. Kellogg Foundation |

**Allen Blue** is the vice president of product management and cofounder of LinkedIn, the online professional network. At LinkedIn, he is responsible for the company's overall product strategy. He also sponsors LinkedIn's work and education products within the Economic Graph team, including the products and platforms supporting the Skillful Initiative (a joint effort including LinkedIn, Microsoft, the state of Colorado, and the Markle Foundation to close the middle-skills gap in the United States). He advises several Silicon Valley startups, most of which are focused on improving health and education. He sat on the U.S. Department of Commerce's Data Advisory Council, helping guide the department's efforts to make its data broadly available to U.S. businesses. Blue serves on the boards of the Hope Street Group, a nonprofit that focuses on bringing economic opportunity to Americans through a combination of policy and practice, and Change.org, an online destination for making grassroots-driven change easier. Before LinkedIn, Blue cofounded SocialNet.com, an online dating service, and graduated from Stanford University.

# Networks and Ecosystems for the Future of Work

By Allen Blue, Cofounder and VP Product Management, LinkedIn

In 2004, when LinkedIn wasn't yet a year old, we started taking the fledgling network out on the road. I distinctly remember meeting a group of curious professionals in a borrowed room at a law office in downtown Mountain View, then the location of LinkedIn's own tiny office.

Standing at the front of the room with the website projected live over my shoulder, I explained that LinkedIn was professional people search and that a LinkedIn member could solve any business problem using it. I asked the audience to suggest a problem, and someone gamely offered that she needed help designing compensation policy.

A search using the clunky V1 interface found 15 professionals who had mentioned compensation policy in their profiles. The LinkedIn network at that point had only a few hundred thousand members, but our searches rarely came up empty. Two of the resulting profiles belonged to people who were two degrees away from me: Each of them knew someone whom I also knew. I explained to the audience, which was starting to get the idea, that now I just needed to ask someone for an introduction. Soon I could be buying breakfast for the compensation policy specialist who would help solve my problem.

I tried two or three more suggested problems and some members of the audience seemed intrigued about the possibilities.

Normally when I tell this story, I follow up by saying that none of the people at that early show-and-tell started using LinkedIn the next day, week, or even year, despite their interest. It turns out that using professional people search requires people to think differently about how they work, and that kind of change is always difficult.

But what they saw at that meeting was the core idea that had led us to create LinkedIn:

*Networks are powerful, and a professional with the combined knowledge of and access to hundreds of others can achieve more than anyone trying to go it alone.*

That idea should have been obvious to me, but I have to admit it wasn't. I had started my working life in a very traditional business, the theater. As a theater designer I was about as disconnected from the world of high tech as I could be, coming close only when operating lights and sound for the occasional shareholder meeting or company all-hands.

But in 1997, my friend David, someone I had worked with in the theater, called and asked what I was up to. Might I be interested in joining his team at a new company, an online dating site?

I was at a point in my career where I was happy to consider new things, so David introduced me to the leader of this new startup, a guy named Reid. We had dinner and a great conversation, and he asked me to come by the next day to talk to the team about joining it as the creative director.

My entry into the world of technology came through my network, as had nearly all my other job opportunities. Which productions I designed, which gigs I got to work, and which jobs I could take were almost entirely governed by who I knew and had worked with previously.

So why, when starting LinkedIn with that very same Reid Hoffman in 2003, did I ignore the power of a network?

At the time, I thought of "networking" as something artificial, unpleasant. I didn't trust the people who flourished at it. But I also saw that networking is different than networks. Why did I not actively make networks part of my professional life?

It wasn't until much later that I could articulate my resistance. I was speaking with Gustavo Rabin, a legendary executive coach, when he asked me a question: What makes a professional successful?

I gave him what I thought was the obvious answer: Successful professionals have great ideas and are very good at their jobs.

He smiled and pulled out a piece of paper. He wrote "great ideas" and circled it, and then he wrote "great at your job" next to it.

Then he told me there was a third element essential to success and that most Americans overlook it. Alongside the first two items, he wrote,

*"gets help from others."*

I've tried to adopt this third principle in my work and to pay it forward to others. But Gustavo's point about U.S. professional culture (the same applies to many other business cultures) really sticks with me: Most professionals overlook the importance of relationships and getting help from other people.

# Profiles and Networks

In the real world, we manage our networks in our heads. When faced with a question, we perform a mental survey of our relationships, seeking someone we know who can help.

It's not a perfect system; we frequently miss people who can help. We expend a lot of effort on this sorting. And, crucially, we can only seriously consider the people we already know, and they make up but a tiny fraction of those who might be able to help.

LinkedIn allows members to create professional profiles for themselves, to post their experience, education, skills, and interests, as well as the kinds of opportunities they seek. For example, I can indicate where I went to school, my previous jobs, and my current work at LinkedIn, all typical résumé stuff. But my profile also includes what I've written, and those articles, published on LinkedIn and elsewhere, clearly indicate my knowledge and interests. When I answer questions publicly or follow topics that interest me, I'm not simply participating in a public professional conversation, I'm establishing who Allen Blue is in a way that allows others to understand who I am and what I know.

Further, the LinkedIn system can extract additional information from profiles. For instance, I might not mention a specific programming language I've used, but LinkedIn can frequently infer my expertise in that language from other information in my profile. LinkedIn then presents such inferences to me so I can add them if I want.

Most importantly, LinkedIn allows me to form relationships, called connections, with other users. Those connections can, with my permission, add content to my profile. They can write a long-form comment on my skills and contributions and detail what working with me is like. And each can endorse individual skills on my profile, sometimes reinforcing my mastery of a skill (for instance, they might be the third person to give me a shout-out for product management) and sometimes patting me on the back for something new (being the first to suggest, say, that I excel at strategy).

While not everyone keeps a full and up-to-date profile, a professional can now effectively search the knowledge of the people around her. She's much more likely to find someone she knows who can help with her specific problem than if she were trying to solve this problem from her own memory.

Search lowers the cost of the network survey, turning it into a tool professionals can apply more frequently and to more than just the most urgent or intractable problems. As I mentioned earlier, professionals usually don't think about people search first. LinkedIn works hard to build the idea of personal knowledge and expertise into all its products, including search.

Those connections also give our members the ability to search the knowledge of my connections' connections. My search extends to all LinkedIn members, who are ordered by their degree of distance from me: My connections are first degree, their connections second degree, and so on.

For the first time, the network survey can include more than just a professional's direct connections. Her connections connect her to exponentially more professionals: If she has 100 connections and each connection has that many, she can tap into the knowledge of up to 10,000 professionals in a single search.

Let me return to 2004, when we were trying to demonstrate this power. With LinkedIn, I could have searched for that compensation policy expert by quickly finding a person I knew, or a person I knew who could help by making an introduction.

This capability does not replace our networks, but it does make them easier to use effectively. We still keep in our heads a core part of our networks – our knowledge of each of our direct relationships.

I can't remember the full list of relationships I have. But if someone asks me about my relationship with a specific person I can quickly and easily characterize it. How do I know that person, and how well? How well do they know me? Can they help with this specific need? And is now a good time to reach out?

So if during my search for a compensation policy expert I find exactly the right person in the second degree, I still need to decide whether our mutual connection is the right person to ask for an introduction. Because I have a notion of the strength and quality of each of my own relationships, I can determine whether to ask for that introduction and, if so, how.

While network technology will someday be able to represent the nuanced quality of any person-to-person relationship, it can't do so now. Machines can draw some coarse conclusions about a given relationship and even about a given person's relationships in general, but knowing at a given moment whether a specific relationship can be helpful for a particular need still requires a person.

*This teaming up of human and machine lets any professional get help more easily, help that can make her more successful. A professional with a strong network can simply do more and do it better.*

\*

258

A network, of course, is not enough. "It's not what you know, but who you know" doesn't mean you don't need to know anything. Skills form half of one's ability to perform, attitude, the other half.

I'm using the word "skill" to include the notion of competency: the demonstrated ability to do something at a particular level. If skills are what you know how to do, competencies are the things you do well. Generally, professionals build competencies through practice and experience.

Employers, educators, assessors, certifiers, and unions have long cataloged, codified, and evaluated skills using tools such as apprenticeship systems, civil service exams, assessment tests, and professional certification. These systems grew because employers needed certainty that a given person could actually do a particular kind of work. A guild would certify the quality of its members' work by setting and maintaining high standards for apprentices to progress to journeyman and later master. Certifications allowed employers to know that a given service provider (for instance, a doctor or electrician) would perform his or her work at a high standard.

Over the years, some certifications have become mandatory. Lawyers must pass the bar; doctors must receive MDs and board certifications; pilots must be flight-rated. Other certifications, while not legally required, give professionals access to opportunities that aren't available to those without. Whole credentialing industries have appeared, producing a vast variety of certifications – some with little or no value.

A common general certification is the college degree. A bachelor's degree, of course, doesn't express fitness for any specific profession. Employers, however, treat a bachelor's degree as a necessary requirement for many jobs, believing the degree assures a certain basic level of education and skills.

Employers and educators generally divide skills into two groups, hard and soft. A person who can perform something specific and detailed – say, Microsoft Excel – has that hard skill. Soft skills apply more broadly to most work situations and include, say, the ability to collaborate, to communicate well, and to problem-solve. Employers typically see a bachelor's degree as an indicator of some competency in these soft skills.

Knowledge of technology, which doesn't usually come with a certification, does provide a similar degree of validation in helping professionals get help from others.

*Technology can also help professionals get more leverage from skills and competencies. We now have the ability to fully understand the value of many kinds of certifications.*

Certifications were developed so employers would know they were engaging qualified workers. But as economies grew more complex and employers began to consider workers from other regions, they had to decide whether or not to take an unfamiliar certification seriously. I need to hire glassblowers, but should I trust the ability of a glassblower from the next town over?

I could have one of my own workers assess the quality of this stranger's glasswork. That's easy to do when you're hiring just one glassblower, but harder when you need to hire hundreds or thousands, each of whom has certification from a different source, or when the person in charge of hiring doesn't do the same job as the worker to be hired.

Some people and businesses have taken advantage of the complexity and ambiguity of such situations to create certifications – degrees, certificates, memberships, etc. – that have no real value. By using LinkedIn, however, we can observe how much stock employers actually put in a specific credential because we can see, in detail, how hiring happens.

Several years ago, LinkedIn experimented with a product called Outcomes-Based College Rankings. We looked at the most competitive jobs in a given field (say, accounting) and cross-referenced them with the detailed profiles of accountants who actually were hired. We were able to say, with high confidence, that employers consider degrees from certain institutions to be strong indicators of value in a given role because they tended to hire the alumni of those schools.

If a system records information about people and their certifications, about their jobs, and about their hiring, that system can rank certifications, going from most reliable to least reliable. Students and professionals can understand immediately which certifications matter in certain circumstances and which matter in none.

Such a system can also break down the primacy of certifications, specifically the university degrees that employers use as a minimum hiring requirement for certain jobs. Employers could consider many more candidates for jobs if they removed the requirement of a college education, but that would demand an alternative, trustworthy way to provide direct assessment of skills.

A system that looked beyond a college education could allow a single professional to bring together assessments of all of his or her skills and competencies. I could, for instance, show successful completion of classes in specific skills; online samples of my work that demonstrate others; results of assessment tests I have taken, including perhaps assessments from the potential employer; a skill mastered during military service that had a name different than the one recognized by a civilian employer; and social certification of my skills from reputable people.

Employers – both companies and individuals – could see all of that information and determine the value of each microcertification by outcomes-based analysis. This could open up ways to build much broader and more inclusive hiring pipelines that include candidates who didn't finish college but, say, gained their skills in the military or mastered a skill without obtaining a well-known certification or degree that can act as a proxy for their employability.

Earlier I mentioned the importance of one's attitude toward work. A successful attitude may be reflected in one's drive, promptness, grit, and passion for the work. Importantly, professional attitude will also be shaped by a candidate's values, which will, ideally, align with the hiring company's culture. Employers typically can test a worker's attitude through interviews and references. A network-based system allows more powerful referencing, although nothing is likely to replace human judgment about whether a worker has an attitude that will make them successful in a specific work situation.

## Changing Skills

Technology changes things dramatically. It brings us new capabilities. It allows for the creation of the social network powering LinkedIn and the big data that paints a portrait of the whole economy.

And it transforms work. A lot of technological innovation targets improving how we work, making us faster, stronger, more accurate, more predictable, and more profitable as we do our jobs.

*But two things are different in how technology changes work now. First, the pace. Technology has never changed work so quickly. Second, the scope. Technology has never had the potential to transform so many types of work.*

Every year LinkedIn looks at the top emerging skills. Because most LinkedIn users keep their profiles up-to-date, the system is able to identify new skills as they emerge in the marketplace. In the past few years, skills such as Node.js, Kafka, Facebook ad-targeting, and machine learning have emerged. We've found that tech skills dominate each year's list of new skills.

Why? Companies and individuals constantly create new technologies, some of which are adopted widely enough to count as important skills. Engineers and designers can easily create technologies because the tools they use – code editors, compilers, cloud computing – are cheap when compared to nearly any other form of technology. In addition, these technologies are especially good at making other information-based technologies successful. A new programming language allows easier development of internet-based technology; a new collaborative word processor allows a high-tech marketing firm to market online more easily.

The concentration of productivity in this area also touches "real world" technologies. Think of biotechnology, medicine, architecture, construction, entertainment, and journalism: Information technology can improve any work with an information component.

The more that work becomes mediated by technology, the more easily it can adopt these kinds of transformations. It's easy to see how technology impacts a job like journalism; it isn't as easy to see how it would transform truck driving. But maps are information, logistics are information. And as sensors have become more readily available, truckers have turned to high tech to ensure they're on the right roads at the right times carrying the right loads to the right destinations.

As more companies become information technology companies, information technology skills become more valuable. And information technology skills rise (and fall) faster than any others.

Information storage and processing power also change work. Early techniques of information storage limited storage to just a few kilobytes per machine – enough to store text and a few pictures, but little else. And processing power was equally limited.

Information technology, according to Intel cofounder Gordon Moore's famous law, now doubles in power about every two years. This exponential progress makes processing power and storage plentiful and brings us a whole new set of capabilities.

Where once machines could make only limited decisions, which were governed by strict rules and specific situations, they can now outperform human minds on a large number of tasks.

A machine that is able to make decisions can now do things that five years ago only a human could do. As Erik Brynjolfsson and Andrew McAfee wrote in their book *The Second Machine Age*, technology once augmented muscles, but now it augments minds.

And the power behind this technology increases exponentially, driving ever more applications and doing so faster and faster.

Let's set aside the likelihood that machines will fully replace people in some jobs. This happens regularly – after all, a "computer" used to be the title for a person who did calculations. But before a role is replaced, it will first be changed by technology. The role will typically evolve from having a human doing the work to having a human operating a machine that does the work.

Surgeons now rely on automation while they operate; drivers rely on geo-positioning and navigation systems to find their way; authors rely on word processors to catch spelling errors.

Every job in which some bit of decision-making can be off-loaded to a machine can, in theory, become faster, safer, more productive, and more profitable. Eventually, an entrepreneur will seize the opportunity and make the change real.

The increasing pace of change puts a lot of pressure on older systems, such as the certifications system I sketched out earlier. If I have a generation to embrace a new skill, my trade guild will take it in stride. The apprentice system will graduate journeymen and masters who have that skill and who will, in turn, start teaching it. If I only have a decade, I can still count on O*NET, the Occupational Information Network, from the U.S. government to identify skills that my university should begin to teach.

If I only have five years, these tried-and-true systems can't keep up with the pace of change. Schools may end up teaching skills that have already become outdated, and they may not teach what individuals and companies need to be successful. Company training materials may not evolve as quickly as workers need them to.

At LinkedIn, we have a front-row seat for these changes. CEO Jeff Weiner coined the term "Economic Graph" to describe what LinkedIn can see: As individuals, companies, and schools use LinkedIn for job-seeking, hiring, sales prospecting, business formation, information exchange, purchase decisions, and much more, the network effectively becomes a living portrait of the world's economy.

When we look at the LinkedIn network as the Economic Graph, it offers us an additional and more up-to-date system to react to the changes occurring in the world of work. When a new skill arises in professional profiles or in job listings, the graph can flag it quickly. When we are able to identify skill gaps – gaps between the supply and demand for a specific skill in a particular labor market at a given time – individuals, employers, and educators can act on that information for their own success.

Let's take an example. One recent LinkedIn study of the Denver area showed a skills gap for medical coding technicians, professionals who place standard codes on treatments and diagnoses for record-keeping purposes and insurance payments. Denver's economy was expanding and people were moving to the metro area, increasing the demand for health care. Hospitals, in turn, needed people with coding skills. Three local schools taught people these skills, which created an opportunity for those institutions to work with the hiring hospitals to improve curriculum and to attract more students.

Government can also deploy such insights. For example, LinkedIn worked with the mayor's office in New York City to identify the skill gaps around technology jobs. The city responded to the data by working with local schools – some public, some not – to increase training for key skills.

264

The demand for medical coding in Denver will go up and down. And while the need for tech workers in NYC will continue to rise, the specific skills and skill gaps will change, especially as new skills come on the scene. Many factors will determine when and how these changes will occur, and we can't confidently and responsibly claim we know in advance what will happen.

Our goal should not be to predict the future, but to support an ecosystem of people, organizations, and data that will respond to change quickly, constructively, and compassionately.

## Building an Ecosystem

We pay a lot of attention to large-scale efforts, whether in developing new federal tax policy or social safety net programs, to change our economy for the better. But many of the things that affect us are local: my employer, my employer's suppliers and competitors, my kids' schools, the amount of traffic on my commute, construction in my neighborhood, the distance to my doctor's office, beliefs and prejudices held by the people with whom I interact, and so much more.

While these local forces ultimately connect to large-scale institutions that have impact on tax policy and international law, all of us feel the local effects most strongly.

In the last few years, I have met thousands of people trying to change the economic prospects of their local communities. Some run mentoring programs, manage community colleges, run businesses, or attempt to bring entrepreneurship training to the local prison population.

Each one faces a problem: How do I gain customers, attract students, or recruit mentors? How do I develop the right curriculum, increase revenue, or get in front of individual workers?

Organizations address many of these problems through networks, reaching out to customers, partners, and employees. Each part operates with its own goals, a classic economic ecosystem. But we know this ecosystem leaves too many people behind, and as technology changes, our economy risks leaving even more people behind, especially as jobs change and even disappear.

We know some of the circumstances under which the economically at-risk can be successfully brought along. For instance, we know skills training can open up brand-new opportunities for them. We also know individuals sometimes need expert advice to find that training and discover its value. We also know that many of the people who need this training the most can't afford it, can't take time off work, or can't leave their kids.

Some problems are deeply rooted. For instance, needed soft skills rarely change while needed hard skills change often and quickly. Hard skills are easier to pick up if your soft skills – particularly curiosity, grit, adaptability – are robust. But soft skills begin developing in childhood, so that a flexible workforce requires good early childhood education to prepare it for constant learning and retraining.

Our goal is an ecosystem that achieves three things:

1. It must function at the local level with local players

2. It must help remove barriers blocking valuable ecosystem participants

3. It must encourage innovation on unsolved problems

The valuable participants in this ecosystem must include at least:

- Employers of all sizes and types, including gig work, contract work, and entrepreneurship

- Trainers and educators at all levels

- Individual workers

- Assessment and certification providers

- Navigators (mentors as well as career and social benefits guides)

- Governments at all levels and across many functions

- Chambers of Commerce and other employer organizations

- Unions and guilds

All of these participants are already in the market. But to make them successful, the ecosystem needs at least two additional elements, both of which I've discussed before.

First, reputation. For any participant to choose the right partner or provider, she must know what solutions actually work. Individuals should feel complete confidence choosing a training provider; mentors should feel they can direct mentees to solutions that will actually work.

Reputation can also drive innovation. An entrepreneur may not be able to outcompete a well-known, established player. But if a new business can find a quick way to prove its effectiveness, it can shake up the established order and maybe even see its way to the top.

Second, data. An informed educator who has an up-to-date view of the local skill gaps can find business partners and develop curricula that attract students. An informed union can make sure it prepares its members for the changing needs of their employers. An informed government can understand which skill development courses will need additional funding or require child support provisions that recognize the difficulties posed by long classes.

And like reputation, data helps innovators discover opportunities. In a region where skills training is insufficient, an entrepreneurial educator can see a chance to enter a hungry market.

LinkedIn's vision is to create economic opportunity for every member of the global workforce. Even though LinkedIn started as a network of white-collar professionals, it has become a network for people in all types of work. In the end, we hope it will include all 3.3 billion people in the global workforce.

Economic opportunity means having the resources necessary to control one's own life. And that means enough income to live on, to support others, to manage downturns, to invest, and to enjoy a secure life. And it also means enough income and economic power to be a good citizen, which influence and perhaps change the world in ways small or large.

We provide a network to help the ecosystem function. We already share our data with governments, and we have developed products to help companies make better decisions, with more to come. And we hope to build that notion of reputation into how the network functions.

We are not and will not be the only provider; many organizations are building powerful sources of data and reputation. So regardless of which sources support it, a healthy ecosystem will be able to respond more quickly to change and will enable the economy to leave fewer behind.

# Changing a Culture

Some of the problems that must be solved to make our ecosystem successful will require cultural change.

As I said earlier, Americans don't typically see getting help as a key part of success. This blindness is cultural: Our heroes almost always achieve their goals on their own – they pull themselves up by their own bootstraps. That notion aligns with the country's veneration of individualism and achievement, and most U.S. workers carry this mythos with them from the greater culture into the company culture.

As business executives often acknowledge, institutional cultural changes are the hardest to make. If culture is the way we act together, then company culture is the way we work together. Once a company settles on a habitual way of doing things, executives must exert a lot of leadership to change it. Without such leadership, cultural change rarely happens quickly.

Culture affects hiring. A given company may hire people from a certain university, say, or people who look or act a particular way. Promotions and internal opportunities may happen the same way.

Culture frequently expresses itself in processes. A hiring process, for instance, might include a step where the hiring team will discuss what it knows about the school someone has graduated from. That becomes part of every hiring conversation and, from that point on, the culture selects in particular ways.

Companies find building diverse workforces difficult because it involves all three of these forces: external culture, unspoken internal culture, and process. Diversity hiring requires extraordinarily focused and consistent leadership from the very top of the organization.

Convention can also stand in the way of organizations hiring employees who don't have a college degree. How can a company that wishes to broaden its pipeline embrace the idea of nontraditional candidates? How can an individual worker comfortably select a nontraditional entrance into the workforce, rather than seeking the traditional four-year degree? How can a career counselor recommend an unconventional path with any confidence?

Organizations will need to pay more attention to high-quality, nontraditional candidates who succeed at their company. As confidence grows in the abilities of workers who don't have college degrees, so will their presence in hiring pipelines. But such a change may be generational. Cultural change that takes place in less than a generation requires tremendous focused effort from leaders. If that effort comes, from either government or extremely influential employers, and it is reinforced by a system, major cultural shifts could happen more quickly. This may be an issue on which influential participants in the ecosystem have to act in concert.

# A Stable and Just Ecosystem

It's certainly not a new observation that economic power allows some people to influence our societies while excluding others. Economic opportunity is the first step on the path to a powerful voice in the way the world works. And people will become angry and act out if they feel cut off from that opportunity.

A few years ago, for example, people threw rocks at Silicon Valley.

Well, the target was actually the commuter buses chartered by Google to bring employees from San Francisco to the company's main offices in Mountain View, 30 miles south. Buses from other tech companies were also attacked.

The rock-throwers turned out to be activists protesting the use of San Francisco streets by these buses and what they saw as the growing economic inequality in the city. San Francisco was already changing profoundly as high-tech companies transformed everything from the skyline to housing prices to the way city government works.

The Valley has definitely changed the city, introducing problems typically caused by rapid gentrification. In a way, the protests made sense – especially in a city like San Francisco that has a long history of labor and political activism.

At the time, a friend pointed out that these protests were also part of something larger. The eager young people working at tech companies were a new kind of haves, and the activists were fighting on behalf of a new kind of have-nots. The direct beneficiaries of the tech boom were resented by those on the outside who were simply hoping to enjoy some residual uplift.

In many cases, of course, they have. Application of technology has lifted billions out of poverty, improved our health, and enriched our lives. But our societies are becoming more unequal, as meaningful power is held in the hands of fewer people with stronger tools for maintaining their advantage. We still don't know the outcome of the rise of social media and ubiquitous, technology-mediated communication. But some people, organizations, and governments are already using these new communication tools to advance their own agendas in ways we did not anticipate. These tools, amplified by machine learning and artificial intelligence, will only become more powerful as time goes on.

In the face of this growing inequality, we struggle to understand the new economy and new way of working. We know that the cultural and economic dislocations of the last industrial revolution swiftly brought war, famine, depression, and ideologies that killed millions. Change is likely to come even faster this time.

The ecosystem we support must produce ways for individuals to roll with the punches and must also generate economic opportunity and power for more of us. Our new ecosystem will be the product of millions of organizations and billions of people and, to be stable and just, will require the participation and creativity of workers at every level and from every corner of the globe.

I wrote earlier about leadership: Where does it really come from? In a truly networked world with a flourishing ecosystem, it comes from everywhere, arising when potential leaders have the economic power to assert influence. And power is only fairly applied when those who will be led have the economic power to push back.

### #

Patricia Olby Kimondo is the CEO and founder of People Productions, a Swedish based company passionate about finding true talent. After hiring over 20000 young people Patricia learned that talent comes in many shapes and sizes and that potential is stronger than past. And almost always a better predictor for future success than hard skills. So People Productions uses their experience, data and AI to develop brands and solutions that help people and organizations move into the future of work. The current portfolio of brands includes Lärarförmedlarna & Vikarie Direkt, Sweden's leading recruiting and temp agencies for schools, Pamoja Solutions software development and Naked Work media platform and broadcasting.

# THE SUCCESS OF DUAL CUSTOMER LOVE IN MODERN TEMP BUSINESS

by Patricia Olby Kimondo

*In the last 20 years the world has seen amazing technological change at a faster pace than any time before in history. Regardless of whether we like it or not, humans are now entering a global, transparent, data-driven world whose logic will be all digital connected 24/7. Technology is changing everything, everywhere. We already see job automation replacing humans in the workplace, and there is little evidence that we can change this trend. What can we do? The answer I believe, is to use technology to become more human. To use it to enable us to be more caring, curious, creative, and -- most of all -- empathetic and kind. As we at People Productions engage in developing solutions for the future of work -- for those looking for good jobs and for those looking for great people -- this is what we aim for: To become more human.*

# Where it started

I grew up in Sweden in the 70s and 80s. My parents had immigrated in
the late 60s, when my father left his native Kenya in the aftermath of
the independence movement. My grandfather had decided it was best
for my father to study in Europe, so he ended up in Sweden where he
met my mother. My parents often told me stories of how, when they
were young, lived an exciting life in international and intellectual
circles. This was a time when Sweden welcomed immigrants to work in
blue-collar industries. My father was a business student who looked for
opportunities in business, but being an African immigrant in Sweden
at that time was unusual, and employers were reluctant to hire him.
The struggle to find a job became a little too hard after my siblings and
I came along, so he ended up working as an industry technician. He
eventually became very skilled at his job, though I am sure he would
have excelled in other areas. I never heard him complain. On the
contrary, he was always proud of his accomplishments; he just
reframed, adapted to circumstances, and made the best of it. He
eventually became an elder in the Swedish-Kenyan society and used
his experience and the skills he developed as an early immigrant to
help new immigrants adapt and flourish.

My mother was a preschool and kindergarten teacher with a deep
passion for her work, pioneering as one of the first in Sweden in the
late 1980s to start a charter preschool and kindergarten. The core idea
of putting children first and teachers second defied accepted
pedagogical methods at the time.

As an entrepreneur in a field where most people had no concept of
what an entrepreneur does or how a company functions, she
experienced the same skepticism that has met many entrepreneurs
and early thinkers. Luckily she was a strong-headed woman and was
seldom deterred by people's opinions. I tell this story of my parents
because I am sure it has influenced the way I see the world.

I learned early that life is full of struggles and hurdles -- as well as
opportunities -- and that people's potential can easily be overlooked
where there isn't enough variety and diversity. I also learned that if you
want to go somewhere where there is no road you probably have to
build it yourself. So in 1999, when I left my job in recruiting and HR at
a large global IT-company to start a recruiting and temp agency for
teachers, most people around me thought I was crazy.

At that time my sister, who had graduated from a teaching school, was travelling the world to broaden her experience. But when she came home and started looking for work, it became apparent that job matching in this sector was inefficient. Schools were desperate for teachers, but there was something about the job matching process that didn't work. My idea was to use insights from my work in HR to better match work with opportunity in education. Because of the shortage of teachers on the market, we wanted to target talented people who might be curious of a possible teaching career.

The early years were a rollercoaster. A lot of effort went into "building a road" explaining the business idea to our potential school customers. Schools were not used to buying services. But I firmly believed it was time to say goodbye to the old temp lists and endless calls, and help schools move to the 21st-century method of hiring temps. Quite soon I realized an interesting fact that had nothing to do with the actual service. I found that a key component to the mismatch in the hiring process seemed to be a lack of empathy among employers for the jobseekers. So that became our starting point.

# What we did

## From candidate to customer

Early on we experienced a huge need among teachers to be able to discuss work-related opportunities, but there was no logical place for them to do that. So we arranged different settings to meet that need. We met, talked, and created a platform where they could act as professionals. More than anything, we listened. We took time to connect to the human person behind the temp label. A very basic human need that helped both our temps and us to perform better.

We also took on the role of an agent looking out for our temps interests. In cases where the customer was not satisfied, we decided we would represent our temps the same way we listened to our customers. As you can imagine we took a rather radical stance. But we had made the important realization that we did not have just one customer, but two. Our temps were as important for business success as the schools. Without the loyalty of our temps, we would never be able to deliver real value to our customers. So our success would be determined by our ability to cater to the needs of both groups.

## From trusting the candidate to trusting the company

One might assume that the dual-customer perspective would be risky to apply to the conventional business model. But it turned out that looking out for our temps brought clear benefits. Among other things, we became experts on their abilities and needs. The better we knew them, the more value we could deliver to our customers. Over time, that value creation helped us earn our customers' trust. Because of the trust in our relationship, our customers gained confidence in us. One result was a very low number of complaints despite making thousands of assignments every month. That confidence and trust later turned out to be one of our biggest assets in building a sustainable profitable business.

There are of course also many other reasons to our success. First of all we have been fortunate enough to have amazing people in and around our company -- dedicated, curious, creative, persevering. They have all been key to solving our customers' real needs.

Our business was initially a quite simple but sophisticated service offering qualitative screening and matching. On top of that we developed a production process and built an on-demand service for temps that enabled customers to order and receive temps in a matter of hours (remember, this was in the era before the internet was mature). Such results are still almost unheard-of in our industry. Also, we had become the facilitator that could create movement in the otherwise static teacher work market. We obviously filled a need. By now our company has been growing and profitable for 18 years straight. How is that possible? The answer, I believe, is in our culture -- one that fosters hard work, lots of pride, and above all -- customer love.

## Building the business

Without even realizing it, we had created a new logic. We had built a two-sided business model that had two customer groups and combined classic recruiting and staffing agency services with an on-demand temp service -- long before the gig-economy was a concept. But is was still performed analog and manually.

Despite our proven business success we had also gotten used to being disregarded by both public officials and business representatives as "the

274

substitute teacher temp agency." It seemed that most people's notion of a "real business" did not include teachers, schools, or temps. Also, as an entrepreneur I was considered to have no formal business background. All I had was my idea, a strong will, and lots of perspective on what hurdles you face if you are outside the work market trying to get in or if you are trying to explain an idea nobody heard of before.

To this day, we still have to deal with the biases that comes from a lack of diversity, creativity, and collaboration in our field. We operate in a rather traditional and regulated market where innovation is seldom the top priority. We could choose to see this as a problem, or -- our choice -- as an opportunity. The culture we built in our company has always been our lifeline and has enabled us to focus on our vision and our objectives. So we envisioned creating a talent platform for those curious of a career in education, and those looking for talent and aimed at the position as Sweden's largest provider of recruiting and staffing services in the education area. We not only reached and kept that position, today we have built a portfolio of brands and solutions aiming at solving needs in the future of work.

How did we get here? Let me answer with a short story. Back in 1999, during the first rocky-road years, there was a moment when we were unsure of the future of the company and decided we to had downsize. But we kept the company alive "on the side" while working with other projects. Out of the blue, it seemed, our persistence suddenly began to pay off. One day customers started calling asking for temps. I quickly needed to find an office space to interview candidates. With real clients waiting for delivery, there was just no time to go office hunting, and we really didn't have any money. So I asked my brother to help me move some furniture out of my apartment to turn it into something resembling an office. I put a handmade sign on the door, and voila! I had an office, and in that same impromptu setting I closed my first big deal. Perhaps this says something about the entrepreneurial mindset that has influenced who we are and how we think and act -- to be able to frame a situation and then reframe it to move forward. Since that day we have used this mindset and skill set over and over again.

## A new world

It's probably worth noting that we started out very early in the history of the Internet in business. And like most other companies, we initially imagined that our business would grow in a world that was rather linear and predictable. Fast forward 15 years, and we suddenly found ourselves in a totally different world, in a short time radically changed by new technology and globalization. Our analog business quickly needed to move into a world of all digital, mobile first, and 24/7 connection.

The first signals of change came from our customers. They told us they loved us and our services, but that they expected faster and better service. It didn't matter that we already delivered value way beyond all our competitors. We had raised the bar by being fast, efficient, and qualitative. Now our customers wanted more, and we needed to respond.

## Scaling trust

Our first step was to focus on automating any manual process and task that could be automated. The next step was to look at what we could do with AI to create real digital transformation. Just automating processes wasn't enough. We had already launched our first app 2011 but this time it was different. We had the feeling that if we could combine our 15 years of experience with smart technology we could potentially solve problems in a totally different way. That insight was thrilling. We knew we had the skills and the experience, because over the years we had hired more than 20,000 people who had gone through the processes of screening, matching, and coaching. From those hirings and the matching transactions, we had the data we needed. We also knew we had happy customers.

Approximately 50 percent of our temps were receiving permanent work offers within a year, and 8 out of 10 of them would recommend a friend to come work for us.

We started off by analyzing our business processes. We decided that our first step would be to rethink the application and screening process. We ditched the old CV custom simply because we saw no evidence that it actually added any value to our business. Instead of evaluating CV's, which mostly functions as a rearview mirror, we wanted to look for future potential in our job seekers. One part of this was to custom-build an automated screening tool for temps based on our own validated success factors for temps and customers. We worked with leading psychologists and our customers to create our tool. Then we moved on to develop matching algorithms -- a considerable challenge, given the 15 years of skills and experience we wanted to translate into algorithms.

In 2015 we launched the beta "Vikarie Direkt" and in August 2017 our full solution -- a platform and app that delivers recruiting and temp services on demand -- as well as supporting movement on the work market. Our solution offers faster, better ways for those looking for work to meet and match those looking for talent. We have been profitable from day one and business is growing. We will be hiring more than 2000 people onto the platform in 2018.

# Vikarie Direkt and real on-demand

Vikarie Direkt (which roughly translates to "Temp Direct") is a solution for great temps and good jobs. Here are some of the features.

## Paying customers

Customers can order temps in the app 24/7. Confirmation is instant and a suitable (depending on requirements) and vetted temp will show up at the desired hour. Customers handle the entire process through the app and also have the option to curate a talent pipeline for future temporary or more permanent recruiting needs. A built in recruiting tool will make sure those future hiring decisions are supported by validated data from previous assignments. This means less headache for managers and less bias in the process.

## Temps

Our temps are looking for a flexible way to work – and the opportunity

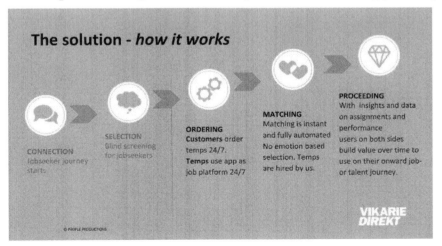

277

to build a career. They use the app to plan and manage their everyday work. Every hour a temp works counts and builds value over time.

## What makes us different

All our temps are hired with full benefits by our company. They have full flexibility and can choose to work extra hours, part time or full time. Because we are their employers, albeit temporary, we know who our people are, and that we can be confident that they will do a good job.

They stay as our employees for as long as they choose. Their habits vary; approximately 50 percent leave and then come back within a year. Temps have the option to move in and out of the platform as they choose.

Our temps for their part, offer us time and skills. In some ways, this resembles the way a staffing company works, with an important difference: Our solution is built for movement, flexibility and learning.

When our people move on to another job, we judge it to be a sign of success. It means our role as facilitator worked out as planned. The more people we move the more impact we have on the labor market.

## Our most important task. The learning journey.

Quite a few of our temps are young and inexperienced. For some of them we provide their first real job experience. So what is a job? Well, if you are young or and have limited experience it actually starts with understanding what it means to work. It starts at the very beginning preparing for the day ahead, planning to wake up in time to get to work, and knowing what you do when you arrive and what other people will expect from you during the day. A large part of our work is around supporting that learning process, to help create a foundation of clarity and safety to continue to build on. We then add AI to enhance learning and development. With data-driven and personalized feedback we help switch focus from doing the job to also learning and developing skills. Work at Vikarie Direkt becomes more than "just a job". It's a platform for earning, learning and proceeding, all in real-time. Our model for potential-based hiring, work-based learning and personalized development is summarized in what we call the HI-LEAP process ™.

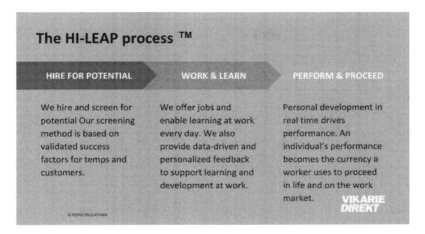

## We do the matching.

When a paying customer orders a temp, and when a temp is assigned to a job, there is no choosing, swiping, or liking involved, procedures that lately have been made popular by dating and matching apps. Instead, assignments are matched instantly, based on our experience, matching algorithms and data telling us what actually creates a successful match. The benefits are obvious: high-quality matching, at lightning speed, with a minimum of bias. Once a successful match has been made between a temp and a customer, the can - if they choose to - continue to work together on future assignments.

The fact that we decide the matching for customers and temps, is core in our solution. First of all, we believe it's the key to a real on-demand service. We don't want our customers to be saddled with the headache of posting job ads, searching among available temps, and guessing at who will be a good match before actually making a choice that may or may not be a good one. Secondly, and more important, we don't think that "swiping" is a good practise. The risk of arbitrary selection is obvious.

Choosing workers based on superficial attributes like good looks, star ratings from users in other companies, or what school a person attended is not an accurate method for assessing a person's capabilities. Just because it's offered in an app doesn't make it valid.

# People power

The current climate in the social media landscape has unfortunately played a highly influential role in nurturing superficial job-matching techniques. Far worse, it has inspired an obsession with growing followers and likes. Just like tabloid journalism, social media sell exciting stories, they are the new yellow press. That's fine in the entertainment industry, but is it good enough for people business? I generally embrace the idea of looking outside your industry to find inspiration and discover new things. In this case, however, I think it's more complicated. We're entering an era when technology is rapidly changing the power balance in the world. People who yesterday had no access to information now have access to everything as well as the power to interact with others, raising their voices and using their consumer powers to influence how big-name brands make decisions. The digitized world has increased people power over the old logic of knowledge advantage. The time is over when brands or experts corner the valuable information and use it to build competitive advantage. In this new world, anyone can be an expert -- even the workers who are judged by non-validated assessment methods like star ratings.

I believe the function of the star rating is primarily entertainment. My brain might feel a certain comfort from having the ability to grade a service I have used, but in our company we don't see such ratings in any way useful in predicting future success -- for the company or the worker. Instead, we experiment with other ways to share information between temps and customers to gain insights in how our business development can create value for people. And there is one more thing. We don't feel the need to control our people, because we already trust them.

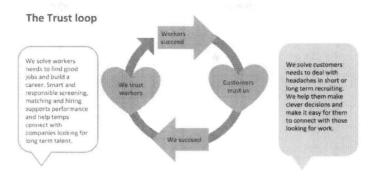

The Trust loop

We solve workers needs to find good jobs and build a career. Smart and responsible screening, matching and hiring supports performance and help temps connect with companies looking for long term talent.

We trust workers

Workers succeed

Customers trust us

We succeed

We solve customers needs to deal with headaches in short or long term recruiting. We help them make clever decisions and make it easy for them to connect with those looking for work.

# Summary and Conclusion

I was lucky enough to be born in one of the wealthiest and egalitarian countries in the world. Naturally it has influenced the way I do business. In Sweden we have always been innovators, but as a small country far north in Europe (we are only 10 million people), we learned early on, to look outside and build relationships. This helped us understand that collaboration is clever. Education has also played an important role. It starts as early as kindergarten with a national curriculum for learning, and helps foster a non-hierarchical, consensus-driven culture that's open to diversity -- and key to innovation.

Our company is built on the simple idea of a dual customer perspective and that we should be doing what customers really need. Our job is to find out what that is. It's certainly not always an easy task. But it helps to put people first. When people's needs are fulfilled, they have greater chance of feeling safe and confident. That safety and confidence creates trust -- an important basis for good performance in any job, for both employees and managers. This is especially true in a world that's changing fast, is hard to predict, and where all of us will have to extend ownership over our individual and joint future. Another guiding principle we have is that no worker "is" or "has" talent, but rather "becomes" talented - if we support them. To achieve this we need to believe in humans and their potential. Both as individuals and as a collective force that builds our company as well as contributes to society at large. Today there are endless opportunities to use intelligent technology to not only solve problems but to also support this idea and become more human. We should all try to seize those opportunities.

Jamie Merisotis is a globally recognized leader in philanthropy, education, and public policy. Since 2008, he has served as president and CEO of Lumina Foundation, an independent, private foundation that is committed to making opportunities for learning beyond high school available to all. His work includes extensive global experience as an adviser and consultant in southern Africa, the former Soviet Union, Europe and other parts of the world. He previously served as CEOof the Institute for Higher Education Policy in Washington, DC, and as executive director of a national commission on college affordability appointed by the U.S. President and Congressional leaders.

Merisotis is the author of the widely-acclaimed book *America Needs Talent*, named a Top 10 Business Book of 2016 by Booklist. A frequentmedia commentator and contributor, his writing has appeared in *The Washington Post,New York Times*, *Wall Street Journal*, *Stanford Social Innovation Review, Washington Monthly, Huffington Post, Politico,* and other publications. He is a member of the Council on Foreign Relations, and serves as a trustee for diverse array of organizations around the world including The Children's Museum of Indianapolis, which he chairs, Bates College in Maine, and the Council on Foundations in Washington, DC.

# How Talent Drives the New Ecosystem for Work

## by Jamie Merisotis

*The people-centered economy needs a talent-based labor market. Talent is more than skills; it gives people control over their own destiny and makes society work. We urgently need systems that help individuals develop their talents, because postsecondary credentials are already a requirement for most good jobs. In this system, "first you learn, then you work" will be replaced by continuous, integrated, talent development and deployment. The goal is to build a talent system where 60% of all Americans possess high-quality credentials. The Lumina Foundation is now building new directions for philanthropy to reach this goal and has established Lumina Impact Ventures, investing in portfolios of startup companies, dedicating one of the nation's largest private endowments to making the talent system grow.*

In 2008, Lumina Foundation began to focus on a specific, measurable goal – that 60% of Americans hold high-quality postsecondary degrees, certificates, or other credentials by 2025. While we recognized that setting a goal was a significant step in our work, at the time we didn't fully realize how important the goal would prove to be – both for Lumina as a national foundation and for the field in which we worked.

The first hint about the importance of the goal came from the reaction of our stakeholders. The initial reaction was, frankly, a certain level of shock. Most were unfamiliar with the concept of "attainment" (a measure of the proportion of the population that has reached a given level of education) and many had no idea that the U.S. had fallen so far behind other nations in providing opportunity for high-quality postsecondary learning. Soon after, once the shock had worn off, reactions to the goal fell into two camps. One camp saw the goal as close to absurd – on one hand, likely impossible to reach, and on the other hand, an act of extreme hubris. The second camp reacted more positively to the goal, both as a clear statement of the national need to increase postsecondary attainment and as an indication of the Foundation's willingness to assume a leadership role.

We didn't realize at first that articulating the goal completely changed our perspective on what Lumina was about. The reason was hiding in plain sight – the fact that the goal is measured by the number of Americans who obtain a high-quality postsecondary credential. The goal is not about the educational system or its providers—colleges and universities, workforce programs, or, for that matter, any other institutions and systems. It is about people and their needs, aspirations, and accomplishments.

In 2015, I wrote a book that investigated the implications for the U.S. as a whole of this shift in focus from institutions to people. That book, *America Needs Talent,* suggests that the acquisition and development of talent will drive America's future. Of course, the ever-increasing employer demands for "skills" is part of what's driving the need to focus on talent, but it's about so much more than simply skills, as that term is understood in the public dialogue. Talent is what gives people the chance to bend the trajectory of their lives toward something better. It is this ability of people to control their own destiny that makes a society function. Sadly, in America today, too many people have, through no fault of their own, lost the ability to improve the quality of their lives because the systems that could nurture and develop their talent do not exist. Aside from representing a personal tragedy for innumerable people, the erosion of talent is deeply threatening to the future of the U.S. as a nation.

# The nature of talent

In the book, I define talent as the "reflection of the synergies that result when individuals acquire a mix of capabilities that lead to prosperity in their careers and personal lives—synergies that not only impact them as individuals, but all of society." This kind of talent is elusive and difficult to categorize, but that doesn't make it any less real. We can begin to understand it by recognizing both its cognitive and non-cognitive components:

- *Knowledge*—understanding in a particular subject matter, such as math, science, or the humanities, as well as applied subjects like accounting.

- *Skills*—like critical thinking and problem solving; competencies that allow individuals to use their knowledge to solve many kinds of problems as well as to generate new knowledge.

284

- *Abilities*—like memory, creativity, and reasoning; these are enduring personal attributes.

- *Values*—like recognition, achievement, and authority; values reflect preferences for outcomes, goals, or ideals.

- *Interests*—like social or investigative; the characteristics of the kinds of environments where people prefer to locate themselves.

- *Personality traits*—like conscientiousness or extroversion; habitual patterns of behavior, thought, or emotion that are relatively stable over time.

However one might define talent, there is one immutable fact about it that we must recognize: it can be nurtured and developed. Some of the components of talent are innate to an extent, but all can be developed through formal and informal learning – even values, interests, and personality traits.

*Talent is not born or bought; it is created within supporting families and social institutions, including schools and colleges, and developed through the experiences of learning and working over the course of a lifetime.*

## Talent and the knowledge economy

Talent has emerged as the primary determinant of a person's level of employment. It's easy to lose sight of the fact that a massive transformation of the U.S. employment market has already occurred, with profound implications not just for the economy but for the lives of millions of Americans. The demand for talent puts *people* – learners/students and workers – at the center of a new education-employment ecosystem. Since this ecosystem is centered around people and their talent, credentials are its currency in all sectors. This meant that the demands for different and more robust talent began increasing across the board as, one-by-one, occupations were transformed. Little by little, those without more advanced skills were cut off from good jobs and opportunities for advancement. Because this transformation was not widely recognized, employers, policymakers, and educators were slow to respond.

285

All this came to a head in 2008 with the Great Recession, described by labor economist Tony Carnevale as "a smart bomb targeting low-skill jobs." It was worse than that; entire industries that employed large numbers of low-skilled workers were wiped out. Jobs have come back from the depths of the recession, but they are not the same ones that were lost. From December 2007 to January 2010, the economy shed a net total of 7.4 million jobs – 5.6 million of them held by people with a high school education or less. Yet between the end of the recession and 2016, of the 11.6 million new jobs created in the U.S. economy, 11.5 million of them required at least some college education. Put more bluntly, the new ecosystem for work requires workers with postsecondary credentials.

Why are postsecondary credentials so valuable? It's a very important question, and one that some want to trivialize. In the view of many, students are merely sheep pursuing unneeded postsecondary learning simply for its prestige value. These critics say that employers' preference for people with postsecondary credentials is mere "signaling" or a symptom of "credential creep." But, of course, these arguments are at best wishful thinking and at worst an attempt to hang on to the perceived privilege a college degree conveys to its holder (including those who are making these arguments). Both students and employers are responding to a real shift that has taken place in the knowledge economy – the shift to a talent-based labor market.

Today, it seems impossible to overstate the effects this transformation of the labor market has had on Americans. A good job as we know it today – one that pays middle-class wages and allows a worker to have health care and save for retirement – now requires postsecondary learning. Moreover, in the modern economy, holding a good job has become inextricably linked to well-being and the quality of life.

*The knowledge economy creates many opportunities for those with the necessary talent, but for those without it, it is ruthless.*

The consequences of being left out of the economy are no longer abstract – they are directly measurable in terms of life expectancy and other key social indicators. The U.S. is now slipping backward on many of these indicators, and our failure to nurture and develop talent looks more and more to be the culprit.

Anne Case and Angus Deaton's groundbreaking 2015 paper[50] and their 2017 follow-up[51] showed exactly what is at stake in the growing relationship between talent development and quality of life. Their analysis of mortality data, disaggregated by race and level of education, shows a truly disturbing rise in "deaths of despair" among the working class without postsecondary credentials. What seems to be happening is that millions of Americans are losing faith in the belief that economic opportunity and social mobility – the American Dream – are attainable by all of those who are willing to work. These trends will only get worse unless we can nurture and develop the talent of all our people.

## Talent and the ecosystem for work

To survive in the knowledge economy, employers must find people with the specific talent they need. And workers must find employers who are willing both to recognize and continually invest in their ongoing need for talent development. Employers believe postsecondary credentials – including but not exclusively defined as college degrees – represent the talent of their holders, which is why they have become so valuable. Workers need to develop the talent that employers are seeking and must continually update it to remain marketable. But even if employers understand their talent needs and workers have the opportunity to develop the talent employers demand (both conditions being imperfect at best), it doesn't do any good if employers and employees can't find each other. All too often in today's labor market with today's credentials, they can't.

In a talent-based market, a common frame of reference is essential, as are systems to match the skills of workers to employment opportunities. But it's not just employers and workers who must speak the same languages. The role of education providers is essential in a talent-based market as the range of skills in demand and the number of people who need to learn them both grow exponentially. To a certain extent, education providers have tried to respond to the needs of employers and prospective workers by developing programs in in-demand fields, collaborating with large employers around customized

---

[50] *Rising morbidity and mortality in midlife among white non-Hispanic Americans in the 21st century*, Proceedings of the National Academy of Sciences (PNAS). December 8, 2015.

[51] *Mortality and Morbidity in the 21st Century*, The Brooking Institution, March 23, 2017.

training programs, and other such efforts. But these approaches, however worthy, are inadequate in the knowledge economy.

*What is needed is a new ecosystem in which two systems – learning and working – are fully integrated into a talent ecosystem based on flexible pathways to transparent, quality credentials.*

In this system, the temporal idea of "first you learn, then you work" is replaced by a continuous and integrated model of talent development and deployment. This takes us well beyond the historic concept of "lifelong learning" and more toward the idea of a continuous, fully-connected system for talent. These are the characteristics of this new learning/working ecosystem:

- **It is based on transparent credentials**. Credentials are the currency of talent. Almost everyone will have multiple credentials that represent their talent to employers and education providers. Employers will be able to quickly determine the meaning of all credentials in terms of the talent they are looking for. Individuals will know what kinds of work their credentials qualify them to hold.

- **A common language unites the learning providers and employers**. Both learning providers and employers will use the same terms to describe talent. With this common language, educators can design programs to meet the talent needs of the knowledge economy and employers will be able to understand how the learning outcomes of education programs relate to the talent they need and are looking for.

- **Assessment of talent is widely available**. Anyone will be able to have their talent assessed and receive an appropriate credential based on the assessment.

- **Flexible pathways are ubiquitous**. Through the integration of learning and work, everyone will have access to flexible pathways to develop their talent.

While actually creating such a system may seem far-fetched, it is already coming into being. New kinds of employer-recognized postsecondary credentials – micro-degrees, badges, and many more – are being created by new kinds of learning providers like edX.

Traditional colleges and universities are also getting in on the act by offering a growing numbers of occupation-specific undergraduate and graduate certificates in many fields. Platforms like LinkedIn allow individuals to create their own profile highlighting relevant learning, work experience, and demonstration of mastery.

On the employer side, things are changing, too. Industry sector groups continue to develop and refine talent frameworks that are used primarily to guide training programs for incumbent and prospective workers. Automated hiring processes are widely used by employers to screen candidates against defined criteria, and artificial intelligence and predictive analytics promise to make these systems even more powerful.

This system is still evolving, and it is already stymied by at least one significant challenge: an almost complete lack of transparency across these efforts caused by the lack of common standards. As a result, learner-workers don't know what credentials employers are seeking. Employers don't know how to define their talent needs in terms that education providers can respond to. Few know what degrees and other credentials represent in terms of talent.

# Talent and new ways of working at Lumina Foundation

This leads us back to Lumina Foundation and our role in this talent system. The Foundation, one of the nation's largest private endowments and unusual in its singular focus, has been working for many years to improve college access and success; we've learned a lot, and the lessons we've learned have informed the development of what we've called a leadership model of philanthropy. Now, when I say "philanthropy" here, I do so quite intentionally and specifically. There's a difference between charity and philanthropy; charity is about helping ... providing direct service or assistance. That work is vital and will always be important. There is no substitute for charity or the human generosity that fuels it.

But if charity is about help, philanthropy is about change. Its goal is not so much to provide assistance or service; rather, it seeks to alter the conditions that make assistance necessary. Philanthropy gets to root causes, not symptoms. It is systemic, not episodic, and ideally more proactive than reactive.

Lumina's agenda is a change agenda and for us, it all started with the bold, atypical decision made by the Foundation's founding board to commit to a single topic: boosting postsecondary education attainment. This was unusual for a large, national foundation, blessed with lots of resources. In 2008, we took that focused approach even further, committing to serve as a catalyzing organization to help the country achieve the time-limited, quantitative goal mentioned earlier — that 60% of Americans will earn a high-quality degree, certificate or other credential by 2025. This decision has affected everything we do.

With the goal, Lumina has evolved from a very good grantmaking organization to one that uses all of the tools in the toolbox, from traditional grants, to serving as a convener, to using its bully pulpit of expertise to inform public policy and stimulate thought leadership across different domains.

I remember quite clearly the day I realized that the 60% attainment goal meant that Lumina was no longer a "higher education" foundation. By that, I mean that goal shifted Lumina from being a good grantmaking organization with a thematic focus to one highly mission-driven and outcomes-focused. Our raison d'etre was no longer on improving higher education to serve students more effectively. Because of the goal, our focus was now fixed on increasing the number of Americans with postsecondary credentials that lead to good jobs or fulfilling work, and an overall better quality of life.

Ironically, this narrowing of focus broadened our perspective about how – and with whom – we work. As our understanding of the interconnected issues affecting talent and attainment deepened, we came to realize we were building a people-centered ecosystem involving both the learning and work sectors to grow talent. We recognized the need to partner with all those who will play a role in building this system, and were gratified by the eager response of many actors who we did not know and who did not know us. These broad and inclusive partnerships – involving workforce development systems, employers, unions, policymakers, think tanks, community and regional leadership, national and local funders, as well as colleges and universities – are now central to our work.

We also realized we had to re-engineer our philanthropic role from "funder" to "investor." For Lumina, the return on investment that we seek has little to do with money – but it has everything to do with innovation and long-term sustainability. We found we needed to expand our financial tools beyond grants to possess a spectrum of strategic investments.

One of these tools is strategically-focused impact investing through an integrated platform that we call Lumina Impact Ventures. LIV's primary approach is to invest directly in companies – mostly early/seed stage enterprises – or secondarily in organizations and managed funds, that can advance Lumina's goal. Lumina works with a range of partners to identify promising and innovative solutions to increase attainment and turn them into scalable and investable opportunities. The idea is simple: use these private investments to catalyze progress toward the 2025 goal the same way that grants, convenings, et. have always been used.

## Building the people-based talent ecosystem

Ultimately, the work that Lumina and many others are doing to change the talent ecosystem is about more than jobs.

*By focusing on nurturing and developing talent on a massive scale, we have the opportunity to make an enormous difference in the quality of the lives of millions of Americans. Just as important, we can create a society where genuine opportunity is available to all. This is the promise of the people-centered economy.*

Moreover, in a future where what we today call "jobs" may become less common than differentiated models of work—extensions of today's "gig economy" work that include everything from highly-individualized work experiences to team-based employment models. Given this trend, the need to develop and deploy a people-based talent ecosystem grows ever more urgent.

The way forward is clear. First, in a people-centered economy and its talent-based labor market, the talent demands of work must be clear and transparent to all. At the same time, everyone must know what their own talent is, have opportunities to develop it, and know what it can lead to in terms of jobs, other forms of work, and further education. Finally, they must be prepared to use it as they see fit to earn a living and improve the quality of their life. These are all essential pillars of the new model of people-centered learning and work. They are based on transparency of learning and flexible pathways through an integrated, continuously changing ecosystem of talent development and deployment.

*Jamie Merisotis is president and CEO of Lumina Foundation and author of the book **America Needs Talent**.*

291

Jacob Hue is the CEO of Catalyte, a software development and engineering company that uses AI to identify anyone who has the aptitude, regardless of background, to become a software developer. Catalyte identifies, upskills and deploys high-performing teams to deliver product engineering and enterprise applications for Fortune 1000 companies. Prior to joining Catalyte, Jacob was CEO at Symbio, a global IT services company with development centers across China, Philippines and Scandinavia. He transformed Symbio from an early stage startup to a global IT services company with over 23,000 employees around the world. Jacob has also co-founded or been a founding investor in over thirty other companies in the United States and Asia.

Jacob is a Young Global Leader of the World Economic Forum and has been named as one of the world's Top 12 CEOs by Chief Executive Magazine. Additionally, Jacob is a founding member of the Markle Foundation's Rework America Task Force, focused on modernizing the United States' outdated labor market and unlocking economic opportunity for American job seekers, workers and businesses. He is also a board member of Welcoming America, which helps cities in the US be more welcoming of new immigrants.

# Advancing human potential for the digital economy

## -- How Catalyte is transforming skills-based hiring to extend software development careers to anyone

by Jacob Hsu, CEO of Catalyte

## The Catalyte story

The mechanisms that Catalyte uses to connect aptitude with opportunity are born of the 21st century: artificial intelligence, machine learning, big data and predictive analytics.

But the idea for Catalyte was born from something that has happened for generations: a kid not being invited to a friend's party.

Our founder Michael Rosenbaum grew up in Bethesda, Maryland, a well-to-do, inner-ring suburb of Washington, D.C. Bethesda was, and continues to be, a professional, cosmopolitan neighborhood. While it has grown to be more diverse, even in the 1960's and 1970's it offered exposure and proximity to differing cultures and communities.

Despite the trappings of a well-to-do upbringing in this self-proclaimed open-minded community, Michael was still often on the outside looking in. The Chevy Chase Club was the local country club where many of his school peers would spend their summers poolside. But not Mike.

He quickly figured out that he and his fellow Jewish classmates, his African American classmates and other minority classmates were never invited to the Chevy Chase Club. This was his first realization that those with the power to make decisions often let their own biases cloud their decision-making processes.

Fast forward to the mid-1990's. Michael is a Harvard economics and law fellow working as an economic advisor in the Bill Clinton White

293

House. He is advocating for an inclusive economic policy that was partly shaped by his Chevy Chase Club experience.

He is advocating that workforce talent is equally distributed among populations, but that inherent biases make it impossible to identify individuals with the ability for a certain job or career. Urban, economically distressed communities are passed over for employment and economic development because of these biases.

These communities have just as many individuals with the inherent aptitude to be great employees. But, because they lack the traditional societal markers of pedigree - class, education, resume, previous job experience, etc. - they aren't given the opportunity.

*If you could remove the bias inherent in the current job market, and assess individuals based on their inherent abilities, not the rewards of privilege or pedigree, you could create a more productive, equitable job market that could increase sustainable economic growth.*

After his time in the White House, Mike took this idea back to Harvard. He was convinced that he could conduct the substantive research to prove his theory. However, if he remained in the Ivory Tower of academia, his theory would remain just that - theoretical. But if he could prove his theory in the "real world," by starting a private company based on this idea that talent is equally distributed, but opportunity is not, he could make a substantial impact on the lives of underserved individuals and begin to change the job market at a practical level.

In 1999, Michael relocated to Baltimore, Maryland, a post-industrial city struggling to make an economic comeback. Here, in Charm City (as Baltimore is nicknamed), among the crab cakes and row homes, he founded Catalyte to prove: if you could identify the under-represented individuals with the innate aptitude for a job, you could create a more productive, diverse and equitable workforce.

## CatPlat: The engine that drives us

To find extraordinary, untapped talent that would comprise a more productive, diverse and equitable workforce, you first have to quantify what being a "great" employee means and create a way to screen for greatness.

Catalyte does this with our Catalyte Talent Platform, or CatPlat for short. This is the artificial intelligence, predictive analytics engine that powers our talent discovery, hiring and training processes. It's evolved into a robust and intricate interaction of around 5,000 variables.

But it didn't start this way. As with any machine learning, it takes a while to fine tune the algorithm and separate the signal from the noise.

When Michael started building CatPlat, he knew that software engineering would be the perfect field in which to test his hypothesis. It was a growing and in demand employment market, so he could attract and employ an ever-increasing number of developers. And in software development, unlike other more subjective fields, there is concrete data on what makes an employee great. These include velocity, speed of ramp, points delivered, productivity, etc.

*By capturing the results of the best engineers, Michael couldwork backwards and figure out what traits they possessed, and then screen future applicants for those traits.*

As the sample size of both applicants and outcome data grew, a few patterns emerged. Great software developers shared some common traits of curiosity, mental dexterity and cognitive agility, problem solving and the willingness to change their opinion when presented with new or contrary facts.

CatPlat currently takes into account 18 years of software engineering outcome data, historical data from our 50,000+ applicants and ties those pieces together to screen all new applicants. Because we know which applicants have proven their greatness in the past, we can screen for those attributes in new applicants, and hire those with the greatest aptitude for software development.

Like our engineers, CatPlat is set up to evolve when presented with new information. The feedback loop between outcomes and applicants means that CatPlat is constantly learning and finding better talent over time.

# The three surprises

We were always confident in our hypothesis that talent was equally distributed, but opportunity was not. It has sometimes been a challenge to convince others of the benefits of skills-based hiring. We, as a society, are so deeply invested in the notion that hiring based on arbitrary markers of success - educational degrees, previous work experience, network connections - automatically leads to an optimized workforce.

When you challenge peoples' fundamental core beliefs on how the labor market operates, and hire for aptitude rather than pedigree, you get three surprises:

- When you take human bias out of the hiring process, you get a more diverse workforce.

- On top of a more diverse workforce, you create a more productive workforce.

- By not relying on pedigree, you can build a workforce wherever, without overpaying for in-demand and low-supply talent.

The fact that you get a more diverse workforce when we take human bias out of the hiring process and screen for aptitude shows that our founding hypothesis is correct: talent is everywhere, opportunity is not. Humans of different races, ethnicities, genders or classes aren't somehow born with more or less innate ability than others. These abilities are distributed widely throughout the general population, regardless of the societal makers we give credence to in the hiring process - class, education, age, job experience, etc.

*Catalyte's workforce mirrors the communities from which we draw applicants.*

In a diverse metro area like Baltimore, 26 percent of our developers are African American. This mirrors the area's population, which is about 28 percent African American.

In fact, this ratio holds true across the entire country. The percentage of the American populace that is African American is roughly 13 percent. The percentage of Catalyte developers who are African American is also roughly 13 percent. To put this into perspective, in

296

Google's recent diversity report, only two percent of its tech hires in 2017 were African American.

We're working hard to reach gender parity. Part of this process is overcoming self-selection bias. When pervasive societal messages and representations of software engineers are anti-women, it becomes a hurdle to convince many that they belong in this field.

Diversity goes beyond race and gender. Tech talent isn't a Millennial-only trait. We have a broad spectrum of ages applying to Catalyte. In one of our most recent training cycles, we had new graduates working side-by-side with a retired public school teacher starting a second career.

Most interesting is the educational diversity this skills-based model produces. Around 45 percent of our employees don't have a four-year college degree. The other 55 percent have a four-year or advanced degree. In other words, for software development, having a degree doesn't mean you're a great engineer. This should be obvious, as many of our tech heroes - Jobs, Wozniak, Gates, Zuckerberg - didn't have this marker of pedigree when they first made their impact on the industry.

Having a more diverse workforce doesn't mean sacrificing the level of employee talent. You can create both a more diverse and productive workforce. Stats released by our clients show that Catalyte's teams of diverse developers from untraditional backgrounds outperform traditional software development teams 3-to-1.

*This pokes a giant hole in the notion that hiring someone based on pedigree of where they went to school, what degree they have, what job they've held before or who in their network recommended them for the position means you'll get a better, more productive employee.*

This is important because of the tight supply of and competition for great developers. Colleges and universities can't graduate enough computer science majors to keep up with demand. Even if they could, many people can't afford the four years and tens, if not hundreds, of thousands of dollars it takes to get a degree. Throw in geographic roadblocks that reduce access to elite educational opportunities, and you have large populations that will continue to be undeserved and languish in the expanding knowledge economy.

Skills-based hiring can overcome these challenges by creating workforces wherever needed. You can enter any community, screen and select those with the aptitude to become great software developers, train them and then put them to work in a lucrative, knowledge economy career. These individuals then reinvest in their local communities, raising the economic level of everyone around them. And this builds long-term, sustainable talent pipelines that attract new businesses, development and capital into previously overlooked communities.

# Tim Reed

It's hard to put into perspective what skills-based hiring really means without telling the story of one of our extraordinary employees.

Tim Reed has been with Catalyte for over three years. A product of our CatPlat screening and training program, Tim now specializes in quality assurance engineering and is a leader in our QA Center of Excellence.

Tim's story is remarkable in the general sense, but exemplative of the Catalyte experience of finding exceptional engineers from unexpected places. He is Baltimore born and raised, to parents who were Baltimore born and raised. Always mechanically inclined, he was the go-to person in the house when something needed fixing. He enjoyed taking things apart, learning how they worked and then putting them back together.

Tim took this engineering inclination to the next level when he enrolled in Morgan State University, becoming the first member of his family to attend college. But college couldn't contain his enthusiasm. More interested in practical, hands-on learning than rote studies, Tim left Morgan State.

Reorganizing and reassessing his priorities, Tim once again enrolled in college, this time at the Community College of Baltimore County. Unfortunately, this time on his way to a degree, finances reared their ugly head and Tim had to withdraw again.

With a natural ability for engineering, Tim plotted his next move. While looking for jobs on Craigslist, Tim ran across a recruitment ad for Catalyte. He took the CatPlat screening, and we identified him as having the potential to be a great developer. He joined a cycle training cohort and in less than six months, graduated and became part of the Catalyte family as a junior developer.

Tim continues to show that natural curiosity and drive that lead him as a kid to disassemble and reassemble electronics. He's taken it on himself to become an expert in quality engineering. And, with the help of our educational stipend, Tim returned to school to earn his associate's degree.

Tim is the type of person Catalyte discovers. He is someone others might have overlooked due to his background or pedigree. But Tim, and the hundreds of Catalytes just like him, have the aptitude and ability to thrive and build better careers, lives and futures for themselves, their families and their communities.

## The future is now

Something has to change soon, or we risk major disruptions to our economic order and stability. The ascension of automation presents the possibility of displacing large percentages of current service or labor economy workers. At the same time, digital transformation of the enterprise has left businesses with a crushing skills gap that no one can seem to fill.

Skills-based hiring presents an opportunity to reduce the impact of both of these trends.

*We can identify service or labor economy workers who have the aptitude to succeed in the knowledge economy. We can quickly and economically train them and put them to work*

building the digital products and services for enterprises struggling to find quality development talent. The future of our labor market and economy depends on it.

Tess Posner is a social entrepreneur focused on increasing equity and inclusion in the tech economy. As CEO of AI4ALL, she is working to make artificial intelligence more diverse and inclusive and to ensure that AI is developed responsibly. Before joining AI4ALL, she was Managing Director of TechHire at Opportunity@Work, a national initiative launched out of the White House to increase diversity in the tech economy, where she oversaw the network of 72 cities, states and rural areas and 1300+ companies creating more inclusive education and hiring pathways. Earlier in her career, Tess built and ran Samaschool, a nonprofit that equips low-income people to find work in the digital economy through an online platform training 50,000+ students worldwide and a dozen diverse locations from New York City to rural Arkansas and East Africa. Tess's work has been featured by the Wall St. Journal, the Atlantic, VentureBeat, Business Insider, TechCrunch, and Fast Company and funded by the Tipping Point Community, JPMorgan Chase, the California Endowment and the Robin Hood Foundation. Tess holds a master's degree from Columbia University School in Social Enterprise Administration and a bachelor's in liberal arts from St. John's College.

# Diverse and Inclusive Artificial Intelligence for a People-centered Future

By Tess Posner

*"AI and computer science are the future of our world, but how can we continue to move forward if only a portion of society understand or have access to it?"*

-Priyanka, AI4ALL graduate

There is a diversity crisis in AI and computer science. Today, a homogenous group of technologists is building AI solutions for our diverse population. Artificial intelligence is powering the fourth industrial revolution and has been called the "new electricity." The global economic impact of AI applications is expected to reach \$2.95 trillion by 2025, and we're already seeing AI incorporated into areas and tools like medical diagnosis, personal assistants like Siri, self-driving cars, and Google Translate.[52] A recent Gallup poll showed that 85% of Americans use AI technology every day.[53] This tremendous growth has led to a talent gap and skyrocketing demand for AI skills. The number of jobs requiring AI skills, including machine learning and natural language processing, has grown 4.5 times since 2013,[54] and employer demand for AI-related roles has doubled over the last 3 years.[55] Element AI, a Montreal-based AI platform company has said that there are fewer

---

[52] Chen, Nicholas et al, "Global Economic Impacts Associated with Artificial Intelligence." *Analysis Group.* http://www.analysisgroup.com/uploadedfiles/content/insights/publishing/ag_full_report_economic_impact_of_ai.pdf

[53] Reinhart, RJ, "Most Americans Already Using Artificial Intelligence Products." *Gallup.com*, 6 Mar. 2018, news.gallup.com/poll/228497/americans-already-using-artificial-intelligence-products.aspx. Accessed 17 May 2018.

[54] Artificial Intelligence Index. *2017 Annual Report.* https://aiindex.org/2017-report.pdf. Accessed 17 May 2018.

[55] Rayome, Alison DeNisco. "Demand for AI Talent Exploding: Here Are the 10 Most in-Demand Jobs." *TechRepublic*, 1 Mar. 2018, www.techrepublic.com/article/demand-for-ai-talent-exploding-here-are-the-10-most-in-demand-jobs/. Accessed 17 May 2018.

than 10,000 individuals [56] with the skills needed to fill specialized AI research roles. As a result, recent Ph.D. graduates and researchers with only a few years of experience can make up to $500,000 in salary and stock options, according to a 2018 New York Times article, and specialized AI researchers have received salaries of up to almost $2 million. [57]

Additionally, the average person in the future will need "AI literacy" as AI will touch and get embedded in most industries. A January 2018 article in MIT Technology Review looked at 19 studies about automation-fueled job change from groups like McKinsey and Gartner and found that the predictions were all over the map.[58] Despite this note of uncertainty, we do know that many jobs will not be replaced by automation but instead will shift as a result of incorporating automation, where AI and humans will need to collaborate. Jobs likely to be most impacted in the coming years include financial analysts, lawyers, construction workers, taxi drivers, farmers, journalists, telemarketers and even software engineers. And McKinsey reports entire 'backbone' industries in the economy will be disrupted including marketing, sales, manufacturing and customer service. [59]

Most people don't know about or have access to the opportunity to develop these skills, exacerbating the AI talent, literacy, and diversity crises. If jobs requiring AI skills are only accessible to a few, then large swaths of society will not be prepared for the changing economy and are excluded from the lucrative opportunities in AI and upward mobility this sector will offer.

---

[56] Metz, Cade. "Tech Giants Are Paying Huge Salaries for Scarce A.I. Talent." *The New York Times*, The New York Times, 22 Oct. 2017, www.nytimes.com/2017/10/22/technology/artificial-intelligence-experts-salaries.html. Accessed 17 May 2018.

[57] Metz, Cade. "A.I. Researchers Are Making More Than $1 Million, Even at a Nonprofit." *The New York Times*, The New York Times, 19 Apr. 2018, www.nytimes.com/2018/04/19/technology/artificial-intelligence-salaries-openai.html. Accessed 17 May 2018.

[58] Winick, Erin. "Every Study We Could Find on What Automation Will Do to Jobs, in One Chart."*MIT Technology Review*, MIT Technology Review, 9 Apr. 2018, www.technologyreview.com/s/610005/every-study-we-could-find-on-what-automation-will-do-to-jobs-in-one-chart/. Accessed 17 May 2018.

[59] Columbus, Louis. "Sizing The Market Value Of Artificial Intelligence." *Forbes*, Forbes Magazine, 30 Apr. 2018, www.forbes.com/sites/louiscolumbus/2018/04/30/sizing-the-market-value-of-artificial-intelligence/#205307edffe9. Accessed 17 May 2018.

Financial exclusion is just one risk. The lack of diversity in AI is already leading to harmful impacts on the development and deployment of the technology. Only 13% of AI companies have female CEOs,[60] and less than 3% of tenure-track engineering faculty in the US are black.[61] As machines are getting closer to mirroring human-like abilities, they are also absorbing and sometimes amplifying the deeply ingrained unconscious biases in our society including sexism, racism, and other forms of discrimination.

The lack of diversity is a root cause.

For example, a recent paper called Gender Shades by Joy Buolamwini and Timnit Gebru reveals that widely used facial recognition software can only recognize white male faces with high accuracy. They tested common facial recognition software (IBM, Microsoft, and Face++) using a set of 1,270 images (a dataset created by the authors as existing benchmarks were overwhelmingly homogenous). The images were taken of subjects from 3 European countries and 3 African countries. Subjects were grouped by gender, skin type, and the intersection of gender and skin type. While the 3 companies' software products appear to have relatively high accuracy overall, there are notable differences in the error rates between different groups. All 3 companies's software products performed better on facial recognition of males than females, and all software performed better on lighter-skinned subjects than darker-skinned subjects. All software performed worst on darker-skinned females. The Gender Shades website notes that "inclusive product testing and reporting are necessary if the industry is to create systems that work well for all of humanity." As of September 2018, IBM and Microsoft have responded to this research to share that they have worked to improve the accuracy of their facial recognition products since the release of the Gender Shades study. Face++ has not responded. [62]

---

[60] Faggella, Lauren D'Ambra. "Women in Artificial Intelligence – A Visual Study of Leadership Across Industries -." *TechEmergence*, 15 Sept. 2017, www.techemergence.com/women-in-artificial-intelligence-visual-study-leaderships-across-industries/. Accessed 17 May 2018.

[61] Yoder, Brian L., "Engineering By The Numbers." *ASEE.* https://www.asee.org/documents/papers-and-publications/publications/college-profiles/16Profile-Front-Section.pdf. Accessed 17 May 2018.

[62] .https://www.media.mit.edu/projects/gender-shades/faq/#faq-what-did-ibm-say-about-this-work

Despite the potential dangers and ethical risks in AI development, this technology has tremendous promise to create breakthroughs and to be applied to solve some of the world's most pressing problems. For example, in agriculture, AI can help people efficiently monitor the health of farms in real time. By 2050, farmers must produce more food, on less arable land, and with lower environmental impact to feed the world's rapidly growing population.[63] AI is also being used to tackle climate change.[64]

*"Machines can analyze the flood of data that is generated every day from sensors, gauges, and monitors to spot patterns quickly and automatically. By looking at data about the changing conditions of the world's land surfaces that is gathered by NASA and aggregated at Landsat, it provides a very accurate picture of how the world is changing. The more accurate we're able to be at the current status of our climate, the better our climate models will be." - Bernard Marr, Forbes*

AI is also helping seismologists detect earthquakes they'd otherwise miss.[65] In the healthcare field, robot-assisted surgery enhances the physician's instrument precision, leading to a 21% reduction in a patient's length of hospital stay post-operation and a reduction of damage in heart surgery.[66]

*"You don't have to be an AI expert to know that we, in this day and age, are in the middle of something almost magical, infinitely creative, and beautifully applicable in a variety of settings."- Ananya, AI4ALL Graduate*

---

[63] Associated Press. "UN: Farmers Must Produce 70% More Food by 2050 to Feed Population."*The Guardian*, Guardian News and Media, 28 Nov. 2011, www.theguardian.com/environment/2011/nov/28/un-farmers-produce-food-population. Accessed 17 May 2018.

[64] Marr, Bernard. "The Amazing Ways We Can Use AI To Tackle Climate Change." *Forbes*, Forbes Magazine, 22 Feb. 2018, www.forbes.com/sites/bernardmarr/2018/02/21/the-amazing-ways-we-can-use-ai-to-tackle-climate-change/. Accessed 17 May 2018.

[65] Vincent, James. "AI Is Helping Seismologists Detect Earthquakes They'd Otherwise Miss."*The Verge*, The Verge, 14 Feb. 2018, www.theverge.com/2018/2/14/17011396/ai-earthquake-detection-oklahoma-neural-network. Accessed 17 May 2018.

[66] Zaidi, Deena. "The 3 Most Valuable Applications of AI in Health Care." *VentureBeat*, VentureBeat, 22 Apr. 2018, venturebeat.com/2018/04/22/the-3-most-valuable-applications-of-ai-in-health-care/. Accessed 17 May 2018.

These are just a few of the potential areas where "moonshots" in AI could massively improve the cost-effectiveness of important interventions, prevent disasters, and improve health and wellbeing of people and planet.

So how do we ensure AI is created ethically and equitably, living up to its potential to address big problems facing our world? The answer is to prioritize inclusion and diversity of voices in the AI field at all levels: leadership, development, policy, and education. By broadening access to the field, we can ensure that AI is being used to its fullest potential, that new questions and problems are addressed, and that more useful products created.

The organization I lead, AI4ALL, aims to ensure that AI technology represents the needs of a diverse society, to mitigate negative impacts, like bias, of AI development, and to raise awareness of AI so that everyone impacted will be informed consumers and have the opportunity to benefit from AI technology. We do this through three core initiatives. First, by educating and inspiring underrepresented youth to pursue AI by partnering with universities including Stanford, Princeton, Boston University, and Carnegie Mellon. The programs teach students technically rigorous AI concepts in the context of societal impact. Students engage in a combination of lectures, hands-on projects, field trips, and mentoring activities that enable them to develop technical skills and motivation and self-confidence to pursue AI and related field. Students then apply their skills to a final project they present to fellow students, teachers, and parents. For example at the 2018 program at Stanford, students completed a project that used natural language processing rendered in Python to classify tweets from Hurricane Sandy in order make disaster relief more efficient.

AI4ALL's second initiative is focused on increasing awareness of AI through educational outreach to communities at risk of being left behind. In July 2018, AI4ALL announced that we will develop and launch a free, online AI education program focused on increasing access to AI education that will reach 1,000,000 people by 2023. This program, called AI4ALL Open Learning, will launch in early 2019 and will be built with with an audience of underrepresented talent mind in a culturally responsive, relevant way that focuses on the social and ethical impacts of AI.

Finally, AI4ALL expands and promotes beneficial uses of AI by pairing its alumni with AI professionals from companies like OpenAI, IBM, Ford, and Accenture to solve problems and create positive impact using AI, including early detection of wildfires, personalized education, and more effective disease diagnosis.

91% of graduates feel like they're part of a community in AI, and 98% know how to find resources to learn more about AI and computer science. A program graduate shared:

*"I used to think I wasn't smart enough to do computer science and AI. But now I've gained so much confidence because of all the support, and being around other girls who are into the same thing. They make me feel comfortable to speak out and ask questions."*

I want to present three case studies that demonstrate that when we broaden access and prioritize inclusion in AI, we:

1.  see more creative ways to leverage AI towards solving important challenges,

2.  uncover hidden geniuses that might develop the next big thing and moonshots in AI, and

3.  spur a powerful network effect that involves even more people and communities in shaping and informing this important technology.

# 1. Creative Solutions

*Photo credit: Stephanie T.*

*"Despite our different cultures or backgrounds, all of my Stanford AI4ALL peers were able to connect through our passion for AI and*

*tech. I learned that our different cultures and backgrounds were the key to connecting and fusing our bright ideas. We brought Stanford AI4ALL to life because we created a diverse environment and brought unique ideas to the table." - Stephanie T. (Stanford AI4ALL '17)*

Stephanie T., a current high school junior in Salinas, California, is a first-generation Mexican-American deeply interested in using AI to solve tangible problems in her community.

Salinas, a booming agricultural community, exports over 79 million pounds of fruits and vegetables to other countries.[67] Stephanie's mother is a farmworker, contributing to this vibrant agricultural community by picking strawberries. Due to the high concentration of agricultural activity in the area, the groundwater in Salinas and the surrounding areas are susceptible to contamination due to agricultural pesticide, waste, and fertilizer runoff, among other factors. A 2012 study estimated that 2.6 million people in the region rely on groundwater, leaving them susceptible to consuming or using contaminated water.[68]

Although Stephanie hasn't experienced this water contamination directly yet, the risk is ever present in her community. Because of this, she's passionate about using the power of technology to investigate and try to mitigate this risk for her community.

She first began to investigate the issue through a science project in 9th grade, where she examined the rate at which Daphnia Magna (a water flea that can detect water toxicity) dies in water from agricultural river versus a river in a non-agricultural city. After learning about artificial intelligence through Stanford AI4ALL in the summer of 2017, she realized that she had a new set of tools to examine the issue of water contamination in agricultural areas. She was accepted into AI4ALL's Alumni Research Fellowship Program, where she chose to focus on using data analysis and AI techniques to monitor water flow and distribution throughout specific counties along the Colorado River in the western United States to predict where contaminated water might be flowing. She plans to adapt the project to be applicable to the water sources in her own community in Salinas, CA.

---

[67] "Facts, Figures & FAQs." *Monterey County Farm Bureau*, Central Coast Regional Water Quality Control Board, montereycfb.com/index.php?page=facts-figures-faqs.Accessed 17 May 2018.

[68] Harter, Thomas et al,. *Addressing Nitrate in California's Drinking Water*. California State Water Resources Control Board, groundwaternitrate.ucdavis.edu/files/138956.pdf. Accessed 17 May 2018.

Although still in high school, Stephanie intends to further her education in computer science in college, with a focus on AI. She is particularly attracted to AI because of its potential to solve tangible problems. While attending Stanford AI4ALL, she noticed that the program was brought to life because so many diverse ideas and voices were brought to the table. These voices were supported, uplifted, and valued - all of which contributed to an atmosphere that helped inspire her to use the power of AI and technology to creatively investigate water issues in her own backyard. Bringing diverse voices like Stephanie's into AI will allow for creative solutions to problems which conventionally heterogeneous groups working in AI risk ignoring.

# Hidden Talents

*Photo credit: Sahana Srinivasan*

*"Stanford AI4ALL...showed me how powerful AI and computer vision are in addressing real-world problems." (Amy J., Stanford AI4ALL 2015)*

Stanford AI4ALL was the springboard that launched Amy J.'s research journey in AI. She's a college freshman at Harvard University with a keen interest in developing solutions to human problems using ethical AI. She was itching to learn more about the AI subfield computer vision after her AI4ALL program ended, so continued to pursue the field by auditing Stanford computer vision courses, creating educational tools--like an intro to computer vision website hosted on Stanford.edu--and interning in Stanford's computer vision lab.

Through her persistence and curiosity, and with the encouragement and support of female mentors in Stanford's computer vision group,

Amy has been able to make significant contributions to computer vision research. In 2017, she was lead author on the paper, Tool Detection and Operative Skill Assessment in Surgical Videos Using Region-Based Convolutional Neural Networks, which reports on results of the research she undertook with computer vision faculty and Ph.D. candidates at Stanford.[69] The research assessed surgeons' operative skills for laparoscopic gallbladder removal surgery using deep learning to provide feedback to surgeons on their performance, improving on results obtained by other researchers by 28%. By providing surgeons with feedback--something they don't regularly get in professional settings--the researchers' goal is to reduce patient complication rates.

Amy's research contributions were recognized for their merit at what is widely considered the industry-standard machine learning and computational neuroscience conference, NIPS. As one of the youngest conference participants, Amy was awarded "best paper" in the Machine Learning for Health workshop at NIPS 2017, beating out hundreds of other submissions made by adult professionals in the field.

Amy hopes to further this research and expand the scope of the project by increasing the size of the dataset used to train the algorithms. She also wants to develop an automated method of scoring a surgeon's skill based on a standardized assessment rubric.

Amy has managed to accomplish all this while still in high school. Her unique and valuable contributions to the field demonstrate the importance of uplifting diverse voices in AI. Amy is interested in following a pathway to a career in AI by interning at a research lab. She also plans to pursue computer science in college.

If underrepresented groups in AI aren't given the opportunity to actively participate in AI, we miss out on untapped talent who have the potential to make a huge potential impact on the field of AI and on humanity at large. Bringing more diverse people into the field is valuable because it will also bring forward varied and diverse interests. In Amy's case, she's passionate about the ethical dimension of AI and building ethical AI systems that solve tangible social problems.

---

[69] Jin, Amy, et al. "Tool Detection and Operative Skill Assessment in Surgical Videos Using Region-Based Convolutional Neural Networks." *31st Conference on Neural Information Processing Systems (NIPS 2017)*, 2017.
http://ai.stanford.edu/~syyeung/jin_nips_ml4h_2017.pdf

# Network Effects

*Photo credit: Manish Dogra*

*"During my time in the Bay Area, I learned of the numerous opportunities available for women and minorities in STEM, something that I saw lacking in my Seattle-area hometown. I felt that I had to bring these opportunities back to my community and resolved that I would try to help others find the same passion for STEM that I did." - Archika D. (Stanford AI4ALL 2017)*

Archika's first ever encounter with computer science wasn't a particularly welcoming one. "Walking into my first computer science camp, I was one of two females in a class of thirty and was completely new to programming—two things that proved to be a problematic combination. After spending two weeks programming a car racing game that I frankly had no interest in ever playing, my first taste of CS was rather discouraging," Archika said of her experience. Because the lessons were a bit alienating, she found that she wasn't engaged with the field. After attending Stanford AI4ALL in 2017, however, her experience with computer science was transformed into a positive and welcoming one. She worked with inspiring mentors and girls like herself, and she came away from it convinced that she had the power to make a positive impact on her community through AI.

In particular, she was motivated to replicate her experience at Stanford AI4ALL with other underrepresented groups in her hometown of Seattle, Washington. As a result, she co-founded EduSTEM, an organization that aims to increase diversity in STEM by exposing young people to supportive and positive impact-oriented STEM education. In particular, the program focuses on serving underrepresented ethnic, socioeconomic, and gender minorities. Workshops and events are geared toward students in 3rd through 7th grade, emphasizing topics like science, physics, and even robotics. Through EduSTEM, Archika is able to reach students from lower-income families who otherwise may not have had the resources or opportunity to access STEM education programs.

Archika's outreach exemplifies the power of network effects, one of the core benefits of AI4ALL programs and of inclusive STEM education in general. After her interest in STEM was nurtured and valued at AI4ALL with supportive peers, she felt empowered to do the same for other young people in her city. What started as an initiative in the Greater Seattle Area has grown to impact over 200 students in 5 cities across the United States, including San Ramon, CA; San Mateo, CA; New York, New York; Kent, Connecticut; Seattle, WA. If diverse talent are given opportunities to pursue their interest and passion in computer science at large and AI in particular within a supportive environment, they're able to effectively contribute to this growing field and bring their peers along with them.

# Conclusion

Inclusion and diversity must be a critical and urgent priority to mitigate the potential risks in AI development and to allow AI to live up to its full potential. Additionally, the public sector and private sector both have an important role to play in ensuring both responsible AI development and to prepare for AI's disruptive impact on the workforce and jobs. In addition to pushing for greater diversity in the field, we also must create and adopt ethical standards and training for the development and use of AI. Though no single set of ethics or standards has been put forward, there are groups working on or advocating for ethical standards including: the IEEE Global Initiative on Ethics of Autonomous and Intelligent Systems; Fairness, Accountability, Transparency in Machine Learning; Partnership on AI and internal efforts from industry leaders. In order to make the most broadly useful standards and policy, we need to take an interdisciplinary and human-centered approach, calling on people from a variety of disciplines to contribute to the responsible development and regulation of AI. And lastly, we also must focus and fund research on the impacts of AI and society to proactively mitigate risks and take advantage of critical opportunities for AI to create public benefit. Current groups include AINow, The Berggruen Institute, AI100, and Data and Society.

The impact of AI on society is one of the more important questions facing humanity today. If we aren't including a broad range of doers and thinkers in shaping and creating AI, we risk dangerous impacts like bias and miss out on the potential benefits this technology could bring to the health and well-being of people and planet.

*"Through lines of code, I was able to create an algorithm that, when implemented in society, could actually change people's lives."*

-Stephanie, AI4ALL Graduate

Monique is President and Co-Founder of the Humanized Internet, a non-profit organization focused on providing digital identity for those individuals most underserved, blockchain is certainly a potential mechanism for this billion people challenge, see: https: www.thehumanizedinternet.org.

Monique has already advanced Cisco's technology footprint through the ideation and conception of disruptive technologies spanning Artificial Intelligence and Mixed Reality (AI/MR), Blockchain, IoT and M2M services, Semantic Web, Cloud Federation, and the Tactile Internet. Her greatest success has been in infusing a big-picture perspective that helps engineers and business leaders understand how existing and future technologies align with the needs of business, government, non-profits, and society-focused organizations. To this end, Monique was honored as *Business Worldwide Magazine's* 2016 Visionary of the Year (Technology, Social Change and Ethics) and 2016 Social Media Champion of the Year.

Monique began her journey with Cisco in 2000 as an SP Solutions Engineer in Europe where she helped embed a service provider DNA into the company. In 2001, she became the CTO Consulting Engineer for the service provider segment in Europe and Asia. By 2005, Monique was building a technical leadership team in Hong Kong and directing strategic initiatives for technology globalization for the Office of the CTO. She became Cisco's first Services CTO in 2012, effectively aligning the

vision and architecture for services technology across the organization.
In this role, Monique helped to prepare Cisco for the transition from
hardware to services as the core business, growing the monetary impact
of services for software, security, and analytics.

# Restoring Certification of Refugee Health Professionals and Caregivers through a Blockchain-Based Ecosystem

By Monique Jeanne Morrow

*The world will face a shortage of up to 4.3 million doctors, midwives, nurses, and other healthcare professionals over the next decade. At the same time, there are many trained experienced healthcare professionals among the world's many millions of refugees and displaced people who cannot practice their skills due to a number of reasons, often relating to validation of credentials. There exist today organizations that help foreign-educated healthcare professionals live and work in their country of choice by assessing and validating their academic and professional credentials. This chapter presents a proposal how the this could reach most refugees with healthcare skills with the help of smartphone and blockchain technologies.*

In June 2016, the United Nations High Commissioner for Refugees
(UNHCR) reported that the number of refugees, asylum-seekers, and
internally displaced people around the world had topped 65 million.
That number is likely to have increased significantly since then. Not
only does this number indicate "immense human suffering," as
reported by the UNHCR, but it is also likely to include an enormous
and unused resource of professional skills in the form of thousands of
health care professionals.

Such displaced populations represent a potential productive
workforce, whether in their host countries, their home countries once
repatriated, or any other country with shortages of important skills. It
has been estimated that the world will face a shortage of up to 4.3
million doctors, midwives, nurses, and other healthcare professionals[70]
over the next decade. *Therefore, without adequate and timely*

---

[70] Source: The National Center for Biotechnology Information NCBI

*intervention in the form of professional credential restoration and professional development, nurses and other healthcare professionals within these displaced populations represent a huge economic and health resource loss.*

One proposed remedy offers restoration of the professional development and identity of these individual caregivers. This remedy would afford them increased ability to be considered for licenses to practice and gain work visas. These visas could be to the countries of asylum or countries with important healthcare shortages, such as the UK, Canada, Australia, and New Zealand.

Middle-income countries are predicted to experience the largest and most rapidly increasing demand and shortages of health workers between 2013 and 2030. The average annual growth in the supply of health workers is lower in high- and upper-middle-income countries than in the lower-middle income countries. However, the comparatively higher growth in demand will lead to the largest health worker shortages in the labor market in upper-middle-income countries. The growth in the supply for workers is predicted to be the slowest in low-income countries, but the growth in demand there is also slow.

*As a result, the net shortage of health workers in low-income countries will be reduced by 2030, but still fall significantly below the threshold level.*

Timely credential restoration and professional development would also provide displaced health care professionals with the profound psychological benefit of being able to maintain and develop their personal and professional identities at a time of great physical and emotional upheaval. The intervention is therefore key to helping displaced persons maintain resilience and some degree of psychological equilibrium during their period of displacement.

# Global Needs Assessment for Caregiver Skills

The undersupply of healthcare professionals is concurrent with globalization and the resulting liberalization of markets, which allow health workers to offer their services in countries other than their own. *High- and middle-income countries will have the economic capacity to employ tens of millions additional health workers. By contrast,*

315

*low-income countries will face both low demand for and supply of health workers.* This means that even countries that can produce additional workers may not be able to employ and retain them without considerably higher economic growth, especially in the health sector.

The United Nations Secretary-General announced on June 2, 2016 the appointment of a High-level Commission on Health Employment and Economic Growth with the goal of supporting the Sustainable Development Goals' (SDGs) ambitious agenda to improve the lives of all, including improved health and prosperity. The 10 recommendations from the Commission include:

1. Job creation

2. Gender equality and women's rights

3. Education, training and competencies

4. Health service delivery and organisation

5. Technology

6. Finance & fiscal space

7. Partnerships and cooperation

8. International migration

9. Crisis and humanitarian setting

10. Data, information and accountability

Most of these priorities would be addressed through the current project.

Recent developments have additionally confirmed the urgency to build resilient health systems and to strengthen global health security. Health workers and health employment function at the heart of the SDG agenda (specifically SDGs 3, 4, 5 and 8). The rising global demand and need for health workers over the next 15 years present significant challenges. Importantly, this need also offers the opportunity to generate employment in areas where decent jobs are most needed - for example, through involvement of refugees with a background in healthcare - who can be valuable contributors not only in their home countries, if return is possible, but in other places where health workers are scarce and needed. The number of migrant doctors and nurses working in OECD countries has increased by 60% over the past 10 years - up from 1,130,068 to 1,807,948[71].

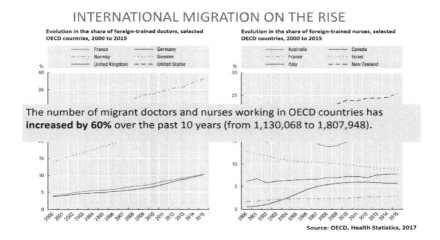

INTERNATIONAL MIGRATION ON THE RISE

The number of migrant doctors and nurses working in OECD countries has **increased by 60%** over the past 10 years (from 1,130,068 to 1,807,948).

Source: OECD, Health Statistics, 2017

# Recognition of standards, skills, and education certification by third countries

It is not enough to provide a caregiver standards, skills, and education certification, these assets must be recognized by countries and organizations. CGFNS has a large network of health profession regulators they work with around the world. It is through this interface we aim to assist people in obtaining recognition for their qualifications and professional licensure. This fact is not a technology problem but one that needs to be part of a proposed pilot process.

The program suggests a partnership with the internationally recognised Certification Body CGFNS International, Inc. (Commission on Graduates of Foreign Nursing Schools). CGFNS International is an immigration-neutral nonprofit organization that helps foreign-educated healthcare professionals live and work in their country of choice by assessing and validating their academic and professional credentials. It provides foreign students and healthcare professionals with a comprehensive assessment of their academic records to facilitate their successful admission to schools in the U.S. and other countries.

---

71 Source: WHO.org

CGFNS also helps protect migrating healthcare professionals by advocating for ethical recruitment practices and continuously monitoring the global landscape for developing trends in recruitment and workplace norms. It has NGO consultative status with the United Nations Economic and Social Council (ECOSOC).

Once displaced health care professionals are identified through informal interviews or a similar process, CGFNS attempts to obtain hard-copy credential information, such as licenses and educational transcripts, in his or her possession.

Should a displaced professional not have access to hard-copy records, CGFNS has the expertise to administer a *predictor exam* that ascertains the skill level of the professional as a first step in resurrecting his or her professional identity. Harnessing the technology of comparability for its unique credentials assessment approach, CGFNS will next perform a forensic assessment to compare any produced documentation with education/license information from its state-of-the-art database. The goal of this assessment is to verify and ultimately restore formal education, training, and licensure histories that have been lost or destroyed.

Once a displaced professional's "preliminary credential portfolio" is assembled, CGFNS proposes adding an additional level of scrutiny by its Professional Standards Committee, whose members are health care experts qualified to further assess and verify each credential and portfolio. CGFNS has a proven track record of successfully restoring or "recreating" reliable professional histories of migrant health care workers utilizing both its educational database and its Professional Standards Committee. Once a displaced professional's identity is restored, the credentials are stored in the blockchain and certified by CGFNS.

# The case for blockchain technology

This careful process of assessment and record-keeping is designed to take into account situations where the records no longer exist or access to them is prevented. Health professionals who have fled to Jordan, for example, could be residing both in camps or in urban situations, in neither of which could they have access to their degree materials or to the institution that issued them.

318

To enhance the security of these records once they are recreated, the proposed pilot mechanism involves the creation of an online platform based on blockchain technology. Because blockchain is decentralized by nature, we can leverage this technology to enable individuals to hold and control their own personal data that can still be assessed and used in humanitarian crises, such as wars, natural disasters, and refugee flight.

This system differs from classic methods of data preservation. Those systems are largely centralized, and access to their content, such as university certificates and land registry titles depends upon the survival and availability of the institutions. Key questions include the characteristics of content preservation, data integrity, and the continuing control of access. The advantage of blockchain technology is its ability to protect the information through privacy and security mechanisms. Via blockchain, for example, we could create a closed permissioned group where only the known persons or organizations are allowed to exchange data. The technologies to develop such a sustainable platform exists today through interfacing to a smartphone with biometric authentication. It seems safe to assume that a smartphone will be the tool used by refugees, and already UNHCR is working with GSMA members to obtain approval of SIM cards for refugees. This enabling innovation, which seems likely to move into the stage of practical and effective availability, seems likely to help close the global caregiver profession shortage.

*Other Contributors to this proposal include Paola de Leo, Andan Foundation; Dr. Frances Hughes; Lilian Furrer; Akram Alfawakheeri; and Mark Kovarski.*

*References:*

*https://www.ictworks.org/united-nations-agencies-using-blockchain-technology/*

*http://www.unhcr.org/blogs/promise-hype-provides-blockchain-safe-identity/*

Daniel Pianko is co-founder and managing director at University Ventures. With over a decade of experience in the education industry, Daniel has built a reputation as a trusted education adviser and innovator in student finance, medical education, and postsecondary education. Daniel began his career in investment banking at Goldman Sachs, and quickly became intrigued by the potential of leveraging private capital to establish the next generation of socially beneficial education companies. After leaving Goldman, Daniel invested in, founded, advised, or managed a number of education-related

businesses that led to the creation of University Ventures. Daniel graduated magna cum laude from Columbia University, and holds a M.B.A. and M.A. in Education from Stanford University.

# Income Share Agreements: the I-Thou Answer to Student Loans

## By Daniel Pianko

College is supposed to lead to a good middle class life. For increasing numbers of people, this is no longer true. After 10 years of struggling with student debt, a social worker named Jessica reached out to me Within minutes I ascertained that there was effectively no way for her to ever pay down her loans. While her family income of almost $100,000 should put Jessica solidly in the middle class, her $150,000 of loans meant that her monthly student loan payments exceeded $1,000 per month. Even with that payment, her loan balance would take almost 30 years to pay down. Between rent and the standard expenses of a young family, she was unable to save enough for a down payment or to do anything but pay down debt. Even bankruptcy was not an option as loans are not dischargeable. The US government made free debt available to Jessica, but failed to alert her that the consequences of the debt meant that she would never live the financial side of the American dream.

In 1965 with the passage of the first Higher Education Act, America embarked on an experiment in which the government created a program that appeared to empower students: students choose what school to attend and the federal government guaranteed tuition payments. The process has actually *disempowered* people like Jessica through a massive case of three card monte – students are making perhaps the largest investment decision of their lives (e.g. $100,000+ for college) with little information and a perception of "free" debt that is, in reality, quite costly.

The process appears to benefit all players in higher education. The schools get their money as soon as a student enrolls. Students have their choice of institution. The nation gets a more educated populace prepared for modern work.

Everyone benefits, that is, except the student. At first blush, the student is ecstatic: receiving a large amount of (relatively) low interest debt to finance an education that is the best pathway to the middle class. The only problem is that fewer than 50% of students who start a degree, finish. Many that do finish, finish after many years of struggle and find jobs that do not generate enough income.

The net effect is quite pernicious: the federal government functions is functioning as the ultimate loan shark – the ability to garnish social security wages and other benefits to ensure payment, collecting from the basic welfare that no private creditors are allowed to touch. . The results have been staggeringly bad for students.

*There is over $1.4 trillion of student debt – more than 3 times the total debt 10 years ago on the eve of the subprime crisis and the Great Recession that followed.*[72]

There are over 4.6 million Americans in default on their student loans – *double* the number four years ago[73]. Even worse, only two out of five pay enough each year to reduce their principal balance. Brookings

---

[72] https://fred.stlouisfed.org/graph/?id=SLOAS,#0

[73] https://www.wsj.com/articles/nearly-5-million-americans-in-default-on-student-loans-1513192375

recently released a report that by 2023 student loan defaults for students who graduated in 2003 could reach 40 percent of all such borrowers[74]

The solution is not to make slight changes around the edges of a broken system, but instead to re-imagine how to put the power of higher education finance in the hands of students. Furthermore students (and the federal government) should not be bearing the risk of the efficacy of education.

*Instead, America should shift from debt to financing higher education with a percentage of future income flows. In this model, each school has "skin in the game" whereby if a student is highly successful then the school benefits.*

If the student does not receive an education that leads to employment, then the school suffers the consequences and the student is not subjected to the modern day debtor's prison that is student loans.

The mechanism of risk sharing is called an Income Share Agreement ("ISA"). The rise of ISAs creates perhaps the most important change in the power dynamic between student and school. Currently the pricing and outcomes of school are highly opaque. There is limited outcomes data by school and by program (e.g. what does an engineering major at Purdue make vs. NC State?) By having the private sector "price" the economic return of any degree, then students can have a clear understanding of the return on investment for that program. If the Purdue program requires 3.5% of income for 7 years for an ISA, whereas the NC State program requires 4.8% of income for 10 years, the Purdue program is clearly superior in economic return. Students can make decisions to attend a school based on a number of factors from proximity to home to quality of sorority life. What ISAs do is make the economically rational decision clear.

---

[74] https://www.brookings.edu/research/the-looming-student-loan-default-crisis-is-worse-than-we-thought/

# The Modern Income Share Agreements: Returning Financing Power to the Student

The University of Chicago Economist Milton Friedman created the concept of ISAs in the 1950s. Freedman argued that instead of charging tuition to students, schools should instead charge a percentage of a graduates' income. The first school to try ISAs was Yale University. The first experiment is roundly regarded as a failure because all the students were responsible for all the debt. However, Blair Levin, an early recipient of the failed Yale program recently wrote "When I was accepted [to Yale], I had no idea how to pay for it... Like many aspiring students, I knew that a traditional loan was a financial burden difficult to discharge."[75] The ISA program made it more important that Blair was accepted to Yale, then whether he had a father who could pay for the education.

The modern ISA was created by Vemo Education founder Tonio DeSorrento[76]. What DeSorrento realized was that ISAs only worked when incentives of all parties – the students and schools – are aligned. DeSorrento re-created the ISA as an installment contract between the student and the school where the student pays a percentage of their income but only within certain key criteria:

- **Money cap**: no student will pay more than 2.0-2.5X the value of their tuition, and the money cap is more frequently 1.0X the total tuition value

- **Time cap**: no student will pay an ISA for more than 10 years, with certain extensions for standard reasons (e.g. if a student re-enters school)

- **Minimum income**: If a person makes less than a preset minimum income level, than student is not required to make any payments under the ISA (e.g. no payments due for any students who make less than $40,000 per year).

---

[75]https://www.realcleareducation.com/articles/2018/05/15/how_yales_failed_income_share_experiment_worked_for_me_110277.html

[76] The author, Daniel Pianko, is an investor in Vemo Education and a member of the board.

Vemo estimates it is structuring and servicing over 95 percent of all ISAs being written today. Vemo is religious about making sure that each school maintain some of the "risk" that students repay. By forcing schools to keep 10-30 percent of the "risk" of repayment, the risk for the quality of the education is being switched from the student bearing the risk to the schools having "skin in the game".

The first major client was Purdue University. Every senior at Purdue who qualifies receives an offer to receive an ISA. Students are told to first access all federal aid, grants, scholarships and other "cheap" forms of financing first. After those sources are Every major from dance to engineering can qualify for an ISA, but with slightly different terms. After entering their major and year of graduation, students see the following option to accept an ISA:

### Income Expectations

For students in the group of majors that includes **Management** and who expect to graduate in 2020, their expected starting income would be approximately **$41,000**. Assuming that income grows at **3.8%** per year on average, this chart shows expected income for the first 10 years after leaving school:

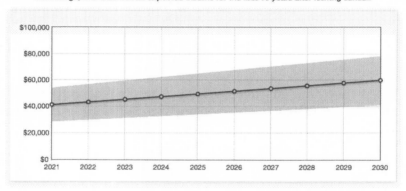

Then the student can compare an ISA to their alternative forms of financing:

## Total Payments

Based on your expected income, this chart shows what your total payments would be if you were to accept an ISA of **$11,000** with an Income Share of **4.91%**. For comparison, this chart also shows total pre-tax payments for a PLUS loan at **7.00%** (click to change parameters) and a Private loan at **9.50%** (click to change parameters):

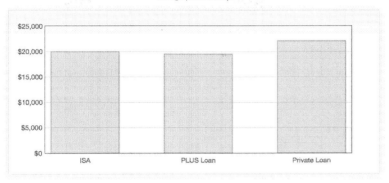

A PLUS loan is a federally subsidized loan program that requires a parent to co-sign. Many students do not have parent a parent who is willing/able to co-sign. A private loan generally requires a high credit/FICO score to receive a loan, which many students do not have. Private loans are also available to students with parents who have high credit scores and are willing to co-sign the loan.

Today over 30 schools have announced ISA programs with Vemo. Besides Vemo, there are a handful of providers, including LEAF Education and Better Future Forward, that have experiments with ISAs in process.

# Future State: ISAs as Student Comparison Tool

While traditional colleges and universities have begun implementing ISAs in small numbers, the coding boot camp market has become a rapid first mover of this new student finance technology. Coding boot camps are an ideal testing ground for ISAs: they are short (3-6 month) in duration programs where graduates frequently make $60,000-$100,000 per year. The return on investment for these programs is extremely high so the ISA is an effective financing mechanism. Since a 2014 launch at Make School, a coding bootcamp, now over 25 of the 90 code schools have initiated ISA programs.

The ISA has empowered the students. Many students will only enroll at coding schools that have ISA programs – the zero-upfront cost with the school bearing 100% of the risk is a compelling value proposition to students. Many students will only select a code school that has an ISA offering. Some schools like MakeSchool are even functioning as a college alternative. MakeSchool is a 2 year program whose graduates make on average a salary of $95,000 in full time coding jobs at companies like Facebook, Google, Apple, Tesla and even NASA. The entire program costs 25% of the students income upon graduation for 42 months after graduation – and the student owes nothing if they make less than $60,000 per year. Students can alternatively opt to pay $60,000 in cash instead of the ISA (but few take the cash option).

Perhaps the most transformative is how ISAs could impact the pricing and academic offerings of traditional universities. Tuition at universities has risen at over twice the rate of inflation for over a generation. To put this in perspective, in 1978 a person attending community college in New Jersey would have to work 2.5 hours per week to fund tuition. Today, the same student must work 16 hours per week to afford tuition.[77] While the value of a college education is clear – graduates make over $1 million more in their lifetime than non-graduates, Americans are losing faith in the value of higher education. 58 percent of While Americans will likely spend more on their higher education than any other consumer good other than their house, it is extremely difficult to show "quality" higher education. Currently consumers rely on poor indicators of quality like US News and World Report rankings or the federal "college score card". With pricing high and rising and quality virtually impossible to understand, Americans have intuitively realized that the cost of higher education is far beyond the return on investment.

College pricing is almost intentionally opaque. Websites abound about how to "decipher" financial award letters[78]. Campus Logic recently raised $55 million to help colleges simplify award letters.[79] Imagine if instead of getting a complex financial aid package upon admission to a school with multiple types of loans, work student, required parent contributions, etc students received the following economic proposal:

---

[77] http://www.insidehighered.com/blogs/confessions-community-college-dean/it-doesn%E2%80%99t-just-seem-harder%E2%80%A6

[78] see, for example: https://studentloanhero.com/featured/ways-compare-contrast-financial-aid-offers/

[79] University Ventures was an investor in Campus Logic.

- Tuition will be 10% of your income for the first 10 years of your professional career

- Your total payments will be capped at $100,000

- If you don't reach $100,000 in payments after 10 years, you will owe nothing.

- If you earn less than $40,000 in any given year, then you own nothing.

This is a simple, easy to understand financial relationship that removes the risk from the students. Assuming a standardized ISA form, there are only 4-5 variables that matter to the student. With a few simple variables, students can assess the relative economic worth of a higher education program.

The differential pricing of the ISAs is driven by two simple variables: the salary received from achieved from the degree divided by the cost of the education. Schools can improve their ISAs percentages in two ways: 1) lowering the cost of attendance and/or 2) improving the income of their graduates.

Cost containment is easy to understand. The more interesting variable is increased earning power. In an ISA heavy future, schools will be incentivized to invest in academic and non-academic areas that increase the percentage of students who graduate and their income post-graduation. For example, today, most colleges have more staff in their alumni relations office soliciting donations vs. career services. The focus on outcomes would transform the career services office into a job hunting machine. Similarly, if a graduate lost a job, the school would be incentivized to re-engage career services and alumni resources to find that student a job.

On the academic side, schools would be encouraged to modernize curricula. For example, study after study shows the value of a liberal arts degree is increased exponentially by requiring 5-6 courses in key financial areas (e.g. statistics, economics), then schools might require such subjects. Schools will be incented to partner more closely with businesses that offer internships. Accounting programs will be more likely to prepare students for the Certified Public Accountants exam. In an era where over 90 percent of students attend higher education to improve their job prospects, the ISA creates a powerful incentive for schools to meet the needs of their students.

# Tale of the Tape: ISAs vs. Student Debt

There are some serious potential criticisms of how ISAs that require consideration. The immediate critique of the ISA structure is that it is a form of indentured servitude. While the initial experiments with Yale students might of some elements of indentured servitude (e.g. a 30 year life), the modern ISA is both time and money capped at levels that are reasonable for any form of obligation (e.g. 2X value of education and 10 years).

ISAs function like a progressive insurance policy. Students who make a lot of money pay more than those who do not have strong financial outcomes. In addition, one of the most noxious issues is that student debt is non-dischargeable in bankruptcy so once a student takes a loan, they will be responsible for that loan through any hardship.

The more appropriate way to consider ISAs as a mechanism for social good is to compare ISAs to what they are replacing: private student loans.

The real issue is that the Obama administration attempted to ease the burden of student loans by creating an income based repayment program and other mechanisms that made forbearance (or the postponement of payments easier). While well intentioned, these changes set the required payment rates too low. The required repayment rates are so low that only 37% of students are paying down principal on their loans.[80] That means that 60+% of Americans have negative amortizing student loans – in other words that each year their student loan balance goes up each month. This has created a situation where there is no way many students will ever repay their loans.

|  | Student Loans | ISA |
|---|---|---|
| Duration | 10 years | Up to 10 years |
| Interest rate | 8-19% | No interest rate; percentage of income varies based on cost of program and projected annual salary |
| Minimum required payments | Required monthly payments | If a student makes below a set amount (e.g. $40,000) then the student owes zero for that period. |

---

[80] https://www.wsj.com/articles/writing-off-student-loans-is-only-a-matter-of-time-1471303339

| Bankruptcy | Non-dischargeable in bankruptcy | Students owe anything post bankruptcy |
|---|---|---|
| Dance vs. Engineering | No information on impact of major | While aggregate amount paid is the same (e.g. tuition is set), different percentages of income depending on program choice |
| Progressive Repayment | Students with successful outcomes and poor outcomes pay the same amount; creating a regressive repayment structure | Progressive repayment where rich pay more than those less well off. |
| Underwrite program vs. person | Students or parents with credit worthy FICO score, co-signers, etc. | Qualification based on program of attendance; Limited number of "knockouts" such as prior bankruptcy, lack of attendance |

Some critics of ISAs claim that transparent pricing will force students to select STEM or other employable majors. What ISAs actually do is give students the ability to choose a program based on information. Students can of course choose to study dance, they should just know the ramifications of the choice (e.g. a higher income share). Social worker Jessica attended an expensive undergraduate private school followed by expensive graduate programs. She likely would have chosen a cheaper or shorter program if she had understood the ramifications of $150,000 of student loans.

Perhaps more importantly, it is highly possible that with some tweaking, the liberal arts may become more attractive as ISA programs than certain STEM fields. For example, while colleges charge the same for a liberal arts vs a STEM degree, the liberal arts generally subsidize the hard sciences (lecture courses are far cheaper to deliver than laboratory time). Furthermore, the long-term income of liberal arts students, especially at stronger universities do even out or even exceed their STEM colleagues.

# International Comparisons

Increasingly western nations are experimenting with shifts towards ISAs or other forms of income based repayment schemes. The United States allows certain students to apply for income based repayment options, which tend to be for longer time periods and higher percentages than private sector ISAs. However, the most radical forms of experimentation are coming from overseas. Australia, the Unikted Kingdom and other countries are creating government funded income based repayment schemes for effectively all students. In Australia, where the average student borrows as much as in the US, The government automatically deducts 4 percent of earnings from former students, but only if the student makes more than AUD 40,000.[81] The UK has a similar scheme but creates the obligation as a "loan" which needs to be repaid. Unlike the US income based repayment options (or private ISAs in the US), there is no obligation to repay after 20-30 years.

# Conclusion

The student loan market in the United States is fundamentally broken. With default rates likely to exceed 35 percent for many loan programs over their lifetime, it makes no sense to continue the system of loans that require fixed repayments. The US should move to an ISA model where students face limited negative consequences if they fail to receive the economic return from education. Instead, the allocation of risk should shift from the federal government and the student to the schools which have the most control over the costs they charge and the outcomes they achieve.

# The I-Thou Alternative

Perhaps what is most exciting about ISAs is that they have the potential to create a series of I-Thou interactions. When schools have a stake in their students' long-lasting success, administrations have incentive to see to that their students help each other, which would align financial and purely human interests. One of the most important outcomes of college educations are the friends people make. College is for many the crossroads between youthful play and adult responsibility and college friendships are often at the same time deeply personal and supportive, as well as a social capital for career opportunity. As a part of the ISA contract, students could be asked to mentor future students t, for the purpose of seeding long-lasting personal friendships, where people support each other through both good and testing times. A recent graduate from a particular demographic, for example a first-generation college goer, could be asked to mentor a current student as part of their ISA contract. Alumni from a specific school will be encouraged to hire other alumni or assist in a job search. In effect, the ISA creates a village of people with committed friends helping each other to achieve the economic promise of higher education.

---

[81] https://www.nytimes.com/2016/07/10/upshot/america-can-fix-its-student-loan-crisis-just-ask-australia.html

**Gi Fernando MBE, Founder of Freeformers**

Gi is an engineer, social impact entrepreneur and investor, who founded Freeformers in 2012 having previously built successful technology businesses, including Techlightenment (sold to Experian Plc). The father-of-three received an MBE in the New Year Honours 2017 for services to the Digital Economy. A thought-leader on the Future of Work, Behavioural Change and the impact of Automation and AI on employment and society, Gi holds positions on various boards including Apps for Good, Duke of York IDEA and Craft.co. He also invests in innovative startups such as Technology Will Save Us, BookingBug, Citymapper and Playmob. In September 2017, Gi was named Entrepreneur of the Year at the Asian Achievers Awards.

# Banks at the heart of a people-centered economy

By Gi Fernando MBE, Founder of Freeformers

## Banking is going back to the future

Traditional retail banking faces an unprecedented set of pressures from today's fast-paced technological change - but it already has the historical evidence of how to face down these challenges.

Throughout this book, the authors demonstrate how a people-centered economy is the best route to effect real change in the world moving forward. Banking should be held up as a prime example; it has a distinct opportunity to show how and why people will stimulate a renaissance in an industry tainted by mistrust and an uncertainty over its role within society.

Modern retail banking has become far too task-centered. In a task-centered economy we optimise transactions. But AI can do this far easier and faster than humans and so there is no business advantage to be gained from it.

With a people-centered economy, we can instead build thriving ecosystems with money, products and relationships at the heart, starting as locally as possible - and this is where banking first began.

Throughout banking's history, whether the early traders and merchants in ancient Greece, the Medicis in the 1400s, the Bank of England's foundation in 1694, the First Bank of the United States in 1791 or the Quaker movement, banks were always designed and operated with people as their focus.

They existed to forge and build communities, and in the centuries before computers could crunch data in seconds to assess risk, so much of their transacting was carried out on trust, solely based on people-centered relationships.

And it is this theory of banking's historic place in the advancement of people that underpins my belief that a people-centered model for the industry, to replace today's failing task-centered one, is the way in which banking becomes relevant again.

# Task-centricity is the main challenge for modern retail banking

At my company Freeformers, we work with retail banks around the world to show how through a fusion of people, digital skills and data you can change outdated mindsets and practices to meet the demands of new generations of customers.

The CEOs and boards we work with are fighting on two fronts.

First, there is the threat from leaner, faster and nimbler Fintech startups, building digital products and offers at a speed the incumbents cannot match. They do not have the same inherent barriers to innovation whereas banks cannot afford to fail fast and then try again and fail again. There are large-scale costs involved to roll out new digital services and due to legacy infrastructure, outdated systems, economic uncertainty and the aforementioned old-style mindsets and practices, today's incumbents have become very risk-averse.

They are now mired in a laser focus on the micro transactional elements of their businesses and the aggregation of these transactional elements into products, which are very well executed but lack any demand. This task-centered approach is returning less and less each minute in profits and wider value to customers, to businesses, to the economy and to their own banking employees.

This cannot go on. Much of their current income, for example at a retail bank, comes through charging customers for a wide-range of elements such as paying in a cheque, the interest on a loan or the fee for going overdrawn and these tiny transactional elements are becoming increasingly commoditized.

Similarly for investment banks,increasing amounts of far larger transactions such as Mergers and Acquisitions can be automated - particularly the heavily data-driven risk assessments, due diligence, ratios and so on. Again, all these lenses are purely an aggregation of moving data points, which are much better handled by machines.

Replicated into their billions, small micro transactions and charges may show as a strong number on the balance sheet but in a world where everything is now connected with effectively unlimited processing power, low-cost mass security checking and cheap storage, moving 1s and 0s from one place to another is now practically-free to all.

When the margin on a micro transaction is near enough at zero, and everyone is competing to drive that margin down even further, you have to find a different way to grow. Charging a percentage or fixed fee on moving a piece of information is no longer sustainable. It is dangerous to continue this as a business model.

Banks however have one thing none of the new digital challengers have: the sheer volume of PEOPLE working for them and the sheer volume of customers, both personal and commercial, they are serving.

They already have the tools to return their gaze to a people-centered model, rather than a task-centered one; it would not be difficult and offers far more innovational opportunity and positives for social change than continuing with this mass micro focus on money being lent and stored. This may mean a short-term hit financially but over years and decades it will return far more in monetary gain, economic prosperity and game-changing solutions for a better world.

A new core mission should now be at the heart of the retail banking industry: To make all of the people banking serves and employs to be the best that they can be!

# It's time to leverage people not 1s and 0s

The general measure of value has always been money; the notes and coins exchanged over a counter, the balances in an account or the debt outstanding on a loan or credit card. But people have value too and this can and must be measured through data, only then can we can develop the human growth that powers financial growth.

At Freeformers, we are already doing this with many retail banks, showing how a measured increase in the digital mindset and skillset - soft and hard - of their people is leading to greater profits as employees gain the tools to show customers how new products and services are, and can be, relevant to their lives. It means take-up surges and their use is far more effective on a day-to-day basis.

Banks today have something of value that is woefully underused and underutilised, the tangible everyday relationships between customers and those serving them or managing their assets and loans. But these direct relationships have been diluted to make transacting faster and cheaper.

Banking's history shows us that when customers aren't just numbers on a spreadsheet, and money itself is not always the dominant factor for one-to-one engagement, connections are made, advice is offered, knowledge flows, new ideas germinate, trade is be facilitated and communities thrive.

AI and automation can take care of the machine transactions, banking's people must be shown how to fully harness and optimise the human 'transactions'.

Banks can take greater, faster and more confident strides in this respect because they have the people and the data already to hand. Few other industries have this chance for change on such a huge scale. They just need to use the opportunity more effectively.

## People-centered conversations sow the seed for task- centered transactions

Banks need to talk to their customers more. Not just on the phone or via email, and not through a faceless online live chat. Right now it is practically impossible for banks to do much about personalising a service purely for an individual customer but this is the key to the industry's future in a people-centered economy.

Business plans and spreadsheets tell you very little about the person presenting it or their innate and potential abilities to develop a proposition over time. But that too can be measured using data and welded with the knowledge gained from personalised interactions over months or years. This changes the game.

Machines have made it simple and fast for loans and credit cards to be applied for and approved in minutes with a few clicks without the need to talk. Algorithms work out someone's risk in seconds - not always accurately - but there is no inherent advantage to this technology. The inherent advantage comes through a people-centered approach to gain insights into a customer's psyche and aspirations.

As a bank, when you understand why that customer is taking out that loan or credit card and what they are using it for, you can begin to personalise your approach. This information is a valuable commodity, it has a real premium that a few pennies in interest charged on a monthly overdrawn balance does not.

Information drives change and returning banks to being places where valuable information about people is stored in the 'vault' alongside the money is what can change lives and refuel local and then national economies. It creates an ecosystem.

# The people-centered ecosystem at the heart of a bank

Knowing why a customer is doing something is the currency that can be used to develop a successful ecosystem and it is these ecosystems that can make a bank more successful and sustainable in the long-term.

The McKinsey report "Remaking the bank for an ecosystem world" shows how you get equity by building connections around money and products in the middle. In the future we will see a whole bunch of new services banks can charge for that don't connect to the traditional monetary ones; these will be powered by the burgeoning ecosystem.

This ecosystem doesn't have to be built around a branch although they are still an important place. But so is someone's home or a coffee shop or a supermarket. In all of these places, banks can have real conversations with real people, observe their body language and develop rapports and relationships. It could be truly transformational in rural communities that have lost a branch and where people are now feeling disconnected from ecosystems in larger metropolitan cities.

Understanding everything that a customer is up to at any particular moment is critical for the future of banking. This is how a bank helps customers to be the best that they can be. Transactions are of low or negligible value but aspirations are of high value because they can be used to make connections, not just financial ones, but to much-needed and useful support such as benefits, legal advice or professional collaboration. Banks that put themselves in pole position to make and use these trusted and powerful connections put themselves at the heart of this ecosystem.

What better place than a bank - which already exists around the currency of our lives, namely money - to facilitate somebody's whole life journey within a thriving ecosystem that connects them to, and crucially provides them with, all sorts of new opportunities and chances.

# People-centered banks start by rocking the cradle

The birth of a baby presents a whole change in lifestyle for an individual and a family. This example clearly shows the value in a people-centered approach to banking. If an employee knows a credit card has been applied for to fund a new arrival, that local ecosystem can kick in at various levels.

It can be used to connect that customer with appropriate services from local and national government from benefits to healthcare and it is in prime position at a local level to offer them discounts at relevant nearby stores, fuelling the area's economy.

Employees could hold knowledge-sharing sessions in branches, community centres or schools between parents-to-be and those with children already in order to give them advice on the hidden costs of having and raising a baby they'd perhaps not thought of.

Ensuring they are as financially-prepared for their new arrival as possible is the responsibility of a modern 21st century retail bank and it pays dividends because of the varied financial implications and opportunities a bank can make money from in the long-term.

For example, it could work with the customer to develop a personalised savings plan for their new child towards educational tuition or a home in the future and target ways in which the parent could earn money going forward if they chose not to return to work full-time. This means it could introduce them to, and educate them on, flexible working opportunities providing practical advice and help to set up as a solopreneur and connect them to others doing the same successfully nearby.

Offering such personalised services fosters and creates long-term committed customers. This is more advantageous than a quick-fix transactional focus on some interest charged on a credit card purchase of a pram or cot.

# People-centered banks do business better to ensure people thrive

Technology should always be used to augment real relationships. If AI that is continually processing financial data highlights someone has missed a payment, or stops paying in a salary, a people-centered relationship with that customer quickly identifies why.

If they have lost their job, assistance can be given by the bank on where to turn next and the bank could adapt their credit line in the short-term to ensure they can pay their bills. The bank could even connect them to new money-making opportunities in the gig economy or to state benefits they could claim to stay afloat in the short-term.

At Barclays, when someone falls into problems paying their mortgage, people are connected to sources of help that could prevent this from happening. The costs of a repossession dwarfs the short-term loss on a few postponed mortgage payments.

This could happen at an earlier stage. Rather than notifying someone when they go into their overdraft and are at risk of charges, why not text them before they fall into the red? If the technology knows they have money in a savings account, encourage them to transfer it over. A bank may lose a little in fees but it will gain much more in goodwill.

People-centered banks can also become the hub for financial education from an early age for the next generation of customers. The more they understand about money and living within their means, the greater chance for their prosperity in the future - and the economy's

Banks could foster links within their communities with schools and colleges. Young people may never even go to a branch, or know what one is, but that doesn't mean they can't become a 'fan' of a bank. You may not even need to give them an account when a membership will do just fine.

Young people love events and experiences and they may be encouraged to go to an event about being an entrepreneur or to join a coding club or learning community that is going to help them build their future - all of which are hosted by the bank. Your membership card just happens to also be a bank card allowing you to transact.

People-centered banks built around empowering people means people ultimately earn more, save more and live their lives more enjoyably and effectively.

# People-centered banks do business better to ensure companies thrive

Small business growth can also be underpinned by a people-centered approach, not least to help that customer who has quickly been identified as unemployed to find a new job, especially if they have an in-demand skill.

A people-centered bank will have already identified businesses it is lending to who are looking to grow. They may be hiring new staff locally and have a need for those specific skills of the unemployed customer and so the connection can be made.

This process could be carried out through technology but it is the people-centered knowledge and informational power that makes it work. Then a charge can be made for the successful introduction turning the bank into a broker of people and not just cash.

Trust being restored in banking is so important here because if a bank was to recommend a new employee to one of its commercial customers, the business would have trust in that introduction while the potential employee would also trust it is unlikely the said business would be on the brink meaning they are risking their livelihood yet again.

Similarly, if a people-centered bank knows a company in one sector is heading towards a cliff edge but also knows a similar company is thriving, rather than losing money when the former defaults, it could connect the two. The one in trouble can learn to do things more efficiently or the pair could collaborate or merge.

In the case of the latter example, by helping to transform the two into a more successful business, the bank can lend more securely against this potential, boost growth fast and make more money over time. This is less costly than seeing a new or existing business fold, with the bank getting only a fraction of a return, if any at all, when assets are liquidated.

A people-centered approach is not always about the money a bank can make or lend. For example, if someone comes in for a loan to start a new business, the bank may recommend to them a variety of grants available locally or nationally instead. For a fee it could help them to successfully obtain that grant or even advise of a tax credit they were not utilising, such as for R&D. That banking employee who knows that business well would realise they are innovating by building some kit or technology, even if the business did not. The bank employee could utilise their wider knowledge to negate the need for that loan and free up funds because of the money returned on the tax credit. How many people miss this because they just don't know? The person in the bank who knows them, they will know.

# Don't confuse people-centered with user-centric

What is important to note is that a people-centered approach does not necessarily mean user-centric. User-centric might mean a slick web app or mobile app for banking but that's not the same thing as building a relationship and engendering trust while building an ecosystem founded on local knowledge and connections. That is of far higher value than a super slick app, which may not even resonate at all with someone from a certain generation or living outside of a large metropolitan city.

People-centered means re-training existing employees in soft skills such as empathy so they understand a customer's own personal situation better and then giving them the tools to adopt new digital skills,tools and mindsets to tailor help, advice and offers in an ultra-personalised way.

When this is templated multiple times for people in a single community, that ecosystem grows and can be replicated across a whole country so that ecosystems interconnect.

It is the same way the industrial revolution helped us template everything to become more efficient. It worked brilliantly. But now the people revolution will help us personalise everything and become more efficient. It will also work brilliantly. When everyone can do things more or less the same, there is no value to be found. But every person is different and knowing that difference is an opportunity.

Imagine in the future a bank selling you your dream home because it knows what you can afford to spend and can package up a property with a mortgage, utilities, services, local suppliers and all the legalities taken care of. It becomes a personalised experience, not just a series of disconnected transactions.

Imagine too if that process was started at an even earlier stage and a bank gave you that option sooner, presenting you with a plan showing how you could eventually afford it, all developed from the conversations it had with you over months and years rather than numbers tapped into a digital form on any given day.

And when things go wrong for some people, which they will, it is these strong bonds formed over time that allow a bank to help a person through their difficulties in the short-term but still make money from them in the long-term.

The successful people-centered bank with an ecosystem can stitch these lifelong services together around an individual and be the glue. This makes it difficult for you as a customer to switch because all of your support services are orchestrated by your bank

A people-centered approach to banking, rather than a task-based or user-centric one, can increase the value of human relationships, reduce risks and heighten people's inherent value through personalisation.

Technology has enabled us to be more relevant with our relationships, but we now need to add more value; longer lifetime value. If you build value around a person growing and take a percentage of their growth, that is a much better model than taking their assets. If you do the latter, you lose them as a customer forever. If you help them develop, even when times are tough, you keep them as a customer forever.

# Banks create longer lifetime value through people- centered networks

People must be introduced into the two pervasive scale drivers in the digital age. These are:

1. Network effects

2. Data Network effects

Network effects are situations where goods or services become more valuable when more people use them. There are many examples out there from the telephone system (the value of a phone increases if everyone has a phone) to Facebook to many marketplaces (with some nuances for the latter).

Data network effects occur when your product, generally-powered by machine learning, becomes smarter as it gets more data from your users. In a task-centered world you will drive people out of this flywheel, but in a people-centered world you would add people to both of these flywheels.

341

These relationship-strengthening network effects mean if you add people relationships such that you define network effects as "the more relationships between people that exist as a result of a product or service, the more valuable it is" then the more valuable the product or service is and the stronger your relationships are, the more likely you are to build advocacy and hence more relationships.

This is what we mean when we talk of using branches to strengthen relationships between customers and staff and also customers to customers and staff to staff with technology assisting the personalisation of the product and service. This would increase the network effect and strengthen the ecosystem-centrality a bank plays in the community.

When it comes to relationship-enhanced data network effects, in a task-centered world AI and data crunching would drive better products. But in a people-centered world your product would involve relationships and the data would be split into transactional machinable data which strengthens the product AND nuanced relationship insight, such as empathy, body language, touch. These would add value over the data as data crunching and AI becomes commoditized, creating a stronger relationship and better perception of the product.

Both scenarios play to banks at the heart of a community and repurpose banks being the hub of relationships where products and services and data are enhanced by relationships.

## Yes, you can measure it

People measurement has very much been task-centered, so how do you measure people centric economics? One hypothesis that Freeformers has been working on with its customers is that you can measure how people change and adapt over multiple dimensions (attributes) and link this change over time to traditional business metrics.

These attributes[82] are characteristics such as metacognition, empathy as well tooling, automation and relate to four categories: How you see yourself, how you approach the world, how you communicate and your relationship with technology.

---

[82] https://freeformers.com/products/future-workforce-model/

Each attribute is viewed in three coordinates: Mindset, the attitudes, values and beliefs that make you Want to; the Knowledge that makes you Able to; and the Behaviours (actions) that show you Doing. These create a vector set where a vector is [Mindset, Skillset, Behaviour, Impact, Time] = Attribute and it is used to measure how people change.

We have proved that a change in Mindset, Skillset and Behaviour over time will strengthen relationships and create an impact that can be "hard" measured in terms of financial data such as increased sales or reduced costs of operation, for example from increases in productivity. By looking at this attribute change over time, Freeformers have created a people-centered vector model that can be linked to productivity.

At Freeformers we have also shown that a change in attributes such as empathy - which directly correlate to building relationships between people - make you more money, especially in organisations undergoing massive digital transformation with large workforces.

*Case Study - CYBG*

*CYBG (https://www.cybg.com/ Clydesdale Bank PLC) wanted to increase the "Digital Fitness" of their existing branch workers in their branch network, as the nature of their roles move from transactional to people centric.*

*Using Freeformers Future Workforce Model (FWM) (https://freeformers.com/products/future-workforce-model/) a number of advocates were scientifically identified (looking at mindset, skillset and behaviours). These advocates were trained on a number of attributes from the FWM, tooled up and empowered to deliver online and face-to-face interventions to their colleagues across the branch network at the bank. Data from the impact on customers, business metrics and perceived value in their lives and their colleagues was measured. A group of branches were designated as group (measurement and survey but no interventions). The other groups were designated as test and learn teams.*

*Not only did business performance improve against the control group, but the bank's annual survey revealed the impact of the programme on employee engagement and advocacy: 90% of colleagues on test and learn would recommend the bank to friends or family - 16% ahead of rest of the bank. 85% of colleagues say 'it is easier for me to learn new skills to support the digitisation of the bank - 25% ahead of the rest of the bank.*

A people centred approach improved the business and improved the relationships staff had with the organisation, on their lives and with their colleagues and customers.

*Case Study - Mortgages at Barclays*

*Sally Moran and her team at Barclays had an idea. Instead of repossessing people's homes if they can't afford their monthly payments due to long term financial difficulty, could they help people stay in their homes and start connecting people to other people and organisations that could help them keep their home or provide support in the next stages of transition.*

*Many people found that there was support from government and other orgs in finding ways to help during difficult times including access to money that they didn't know about. This is also good for Barclays as customers keep being customers.*

*Case Study - Barclays - Digital Eagles and Eagle Labs*

*As part of an intent to create the most digital savvy workforce in banking, Barclays gave iPads to a significant number of people working in branches. Only to find that very few people started to use them. They decided that changing the mindset and behaviours as well as skillset of their workforce was critical to their future. They created a network of Digital Eagles - people who self-identified as being enthusiastic and motivated to lead the change. Barclays empowered these Digital Eagles (along with support from Freeformers) to go and identify advocates across their branch network and help create more skilled advocates. The Digital Eagles movement was so successful, it became part of the Bank's advertising hooked against a motto of "never leaving anyone behind in the digital economy".*

*This also led to Barclays repurposing branches into an ecosystem of community hubs. https://labs.uk.barclays/*

*"Eagle Labs are a community resource available for everybody. Whether you're an inventor, an innovator or a mentor, our spaces are conducive to nurturing and growing your idea with support from Barclays and our network. From accelerating UK business to*

*enabling collaborative innovation and digital empowerment for all, our Eagle Labs are a space to create, innovate and grow. "*

# Banks must learn from other ecosystems

The biggest tech players have won because they have built ecosystems. They are not always the provider of services, they are the aggregator. Banks can learn from this.

Barclays has done it with its Eagle Labs. There are 20 of them around the UK. They are branches but they host small businesses and startups and provide access to training and also equipment like 3D printers.

There is money made from rent, events and services but these branches are back as hubs at the heart of their communities once again. They have gone back to the future supporting local trade and local people and local innovation and growth. That is the right thing to do. It is people-centered.

They are largely manned by the same people who used to be tellers but who have now been re-trained in problem-solving and empathy. Remember, your workers are also your customers. They know what they need themselves and this means they know how to help the customer. This is the essence of one-to-one marketing.

When a bank empowers staff to be better advisors and coaches of people's lives, money will be made. It is a beautiful fusion of technology, people and people development. Banks will also be helping their own colleagues grow as workers and increase their own lifetime value.

Banking's forebears who started in churches, meeting houses and even on street corners would be proud of a return to these origins. There is a human responsibility on us all to build a people-centred economy because if we can't build a people-centered economy, we are doomed to fail.

This is retail banking theory for a modern digital age but like all great ideas, it is based on a simple and proven premise, one that banking once always understood: People and relationships matter and are always your greatest strength and asset.

Wendy Guillies is the president and chief executive officer of the Kansas City-based Ewing Marion Kauffman Foundation, one of the largest private foundations in the United States with more than $2 billion in assets.

Guillies leads the Foundation's work to boost student achievement in Kansas City and to accelerate entrepreneurship across the country. Before becoming CEO, she played an instrumental role in building the Foundation's local, national and global reputation as a thought leader and innovator in its fields.

Guillies has deep expertise in communications, marketing, organizational development and talent management. She serves on the boards of the Greater Kansas City Chamber of Commerce, KCSourcelink, MRI Global, Folience and the Enterprise Bank Advisory Board. The Kansas City Business Journal named her to the Power 100 list in 2016 and 2017, and TechWeek KC named her to the Tech 100 list. She was also selected for the 2014 class of Women Executives in Kansas City by Ingram's magazine.

Guillies is a native of Kansas City, Kan. and a graduate of the University of Nebraska. She currently lives in Overland Park, Kan., where she and her husband are the proud parents of two daughters.

Derek Ozkal is a senior program officer in Entrepreneurship for the Ewing Marion Kauffman Foundation, where he assists with writing and analysis of various Research & Policy initiatives and administers grants, which includes managing and overseeing assigned grant portfolios, monitoring grantee performance, and reviewing grant proposals.

Prior to joining the Kauffman Foundation, Ozkal was the research director for the Kansas City Business Journal, where his duties included survey design, data gathering and analysis in support of weekly lists of local industries and topics, writing articles on local economic topics, and various research tasks in support of editorial content.

Ozkal earned a Bachelor of Science degree in economics from Truman State University and is a cast member of the KC Improv Company.

# The future of work and learning is entrepreneurship

## Wendy Guillies and Derek Ozkal

In between the thought-provoking and often depressing panels that highlight the negative aspects of job loss, societal upheaval, and environmental concerns associated with our future economy, there's generally a sliver of hopefulness that focuses on human potential and creativity.

Our view is that we need to flip this script. And we need to do it now.

Of course, it's necessary to recognize the challenges facing us in the future. We are already facing many of them today. We must be clear-eyed regarding our shortcomings, but we must also be equally (if not more) focused on what we can achieve if we take pragmatic steps toward eliminating barriers so that all people have the ability to take risks, achieve success, and give back to make the world we live in better.

The pessimists seem to forget that we can play an active role in creating our collective future. Instead, they focus on the notion that the future will likely be a dark, dystopian landscape. That view diminishes human creativity. That view diminishes our potential. And we believe that view is wrong.

By focusing first on investing in all people, we can create an economy that prioritizes learning and entrepreneurship, thereby lessening inequality and fostering more opportunity for partnerships between people, communities and even nations.

*We can imagine not only a differentfuture economy, but a better one that'smore inclusive and equitable.*

It will take more than imagining to realize this future, however. We need to act collectively — and soon — to make it happen.

# Invest in what will become our scarcest resource: us

Our first step toward a more optimistic future is to recognize the most important resource we have: people.

While the first Industrial Revolution unlocked economic growth and better lives by augmenting our muscles with machines, machines now augment our minds. As artificial intelligence, automation, machines and robotics become more common, the human element could become the scarce resource. Because of this, we must invest in people.

*We must prepare people for a worldthat focuses on what makes us human.Humans create, learn, trust, reason,connect, solve, dream, and love.*

These are not only nice-to-have "soft skills" — they will be necessary attributes for everyone to achieve economic independence in an interconnected, digital world.

By preparing people for a world in which a person's economic independence is connected to the ability to work under ambiguity, we can open access to an economy that we can't predict but that we know will require high levels of problem-solving. Consistent investment in human learning from an early age and throughout life is the No. 1 strategic imperative to designing the type of future we want.

# Getting the right start: Lifelong learning

We cannot rely on the way we've been teaching our children for the past 100 years to satisfy the needs of the next 100 years.

We must reform the way we instruct students and train workers as we transition from a hierarchical and structured workforce into one in which self-motivation (the entrepreneurial mindset) determines success. Not everyone will need to incorporate a business, but everyone will need to have entrepreneurial skills[83] to navigate the new economy.

---

[83] https://www.kauffman.org/rethink/generation-a

The workplace will require credentials, proof of experience, and an evolving set of skills[84] — by 2020, 65 percent of jobs will require a post-secondary credential. Innovation across the education system is essential to prepare not just a fortunate few[85], but *all* students for the jobs they will take and create to meet the needs of a job market that has already changed and that will be almost unrecognizable in the next 20 years. Fortunately, several promising models are emerging in many communities across the country.

In Kansas City, nearly every school district in the region has an "innovation" program that works with students on credentialing, internships, meaningful projects, professional skills development, and practical job experience. These programs are experiential and focused on problem-solving. Unfortunately, only roughly 10 percent of each district's curriculum is geared toward these activities. We are working together with families, students, educators, entrepreneurs and businesses from across the region to rethink the education pathway and develop more "real-world" application in schools. We believe that providing students with these experiences and the credentials to validate them should be on par with core subjects such as English, history, science and math. Doing so will prepare the next generations for the jobs of the future.

Technology will destroy jobs, but it will also create new jobs and drastically change existing jobs. In fact, to leverage our humanity as technology continues to drive this changing workforce.

*there is strong reason to suspect thattechnology will lead to a net gain of new jobs,albeit very different ones from those we have today — jobs we haven't yet dreamed of and jobs that will require a reformed educational approach*

While entire jobs may not be fully automated, we should expect large components (tasks) of many occupations to become partially automated. Multiple estimates[86] [87] indicate that the majority of jobs

---

[84] https://www.kauffman.org/blogs/currents/2017/11/not-just-a-high-school-diploma

[85] https://bvcaps.yourcapsnetwork.org

[86]

https://www.mckinsey.com/~/media/mckinsey/featured%20insights/Digital%2 0Disruption/Harnessing%20automation%20for%20a%20future%20that%20wor ks/A-future-that-works-Executive-summary-MGI-January-2017.ashx will see 30 to 70 percent of the tasks associated with the job automated by technology. Furthermore, research shows[5] that job growth has taken place only for low-skill and high-skill workers, while middle-skill jobs have declined. Wages are stagnant or declining for low- and middle-skill workers while they are rising for high-skill workers. Plus, workers who are most likely to have their jobs (or large parts of their jobs) automated are also the least likely to receive training.

Let's not think of the future of work as firms and jobs, but as people and work. This will force us to let go of the notion of traditional full-time jobs and the inflexible infrastructure of health care, retirement and status tied to that.

## Why worry? The dreamers, makers and doers will design the future of jobs

Imagine telling a farmer in 1900 that the number of people working in agriculture in the U.S. would decrease from 40 percent to 2 percent in the next 100 years. Professor David Autor posed this hypothetical scenario during a TED talk in 2016[88]. What kind of jobs are those people going to do? Will there be enough food?

There would have been no way to predict employment in jobs that didn't exist, especially in industries that didn't exist (computers, aviation, television, etc.). Even with the power of hindsight, the transformation is almost impossible to comprehend and fully appreciate. Our predictions of the future are often rooted in extensions of the edge of what currently exists, so it's very hard to imagine a world more than a couple of decades away.

How is it that we have more people working today than 100 years ago? How did we prepare workers for jobs that didn't exist? The high school movement[89] was key in preparing Americans for this new work. Economists will refer to this as "investing in human capital," but it's probably more accurate to think of it as better preparing people for jobs.

---

[87] https://www.oecd.org/employment/Automation-policy-brief-2018.pdf

[88] https://www.ted.com/talks/david_autor_why_are_there_still_so_many_jobs

[89] https://scholar.harvard.edu/lkatz/publications/why-united-states-led-education-lessons-secondary-school-expansion-1910-1940

How did we imagine and eventually create those jobs? No one person saw the future in its entirety, but hundreds of thousands of entrepreneurs — the dreamers, the makers, the doers — created the future by adding their vision to our collective existence.

*We do not know what jobs we will have 100 years from now, and that's OK. Future generations of entrepreneurs will figure that out along the way as they innovate and improve the human condition through their endeavors.*

Each entrepreneur succeeding or failing by trying out new ideas advances society, and this occurs without coordination.

What if 100 years from now, much of the work is once again available in jobs and industries that don't currently exist? How do we prepare people for that? In addition to ensuring people know how to access learning opportunities that credential and validate their specific skills, we can transition from an approach to education that values knowledge accumulation to one that invests in agile and adaptive lifelong learning based on both the current economy and the future. It must be a national priority to reform our approach to education to one that prepares Americans for the future of work.

We don't have to look far into the future to see how the digital revolution gives us the opportunity to stand on the shoulders of technology — not be trampled under it — if we adopt an approach to lifelong learning that values agility and adaptability.

David Autor, in that same TED Talk[6], asked why automation hasn't killed the job of bank teller. The number of bank tellers has roughly doubled since the ATM was introduced. The fact is, the efficiency of ATMs freed up tellers to be relationship builders, salespeople and problem solvers. Their roles shifted, and banks opened more locations to better serve customers.

That same technological efficiency is being applied to radiology. Artificial intelligence can enhance the role of radiologists by reading radiographs, MRIs and CT scans, flagging in seconds what radiologists should examine. The time saved gives radiologists more time to examine and analyze results, while the efficiency itself improves client care, service and costs.

These are familiar jobs enhanced by technology. There are also emerging jobs such as XRP Markets retail infrastructure manager[90]. What is that? It's a manager who supports technology that allows financial institutions to send money globally using blockchain. We couldn't have imagined that position five years ago, let alone the jobs yet to come.

# The not-so-secret ingredients for a successful future: Diversity, equity and inclusion

There's an old riddle that goes like this: A father and son are in a serious car accident. The father is killed in the accident, and the son is rushed to the hospital for emergency surgery. Once in the operating room, the surgeon looks down and says, "I can't operate on this boy; he's my son!" How is this possible?

If you are like most people[91], you may try to come up with a story or scenario in which the father is able to operate on his son as a ghost or because he's not actually dead. The more logical answer is that the surgeon is the boy's mother.

This parable highlights something we know is true: Humans have biases, both implicit and explicit. If we are expecting the technology and machines we create to help solve humanity's challenges,

*we must be aware of our personal shortcomings and take intentional steps to ensure we are inclusive in building our future together. Otherwise, we will merely be shifting the problem of bias from humans to machines.*

It also calls to mind how we often overlook the most basic of human realities — that we are better together. We know that more diverse teams are more productive and successful teams[92]. Yet we've been slow as a nation to put this into practice in both our businesses and our

---

[90] https://ripple.com/company/careers/all-jobs
[91] http://www.bu.edu/today/2014/bu-research-riddle-reveals-the-depth-of-gender-bias/
[92] https://hbr.org/2016/11/why-diverse-teams-are-smarter

schools. There's a reason why Diversity, Equity and Inclusion (DEI) practices and policies have developed rapidly in the past few years. It's the right thing for any corporation or organization to pursue, but it's also good for the bottom line and results, both today and in the increasingly multicultural world that lies ahead.

Outside of companies, schools and organizations, we see this bias play out in what we prioritize and measure as success. Despite macroeconomic indicators reporting positive — albeit lackluster — economic growth for the nation, the digitalization of the economy across a very wide spectrum is polarizing.

Rural America, for example, isn't necessarily feeling the glow of a rising Dow, nor are those who face systemic barriers to economic success, such as minorities, women and other underrepresented groups.

Traditional economic measures are no longer adequate indicators. The local economy ("metro ecosystem") is a more relevant unit of analysis for understanding declining dynamism and identifying the specific barriers to job creators. This is why it is ever more important to understand the implications of entrepreneurship in the future economy, specifically the new nature of entrepreneurship[93].

Technology has made the activity of starting and scaling a business inherently different from what it used to be. Fewer jobs are created, as companies are able to reach massive scale in terms of revenue without having to scale employment in the same fashion. There aren't fewer jobs overall, just fewer jobs concentrated in a small number of companies. New industries open and entrepreneurial opportunities become more widely accessible through platforms that lower barriers to entry.

The new nature of entrepreneurship relies on more people — from all races, ethnicities, genders, geographies and immigrant statuses — willing to make jobs.

Our future economy depends on removing barriers so that we can welcome and support more diverse job creators. Additionally, low-wage and low-skill workers must be part of the conversation in developing functional local entrepreneurial ecosystems. We know from research that more business starts in any given community increases

---

[93] https://www.kauffman.org/what-we-do/resources/state-of-entrepreneurship-addresses/2017-state-of-entrepreneurship-address

wages, productivity, innovation and overall quality of life. Put simply, the more startups we have, the better for all of our communities.

# Our future. Together.

The fate of a new American Dream resides squarely at the intersection of entrepreneurship and education, and the future of work is exactly that. Today's economy is creating a tremendous amount of wealth, but it is increasingly shared unequally. We must empower the dreamers, makers and doers to pursue economic independence to build stronger communities and design a future for *all* humans in a digital world.

Simply put,

*we must reform education and training to empower everyone to be an entrepreneur, regardless of whether they will start a business one day.*

Technology is changing work, but it is on us to prepare people for work by changing mindsets and increasing the entrepreneurial capabilities of every person.

Technology can replace us, but it can also empower us by augmenting human activity. We can let technology stand on our shoulders, or we can stand on its shoulders. We'll take the latter. It's probably easier to get a glimpse of the next 100 years from up there anyway.

All of this is not to say that there are not important issues that we need to address (inequality, changing demographics, wage stagnation, skills gaps, firm concentration, cost of living, and a host of others). Rather, this is purely to give context to the vital importance of an inclusive, human-centered design at the intersection of learning and work for the next century.

- Perhaps it is because we see the flaws in ourselves that we are so fearful of the machines we can and will create. Perhaps it is easy to imagine a dystopian future because we are aware of our own shortcomings. Perhaps it is because we imagine a future where disturbing trends continue that we often lose sight of the powerful potential of technology to unlock human potential.

355

While it might be possible that technological advancement could usher in a dystopian world in which machines come to life and take over[94], we prefer to envision a tech-fueled future where empowered entrepreneurs create a world in which humans are freer to pursue more passions and keep the cycle of progress moving forward. If we do these things and do them well, then we will provide everyone with the opportunity to be uncommon and to take initiative and risks, and we will ultimately meet the challenges of the future economy.

---

[94] https://en.wikipedia.org/wiki/Maximum_Overdrive

**JIM CLIFTON HAS SERVED AS CEO OF GALLUP**, a global leader in public opinion research and advanced analytics, since 1988. Under his leadership, Gallup has expanded from a predominantly U.S.-based company to a worldwide organization with 30 offices in 20 countries and regions.

Mr. Clifton is the creator of The Gallup Path, a metric-based economic model that establishes the linkages among human nature in the workplace, customer engagement and business outcomes. This model is used in performance management systems in more than 500 companies worldwide. His most recent innovation, the Gallup World Poll, is designed to give the world's 7 billion citizens a voice on virtually all key global issues.

In June 2015, the Clifton Foundation and Gallup announced a $30 million gift to the University of Nebraska to establish the Don Clifton Strengths Institute. The gift will support the early identification and accelerated development of thousands of gifted entrepreneurs and future business builders.

Mr. Clifton is the author of *The Coming Jobs War*, as well as many articles on global leadership. His blog appears regularly in the Influencer section of LinkedIn and on Gallup.com's Chairman's Blog.

He serves on several boards and is chairman of the Thurgood Marshall College Fund. He has received honorary degrees from Medgar Evers, Jackson State and Bellevue Universities. He is also a Distinguished Visiting Professor at UNC-Chapel Hill and Duke University.

# Born to Build

## By Jim Clifton

Well-meaning and important global institutions, scientists, academics and politicians have never fully understood the rare gift to build something — a God-given natural talent that many are born with — that to some degree, we all possess.

Some refer to this gift as "entrepreneurship," which it is, in part. But this human phenomenon is better characterized as "building." Entrepreneurship has taken on many definitions, and it's often confused with innovation. We need a lot of innovation, but building is a very distinct, separate phenomenon.

An innovation has no value until an ambitious builder creates a business model around it and turns it into a product or service that customers will buy.

An innovator is first and foremost a creator, an inventor — a problem solver with a deep passion for improving something. Innovators are thinkers.

A builder is different from an innovator. A builder creates economic energy where none previously existed. A builder builds jobs for people and booms economies.

Builders can start very young. When an 8-year-old puts a lemonade stand on a corner, they create new economic energy on that corner — goods and services are exchanged for the first time at that place. Years ago, a 14-year-old could take on an existing newspaper delivery route with 25 papers and boom it to 100 papers. This young builder created economic energy that wasn't on that route before. Believe it or not, U.S. GDP actually ticked up a little when that paper route quadrupled.

Builders also create goods and services that customers didn't even know they wanted or had ever imagined. Builders create demand – and jobs When Google or Apple was launched or the first commercial airplane took off in 1914, there was no inherent demand for any of their products or services. Nobody said, "Gee, I wish I had a device in my pocket on which I could search everything humans have recorded since the beginning of time instead of going to a library."

Or, "It would be so cool to fly through the air in a metal tube at 400 mph rather than ride to my destination on a horse."

Or, "I wish someone would invent plumbing and electricity rather than using candles and kerosene — and going to the toilet outside."

Economists and well-meaning thinkers often look at a weak or declining economy and conclude, "We have a declining economy because demand is weak or because there is no demand at all." A more insightful observation is, "There is no demand because there aren't enough builders who *create demand*." Without builders, there is no demand, no growing economy and hence, no good jobs.

There was never an inherent demand for cars, flight, TV, video, indoor plumbing, electricity or the internet, or Starbucks or Amazon — somebody had to take a good idea and build it into something big. And when people do that, they create economic energy that wasn't there before — as well as new good jobs and all the things that build a growing economy.

Is it time for all of us to think about building something. Many of us could build a small or medium-sized business. Or build a huge business — one with $10 million or $10 billion in sales. They all count and add up to the sum total of the world. We need hundreds of thousands of small and medium-sized businesses. All societies need organizations of all kinds continuously starting up and booming — or they can't develop.

Some of us could also build a small, medium or jumbo nonprofit. Nonprofits create economic energy too. They boost GDP and create real jobs and real city and state growth. So do megachurches, a new children's museum, a chain of daycare centers, home-health nonprofits or charities to assist disadvantaged citizens. Every one of these organizations or institutions requires a business model and a gifted builder or they will never take off — they will never create new economic energy in the absence of a born builder.

We need "intrapreneurs" too. Intrapreneurs are people who build startups inside established organizations — people who are given hard assignments to start new ventures inside an institution. Established organizations like Gallup will assign someone to "go start a new division that will sell millions of books" or "start a new analytics division" or "start a new center that specifically serves colleges and universities" or "go open a new office in Dubai or Seoul." These jobs require builders.

Building is a high-degree-of-difficulty task, but natural builders want the impossible assignment. They actually prefer the messiness, the problems, the barriers, the absence of supervision, the improvisation and the rush of a new customer breakthrough.

Builders were made differently than the rest of us were. They were born and put on earth to build.

Builders from Andrew Carnegie to J.P. Morgan to John D. Rockefeller to Henry Ford famously created historic economic energy through steel, electricity, trains and cars. They transformed America and the world because they created *customers* that didn't previously exist. They had a gift to envision, create masses of customers and change how we live. They also made very big bets — they would sometimes bet everything they were worth. Extreme builders will, a few times in their life, bet it all.

Every institution in the world — even nonprofits, schools and churches — has customers. Builders were born with a gift to know how to create demand for those customers — market disruptions that offer a better way to live.

Jack Dorsey and his Twitter co-founders didn't respond to a market demand. They disrupted the media market and created a different way to communicate and socialize.

John Hope Bryant built Operation HOPE, a large nonprofit organization to help low-income people improve their credit scores so they could immediately improve their lives. He created a quick education course on money and credit available at a special desk in bank branches throughout the country. Millions of low-income Americans need this service. John's paying customers are the financial institutions because they primarily fund his nonprofit. It is extremely valuable for banks to have citizens who have good credit versus bad or mistakenly low credit scores.

Banks weren't clamoring for this, and many low-income people hadn't even imagined this type of service. John built a huge nationwide nonprofit through envisioning two customers — the low-income citizens who use the service (for free) and the secondary customers, the banks, who fund it. John created customers and economic energy where it hadn't previously existed. He improved lives and changed the world.

Roy and some of his college friends co-founded an ad agency after attending the University of Texas at Austin in 1971. His agency was going to be different from others because rather than simply focusing on traditional branding and marketing, Roy's agency would help customers identify their values and purpose — and communicate to the world *why* they were in business. Values and purpose, not just positioning and brand differentiation, would drive all of his firm's creative work for clients. And the approach proved to be a huge success. Roy's became famous for his "purpose-inspired branding," and the firm he and his partners built boasted big clients such as Walmart, Southwest Airlines and the U.S. Air Force.

Roy has since passed the torch with his firm, but he can't stop building. He has built the Purpose Institute and has started selling his own brand of Royito's Hot Sauce from an Airstream breakfast food truck where he himself works.

Roy's purpose in life is to help others fulfill their purpose. He always says to young people, "You can make a living and a life becoming great at what you are already good at — and spending your life doing what you love to do." Doing just that is in Roy's DNA.

Emily was a student at George Washington University in Washington, D.C. She joined a national nonprofit, Lemonade Day, and took on the challenge of founding a Lemonade Day chapter on the GWU campus.

Lemonade Day teaches fifth- through eighth-graders how to run a business — in this case, their own lemonade stand — and they get to keep the profits. Emily is a born builder, and, with funding, she quickly built a nonprofit that recruits, trains and transports approximately 500 college students a year to mentor 8,000 elementary and middle school students.

Emily built a nonprofit colossus as a full-time student. New energy exploded from the fifth- through eighth-graders, the college students who received college credit and the local businesses who funded it.

Lemonade Day also created a large-scale mentorship model for universities for its national program. This has inspired universities to adopt this model and bring Lemonade Day to their city through university students.

Emily is a born builder. When she rises in the morning, she sees her world through the lens of "What can I build today?"

Jim and John borrowed $5,000 40 years ago to start a small Midwest market research company. They built it because they wanted to do something on their own. They didn't want entry-level sales jobs at IBM or Xerox, which were the hottest jobs on earth back then.

Like most builders, Jim and John got up every morning to build something because they were primarily driven by a need — not so much for money but a need for independence and extreme individualism. They found a highly inspiring job by building our own enterprise, which, with their colleagues, they are still building and growing today.

But creating a big booming enterprise or nonprofit organization won't happen with just one gifted builder. There is a fragile ecosystem around effective builders.

Gallup has found that there are three key players in the development of any organization, whether it's a new enterprise, a new division within a company or a nonprofit. We call them the "three alphas": the alpha Rainmaker, the alpha Conductor and the alpha Expert. When this combination exists in an organization or on a team, the likelihood of it breaking out and booming grows exponentially.

An alpha *Rainmaker* has unusual drive and persistence — rare grit. Obstacles and failure actually increase a Rainmaker's determination. An enterprise virtually never works without this player.

An alpha *Conductor* has management ability. This is the operations person or manager who knows how to get all players on the team — or in the "orchestra" — to work together seamlessly. This person holds the whole organization together.

An alpha *Expert* provides differentiating expertise to the core product or service. Whether it is an analytic services startup's brilliant statistician, a new restaurant's star chef or a software firm's best programmer, virtually every successful startup has an alpha expert who highly distinguishes it from the crowd.

Many were born to do this. Whether we are an alpha Rainmaker, an alpha Conductor or an alpha Expert, there are no limits to what we can build.

Sven Otto Littorin is an entrepreneur and advisor to Swedish and international companies. In 2002-06 he was the Secretary General of the Moderate Party and in 2006-10 Sweden's Minister for Employment. He has a B.Sc. in Economics and Business and has been a Visiting Scholar at Stanford University.

# Successful Elements of a Humane Policy on Restructuring

## By Sven Otto Littorin

Sweden's Minister for Employment 2006-2010

The making of sausages and politics is something many people don't wish to witness. Indeed, political action is slow and linear. New policy is mainly based on old policy and the rapidly changing reality is rarely at the center of attention, probably because politics is a zero-sum game: if someone is to get in, someone else has to get out, and introducing a new idea is much more difficult than debating an existing one. In this way politics is even worse than sausage making, with politicians constantly competing to eat each others lunch. This is not beneficial to creative thought.

In the four years leading up to the 2006 election in Sweden, I was the Secretary General of the Moderate Party, which had basically gone bankrupt after the previous, disastrous, election. We had been appointed "cleaners," a fresh team of young politicians with everything to win and nothing to lose. There was little value left in the party legacy and we had to think new, and quick. Innovation was our only chance to be in shape for the following elections four years later.

We tried an unorthodox approach to policy making. Without really knowing it, we implemented a degree of design thinking in the process. Design thinking is solving a problem through rapid prototyping with many iterations: design, test; design, test; and so on. In our case, however, we started at the end - asking ourselves how we wanted our society to look a decade or two down the line and then iterating a policy process backwards. It was a kind of policy making in reverse where we tried to innovate the actual process of policy making as well as questioning old truths and old beliefs in policy itself.

The process was questioned, sometimes even ridiculed at first, but the outcome was a success. In 2006, my party secured its best election result since 1928 and formed the first majority government in almost three decades. We came to power with a uniquely new mindset and method for innovating policy.

One aspect of this method is to see policy making as a sort of prototyping. After introducing a comprehensive reform in a very complex system thousands of smaller issues and problems arise that you cannot plan for or anticipate. So we changed parts of the implementation of these reforms all the time to address these issues. I remember once a journalist asked me if I didn't believe in my own reforms since we changed them all the time. The answer was simple: - If reality and the road map differ, reality always wins. And it is more important to focus on the overall mission at hand than showing prestige in the exact implementation of policies.

After the election in 2006, I was appointed Minister for Employment (i.e. Labor Secretary), in charge of the second largest budget of the government. The need for policy innovation in that area was great and we tried to combine an innovative approach with the more "traditional" labor market policies, which labor market economists love to promote.

We did get ample possibilities to apply our mindset, and we set to it without delay. First, we introduced a comprehensive labor market reform package with good results. But soon enough, in 2008, Sweden was hard hit by the Lehman Brothers collapse and subsequent recession. Our mindset of reframing crisis as opportunity could not have come in more handy.

We faced the task of massive restructuring of our economy, triggered by the crisis. Traditional restructuring is a difficult and tedious business. In most cases, a company or a factory closing down will spend as little as possible in severance pay and leave the city or region to fend for itself. If there are few regulations in place, the company can do more or less what it likes to bolster the company's financials in the short run. The long-term effects are of course a very negative public view on the company, business at large, and market economy/capitalism in general. But when these crises happen, the focus is on the moment, not on the future. All politicians are aware of that, because they will be the ones at ground zero when things collapse and all fingers are pointing at them.

So it is not hard to see why politicians in many countries regulate closures and restructuring, making it both more costly and difficult to close those factories and entities thought not to be profitable enough. Many countries in Europe have come to face real problems in this area, where labor laws, taxes, and severance pay have become excessive. The result is unprofitable factories that continue operating with little hope of getting out of the red. This is of course not sustainable, but for many politicians, power-kicking the can down the road until the next election is far more attractive than standing at the center of ground zero with everyone pointing fingers at them. But that wasn't how we had come into power; managing at ground zero had become our winning game.

Back in the nineties, before innovating the party, we had first won our "sea legs" as senior staff members for the ministers during the Swedish currency meltdown in 1992. I was heading the staff of Bo Lundgren, Minister for Fiscal and Financial Affairs, when one day I received the dreaded phone call from Sweden's largest private banks, saying, "We are running out of money tomorrow." The warnings signs had been clear, but preparations were sorely lacking -- not unlike the conditions before the 2008 crisis. It was like changing the engines on an airplane in mid-air: we built our bank bailout program at high speed in parallel with events unfolding on the ground. This was one important reason why Sweden managed so famously well in the Great Recession in the 90's. Fate had already prepared us to manage the situation.

This was also why Austan Goolsbee, Obama's Chairman of the Council of Economic Advisers, visited me in Sweden in 2010 to find out how the U.S. could learn from how we had handled the crisis - both cleaning up the financial crisis in 1992 and pulling through the 2008 crisis without compromising our labor market structural reforms.

In 2011, after stepping down from government, I was about to start my tenure as a visiting scholar at Stanford, hosted by David Nordfors. We had decided to look deeper into how innovation can create jobs, which later led to us to co-found i4j together with Vint Cerf and Anders Flodström, who had then just stepped down as the chancellor for higher education in Sweden.

A thrilling event for us was hearing President Obama say "innovation for jobs" multiple times in his 2011 State of the Union speech. We invited ourselves to visit Austan in the White House and asked him what plans they had to promote innovation for jobs. "No plans," he said. "But it was good to say it. It's off the table for now as we are fighting for the budget and might have to close down the government next week." David and I both understood at that very moment that the idea of innovation for jobs was ultimately important but totally undeveloped as a concept. Basically, it was not yet publicly known, which was a powerful reason for us to pursue what has turned into the i4j Leadership Forum.

# A humane policy for restructuring

One morning in 2009 I read a shocking story in the newspapers. General Motors had announced that the Swedish government must buy SAAB Automobile from them or they would close the factory and lay off all the workers. It was obviously a hostile move, and a calculated bit of political blackmail. The Swedish Government had no intention of becoming an automobile manufacturer, and it was now our task to make that very clear to GM, the unions, and the press.

All fingers were pointing at me and the Minister for Industry, and the tools the government would traditionally use to manage the situation had been blunted by the financial crisis. But such a crisis often offers golden opportunities for brinkmanship. Employers could lay off any undesired workforce, blame it on the crisis, and further threaten to shut down completely if anyone interfered, passing the bill along to the taxpayer.

We knew we needed to innovate new policy, or complement old ones, to handle this situation. The Minister for Industry Maud Olofsson and

366

I had become friends - we both favored entrepreneurial action and had come to trust each other - and we decided to take this on together. Bridging labor and innovation policy is difficult to do, due to political inertia and lack of common language, but it offered powerful potential.

The crisis was our opportunity to combine necessary restructuring with a decent, respectful way of approaching individuals, companies, and regions. In short, we decided that Schumpeter's creative destruction can be made to work alongside a more humane way of making sure individual workers are being treated fairly. We would try to keep these destructive forces from jeopardizing the long-term sustainability of the economy or trust in the market economy itself. It made good sense for companies as well: we saw that if they would just spend a little extra time and effort, the rewards will be plentiful.

This approach had been tried before; the fact is that it seems to be in the DNA of the Swedish model. But incentives have to be appropriate across the board, and every crisis approached in the right way, keyed to the situation.

All such restructurings have one thing in common, though: they take cooperation. And a crisis is the best time for people to show that they can cooperate. I have applied this method several times, with good results every time. It is a policy that works.

Based on the Swedish experience of this policy innovation, I would say there are five main elements of a more humane policy on restructuring:

## 1. Focus on employability and job creation instead of keeping dying industries alive

It is necessary to close down unprofitable factories and even companies in order to keep the economy competitive. Using public funds to try to save dying industries is for the most part completely useless as we know from bitter experience. In the 1970's, when the oil crisis hit Swedish shipyards, the government supported the industry with billions in industrial subsidies. This did not help at all: in the early 1980's almost all of the companies which had received subsidies were gone, as were all the jobs. The government might have done better to just burn the cash.

The fact is that we cannot save every job or every company, but we can work to maintain the employability of our workforce. This has to be a common task, where the public sector and private industry join hands. If they do not, workers and communities -- who are also voters -- will demand more regulation, higher taxes, more subsidies, and other distortions to the economy.

It is also the decent thing to do. A society where a severe crisis is attacked jointly by both the private and public sectors is a society without trust - a cold place to be both in good and bad times.

## 2. Apply unemployment insurance cautiously and wisely

In Sweden, as in many other countries, there are support nets in place to alleviate the effects of sudden unemployment, including all kinds of unemployment insurance systems and other benefits. The really important challenge is to get the incentives right. Unemployment benefits should not be used as a wage replacement system, without demands or limitations. Rather, it must be treated as insurance: you pay premiums while you work in order to receive assistance in times of transition.

The important thing, I believe, is to understand that this is not "free cash." On the contrary, individuals may only receive these funds when they are actively looking for a job and willing to accept relocation (both geographically and vocationally) to be offered a new job. One who is unemployed for a longer time must participate in labor market programs, upskilling, or reskilling in order to be more attractive to employers. Being unemployed is, and should be, hard work.

## 3. Apply carrot and stick to make the departing employer a part of the rescue team

If the public sector -- i.e., the taxpayer -- takes a big part of the responsibility for the transitional processes, so must the companies. If companies benefit from a lower degree of regulation and taxation to perform necessary structural reforms and layoffs, it is fair that they should also help out.

Swedish companies are normally extremely good at this. Severance pay is often longer than stipulated by law and companies work very closely with the Public Employment Service to assist people who have been terminated. In larger layoffs, the Public Employment Service is often invited to open up short-term branch offices inside factories to be as close to those terminated as possible. In many cases, companies open their own transitional services in-house, offering terminated people the complete assistance of the HR department to find suitable jobs elsewhere.

In addition, there is a unique mechanism in place. About half of the Swedish labor market is covered by "collective transitional funds", where trade unions and employers have agreed to set aside 0.25 percent of the total wage sum to special companies, own jointly by these unions and employers organizations. The funds are used during termination processes in order to assist individuals by offering them extra education and training, assistance in relocation and search activities.

These funds, and the organizations performing these services, have been extremely successful. During the 2008-09 crisis, 85 percent of people being terminated never had to register as unemployed – they found work before their termination period was up. From a political standpoint this is a huge relief: no tax money was involved and these individuals never had to use public support.

## 4. Leverage on organized labor

In this system, organized labor plays a huge role. In Sweden, the organization rate is over 80 percent and almost 90 percent of the labor market is covered by collective agreements. The legislation regulating these issues were implemented as early as 1928. They were promoted by employers who wanted peace, predictability, and stability in the workplace during the agreement periods. There are of course downsides to this model as well, but the fact is that it makes restructuring processes easier and more manageable.

## 5. Create a startup ecosystem leveraging displaced technologies and workers

Finally - and this is the truly innovative part -- we have found that "getting a job" is not the only option. There are also ways to bridge labor and innovation policy. One successful alternative is for displaced workers to spin out their own company and becoming an entrepreneur. Here, the tradition in Sweden has been weaker: the traditional labor market model is good for larger corporations, but less flexible for smaller companies and entrepreneurs. Taxes have also traditionally been high, and benefit systems are mostly based on regular employment.

But things have changed throughout Scandinavia. When Nokia laid off thousands of people a decade or so ago, they introduced a scheme where the company helped some of the people being terminated to set up their own startup companies. Nokia assisted in training, accounting, and legal issues, and even provided a large portion of the equity. In many cases they even placed orders for the output of these new companies.

In 2013, when Sony Mobile in Lund, Sweden, had to terminate about 1,000 people, I was appointed by the First Governor of the Region of Skåne to coordinate actions to mitigate the effects of these layoffs. Sony Mobile formed a "spinout center," an in-house incubator of sorts, where they took a deep look into patents and products not in their core business that were ready to be sold or spun out to those being terminated. One such example is Sigma Connectivity, where some of the engineers at Sony Mobile spun out a division of the company, taking about 200 people with them. The new company ended up as a subsidiary of another entrepreneurial company. Sony Mobile used them as a contractor, but they were free to look for other business as well. Today, five years later, Sigma Connectivity has more people employed than it did in 2013.

At the same time, Sony Mobile committed SEK 3 million (about USD 340,000) per year for ten years in creating The Mobile and Pervasive Computer Institute at Lund University, an industry research institute studying future system architectures for mobile communications. We managed to get the region to commit the same sum, as did the university. With a combined minimum budget of more than 10 million dollars over ten years, this institute not only employs some of the highly skilled engineers who had to leave Sony Mobile, but is also proving very valuable to the company and to the industry.

Sony Mobile did a very good job in handling their downsizing. They stayed attractive as an employer, created their own subcontractors, formed an alliance with regional government and the university, and spearheaded research which they can benefit from in the years to come. And they did this while cutting costs and protecting their own long-term survival. So there are ways of "doing the right thing" that benefit of both shareholders, employees, and regulators.

# Do structural reforms when you can, not when you need them

The central motto for this business is: Be prepared. Do structural reforms when you can, because it may be too late to start when you actually need them.

When our government came into power in 2006, we did not know that we were about to be hit by the global financial crisis of 2007-2008, followed by the Great Recession, the worst economic disaster since the Great Depression. But because we initiated our structural reforms while the economy was still strong, Sweden passed through the crisis with less pain than almost any other country.

Sweden is an economy where transition and mobility within the labor market is fairly easy; over a million people change jobs in a normal year in a labor market of fewer than 5 million. It is also a stable labor market – we have experienced few strikes and little conflict. Finally, it is a labor market flexible enough to handle the jolts of globalization and change.

When Ericsson cut their staff in Sweden in half around the turn of the century, not one day was lost to strikes; most of the workers laid off found new jobs in reasonable time. The same happened in 2008 and 2009, when the automobile industry was hit especially hard. The combination of traditional economic models with a more humane approach to cooperation delivered good results.

In Sweden, however, the labor market is less a market than a cartel of insiders where almost all efforts are focused on those already on the labor market. The threshold *into* the labor market is still too high, so that labor market exclusion has been a real problem for a long time -- especially for the young, immigrants, and people with disabilities.

Based on research and experience, we embarked on reforms by a three-pillar strategy: 1) making it more worth-while to work, 2) making it easier and cheaper to hire, and 3) improving the process of matching needs with skills in the market. These pillars supported a long list of reforms.

In general terms, we placed our focus on labor supply, basing our agenda on the thinking of French economist Jean Baptiste Say, who in the early 1800s concluded that "supply creates its own demand." In hindsight, this statement seems to have been correct: increase in labor supply seemed to mean a lower pressure on wage increases as well as a better acceptance rate, which in turn meant that employers were more prone to taking the risk of increased hiring.

One of the most important elements was a tax adjustment, when we introduced work-tax credits geared at low- and middle-income earners, in some cases reducing net margin effects from over 80 percent to around 30 percent. The result was dramatic in terms of decreased equilibrium unemployment and increased labor supply – and it left ordinary workers with the equivalent of a month's extra pay.

We also tightened our unemployment benefit insurance system by increasing premiums, reducing dividends toward the end of the period (in effect introducing an outer parenthesis), putting more exacting demands on people entering the system, and finally making sure that our active labor market programs were better synchronized with the later and lower stages of benefit payouts.

We also changed our disability pension system and introduced a much improved menu of rehabilitation activities connected to financial incentives for individuals returning to the labor market.

In addition to this, we reduced payroll taxes, a move specifically geared toward the weaker groups in the labor market, effectively reducing thresholds for entering and re-entering the labor market. This basically compensated for the lower productivity among these groups and made them more attractive to employers.

Finally we improved on the business climate in general both by lowering taxes, abolishing wealth and inheritance taxes, cutting red tape, and improving legislation and education.

# A flexible labor market

Adaptability and mobility of the workforce acts to counter protectionism and stagnation. Adaptability, however, must be viewed from a wide perspective. The starting point is probably a pragmatic view of change, an ability to handle new events, and the capacity to take advantage of development and make us more attractive as a country.

Swedish economic history shows rapid change - but also very peaceful change. The Industrial Revolution during the second half of the 19th century took Sweden from being one of poorest nations in Europe to becoming one of the worlds richest in a period of just 70 years. Much of this progress was based on classical liberal reforms: public school reforms, freedom of trade, credit laws, railway expansion, and the Cobden-Chevalier Treaty on free trade. These reforms, the Swedish engineering tradition, and the emergence of what came to be world-leading companies all led to a rapid and powerful urbanization and industrialization process.

A huge shift in the economy was the decline of agriculture's share of the economy from 95 per cent to under 50 per cent in just a few decades. Remarkably, this enormous change and its many displacements occurred almost entirely without social unrest.

In more recent times, there are many more examples of how the habits of flexibility and adaptability have supported a peaceful labor market. When Ericsson cut its workforce by half in the early 21st century, they did not lose a single day to strike or conflict. When Electrolux shut down its operations in small southern town of Västervik in the early 21st century, the results were similar. And only a handful of years later, employment in Västervik was higher than it was when Electrolux closed down. Employment was much better distributed among a larger number of smaller companies, making the community less vulnerable to economic problems in the future.

The lesson we have taken from all this is that the road to more and better jobs is not through protectionism but through embracing and applying the opportunities offered by globalization.

# Successful Reforms

As a result of the policy changes implemented from 2006, Sweden had the fastest falling unemployment rate in the entire OECD area by 2008. We were breaking records in the numbers of hours worked, in labor participation and in employment. Young people, immigrants and those with disabilities were returning to the labor market faster than the average. In the spring of 2008 one person left exclusion every four minutes to return to the labor market, making this policy of reducing exclusion comparable with the Clinton reform years of the 1990s.

In the Article IV Consultation in 2006, IMF wrote about Sweden: "The government has embarked on a course that is both courageous and necessary. It is courageous because it confronts some long-held beliefs and vested interests. It is necessary because it will help ensure that the much-admired Swedish model of an inclusive society thrives in the face of challenges in demographics and globalization."

In 2007, the OECD wrote in its Economic Outlook on Sweden: "The labor market reforms implemented this year will increase potential employment. Given the strength of the economy, it is an excellent time to pursue labor supply reforms as that will prolong the current expansion."

When the financial crisis swept across the globe in August of 2008, all of that was challenged. The crisis affected our largest trading partners and some of our most important industries. Exports fell, confidence fell, and many feared the financial system would collapse under bad debt and poor prospects.

Sweden, where foreign trade is at about 50 percent of GDP, is of course very dependent on how our trading partners face their challenges. The fact that poor public sector performance in most of these countries coincided with the sharp downturn in the private sector and the financial insecurity created a very direct and difficult impact on the Swedish economy.

In August and September of 2008, the Swedish Cabinet was not sufficiently prepared for the severe downturn they faced head-on. The annual budget bill to Parliament on September 22 was designed to meet a slow downturn of the economy, not a deep financial crisis.

Our immediate focus as the crisis unfolded became to secure a stable financial market, making sure our banks and institutions were ready; by and large, they were. Based on the experiences from our own financial crisis of the early 90's, a lot of safeguards and regulations were already in place.

In less than three weeks, we slid from having the fastest-falling unemployment rate in the OECD to watching more than 20,000 people losing their jobs each month – a situation comparable to the crisis of the early 1990s. Exports, production, and GDP all fell.

On December 5, 2008, the Public Employment Service predicted a net increase in unemployment of 245,000 persons in two years, representing some five per cent of the labor force. These were dramatic days indeed.

My position changed as well: I was no longer the Minister for Employment; I became de facto the "Minister for Unemployment". Every tool in my toolbox, and every policy we had to focus on, was applied to the immediate effects of the crisis. We had no time to think long-term, prepare for structural changes, or adapt to new technology, digitization, automation, and AI.

I remember a press conference at the SAAB plant in Trollhättan in early 2008, together with Mrs. Maud Olofsson, the Minister for Industry. I got the first question: "So the fact that you are here, Mr. Littorin, does that mean it's all over?" It felt as though my title had been changed again to Angel of Death.

# Crisis Response

The budget presented in September 2008 included tax cuts for 2009 and infrastructure investments totaling SEK 32bn, the equivalent to 1 percent of GDP. This was followed by a stabilization plan for the financial system, presented on October 20. The plan had three major components:

- A government guarantee for banks and housing finance institutions in order to improve financing and decreasing costs in times of crises.

- A stabilization fund, where financial institutions were to contribute up to 2.5 percent of GDP for 15 years to finance government support activities

- New legislation giving the Government the right to support individual financial institutions to secure financial stability.

The plan was based on experiences from the 90's, when the government created a system to save the financial system -- but not the equity of individual owners of these institutions. In the early 1990's, the government had supported the financial system with guarantees in the region of SEK 65bn to cover some of the bad debt. Private owners contributed an additional SEK 50bn, and increased interest rate spreads financed an additional SEX 60bn, covering all the bad debt that resulted from the crisis.

In turn for taking over the bad debt, the Government created a holding company for the underlying collateral, giving financial institutions leeway to clean up their balance sheets. More than three fourths of this support was regained during the following 15 years, as the collateral was sold off during better economic times. This plan of action was later highlighted in the U.S. Congress as a paradigm of handling such crises.

On December 5, 2008, the cabinet presented an additional budget, focusing only on immediate actions to combat the financial crisis. Due to the fact that Sweden had exceptionally strong public finances we were able to present an additional SEK 22.9bn in new spending. More than half went to structural reforms that increased tax deductions for hiring. The other half focused on active labor market programs and education.

The car industry was especially hard hit, and in December 2008 the Government introduced a program to help the industry transform itself. The program had three parts: increased research and development, state guarantees for loans from the European Investment Bank for green technology, and finally a government program for emergency loans.

We introduced one additional administrative reform that turned out to be much smarter than we had anticipated. In my discussions with the Minister for Industry, Mrs. Maud Olofsson, we concluded that Sweden had a lot of resources, both in money and institutions, but lack of coordination among them was a major issue.

Starting in October 2008, the Government appointed county governors as crisis coordinators, giving them a strong mandate to coordinate all available resources, across all levels, public and private. The Swedish Agency for Public Management concluded in a report in 2011 that these Coordinators were very effective in both analyzing the specific situation in each region and also in coordinating all available resources. For the Government, the coordinators were extremely valuable as "antennas" to regions and cities, as well as to industries and companies directly affected by the crisis.

The crisis turned out to be rather short-lived. Already in the second half of 2009 came several signs that the immediate crisis was over. The financial systems were stabilizing, and both GDP and exports started to grow again. Unemployment was still rising, but at a slower pace, and turned around by 2011.

The graph below shows what was happening in the labor market. The blue line shows the active population (i.e. the labor market potential) in the age group between 15-74. The green line shows unemployment, age 15 and over. The red line shows the active population minus the unemployed; i.e. active population with jobs.

Until 2005, the labor force was down and unemployment was on the rise. In effect, this meant that more people getting unemployed at the same time as more of the unemployed was giving up. Total effect: significant decline in people with jobs.

Starting 2005 the economy picked up, both domestically and internationally, which showed the labor force increasing and unemployment declining. This was strengthened by the reforms we introduced in 2006.

In 2008 and 2009 the crisis hit, labor force declined and unemployment rose significantly in a short time. The point here is that people lost their jobs but didn't drop out of the labour market. The point here is to set in as many activation activities as possible to refrain people from giving up.

Already towards the end of 2009 things moved dramatically: the graph shows a significant increase in the number of people with jobs.

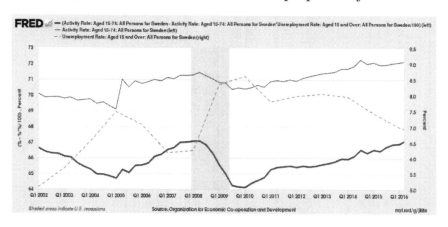

Now compare with the US and we can see how much better Sweden performed in the percentage people with jobs. The big difference is that Sweden's labor force got back into growth quickly after the crisis. In the US however, the rapid drop in unemployment was largely an illusion - much of the drop was not because people were finding new jobs, but because they gave up and quit looking for them.

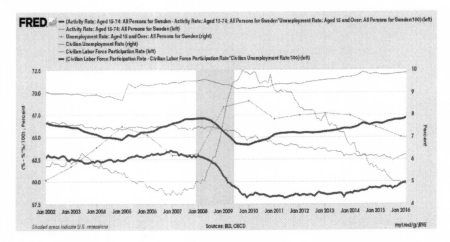

To continue the critique, it seems that stimulus didn't do much good. The US stayed flat from the end of the crisis in 2009 until 2013, while Sweden picked up immediately after the crisis - bounced back, almost.

The reforms we introduced in 2006 was obviously not designed to counterbalance a significant crisis in the world economy. But they did shorten the effects significantly and got people back into jobs quicker than in most other countries.

The SAAB case is instructive. When SAAB in 2011 was forced into the largest-ever bankruptcy in the Nordic countries, over 3,700 people lost their jobs in Trollhättan. Just three years later, over 2,400 of them had found new jobs. Almost 1,000 of them had joined startup companies, and today, seven years on, Trollhättan can boast the fastest-falling unemployment rate in western Sweden and unemployment is lower than before SAAB's bankruptcy.

I would like to take credit for all this, but in all fairness I have to say that this is one of the best features of the Swedish economy: when adversity hits we tend to coordinate all our efforts, private and public, in handling the effects of the situation.

# Conclusion

What lessons have we learned? First, design thinking in policymaking works. Financial incentives work. Supply-side labor market policies work. In combination, these strategies will work together to improve the lives of ordinary citizens in tumultuous times.

In addition: Flexibility is absolutely necessary. Coordination is vital. Crisis programs should be structurally sound but temporary. Preparatory work is crucial – when the crisis hits it is too late to do anything by handle each day's demands as best we can.

By using a degree of innovation in policy making we managed to combine the old truths in economic and labor market policy with new strategies to create policies, which shortened the crisis and actually made us stronger than before. It is a way of handling a crisis that is both humane and also economically sound.

Guido is the Publisher of i4j and active in social enterprise environments with a digital, highgrowth focus as those offer the opportunity to put real change into action in a sustainable way whilst creating a solid business model.

Guido's privileged position in governance, advisory and investment roles inside powerful, both seasoned and young, innovative and market-leading organisations and networks exposes him to many industry trend and player, and pads his network with a roster of interesting and influential contacts.

As CEO of Dutch national news agency ANP Guido created one of the most efficient news agencies and increased digitalisation and entry in to the SaaS-based BtB market of news and information management. A dynamic area with substantial growth potential. ANP is the largest independent BtB news and information supplier to all Dutch media and organisations in public and private sectors. Next to news and information, ANP supplies integrated tools and content that helps customers with itinerary setting, analysing, monitoring and producing content.

Guido is furthermore among other on the supervisory board of World Press Photo, Cinekid, Triodos Cultuurfonds and City Theatre Amstelveen and Advisor to the Dutch Council for Culture.

# Will algorithms take care of people?

## By Guido Van Nispen

*Innovation journalism is the crucial pivot between the innovation economy and the public sphere and it needs urgent further development.*

Technological innovation, and its potential downsides, are attracting mainstream media attention. Series like Westworld and Black Mirror present futures where the machine has taken control. Sometimes it appears that AI might soon threaten all life, and robots directed by algorithms will rule the world. The media juxtaposes this dark view with optimistic product reviews and other lighter news stories spreading technology optimism. The disconnected stories of apocalyptic socio cultural threats on the one hand and the optimism around futuristic smartphone functionalities (which enable the threats) on the other has now been joined by a third prong; the future of work, with news stories making people uncertain about how they will earn their income in the future, not quite knowing if this is a good or a bad thing.

Fate has made it that I am among the far too few people who can be on top of all three types of stories. I have worked in decision making positions at frontiers of both innovation and journalism, being involved with (technological) innovation for 30 years and with media and journalism for over a decade, including five years as CEO of the Dutch national news agency ANP and currently on the Supervisory Board of World Press Photo. Recently, I advised the Dutch government on innovation policy for the audiovisual sector. This acquired split vision has made me acutely aware that the disconnected stories in the news is confusing the general audience, the citizens, which have a considerable way to go before learning to think about technology and society as they need in order for democracy to work in the innovation age.

Journalism must connect the stories, not disconnect them, and enable the readers to understand what is going on so that they can make informed decisions, or else democracy will continue to deteriorate as technology advances.

These technological developments are moving faster than many of us can comprehend, but at least they are still in the hands of humans, and the speed of their development can at least be described.

What is lacking is "Innovation Journalism" that is capable of informing the general public at scale about these developments and helping people gain their footing in this new, uncertain terrain of technological dominance and novelty.

If innovation for jobs is a new way of using technology to create employment and value for people and society, innovation journalism is a new kind of media dedicated to discussing this new kind of value -- along with its advantages and downsides.

Further development of innovation journalism is urgently needed to ensure that technological developments guide us toward a people centered economy, not toward an uncontrolled continuation of the task-centered economy.

The following two quotations suggest the currency and complexity of this issue:

> "In this, the Good Place joins Westworld and Black Mirror in a wave of entertainment preoccupied with the potential humanity of artificial intelligences. Of course, super-smart robots have been a concern from Blade Runner to 2001: A Space Odyssey to The Terminator. But the particular issue of interest right now isn't quite whether Skynet will overpower its creators (though that is a theme of Westworld), nor the life-improving potential of AI (though an episode of Amazon's recent Philip K. Dick's Electric Dreams delved into how an android might offer not only practical but also moral assistance). Rather, the present urgency, according to pop culture, is around this: Will advanced AI deserve human rights? Should we cut back on cursing out Siri as she gets savvier, or outlaw kicking the next generation's Furby?"

> --Spencer Kornhaber, The Atlantic February 13, 2018

> "..., because if algorithms are going to author stories for us, it seems prudent to maintain the ability to author our own. In a world in which algorithms assert their narrative power over us, and entire farms of 'Fake News' write stories substituting one celebrity for another in hopes of generating clicks, human authorship remains an alternate and potentially resistant form of narrative production. While we may not be able to escape

382

*narration by algorithm, we can still publish our own narrative and analysis."*

--Kate Loss (Writer, employee 51 at Facebook), December 22, 2016

Today, there are no popular narratives or stories to help people envision such a radical idea as "innovation for jobs" or the "innovation journalism" that tries make sense of it. So far, most people have found these abstract ideas difficult to parse. Expert language is little help, because it usually exists in silos.

There is, however, experience to build upon. Between 2004 and 2011, Stanford University ran an "Innovation Journalism" initiative, developing conceptual frameworks, academic research projects, hands-on journalism practices, and public policy exercises. Program members worked with governments, universities, newsrooms, journalists, and foundations in the U.S. and elsewhere. They developed national pilot policy initiatives for enabling innovation journalism, running fellowship programs, and building academic research in Sweden, Finland, Slovenia, Pakistan (USAID), and Mexico.

## How can innovation journalism put innovation into perspective?

This question has grown more relevant since the 2016-2018 uproar over 'fake news' and the more recent developments around Cambridge Analytica and Facebook. Those debates have showed that informing the public after things go wrong not only creates a frenzy combined with a witch-hunt, but it does so too late for the public to clearly understand the relevant underlying causes of these events. In The Netherlands, we have a saying: *"After the calf has drowned, we close the pit."* I believe the equivalent in the U.S. and U.K. is, *Don't close the barn door after the horse has bolted.* We need an innovation journalism that is looking forward toward events to come, not backward to what has already gone wrong.

In this chapter, I want to raise two big questions about innovation journalism:

- *If the most significant issues go unreported by popular journalism, what kinds of issues lend themselves to Innovation Journalism?*

- *If journalists mainly comment on events after the horse has bolted, how can they maintain credibility and trust with modern audiences?*

To address these challenges, I asked several innovation thought leaders, including Robert C. Wolcott, Professor of Innovation at the Kellogg School of Management, Robert Hendrickson, Director of NewsCheck and Jim Stolze, Dutch tech entrepreneur and co-founder of Aigency, a global network of AI professionals & TEDxAmsterdam, to share some of their views on innovation journalism. They agreed with me that a people-centered economy only thrives if we can enable society to genuinely understand this new era of technological development. That must be done not only through creating and implementing innovation, but by ensuring that all (human) stakeholders understand what these new technologies imply and how they should be treated. This is a pivotal and essential role for innovation journalism.

# Innovation journalism

In 2008, innovation journalism was listed by the World Economic Forum as one of seven critical dimensions for discussing the redefinition and roles of the media in a global, interconnected society. This message takes considerable pains to state the importance of this form of journalism.

David Nordfors suggested the concept of innovation journalism in 2003, and in 2009 wrote a seminal article on the subject. This brief extract offers an introduction and a definition, and explains the the urgent need to support this form of journalism.

> *"The practice of innovation journalism," he wrote, "or journalism that covers innovation processes and ecosystems, is a crucial pivot between the innovation economy and the public sphere. This is especially true in social situations where decision makers are dependent on the backing of their constituencies, such as a representative democratic system or a publicly traded company."*

*"To the degree that innovation journalism can build an infrastructure for public debate on how we innovate, it will enable open discussion on how we transform ideas into new value. Such an infrastructure for debate connects decision makers with their constituencies across the full spectrum of innovation processes. This in turn provides reasons and means for decision makers to engage in public discussion on what counts in enabling societal innovation and on how to improve the systems that enable innovation."*

*"In an innovation ecosystem, journalism can be seen as an essential partner of the 'triple helix' of industry, academia, and government, just as it has long been considered 'the fourth estate' in a democracy. Journalism is an independent actor that, with industry, academia, and government, is a part of the infrastructure of competitiveness. Innovation journalism has its focus on reporting on the bigger picture of innovation, and enabling journalists to do it." (full article here: http://www.innovationjournalism.org/archive/INJO-6-1.pdf)*

I will address the two questions raised in the introduction separately, with quotes from innovation experts in the field of technology, humanity, and media.

## What kinds of innovations lend themselves to innovation journalism?

Journalism is typically organized in vertical silos by area, such as food, economics, or organic chemistry. Very often journalists are either 'specialists' in a particular field, or generalists who are asked to cover any kind of news. This division offers an insight into the dilemma of covering a topic as broad and interdisciplinary as innovation. Also, innovation is often disruptive (and therefore difficult to understand), cross-functional, or rooted an area remote from the expertise of the journalist. Innovation may also involve a groundswell, or movement, requiring broad experience or expertise to cover. It is therefore not easy for a reporter or editor to decide how best to approach a topic that might lend itself to important innovation -- let alone to produce an article or series that clearly lays out its significance for the general reader.

A helpful explanation is offered by Robert Wolcott:

> *"Like everything... technologies, behaviors, practices that are more sensational, differentiated, perhaps even bizarre tend to get covered. For good and bad. Covering obvious developments isn't satisfying or helpful, but just because someone does something unexpected doesn't mean it's of value. The best innovation journalism ties developments to the missions of their audiences (corporations, policy makers, citizens) which differ widely, and provides insights rather than just reporting 'the news'."*

From this we might conclude that innovation journalism should therefore cover the broader context of the impact of innovation, not just on what is visible from the surface. Another comment is added by Jim Stolze:

> *"Innovation journalism should not report on 'an' implementation of 'a' technology. But it should report either why this is new(s) or put it in a context of other implementations. Unveiling a pattern and explaining why this pattern is relevant. Less about the brand, less about the technology, more about the relevance."*

By creating a clear focus on the groundswell of conditions and actions that underlie innovations, within the general economic, social, and human context, innovation journalism can help to put the societal developments into context.

Good examples of this function of Innovation Journalism are seen in the new custom of the MIT Technology Review to produce every magazine issue on one subject and look at that subject from multiple angles. As they announce in the introduction to one such issue, *"To understand why blockchain matters, look past the wild speculation at what is being built underneath..."*

## How can journalists maintain credibility and trust with innovation ecosystem audiences?

Without trust, the stories from journalists will not be taken seriously. The trust levels for journalism are essential, but they have reached a low point, especially in the U.S. This can be seen by the speed at which we are moving from fact-based to opinion-based journalism. Unfortunately, we seem to be witnessing an outcome of the old saying: *"Facts are expensive, opinions are free."*

The audience needs to trust and rely on the credibility, quality, and independence of journalism. To regain the required levels again will be pivotal in being able to develop good journalism in general, and innovation journalism in particular -- both of which have an enormous challenge in catching up. Here we might consider another useful comment from Jim Stolze:

> *"I know that with the rise of social media there has been a trend for journalists to become their 'own' medium. But I find these reporters to be more bloggers / social media influencers than real reporters. They're just other people with an opinion. The temptation to write about what your followers would want to read about, or to come up with headlines that will receive more 'Likes,' has nothing to do with the objective standard that a newspaper or other serious medium should hold its reporters to."*

Technology and innovation are not only crucial to understand but also crucial to use in innovation journalism. Robert Hendrickson explains: *"Using technology for the transparent scoring of journalists and publishers adherence to journalistic standards will drive confidence in author/content reputation (credibility), and support the rebuilding of audience trust."*

Regaining the necessary credibility for the journalistic profession will require hard work, including monitoring the reputations (credibility) of journalists and their reporting. Just as important is the role of the publisher in adhering to the journalistic standards that can build audience trust. The industry has plenty of tools to make journalist conduct and integrity visible, but they have not been embraced and employed at scale throughout the profession. In general, the news industry is not one of the most advanced technological sectors, and the general decline in their business model has led to more limited R&D budgets and investment funding. This is doubly dangerous, because the use of technology is necessary both to rebuild trust in the journalistic process and to help readers to better understand innovation.

Some urgent needs on the part of innovation journalism are described in stark terms by Robert Hendrickson: *"Many of the current practices inhibit innovation, and the [journalism] community is just beginning to recognize and respond to the technology transformation of the industry. Collaboration and innovation go hand in hand, and are needed more than they are used currently."*

# Some prime examples of innovation journalism

Though there is still a long way to go, there are exciting examples of innovation journalism being used at the intersection of technology and humanity. For example, from Italy comes H-farm's Maize (https://www.maize.io/en); were also have MIT's *Technology Review* (https://www.technologyreview.com, discussed before) and *Wired*, both from San Francisco and London (https://www.wired.com & the European sibling (http://www.wired.co.uk).

These examples must still be regarded as "black swans,"and are mostly geared toward well- educated, experienced audiences with healthy appetites for innovation and technology, as well as human behavior. And building such models of innovation journalism takes significant amounts of time, money, and energy; in addition, they are often combined with and supported by innovation centers such as MIT in Boston and H-Farm in Venice Italy.

## A productive research agenda for innovation journalism

Thus we are far from the outcomes encouraged by the World Economic Forum in 2008 for Innovation Journalism. That is worrying in times where innovation and its impacts on society are becoming more and more critical. The worst outcome, if we do not proceed with care and proper strategy, would be to end up in a journalistic echo chamber exchanging buzzwords.

As Jim Stolze advises, *"One pitfall to avoid is believing that 'share of voice' equals 'share of market.' An example would be for every press release that adds 'artificial intelligence' or 'algorithm' to a headline gets more coverage. Those terms should not be in the lead when reporting on a story. Same goes for blockchain and every other fashionable term."*

If we want a society that supports a people-centered economy, focuses its resources of AI and automation on helping that society rather than seeking maximum profits, journalism has a vital role to play.

Similarly, developing cross-functional innovation journalism, at the intersection of humanity and technology, is a critical lever that can move our society toward a more inclusive future when all people and their talents are valued. Professor Wolcott suggests conscious ways to create an innovative and productive journalistic agenda: *"First, define it clearly. How does it differ from journalism in general? What's included, and what's not? Then, consider the variety of audiences and the roles it plays... Then create an Impact Framework to explore what works and what doesn't in each case... as well as a statement supporting innovation journalism and clarifying the need for journalistic integrity."*

The work done by David Nordfors is an excellent platform from which to leverage such strategies. There already exist valuable initiatives of (financial) support by organizations such as the Omidyar Foundation, Google Digital News Initiative, Facebook, and the Knight Foundation, all of which support and can stimulate innovation in journalism. A specific focus on innovation journalism, combined with such funding opportunities, would be an exciting way to build a stronger and better platform.

# Conclusion

If we do not want a society that values only profitability and market share, makes its decisions by algorithms, and believes the sounds of buzzwords in echo chambers, the development of high-quality innovation journalism will be critical. The crucial next steps will be to create the right impact frameworks. This will not be as easy as just sticking to the traditional business model and old ways of doing journalism, which have already begun to change rapidly.

We have reached a crossroad in the way information is gathered, valued, and communicated in our society. Both the producers and consumers of media are dizzy with confusion about the right direction for their profession. But times of confusion may lead to times of opportunity, as the pioneering platforms of innovation journalism are showing us.

This article is by no means the final answer to the challenge, but I trust it will function as a lighthouse to inspire further research, development, and discussion. It also hope it will push us more quickly toward an exciting new opportunity for (innovation) journalism as a major component of the people centered economy, integrating the tools of technology with the human experience.

If we want algorithms to take care of humans, in whatever extent, shape or format, the general public should be well aware of context and development. Innovation Journalism is the tool to inform them.

*****************

Made in the USA
Monee, IL
28 February 2020